Guide to Computing for Expressive Music Performance

Alexis Kirke · Eduardo R. Miranda
Editors

Guide to Computing for Expressive Music Performance

 Springer

Editors
Alexis Kirke
Interdisciplinary Centre for
 Computer Music Research
University of Plymouth
Plymouth, UK

Eduardo R. Miranda
Interdisciplinary Centre for Computer
 Music Research
University of Plymouth
Plymouth, UK

ISBN 978-1-4471-4122-8   ISBN 978-1-4471-4123-5 (eBook)
DOI 10.1007/978-1-4471-4123-5
Springer London Heidelberg New York Dordrecht

Library of Congress Control Number: 2012942160

Printed on acid-free paper

Springer is part of Springer Science+Business Media (www.springer.com)

Preface

Overview and Goals

In the early 1980s, the seeds of a problem were sown as a result of synthesizers being developed and sold with built-in sequencers. The introduction of MIDI into this equation led to an explosion in the use of sequencers and computers, thanks to the new potential for connection and synchronization. These computers and sequencers performed their stored tunes in perfect metronomic time, a performance which sounded robotic. They sounded robotic because human performers normally perform expressively – for example, speeding up and slowing down while playing, and changing how loudly they play.

The performer's changes in tempo and dynamics allow them to express a fixed score – hence the term expressive performance. However, rather than looking for ways to give the music performances more humanlike expression, pop performers developed new types of music, such as synthpop and dance music, that actually utilized this metronomic perfection to generate robotic performances.

Outside of pop, the uptake of sequencers for performance (as opposed to for composition) was less enthusiastic, except for occasional novelties like Snowflakes Are Dancing by Tomita; computer performance of classical music was a rarity. In the last 25 years, this situation has slowly been changing. Not only has computer performance becoming commonplace, but there has been much progress in learning how such computers can perform more expressively so that they sound less "machinelike". Now there is a thriving research community investigating computer systems for expressive music performance (CSEMPs).

This handbook attempts to provide a broad guide on fundamental ideas as well as recent research on computing for expressive performance. The book aims to cover some of the key issues and a number of the most influential systems from the history of computing for expressive music performance.

Organization and Features

The book is divided into nine chapters, each of which broadly covers a key area or system in computer for expressive music performance. Chapter 1 is an overview of the topic, covering a significant number of the CSEMPs from the last 30 years (including briefs on some which are later covered in more detail in the book). The CSEMPs are classified in this chapter by certain approaches, and a generic CSEMP architecture is introduced. The CSEMPs are also evaluated using a subjective classification scoring to help give perspective. A more recent issue is introduced toward the end of this chapter – that of combined systems for expressive music performance and computer composition. Chapter 2 introduces a key element not discussed in Chap. 1's overview – real-time interactivity in computing for expressive music performance, an example of which is simulated conducting systems. Chapter 3 introduces an actual example system in detail – based on probabilistic methods – one which has won a competition for its successful music performances. Chapter 4 covers a second CSEMP in detail, one using a very different approach to the probabilistic method in the previous chapter – evolutionary computing. Chapter 5 introduces a system that – unlike most CSEMPs – is not focused on classical music but on expressive performance of violin folk music. Another factor covered in some detail in Chap. 5 is the issue of synthesizing non-piano performances expressively. Most CSEMPs have focused on piano music due to its relative simplicity and advanced synthesis technology available. Chapter 6 addresses the technical problems found in polyphonic music expression from a statistical modelling point of view.

Having covered most of the core topics in computing for expressive music performance by this point, the more complex issue of evaluation of such systems is introduced in Chap. 7, mainly through discussion of the most influential CSEMP, the KTH system. Chapter 8 also addresses a more advanced topic, once again through a specific computer system. The topic is automated analysis of musical structure, which by now the reader will have realized is at the core of computing for expressive music performance. The chapter also touches on the idea discussed in Chap. 1 of a system which can be used both for expressive music performance and computer composition. The final chapter, Chap. 9, looks toward the future with the newer area of embodied expressive musical performance – building robots to expressively perform music with traditional instruments.

By the end of the book, the reader should be aware of all the key issues in computing for expressive music performance, the history of the research, a significant number of the systems available today, and the key directions for future research.

Target Audience

This book has a broad target audience. Although some of the chapters are fairly advanced, undergraduate students in computing will find much they can learn here about the field. Certainly postgraduate students and professional researchers in and out of academia will be able to use this as a resource to learn about and reference the field of computer for expressive music performance. A number of the chapters, for example, Chaps. 1 and 2, can be read by people with only a little technical background – for example, music undergraduates – and provide significant under-standing and overview. Popular and classical music practitioners can find much inspiration here for novel direction.

Acknowledgments

We are very grateful to the authors of the chapters for this book who have given their time and energy in providing a new key resource for the field they work in. The authors provided input on the topics suggested to them, moving the book in more productive directions.

We would also like to thank UK EPSRC for providing a grant to the editors that funded our research in this area and Plymouth University at which both the editors are based.

Finally, we would like to thank Simon Rees at Springer publishing for his support and guidance in the production of this book.

Contents

Contributors

Roberto Bresin Department of Speech, Music & Hearing, KTH Royal Institute of Technology, Stockholm, Sweden

Marco Fabiani Department of Speech, Music & Hearing, KTH Royal Institute of Technology, Stockholm, Sweden

Sebastian Flossmann Department of Computational Perception, Johannes Kepler Universitat, Linz, Austria

Anders Friberg Department of Speech, Music & Hearing, KTH Royal Institute of Technology, Stockholm, Sweden

Satoru Fukayama Doctoral Student at Sagayama & Ono Lab (Information Physics and Computing #1) Graduate School of Information Science and Technology, The University of Tokyo

Maarten Grachten Post Doctoral Researcher at the Department of Computational Perception, Johannes Kepler University, Linz, Austria

Masatoshi Hamanaka Intelligent Interaction Technologies, University of Tsukuba, Tsukuba, Japan

Keiji Hirata Department of Complex Systems, Future University Hakodate, Hokkaido, Japan

Tae Hun Kim Audio Communication Group, Technische Universitat Berlin, Berlin, Germany

Alexis Kirke Interdisciplinary Centre for Computer Music Research, School of Humanities and Performing Arts, Plymouth University, Plymouth, UK

Esteban Maestre Visiting Scholar, Center for Computer Research in Music and Acoustics, Stanford University, USA

Eduardo R. Miranda Interdisciplinary Centre for Computer Music Research, School of Humanities and Performing Arts, Plymouth University, Plymouth, UK

Takuya Nishimoto Founder, Olarbee Japan

Alfonso Perez Input Devices and Music Interaction Laboratory, McGill University, Quebec Canada

Rafael Ramirez DTIC, Universitat Pompeu Fabra, Barcelona, Spain

Shigeki Sagayama Graduate School of Information Science and Technology, The University of Tokyo, Japan

Jorge Solis Department of Physics and Electrical Engineering, Karlstad University, Karlstad, Sweden

Research Institute for Advanced Science and Engineering, Waseda University, Tokyo, Japan

Atsuo Takanishi Department of Modern Mechanical Engineering & Humanoid Robotics Institute, Waseda University

Satoshi Tojo Professor, Graduate School of Information Science, Japan Advanced Institute of Science and Technology, Ishikawa, Japan

Gerhard Widmer Department of Computational Perception, Johannes Kepler University (JKU), Linz, Austria

The Austrian Research Institute for Artificial Intelligence (OFAI), Vienna, Austria

Qijun Zhang Interdisciplinary Centre for Computer Music Research, School of Humanities and Performing Arts, Plymouth University, Plymouth, UK

An Overview of Computer Systems for Expressive Music Performance

Alexis Kirke and Eduardo R. Miranda

Abstract

This chapter is a survey of research into automated and semi-automated computer systems for expressive performance of music. We examine the motivation for such systems and then examine a significant sample of the systems developed over the last 30 years. To highlight some of the possible future directions for new research, this chapter uses primary terms of reference based on four elements: testing status, expressive representation, polyphonic ability and performance creativity.

1.1 Introduction

Computer composition of classical music had been around since 1957 when the Illiac Suite for String Quartet—the first published composition by a computer—was published by Lejaren Hiller [1]. Since then there has been a large body of such music and research published, with many successful systems produced for automated and semi-automated computer composition [2–4]. But publications on computer expressive performance of music lagged behind composition by almost quarter of a century. During the period when MIDI and computer use exploded amongst pop performers and up to 1987—when Yamaha had released their first Disklavier MIDI piano—there were only two or three researchers publishing on algorithms for expressive performance of music [5] including the KTH system discussed in Chaps. 2 and 7. However, from the end of the 1980s onwards, there

A. Kirke (✉) • E.R. Miranda
Interdisciplinary Centre for Computer Music Research, Plymouth University,
Faculty of Arts, Drake Circus, PL4 8AA Plymouth, UK
e-mail: alexis.kirke@plymouth.ac.uk; eduardo.miranda@plymouth.ac.uk

A. Kirke and E.R. Miranda (eds.), *Guide to Computing for Expressive Music Performance*,
DOI 10.1007/978-1-4471-4123-5_1, © Springer-Verlag London 2013

was an increasing interest in automated and semi-automated computer systems for expressive music performance (CSEMP). A CSEMP is a computer system able to generate expressive performances of music. For example, software for music typesetting will often be used to write a piece of music, but some packages play back the music in a relatively robotic way—the addition of a CSEMP enables a more realistic playback. Or an MP3 player could include a CSEMP which would allow performances of music to be adjusted to different performance styles.

This book contains a description of various systems and issues found in CSEMP work. As an introduction, this chapter provides an overview of a significant sample of research on automated and semi-automated CSEMPs. By automated, we refer to the ability of the system—once set up or trained—to generate a performance of a new piece, not seen before by the system, without manual intervention. Some automated systems may require manual set-up but then can be presented with multiple pieces which will be played autonomously. A semi-automated system is one which requires some manual input from the user (e.g. a musicological analysis) to deal with a new piece.

1.1.1 Human Expressive Performance

How do humans make their performances sound so different to the so-called perfect performance a computer would give? In this chapter, the strategies and changes which are not marked in a score but which performers apply to the music will be referred to as expressive performance actions. Two of the most common performance actions are changing the tempo and the loudness of the piece as it is played. These should not be confused with the tempo or loudness changes marked in the score, like accelerando or mezzo forte, but to additional tempo and loudness changes not marked in the score. For example, a common expressive performance strategy is for the performer to slow down as they approach the end of the piece [6]. Another performance action is the use of expressive articulation—when a performer chooses to play notes in a more staccato (short and pronounced) or legato (smooth) way. Those playing instruments with continuous tuning, for example, string players, may also use expressive intonation, making notes slightly sharper or flatter, and such instruments also allow for expressive vibrato. Many instruments provide the ability to expressively change timbre as well.

Why do humans add these expressive performance actions when playing music? We will set the context for answering this question using a historical perspective. Pianist and musicologist Ian Pace offers up the following as a familiar historical model for the development of notation (though suggests that overall it constitutes an oversimplification) [7]:

> In the Middle Ages and to a lesser extent to the Renaissance, musical scores provided only a bare outline of the music, with much to be filled in by the performer or performers, freely improvising within conventions which were essentially communicated verbally within a region or locality. By the Baroque Era, composers began to be more specific in terms of requirements for pitch, rhythm and articulation, though it was still common for performers

to apply embellishments and diminutions to the notated scores, and during the Classical Period a greater range of specificity was introduced for dynamics and accentuation. All of this reflected a gradual increase in the internationalism of music, with composers and performers travelling more widely and thus rendering the necessity for greater notational clarity as knowledge of local performance conventions could no longer be taken for granted. From Beethoven onwards, the composer took on a new role, less a servant composing to occasion at the behest of his or her feudal masters, more a freelance entrepreneur who followed his own desires, wishes and convictions, and wrote for posterity, hence bequeathing the notion of the master-work which had a more palpable autonomous existence over and above its various manifestations in performance. This required an even greater degree of notational exactitude; for example in the realms of tempo, where generic Italianate conventions were both rendered in the composer's native language and finely nuanced by qualifying clauses and adjectives. Through the course of the nineteenth century, tempo modifications were also entered more frequently into scores, and with the advent of a greater emphasis on timbre, scores gradually became more specific in terms of the indication of instrumentation. Performers phased out the processes of embellishment and ornamentation as the score came to attain more of the status of a sacred object. In the twentieth century, this process was extended much further, with the finest nuances of inflection, rubato, rhythmic modification coming to be indicated in the score. By the time of the music of Brian Ferneyhough, to take the most extreme example, all minutest details of every parameter are etched into the score, and the performer's task is simply to try and execute these as precisely as he or she can.

So in pre-twentieth-century music there has been a tradition of performers making additions to a performance which were not marked in the score (though the reason Pace calls this history an oversimplification is that modern music does have the capacity for expressive performance, as we will discuss later).

A number of studies have been done into this pre-twentieth-century (specifically baroque, classical and romantic) music performance. The earliest studies began with Seashore [8], and good overviews include Palmer [9] and Gabrielsson [10]. One element of these studies has been to discover what aspects of a piece of music—what musical features—are related to a performer's use of expressive performance actions. One of these musical features expressed is the performer's structural interpretation of the piece [9]. A piece of music has a number of levels of meaning—a hierarchy. Notes make up motifs, motifs make up phrases, phrases make up sections and sections make up a piece (in more continuous instruments, there are intranote elements as well). Each element—note, motif, etc.—plays a role in other higher elements. (This is discussed in more depth in Chap. 8.) Human performers have been shown to express this hierarchical structure in their performances. Performers have a tendency to slow down at boundaries in the hierarchy—with the amount of slowing being correlated to the importance of the boundary [11]. Thus, a performer would tend to slow more at a boundary between sections than between phrases. There are also regularities relating to other musical features in performers' expressive strategies. For example, in some cases the musical feature of higher-pitched notes causes a performance action of the notes being played more loudly; also, notes which introduce melodic tension relative to the key may be played more loudly. However, for every rule there will always be exceptions.

Another factor influencing expressive performance actions is performance context. Performers may wish to express a certain mood or emotion (e.g. sadness, happiness) through a piece of music. Performers have been shown to change the tempo and dynamics of a piece when asked to express an emotion as they play it [12]. For a discussion of other factors involved in human expressive performance, we refer the reader to [13].

1.1.2 Computer Expressive Performance

Having examined human expressive performance, the question now becomes: why should we want computers to perform music expressively? There are at least five answers to this question:

1. *Investigating human expressive performance by developing computational models*—Expressive performance is a fertile area for investigating musicology and human psychology [8–10]. As an alternative to experimentation with human performers, models can be built which attempt to simulate elements of human expressive performance. As in all mathematical and computational modelling, the model itself can give the researcher greater insight into the mechanisms inherent in that which is being modelled.

2. *Realistic playback on a music typesetting or composing tool*—There are many computer tools available now for music typesetting and for composing. If these tools play back the compositions with expression on the computer, the composer will have a better idea of what their final piece will sound like. For example, Sibelius, Notion and Finale have some ability for expressive playback.

3. *Playing computer-generated music expressively*—There are a number of algorithmic composition systems that output music without expressive performance but which audiences would normally expect to hear played expressively. These compositions in their raw form will play on a computer in a robotic way. A CSEMP would allow the output of an algorithmic composition system to be played directly on the computer which composed it (e.g. in a computer game which generates mood music based on what is happening in the game).

4. *Playing data files*—A large number of non-expressive data files in formats like MIDI and MusicXML [14] are available on the Internet, and they are used by many musicians as a standard communication tool for ideas and pieces. Without CSEMPs, most of these files will play back on a computer in an unattractive way, whereas the use of a CSEMP would make such files much more useful.

5. *Computer accompaniment tasks*—It can be costly for a musician to play in ensemble. Musicians can practise by playing along to recordings with their solo part stripped out. But some may find it too restrictive since such recordings cannot dynamically follow the expressiveness in the soloist's performance. These soloists may prefer to play along with an interactive accompaniment system that not only tracks their expression but also generates its own expression.

1.2   A Generic Framework for Previous Research in Computer Expressive Performance

Figure 1.1 shows a generic model for the framework that many (but not all) previous automated and semi-automated CSEMPs tend to have followed. The modules of this diagram are described here.

Performance Knowledge—This is the core of any performance system. It is the set of rules or associations that control the performance action. It is the 'expertise' of the system which contains the ability, implicit or explicit, to generate an expressive performance. This may be in the form of an artificial neural network, a set of cases in a case-based reasoning system or a set of linear equation with coefficients. To produce performance actions, this module uses its programmed knowledge together with any inputs concerning the particular performance. Its main input is the music/analysis module. Its output is a representation of the performance of the musical input, including expressive performance actions.

Music/Analysis—The music/analysis module has two functions. First of all, in all systems, it has the function of inputting the music to be played expressively (whether in paper score, MIDI, MusicXML, audio or other form) into the system. The input process can be quite complex, for example, paper score or audio input will require some form of analytical recognition of musical events. This module is the only input to the performance knowledge module that defines the particular piece of music to be played. In some systems, it also has a second function—to provide an analysis of the musical structure. This analysis provides information about the music features of the music—for example, metrical, melodic or harmonic structure. (It was mentioned earlier how it has been shown that such structures have a large influence on expressive performance in humans.) This analysis can then be used by the performance knowledge system to decide how the piece should be performed. Analysis methods used in some of the systems include Lerdahl and Jackendoff's generative theory of tonal music discussed in Chap. 8 [15], Narmour's implication realisation discussed in Chap. 3 [16] and various bespoke musical measurements. The analysis may be automated, manual or a combination of the two.

Performance Context—Another element which will affect how a piece of music is played is the performance context. This includes such things as how the performer decides to play a piece, for example, happy, perky, sad or lovelorn. It can also include whether the piece is played in a particular style, for example, baroque or romantic.

Adaptation Process—The adaptation process is the method used to develop the performance knowledge. Like the analysis module, this can be automated, manual or a combination of the two. In some systems, a human expert listens to actual musical output of the performance system and decides if it is appropriate. If not, then the performance knowledge can be adjusted to try to improve the musical output performance. This is the reason that in Fig. 1.1 there is a line going from the sound module back to the adaptation procedure module. The adaptation procedure

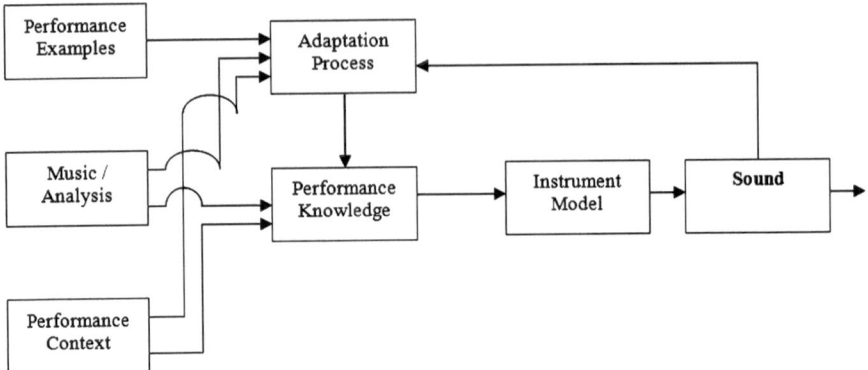

Fig. 1.1 Generic model for most current CSEMPs

also has inputs from performance context, music/analysis, instrument model and performance examples. All four of these elements can influence the way that a human performs a piece of music, though the most commonly used are music/ analysis and performance examples.

Performance Examples—One important element that can be incorporated in the performance knowledge building is the experience of past human performances. These examples can be used by the adaptation procedure to analyse when and how performance actions are added to a piece of music by human performers. The examples may be a database of marked-up audio recordings, MIDI files together with their source scores or (in the manual case) a person's experience of music performance.

Instrument Model—By far the most common instrument used in computer-generated performance research is the piano. This is because it allows experiments with many aspects of expression but requires only a very simple instrument model. In fact, the instrument model used for piano is often just the MIDI/media player and sound card in a PC. Alternatively, it may be something more complex but still not part of the simulation system, for example, a Yamaha Disklavier (e.g. as used in Chap. 7). However, a few simulation systems use non-keyboard instruments, for example, violin (used in Chap. 5) and trumpet. In these cases, the issue of a performance is more than just expressiveness. Just simulating a human-like performance, even if it is non-expressive, on these instruments is non-trivial. So systems simulating expressive performance on such instruments may require a relatively complex instrument model in addition to expressive performance elements. (Chaps. 5 and 9 use more complex instrument models.)

1.2.1 Modules of Systems Reviewed and Terms of Reference

Table 1.1 lists the systems reviewed, together with information about their modules. This information will be explained in the detailed part of the chapter. Note that

Table 1.1 Systems reviewed

CSEMP	Performance knowledge	Music	Analysis	Performance context	Adaptation process	Performance examples	Instrument model (or application)	Performance actions
Director Musices [17] Chap. 2/7	Rules	MIDI, score	Custom	Mood space	–	MIDI performances	All (piano)	T/D/A/P
Hierarchical parabola [18–20]	Parabola equation	MIDI, score	GTTM TSR			–		Piano	T/D
Composer pulse [21, 22]	Multiplier set	MIDI	–		Manual	Tapping	All	T/D
Bach fugue [23]	Rules	Score	Custom		Manual	Books, experts	Keyboard	T/A
Trumpet synthesis [24, 25]	Linear model	Audio, score	Custom		Manual	Audio performances	Trumpet	A/P/O
Rubato [26, 27]	Operators	MIDI, score	Custom		Manual	–	All (piano)	T/D
Pop-E [28]	Rule-based	MIDI, score	GTTM, custom			MIDI performances	Piano	T/D
Hermode tuning [29]	Rule-based	MIDI	Custom			–	All	P
Sibelius [30]	Rule-based	Score	Custom			Unknown	–	Unknown
CMERS [31]	Linear model	MIDI, score	Custom	Mood space		Performances and experiments	Piano	T/D/P/O
MIS [32–34]	Linear model	MIDI, score	GTTM/Meyer		Regression with ANDs	Audio performances	Piano	T/D/A
CaRo [35–37]	Linear model	Audio	Custom	Mood space	PCA, linear regression	Audio performances by mood	All	T/K/D/A
ANN piano [38]	ANN	MIDI	Custom		ANN training	MIDI performances	Piano	T/D
Emotional flute [39]	ANN and rules	Audio, score	Custom	Mood space	ANN training	Audio performances by mood	Flute	T/D/V

(continued)

Table 1.1 (continued)

CSEMP	Performance knowledge	Music	Analysis	Performance context	Adaptation process	Performance examples	Instrument model (or application)	Performance actions
SaxEx [40–42]	Fuzzy rules	Audio, score	Narmour/IR/GTTM, custom	Mood space	CBR training	Audio performances by mood	Saxophone	T/D/V/K
Kagurame [43, 44]	Rules	MIDI, score	Custom	Performance conditions	CBR training	MIDI performances by context	Piano	T/D/A
Ha-Hi-Hun [45] Chap. 8	Rules	MIDI, score	GTTM TSR	Language performance conditions	CBR training	MIDI performances by condition	Piano	T/D
PLCG [46–48]	Learned rules	MIDI, score	Custom	–	Meta-sequential learning	MIDI performances	Piano	T/D/A
PLCG/Phrase-decomposition [49]	Learned rules	MIDI, score	Custom, harmonic by musicologist	–	CBR training, meta-sequential learning	MIDI performances	Piano	T/D/A
DISTALL Chap. 3 [50, 51]	CBR	MIDI, score	Custom, harmonic by musicologist	–	CBR training	MIDI performances	Piano	T/D/A
Music Plus One [52–54]	BBN	Audio/MIDI, score	Custom	Soloist tempo	BBN training	Audio soloist performances	All	T/D
ESP piano [55]	HMM	MIDI, score	Custom	–	HMM training	MIDI performances	Piano	T/D/A
Drumming [56]	Non-linear mapping	Audio	Custom	–	KRR, GPR, kNN	Audio performances	Drums	T
KCCA piano [57]	Non-linear mapping	Worm, score	Custom	–	KCCA	Performance worm	Piano	T/D

Genetic programming Chap. 5 [58]	Regression trees	Audio	IR, custom	—	Genetic programming	Audio performances	Saxophone	T/D/A/N
Generative performance GAs Chap. 4 [59]	Pulse set	MIDI, score	LBDM, Kruhmansl, Melisma	—	GA	None	Piano	T/D
MAS with imitation Chap. 4 [60]	Pulse set	MIDI, score	LBDM, Kruhmansl, Melisma	—	Imitation	None	Piano	T/D
Ossia [61]	Fitness rules	MIDI	—	—	—	None	Piano	T/D/P
pMIMACS	Rule-based (2)	MIDI	Performance skill	Excitability state	Imitation	None	Piano	T/D

Table 1.2 Abbreviations

Abbreviation	Meaning
A	Articulation
ANN	Artificial neural network
BBN	Bayesian belief network
CBR	Case-based reasoning
CSEMP	Computer system for expressive music performance
D	Dynamics
DM	Director musices (KTH system)
EC	Evolutionary computing
GA	Genetic algorithm
GP	Genetic programming
GPR	Gaussian process regression
GTTM	Lerdahl and Jackendoff's generative theory of tonal music
GUI	Graphical user interface
HMM	Hidden Markov model
IBL	Instance-based learning
IR	Narmour's implication/realisation theory of melody
K	Attack
KCCA	Kernel canonical correlation analysis
kNN	k-Nearest neighbour
KRR	Kernel ridge regression
LBDM	Local boundary detection model of Cambouropoulos
MAS	Multi-agent system
CMERS	Computational music emotion rule system by Livingstone et al.
MIDI	Musical instrument digital interface
MIMACS	Mimetics-inspired multi-agent composition system
MusicXML	Music extensible markup language
MIS	Music interpretation system by Katayose et al.
N	Note addition/consolidation
P	Pitch
PCA	Principal component analysis
T	Tempo
TSR	Time span reduction technique (from GTTM)
V	Vibrato

the column for instrument model is also used for CSEMPs without an explicit instrument model so as to show their applicability to various instruments. A number of abbreviations are used in Table 1.1 and throughout the chapter. Table 1.2 lists these abbreviations and their meaning.

Before discussing the primary terms of reference for this chapter, it should be observed that the issue of evaluation of CSEMPs is an open problem. How does one evaluate what is essentially a subjective process? If the CSEMP is trying to simulate a particular performance, then correlation tests can be done. However, even if the correlations are low for a generated performance, it is logically possible for the generated performance to be more preferable to some people than the original performance. Chapter 7 goes into detail about performance evaluation in CSEMPs, but we will briefly address it here. Papadopoulos and Wiggins [62] discuss the evaluation issue in a different but closely related area—computer algorithmic composition systems. They list four points that they see as problematic in relation to such composition systems:

1. The lack of evaluation by experts, for example, professional musicians.
2. Evaluation is a relatively small part of the research with respect to the length of the research paper.
3. Many systems only generate melodies. How do we evaluate the music without a harmonic context? Most melodies will sound acceptable in some context or other.
4. Most of the systems deal with computer composition as a problem solving task rather than as a creative and meaningful process.

All of these four points are issues in the context of computer systems for expressive performance as well. So from these observations, three of the primary terms of reference are extracted for this chapter. The three primary terms of reference which are extracted from points 1–4 are performance testing status (points 1 and 2), polyphonic ability (point 3) and performance creativity (point 4). These first three dimensions will now be examined, and then the fourth primary term of reference will be introduced.

1.2.2 Primary Terms of Reference for Systems Surveyed

Performance testing status refers to how and to what extent the system has been tested. It is important to emphasise that testing status is not a measure of how successful the testing was, but how extensive it was. (This is also discussed in Chap. 7.) There are three main approaches to CSEMP testing: (a) trying to simulate a particular human performance or an average of human performances, (b) trying to create a performance which does not sound machine-like and (c) trying to create as aesthetically pleasing a performance as possible. For the first of these, a correlation can be done between the computer performance and the desired target performance/performances. (However, this will not be a 'perceptually weighted' correlation; errors may have a greater aesthetic/perceptual effect at some points than at others.) For approaches (b) and (c), we have listening tests by experts and non-experts. A wide variety of listening tests are used in CSEMPs, from the totally informal and hardly reported to the results of formal competitions.

Each year since 2002, a formal competition that has been described as a 'musical turing test', called the RenCon (contest for performance rendering systems) Workshop, has been held [63]. This will be discussed in detail in Chap. 7. About a third of the systems we will survey have been entered into a RenCon competition (see Table 1.3 for the results). RenCon is a primarily piano-based competition for baroque, classical and romantic music and includes manual as well as automated systems (though the placings in Table 1.3 are displayed relative to automated and semi-automated CSEMPs, ignoring the manual submissions to RenCon). Performances are graded and voted on by a jury of attendees from the sponsoring

Table 1.3 RenCon placings of CSEMPs in this chapter

CSEMP	RenCon placings
Director Musices	2002 (4th), 2004 compulsory (1st), 2005 compulsory (2nd)
SuperConductor (includes composer pulse)	2004 open (1st), 2006 open (1st and 4th)
Rubato	2004 open (4th)
MIS	2002 (2nd)
Music Plus One	2003 (1st)
Kagurame	2002 (6th), 2004 compulsory (3rd), 2006 compulsory (2nd)
Ha-Hi-Hun	2002 (5th), 2004 compulsory (4th), 2006 compulsory (3rd)
DISTALL	2002 (1st)
Pop-E	2005 compulsory (1st), 2006 compulsory (1st), 2006 open (2nd and 3rd)

conference. Scores are given for 'humanness' and 'expressiveness', giving an overall 'preference' score. It is the preference score we will focus on in the survey. The size of RenCon juries and their criteria have varied over time. In earlier years (apart from its first year, 2002), RenCon did not have a separate autonomous section—it had two sections: compulsory and open, where compulsory was limited to a fixed piano piece for all contestants and open was open to all instruments and pieces.

In these competitions, automated CSEMPs went up against human pianists and renditions which were carefully crafted by human hand. Thus, many past RenCon results are not the ideal evaluation for automated and semi-automated CSEMPs. However, they are the only published common forum available, so in the spirit of points (1) and (2) from [62], they will be referred to where possible in this chapter.

From 2008, the competition had three sections: an 'autonomous' section, a 'type-in' section and an open section. The autonomous section aims to only evaluate performances generated by automated CSEMPs. Performances are graded by the composer of the test pieces as well as by a jury. For the autonomous section, the 2008 RenCon contestants are presented with two 1-min pieces of unseen music: one in the style of Chopin and one in the style of Mozart. An award is presented for the highest-scored performance and for the performance most preferred by the composer of the two test pieces. The type-in section is for computer systems for manually generating expressive performance.

The second term of reference is polyphonic ability and refers to the ability of a CSEMP to generate expressive performances of a non-monophonic piece of music. Monophonic music has only one note playing at a time, whereas non-monophonic music can have multiple notes playing at the same time—for example, piano chords with a melody or a four-part string quartet. Many CSEMPs take monophonic inputs and generate monophonic expression, for example, SaxEx [64] focuses on a single monophonic instrument—saxophone. However, as will be seen, there are also systems like the system in Chap. 6, the ESP piano system [55] and Pop-E [28] which are designed explicitly to work with non-monophonic music. To understand why polyphonic expression is more complex than monophonic expression, consider that each voice of an ensemble may have its own melodic structure. Many monophonic methods described in our survey, if applied separately to each part of a non-monophonic performance, could lead to parts having their own expressive timing deviations. This would cause an unsynchronised and unattractive performance [17]. Polyphonic ability is an important issue for CSEMP research because—although a significant percentage of CSEMP work has focused on monophonic expression—most music is not monophonic. Hence, Chap. 6 is dedicated to a system focusing on polyphony.

The third term of reference in this chapter, performance creativity, refers to the ability of the system to generate novel and original performances, as opposed to simulating previous human strategies. For example, the artificial neural network piano system [38] is designed to simulate human performances (an important research goal) but not to create novel performances, whereas a system like Director Musices in Chaps. 2 and 7 [17], although also designed to capture human performance strategies, has a parameterisation ability which can be creatively manipulated to generate entirely novel performances. The evolutionary computing system discussed in Chap. 4 is partially inspired by the desire for performance creativity. There is an important proviso here—a system which is totally manual would seem at first glance to have a high creativity potential, since the user could entirely shape every element of the performance. However, this potential may never be realised due to the manual effort required to implement the performance. Not all systems are able to act in a novel and practically controllable way. Many of the systems generate a model of performance which is basically a vector or matrix of coefficients. Changing this matrix by hand ('hacking it') would allow the technically knowledgeable to creatively generate novel performances. However, the changes could require too much effort or the results of such changes could be too unpredictable (thus requiring too many iterations or 'try-outs'). So performance creativity includes the ability of a system to produce novel performances with a reasonable amount of effort. Having said that, simple controllability is not the whole of performance creativity; for example, there could be a CSEMP which has only three basic performance rules which can be switched on and off with a mouse click and the new performance played immediately. However, the results of switching off and on the rules would in all likelihood generate a very uninteresting performance.

So for performance creativity, a balance needs to exist between automation and creative flexibility, since in this survey we are only concerned with automated and semi-automated CSEMPs. An example of such a balance would be an almost totally automated CSEMP but with a manageable number of parameters that can be user-adjusted before activating the CSEMP for performance. After activating the CSEMP, a performance is autonomously generated but is only partially constrained by attempting to match past human performances. Such creative and novel performance is often applauded in human performers. For example, Glenn Gould has created highly novel expressive performances of pieces of music and has been described as having a vivid musical imagination [65]. Expressive computer performance provides possibilities for even more imaginative experimentation with performance strategies.

We will now add a fourth and final dimension to the primary terms of reference which—like the other three—also has parallels in algorithmic composition. Different algorithmic composition systems generate music with different levels of structural sophistication—for example, some may just work on the note-to-note level, like [66], whereas some may be able to plan at the higher structure level, generating forms like ABCBA, for example [67]. There is an equivalent function in computer systems for expressive performance: expressive representation. Expressive representation is the level of sophistication in the CSEMP's representation of the score as it pertains to expressive performance actions. We have already mentioned the importance of the music's structure to a human expressive performance. A piece of music can be analysed with greater and greater levels of complexity. At its simplest, it can be viewed a few notes at a time or from the point of view of melody only. At its most complex, the harmonic and hierarchical structure of the score can be analysed—as is done in Widmer's DISTALL system [49, 68]. The greater the expressive representation of a CSEMP, the more of the music features it can potentially express.

So to summarise, our four primary terms of reference will be:

- Testing status
- Expressive representation
- Polyphonic ability
- Performance creativity

At some point in the description of each system, these points will be implicitly or explicitly addressed and are summarised at the end of the chapter (see Table 1.5). It is worth noting that these are not an attempt to measure how successful the system is overall, but an attempt to highlight some key issues. What now follow are the actual descriptions of the CSEMPs, divided into a number of groups.

1.3   A Survey of Computer Systems for Expressive Music Performance

The survey presented here is meant to be representative rather than exhaustive but will cover a significant selection of published automated and semi-automated CSEMP systems to date. Each CSEMP is grouped according to how their performance knowledge is built—i.e. by learning method. This provides a manageable division of the field, showing which learning methods are most popular. The grouping will be:

1. Non-learning (10 systems)
2. Linear regression (2 systems)
3. Artificial neural networks (2 systems)
4. Rule/case-based learning (6 systems)
5. Statistical graphical models (2 systems)
6. Other regression methods (2 systems)
7. Evolutionary computation (6 systems)

The ordering of this grouping is by average year of CSEMP references within the grouping so as to help highlight trends in approaches to generating performance knowledge. For example, most early CSEMPs were non-learning, and most evolutionary computation CSEMPs have only been developed in the last few years. The fourth grouping—rule/case-based learning—is in the middle because it has been used throughout the history of CSEMP research.

1.3.1 Non-learning Systems

1.3.1.1 Director Musices

Director Musices (DM) has been an ongoing project since 1982 and is also discussed in Chaps. 2 and 7 [17, 69]. Researchers developed and tested performance rules using an analysis-by-synthesis method (later using analysis-by-measurement and studying actual performances). Currently, there are around 30 rules which are written as relatively simple equations that take as input music features such as height of the current note pitch, the pitch of the current note relative to the key of the piece or whether the current note is the first or last note of the phrase. The output of the equations defines the performance actions, for example, phrase arch which defines a 'rainbow' shape of tempo and dynamics over a phrase. The performance speeds up and gets louder towards the centre of a phrase and then tails off again in tempo and dynamics towards the end of the phrase. Some manual score analysis is required—for example, harmonic analysis and marking up of phrase start and end.

Each equation has a numeric 'k value'—the higher the k value, the more effect the rule will have and a k value of 0 switches the rule off. The results of the equations are added together linearly to get the final performance. Thanks to the adjustable k-value system, DM has much potential for performance creativity. Little work has been reported on an active search for novel performances, though it is reported that negative k values reverse rule effects and cause unusual performances. DM's ability as a semi-automated system comes from the fact that it has a 'default' set of k values, allowing the same rule settings to be applied automatically to different pieces of music (though not necessarily with the same success). Rules are also included for dealing with non-monophonic music [17].

DM is also able to deal with some performance contexts, specifically emotional expression [70], drawing on the work by Gabrielsson and Juslin [12]. Listening experiments were used to define the k-value settings on the DM rules for expressing emotions: fear, anger, happiness, sadness, solemnity, tenderness or no expression. As a result, parameters were found for each of the six rules which mould the emotional expression of a piece. A more recent development in Director Musices has been the real-time generation of performances using a version of the system called pDM [71]. Unlike pDM, many CSEMPs in this survey receive the inputs and parameters and the whole piece of music and process the data, and when this processing is complete, a generated performance is available to the user. They are not designed for real-time usage.

Director Musices has a good test status, having been evaluated in a number of experiments. In the first RenCon in 2002, the second prize went to a DM-generated performance; however, the first-placed system (a manually generated performance) was voted for by 80% of the jury. In RenCon 2005, a Director Musices default-setting (i.e. automated) performance of Mozart's Minuette KV 1(1e) came a very close 2nd in the competition, behind Pop-E [28]. However, three of the other four systems competing were versions of the DM system. The DM model has been influential, and as will be seen in the later systems, DM-type rules appear repeatedly.

Tempo Parabolas

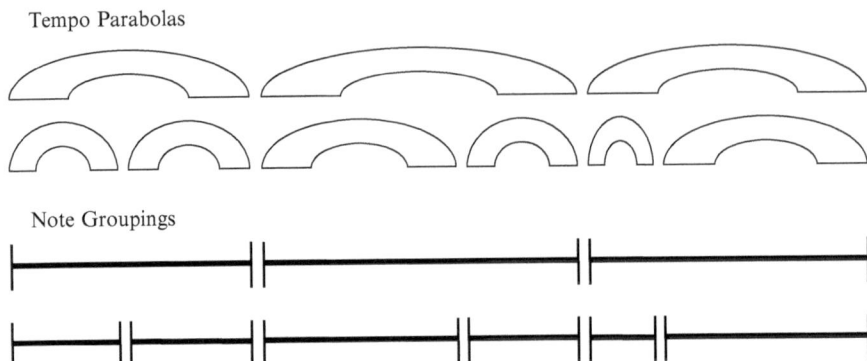

Note Groupings

Fig. 1.2 Todd's parabola model

1.3.1.2 Hierarchical Parabola Model

One of the first CSEMPs with a hierarchical expressive representation was Todd's hierarchical parabola model [15, 18–20]. Todd argues it was consistent with a kinematic model of expressive performance, where tempo changes are viewed as being due to accelerations and decelerations in some internal process in the human mind/body, for example, the auditory system. For tempo, the hierarchical parabola model uses a rainbow shape like DM's phrase arch, which is consistent with Newtonian kinematics. For loudness, the model uses a 'the faster the louder' rule, creating a dynamics rainbow as well.

The key difference between DM and this hierarchical model is that implicit in the hierarchical model is a greater expressive representation and wider performance action. Multiple levels of the hierarchy are analysed using Lerdahl and Jackendoff's generative theory of tonal music (GTTM). GTTM time span reduction (TSR) examines each note's musicological place in all hierarchical levels. The rainbows/parabolas are generated at each level, from the note-group level upwards (Fig. 1.2), and added to get the performance. This generation is done by a parameterised parabolic equation which takes as input the result of the GTTM TSR analysis.

The performance was shown to correlate well by eye with a short human performance, but no correlation figures were reported. Clarke and Windsor (2000) tested the first four bars of Mozart's K.331, comparing two human performers with two performances by the hierarchical parabola model. Human listeners found the parabola version unsatisfactory compared to the human ones. In the same experiment however, the parabola model was found to work well on another short melody. The testing also showed that the idea of 'the louder the faster' did not always hold. Desain and Honing [72] claim, as a result of informal listening tests, that in general the performances do not sound convincing.

The constraint of utilising the hierarchy and the GTTM TSR approach limits the performance creativity. Note groupings will be limited to those generated by a GTTM TSR analysis, and the parabolas generated will be constrained by the model's equation. Any adjustments to a performance will be constrained to working within this framework.

Table 1.4 Level 2 composers' pulses

Level 2 composers' pulses—four pulses					
Beethoven	Duration	106	89	96	111
	Amplitude	1.00	0.39	0.83	0.81
Mozart	Duration	105	95	105	95
	Amplitude	1.00	0.21	0.53	0.23
Schubert	Duration	97	114	98	90
	Amplitude	1.00	0.65	0.40	0.75
Haydn	Duration	108	94	97	102
	Amplitude	1.00	0.42	0.68	1.02
Schumann	Duration	96	116	86	102
	Amplitude	0.60	0.95	0.50	1.17
Mendelssohn	Duration	118	81	95	104
	Amplitude	1.00	0.63	0.79	1.12

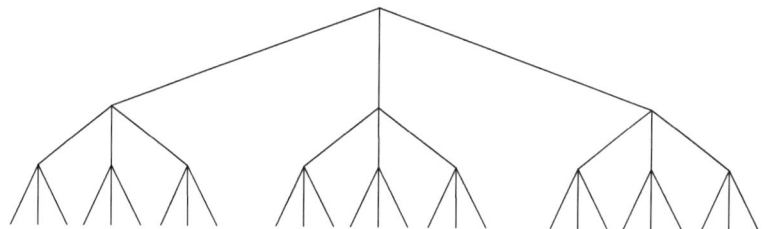

Fig. 1.3 Structure of a pulse set in three-time

1.3.1.3 Composer Pulse and Predictive Amplitude Shaping

Manfred Clynes' composer pulse [21] also acts on multiple levels of the hierarchy. Clynes hypothesises that each composer has a unique pattern of amplitude and tempo variations running through performances—a pulse. This is captured as a set of numbers multiplying tempo and dynamics values in the score. It is hierarchical with separate values for within the beat, the phrase and at multiple bar level. Table 1.4 shows the values of pulses for phrase level for some composers. The pulses were measured using a sentograph to generate pressure curves from musicians tapping their finger whilst thinking of or listening to a specific composer. Figure 1.3 shows the structure of a pulse set in three-time (each composer has a three-time and a four-time pulse set defined). This pulse set is repeatedly applied to a score end on end. So if the pulse is 12 beats long and the score is 528 beats, the pulse will repeat 528/12 = 44 times end on end.

Another key element of Clynes' approach is predictive amplitude shaping. This adjusts a note's dynamics based on the next note, simulating 'a musician's unconscious ability to sculpt notes in this way' that 'makes his performance flow beautifully through time, and gives it meaningful coherence even as the shape and duration of each individual note is unique'. A fixed envelope shape model is used (some constants are manually defined by the user), the main inputs being distant to the next note and duration of the current note. So the pulse/amplitude system has only note-level expressive representation.

Clynes' test of his own model [22] showed that a number of expert and non-expert listeners preferred music with a composer's pulse than with a different pulse. However, not all tests on Clynes' approach have supported a universal pulse for each composer [73, 74], suggesting instead that the pulse may be effective for a subset of a composer's work. Clynes' pulses and amplitude shaping have been combined with other performance tools (e.g. vibrato generation) as part of his commercial software SuperConductor. Two SuperConductor-generated performances were submitted to RenCon 2006 open section: Beethoven's Eroica Symphony, Op.55, Mvt.4 and Brahms' Violin Concerto, Op.77, Mvt.1. The Beethoven piece scored low, but the Brahms piece came first in the open section (beating two pieces submitted by Pop-E [28]). The generation of this piece could have involved significant amounts of manual work. Also because it was the open section, the pieces submitted by Pop-E were not the same as submitted by SuperConductor—hence, like was not compared to like. SuperConductor also won the open section in RenCon 2004 with J. S. Bach, Brandenburg Concerto No. 5, D Major, 3rd Movement. The only competitor included from this survey was Rubato [26] performing a Bach piece. It should be re-emphasised that these results were for SuperConductor and not solely for the pulse and amplitude tools.

In the context of SuperConductor, Clynes' approach allows for significant performance creativity. The software is designed to allow a user to control the expressive shaping of a MIDI performance, giving significant amounts of control. However, outside of the context of SuperConductor, the pulse has little scope for performance creativity—though the amplitude shaping does. The pulse and amplitude shaping do not explicitly address non-monophonic music, though SuperConductor can be used to generate polyphonic performances.

1.3.1.4 Bach Fugue System

In the Bach fugue system [23], expert system methods are used to generate performance actions. Johnson generated the knowledge base through interviews with two musical expert performers and through a performance practice manual and an annotated edition of the Well-Tempered Clavier; so this system is not designed for performance creativity. Twenty-eight conditions for tempo and articulation are so generated for the knowledge base. For example, 'If there is any group of 16th notes following a tied note, then slur the group of 16th notes following the long note'. Expressive representation is focused on the note to phrase level. The CSEMP does not perform itself but generates instructions for 4/4 fugues. So testing was limited to examining the instructions. It gave the same instructions as human experts 85–90% of the time, though it is not said how many tests were run. The system is working in the context of polyphony.

1.3.1.5 Trumpet Synthesis

The testing of many of the CSEMPs surveyed has focused on keyboard. This pattern will continue through the chapter—most historical CSEMPs focused on the piano because it was easier to collect and analyse data for the piano than for other instruments. However, this book shows that this trend is starting to change (e.g. see Chaps. 5 and 9). One of the first non-piano systems was Dannenberg and Derenyi's trumpet synthesis [24, 25]. The authors' primary interest here was to generate realistic trumpet synthesis, and adding performance factors improves this synthesis. It is not designed for performance creativity but for simulation. This trumpet system synthesises the whole trumpet performance, without needing any MIDI or audio building blocks as the basis of its audio output. The performance actions are amplitude and frequency, and these are controlled by envelope models which were developed using a semi-manual statistical analysis-by-synthesis method. A 10-parameter model was built for amplitude, based on elements such as articulation, direction and magnitude of pitch intervals and duration of notes. This system works by expressively transforming one note at a time, based on the pattern of the surrounding two notes. In terms of expressive representation, the system works on a three-note width. The pitch expression is based on envelopes which were derived and stored during the analysis-by-synthesis.

No test results are reported. Dannenberg and Derenyi placed two accompanied examples online: parts of a Haydn Trumpet Concerto and of a Handel Minuet. The start of the trumpet on the concerto without accompaniment is also online, together with a human playing the same phrase. The non-accompanied synthesis sounds quite impressive, only being let down by a synthetic feel towards the end of the phrase—though the note-to-note expression (as opposed to the synthesis) consistently avoids sounding machine-like. In both accompanied examples, it became clear as the performances went on that a machine was playing, particularly in faster passages. But once again, note-to-note expression did not sound too mechanical. Despite the reasonably positive nature of these examples, there is no attempt to objectively qualify how good the trumpet synthesis system is.

1.3.1.6 Rubato

Mazzola, a mathematician and recognised jazz pianist, developed a mathematical theory of music [26, 27]. Music is represented in an abstract geometrical space whose coordinates include onset time, pitch and duration. A score will exist in this space, and expressive performances are generated by performing transformations on the space. The basis of these transformations is a series of 'operators' which can be viewed as a very generalised version of the rule-based approach taken in Director Musices. For example, the tempo operator and the split operator allow the generation of tempo hierarchies. These give rubato a good expressive representation. However, the definition of the hierarchy here differs somewhat from that found in the hierarchical parabola model [18, 19] or DISTALL [50, 51]. A tempo hierarchy, for a piano performance, may mean that the tempo of the left hand is the dominant tempo, at the top of a hierarchy, and the right-hand tempo is always relative to the left-hand tempo—and so is viewed as being lower in the hierarchy. Mazzola also discusses the use of tempo hierarchies to generate tempo for grace notes and arpeggios—the tempo of these is relative to some global tempo higher in the hierarchy. Ideas from this theory have been implemented in a piece of software called Rubato, which is available online. The expressive performance module in

Rubato is the 'Performance Rubette'. A MIDI file can be loaded in Rubato and predefined operators used to generate expressive performances. The user can also manually manipulate tempo curves using a mouse and GUI, giving Rubato good scope for performance creativity.

Test reports are limited. In RenCon 2004, a performance of Bach's Contrapunctus III modelled using Rubato was submitted and came fourth in the open section (SuperConductor came first in the section with a different piece). It is not clear how automated the generation of the performance was. Listening to the submission, it can be heard that although the individual voices are quite expressive and pleasant (except for the fastest parts), the combination sounds relatively unrealistic. An online MIDI example is available of Schumann's Kindersezenen Op. 15 No. 2, 'Kuriose Geschichte', which evidences both tempo and dynamics expression and is quite impressive, though once again it is not clear how automated the production of the music was.

1.3.1.7 Pop-E

Pop-E [28], a polyphrase ensemble system, was developed by some of the team involved in MIS [32, 33]. It applies expression features separately to each voice in a MIDI file, through a synchronisation algorithm. The music analysis uses GTTM local level rules and utilises beams and slurs in the score to generate note groupings. So the expressive representation is up to phrase level. Expressive actions are applied to these groupings through rules reminiscent of Director Musices. The five performance rules have a total of nine manual parameters between them. These parameters can be adjusted, providing scope for performance creativity. In particular, jPop-E [75], a java implementation of the system, provides such tools for shaping new performances.

To deal with polyphony, synchronisation points are defined at the note-grouping start and end points in the attentive part. The attentive part is the voice which is most perceptually prominent to a listener. The positions of notes in all other non-attentive parts are linearly interpolated relative to the synchronisation points (defined manually). This means that all parts will start and end at the same time at the start and end of groupings of the main attentive part.

Pop-E was evaluated in the laboratory to see how well it could reconstruct specific human performances. After setting parameters manually, performances by three pianists were reconstructed. The average correlation values between Pop-E and a performer were 0.59 for tempo and 0.76 for dynamics. This has to be viewed in the context that the average correlations between the human performers were 0.4 and 0.55, respectively. Also, the upper piano part was more accurate on average. (It is interesting to note that for piano pieces whose attentive part is the right hand, the Pop-E synchronisation system is similar to the methods in the DISTALL [50] system for dealing with polyphony.) Pop-E won the RenCon 2005 compulsory section, beating Director Musices [17] (Chaps. 2 and 7). In RenCon 2006, Pop-E won the compulsory section, beating Kagurame [43] and Ha-Hi-Hun [45]. In the open section in 2006, SuperConductor [21, 22] beat Pop-E with one performance and lost to Pop-E with another.

1.3.1.8 Hermode Tuning

The next two subsections describe successful commercial CSEMPs. Despite the lack of details available on these proprietary systems, they should be included here, since they are practical CSEMPs that people are paying money for and illustrate some of the commercial potential of CSEMPs for the music business. However, because of the lack of some details, the four review terms of reference will not be applied. The first system is Hermode tuning [29]. Most systems in this chapter focus on dynamics and timing. However, intonation is another significant area of expression for many instruments—for example, many string instruments. (In fact, three intonation rules were added to Director Musices in its later incarnations, e.g. the higher the pitch, the sharper the note.) Hermode tuning is a dedicated expressive intonation system which can work in real time, its purpose being to 'imitate the living intonation of well-educated instrumentalists in orchestras and chamber music ensembles'. Instrumentalists do not perform in perfect intonation—in fact, if an orchestra performed music in perfect tuning all the time, the sound would be less pleasant than one that optimised its tuning through performance experience. A series of algorithms are used in Hermode tuning, not just to avoid perfect intonation but to attempt to achieve optimal intonation. The algorithms have settings for different types of music, for example, baroque and jazz/pop. Examples are available on the website, and the system has been successful enough to be embedded in a number of commercial products—for example, Apple Logic Pro 7.

1.3.1.9 Sibelius

As mentioned in the introduction of this chapter, the music typesetting software package Sibelius has built-in algorithms for expressive performance. These use a rule-based approach. Precise details are not available for these commercial algorithms, but some information is available [30]. For dynamics, beat groups such as bar lines, sub-bar groups and beams are used to add varying degrees of stress. Also, the higher the note is, the louder it is played, though volume resets at rests and dynamics expression is constrained to not be excessive. Some random fluctuation is added to dynamics to make it more human sounding as well. Tempo expression is achieved using a simple phrase-based system; however, this does not include reliable phrase analysis. The manufacturer reports that 'phrasing need only be appropriate perhaps 70% of the time—the ear overlooks the rest' and that 'the ear is largely fooled into thinking it is a human performance'. Notion and Finale also have expressive performance systems built into them, which are reportedly more advanced than Sibelius', but even fewer details are available for the proprietary methodologies in these systems.

1.3.1.10 Computational Music Emotion Rule System

In relation to the philosophy behind the computational music emotion rule system (CMERS) [31], Livingstone observes that 'the separation of musical rules into structural and performative is largely an ontological one, and cedes nothing to the final audio experienced by the listener'. The computational music emotion rule system has a rule set of 19 rules developed through analysis-by-synthesis. The rules have an expressive representation up to the phrase level, some requiring manual markup of the score. These rules are designed not only to inject microfeature deviations into the score to generate human-like performances but also to use microfeature and macrofeature deviations to express emotions to the listener. To this end, CMERS is able to change the score itself, recomposing it.

CMERS has a 2-D model of human emotion space with four quadrants going from very active and negative to very active and positive, to very passive and positive through very passive and negative. These four elements combine to give such emotions as angry, bright, contented and despairing. The quadrants were constructed from a review of 20 studies of music and emotion. The rules for expressing emotions include moving between major and minor modes, changing note pitch classes and DM-type rules for small changes in dynamics and tempo. It was found that the addition of the microfeature humanisation rules improved the accuracy of the emotional expression (as opposed to solely using macrofeature 'recomposition' rules). The rules for humanising the performance include some rules which are similar to Director Musices, such as phrase arch and emphasising metrically important beats. Creative performance is possible in CMERS by adjusting the parameters of the rule set, and the emotional specification would allow a user to specify different emotions for different parts of a performance.

A significant number of formal listening tests have been done by Livingstone, and they support the hypothesis that CMERS is more successful than DM at expressing emotions. CMERS is one of the better tested systems in this chapter—one reason being that its aim is more measurable than a purely aesthetic goal. Examples of CMERS are available on the author's webpage.

1.3.2 Linear Regression

Learning CSEMPs can incorporate more knowledge more quickly than non-learning systems. However, such methods do not always provide tools for creative performance because they are strongly rooted in past performances. Before continuing, it should be explained that any CSEMP that learns expressive deviations needs to have a non-expressive reference point, some sort of representation of the music played robotically/neutrally. The CSEMP can then compare this to the score played expressively by a human and learn the deviations. Linear regression is the first learning method which will be addressed. Linear regression models assume a basically linear relationship between the music features and the expressive actions. The advantage of such models is their simplicity. The disadvantage is that assuming music expressive performance as a linear process is almost certainly an oversimplification.

1.3.2.1 Music Interpretation System
The music interpretation systems (MIS) [32–34] generate expressive performances in MIDI format but learn expressive rules from audio recordings. This is done using a spectral analysis system with dynamic programming for note detection.

The system is a simulatory CSEMP and uses a set of linear equations which map score features onto performance deviation actions. Its expressive representation is on the note and phrase level. MIS has methods to include some non-linearities using logical ANDs between music features in the score and a way of reducing redundant music features from its equations. This redundancy reduction improves 'generalisation' ability (the ability for the system to perform music or composers that were not explicitly included in its learning). MIS learns links between music features and performance actions of tempo, dynamics and articulation. The music features used include score expression marks and aspects of GTTM and two other forms of musicological analysis: Leonard Meyer's theory of musical meaning [76] and Narmour's IR theory. IR considers features of the previous two notes in the melody and postulates that a human will expect the melody to move in a certain direction and distance; thus, it can classify each note as being part of a certain expectation structure. Meyer's theory is also an expectation-based approach, but coming from the perspective of game theory.

For testing, MIS was trained on the first half of a Chopin waltz and then used to synthesise the second half. Correlations (accuracies when compared to a human performance of the second half) were: for velocity 0.87, for tempo 0.75 and for duration 0.92. A polyphonic MIS interpretation of Chopin Op. 64 No. 2 was submitted to RenCon 2002. It came third behind DISTALL [50], beating three of the other four automated systems—DM, Kagurame [43] and Ha-Hi-Hun [45].

1.3.2.2 CaRo

CaRo [35–37, 77, 78] is a monophonic CSEMP designed to generate audio files which—like CMERS [31]—express certain moods/emotions. It does not require a score to work from but works on audio files which are mood neutral. The files are however assumed to include the performer's expression of the music's hierarchical structure. Its expressive representation is at the local note level. CaRo's performance actions at the note and intranote level include changes to inter-onset interval, brightness and loudness-envelope centroid. A linear model is used to learn actions—every action has an equation characterised by parameters called shift and range expansion. Each piece of music in a particular mood has its own set of shift and range expansion values. This limits the generalisation potential.

CaRo also learns 'how musical performances are organised in the listener's mind' in terms of moods: hard, heavy, dark, bright, light and soft. To do this, a set of listening experiments analysed by principal component analysis (PCA) generate a two-dimensional space that captures 75% of the variability present in the listening results; this space is used to represent listeners' experience of the moods. A further linear model is learned for each piece of music which maps the mood space onto shift and range expansion values. The user can select any point in the mood space, and CaRo generates an expressive version of the piece. A line can be drawn through mood space, and following that line, in time CaRo can generate a performance morphing through different moods. Apart from the ability to adjust shift and range expansion parameters manually, CaRo's potential for creative performance is extended by its ability to have a line drawn through the mood space. Users can draw trajectories through this space which create entirely novel performances; and this can be done in real time.

For testing, 20-s clips, each from three piano pieces by different composers, were used. A panel of 30 listeners evaluated CaRo's ability to generate pieces with different expressive moods. Results showed that the system gave a good modelling of expressive mood performances as realised by human performers.

1.3.3 Artificial Neural Networks

1.3.3.1 Artificial Neural Network Piano System

The earliest ANN approach is the artificial neural network piano system [38]. It has two incarnations. The first did not learn from human performers: a set of seven monophonic Director Musices rules were selected, and two (loudness and timing) feedforward ANNs learned these rules through being trained on them. By learning a fixed model of Director Musices, the ANN loses the performance creativity of the k values. When monophonic listening tests were done with 20 subjects, using Mozart's Piano Sonatas K331 and K281, the Director Musices performance was rated above the non-expressive computer performance, but the neural network performance rated highest of all. One explanation for the dominance of the ANN over the original DM rules was that the ANN generalised in a more pleasant way than the rules. The other ANN system by Bresin was a simulation CSEMP which also used a separate loudness and timing feedback ANN. The ANNs were trained using actual pianist performances from MIDI, rather than on DM rules, but some of the independently learned rules turned out to be similar to some DM rules. Informal listening tests judged the ANNs as musically acceptable. The network looked at a context of four notes (loudness) and five notes (timing) and so had note- to phrase-level expressive representation, though it required the notes to be manually grouped into phrases before being input.

1.3.3.2 Emotional Flute

The emotional flute system [39] uses explicit music features and artificial neural networks, thus allowing greater generalisation than the related CaRo system [35, 36]. The music features are similar to those used in Director Musices. This CSEMP is strongly related to Bresin's second ANN, extending it into the non-piano realm and adding mood space modelling. Expressive actions include inter-onset interval, loudness and vibrato. Pieces need to be segmented into phrases before being input—this segmentation is performed automatically by another ANN. There are separate nets for timing and for loudness—net designs are similar to Bresin's and have similar levels of expressive representation. There is also a third net for the duration of crescendo and decrescendo at the single note level. However, the nets could not be successfully trained on vibrato, so a pair of rules were generated to handle it. A flautist performed the first part of Telemann's Fantasia No. 2 in nine different moods: cold, natural, gentle, bright, witty, serious, restless, passionate and dark. Like

CaRo, a 2-D mood space was generated and mapped onto the performances by the ANNs, and this mood space can be utilised to give greater performance creativity.

To generate new performances, the network drives a physical model of a flute. Listening tests gave an accuracy of approximately 77% when subjects attempted to assign emotions to synthetic performances. To put this in perspective, even when listening to the original human performances, human recognition levels were not always higher than 77%; the description of emotional moods in music is a fairly subjective process.

1.3.4 Case and Instance-Based Systems

1.3.4.1 SaxEx

Arcos and Lopez de Mantaras' SaxEx [40–42, 64, 79] was one of the first systems to learn performances based on the performance context of mood. Like the trumpet system described earlier [24, 25], SaxEx includes algorithms for extracting notes from audio files and generating expressive audio files from note data. SaxEx also looks at intranote features like vibrato and attack. Unlike the trumpet system, SaxEx needs a non-expressive audio file to perform transformations upon. Narmour's IR theory is used to analyse the music. Other elements used to analyse the music are ideas from jazz theory as well as GTTM TSR. This system's expressive representation is up to phrase level and is automated.

SaxEx was trained on cases from monophonic recordings of a tenor sax playing four jazz standards with different moods (as well as a non-expressive performance). The moods were designed around three dimensions: tender-aggressive, sad-joyful and calm-restless. The mood and local IR, GTTM and jazz structures around a note are linked to the expressive deviations in the performance of that note. These links are stored as performance cases. SaxEx can then be given a non-expressive audio file and told to play it with a certain mood. A further AI method is used then to combine cases: fuzzy logic. For example, if two cases are returned for a particular note in the score and one says play with low vibrato and the other says play with medium vibrato, then fuzzy logic combines them into a low-medium vibrato. The learning of new CBR solutions can be done automatically or manually through a GUI, which affords some performance creativity giving the user a stronger input to the generation of performances. However, this is limited by SaxEx's focus on being a simulation system. There is—like the computational music emotion rule system [31]—the potential for the user to generate a performance with certain moods at different points in the music.

There is no formal testing reported, but SaxEx examples are available online. The authors report 'dozens' of positive comments about the realism of the music from informal listening tests, but no formal testing is reported or details given. The two short examples online (sad and joyful) sound realistic to us, more so than, for example, the trumpet system examples. But the accuracy of the emotional expression was difficult for us to gauge.

1.3.4.2 Kagurame

Kagurame [43, 44] is another case-based reasoning system which—in theory—also allows expressiveness to be generated from moods, this time for piano. However, it is designed to incorporate a wider degree of performance conditions than solely mood, for example, playing in a baroque or romantic style. Rather than GTTM and IR, Kagurame uses its own custom hierarchical note structures to develop and retrieve cases for expressive performance. This hierarchical approach gives good expressive representation. Score analysis automatically divides the score into segments recursively with the restriction that the divided segment must be shorter than one measure. Hence, manual input is required for boundary information for segments longer than one measure. The score patterns are derived automatically after this, as is the learning of expressive actions associated with each pattern. Kagurame acts on timing, articulation and dynamics. There is also a polyphony action called chord time lag—notes in the same chord can be played at slightly different times. It is very much a simulation system with little scope for creative performance.

Results are reported for monophonic classical and romantic styles. Tests were based on learning 20 short Czerny etudes played in each style. Then a 21st piece was performed by Kagurame. Listeners said it 'sounded almost human-like, and expression was acceptable' and that the 'generated performance tended to be similar to human, particularly at characteristic points'. A high percentage of listeners guessed correctly whether the computer piece was romantic or classical style. In RenCon 2004, Kagurame came fourth in one half of the compulsory section, one ahead of Director Musices, but was beaten by DM in the second half, coming fifth. At RenCon 2006, a polyphonic performance of Chopin's piano Etude in E major came second—with Pop-E [28] taking first place.

1.3.4.3 Ha-Hi-Hun

Ha-Hi-Hun [45] utilises data structures designed to allow natural language statements to shape performance conditions (these include data structures to deal with non-monophonic music). The paper focuses on instructions of the form 'generate performance of piece X in the style of an expressive performance of piece Y'. As a result, there are significant opportunities for performance creativity through generating a performance of a piece in the style of a very different second piece or perhaps performing the Y piece, bearing in mind that it will be used to generate creative performances of the X piece. A similar system involving some of the same researchers is discussed in Chap. 8 as part of introducing an approach for automated music structure analysis. The music analysis of Ha-Hi-Hun uses GTTM TSR to highlight the main notes that shape the melody. TSR gives Ha-Hi-Hun an expressive representation above note level. The deviations of the main notes in the piece Y relative to the score of Y are calculated and can then be applied to the main notes in the piece X to be performed by Ha-Hi-Hun. After this, the new deviations in X's main notes are propagated linearly to surrounding notes like 'expressive ripples' moving outwards. The ability of Ha-Hi-Hun to automatically generate expressive performances comes from its ability to generate a new performance X based on a previous human performance Y.

In terms of testing, performances of two pieces were generated, each in the style of performances of another piece. Formal listening results were reported as positive, but few experimental details are given. In RenCon 2002, Ha-Hi-Hun learned to play Chopin Etude Op. 10 No. 3 through learning the style of a human performance of Chopin's Nocturne Op. 32 No. 2. The performance came ninth out of ten submitted performances by other CSEMPs (many of which were manually produced). In RenCon 2004, Ha-Hi-Hun came last in the compulsory section, beaten by both Director Musices and Kagurame [43]. In RenCon 2006, a performance by Ha-Hi-Hun also came third out of six in the compulsory section, beaten by Pop-E [28] and Kagurame.

1.3.4.4 PLCG System

Gerhard Widmer has applied various versions of a rule-based learning approach, attempting to utilise a larger database of music than previous CSEMPs. Chapter 3 discusses some of this work. The PLCG system [46–48] uses data mining to find large numbers of possible performance rules and cluster each set of similar rules into an average rule. This is a system for musicology and simulation rather than one for creative performance. PLCG is Widmer's own meta-learning algorithm—the underlying algorithm being sequential covering [80]. PLCG runs a series of sequential covering algorithms in parallel on the same monophonic musical data and gathers the resulting rules into clusters, generating a single rule from each cluster. The data set was 13 Mozart piano sonatas performed by Roland Batik in MIDI form (only melodies were used—giving 41,116 notes). A note-level structure analysis learns to generate tempo, dynamics and articulation deviations based on the local context—for example, size and direction of intervals, durations of surrounding notes and scale degree. So this CSEMP has a note-level expressive representation. As a result of the PLCG algorithm, 383 performance rules were turned into just 18 rules. Interestingly, some of the generated rules had similarities to some of the Director Musices rule set.

Detailed testing has been done on the PLCG, including its generalisation ability. Widmer's systems are the only CSEMPs surveyed in this chapter that have had any significant generalisation testing. The testing methods were based on correlation approaches. Seven pieces selected from the scores used in learning were regenerated using the rule set. Their tempo/dynamics profiles compared very favourably to those of the original performances. Regenerations were compared to performances by a different human performer Philippe Entremont and showed no degradation relative to the original performer comparison. The rules were also applied to some music in a romantic style (two Chopin pieces), giving encouraging results. There are no reports of formal listening tests.

1.3.4.5 Combined Phrase-Decomposition/PLCG

The above approach was extended by Widmer and Tobudic into a monophonic system whose expressive representation extends into higher levels of the score hierarchy. This was the combined phrase-decomposition/PLCG system [49]. Once again, this is a simulation system rather than one for creative performance.

When learning, this CSEMP takes as input scores that have had their hierarchical phrase structure defined to three levels by a musicologist (who also provides some harmonic analysis), together with an expressive MIDI performance by a professional pianist. Tempo and dynamics curves are calculated from the MIDI performance, and then the system does a multilevel decomposition of these expression curves. This is done by fitting quadratic polynomials to the tempo and dynamics curves (similar to the curves found in Todd's parabola model [18, 19]).

Once the curve fitting has been done, there is still a 'residual' expression in the MIDI performance. This is hypothesised as being due to note-level expression, and the PLCG algorithm is run on the residuals to learn the note-level rules which generate this residual expression. The learning of the non-PLCG tempo and dynamics is done using a case-based learning type method—by a mapping from multiple-level features to the parabola/quadratic curves. An extensive set of music features are used, including length of the note group, melodic intervals between start and end notes, where the pitch apex of the note group is, whether the note group ends with a cadence and the progression of harmony between start, apex and end. This CSEMP has the most sophisticated expressive representation of all the systems described in this chapter.

To generate an expressive performance of a new score, the system moves through the score and in each part runs through all its stored musical features vectors learned from the training; it finds the closest one using a simple distance measure. It then applies the curve stored in this case to the current section of the score. Data for curves at different levels and results of the PLCG are added together to give the expression performance actions.

A battery of correlation tests were performed. Sixteen Mozart sonatas were used to test the system—training on 15 of them and then testing against the remaining one. This process was repeated independently, selecting a new 1 of the 16 and then retraining on the other 15. This gave a set of 16 results which the authors described as 'mixed'. Dynamics generated by the system correlated better with the human performance than a non-expressive performance curve (i.e. straight line) did, in 11 out of 16 cases. For the timing curves, this was true for only 6 out of 16 cases. There are no reports of formal listening tests.

1.3.4.6 DISTALL System

Widmer and Tobudic did further work to improve the results of the combined phrase-decomposition/PLCG, developing the DISTALL system [50, 51] for simulation. The learned performance cases in the DISTALL system are hierarchically linked, in the same way as the note groupings they represent. So when the system is learning sets of expressive cases, it links together the feature sets for a level 3 grouping with all the level 2 and level 1 note groupings it contains. When a new piece is presented for performance and the system is looking at a particular level 3 grouping of the new piece, say X—and X contains a number of level 2 and level 1 subgroupings—then not only are the score features of X compared to all level 3 cases in the memory but the subgroupings of X are compared to the subgroupings of the compared level 3 cases as well. There have been measures available which can do such a comparison in case-based learning before DISTALL (e.g. RIBL [81]). However, DISTALL does it in a way more appropriate to expressive performance—giving a more equal weighting to subgroupings within a grouping and giving this system a high expressive representation.

Once again, correlation testing was done with a similar set of experiments to the section above. All 16 generated performances had smaller dynamics errors relative to the originals than a robotic/neutral performance had. For tempo, 11 of the 16 generated performances were better than a robotic/neutral performance. Correlations varied from 0.89 for dynamics in Mozart K283 to 0.23 for tempo in Mozart K332. The mean correlation for dynamics was 0.7 and for tempo was 0.52. A performance generated by this DISTALL system was entered into RenCon 2002. The competition CSEMP included a simple accompaniment system where dynamics and timing changes calculated for the melody notes were interpolated to allow their application to the accompaniment notes as well. Another addition was a simple heuristic for performing grace notes: the sum of durations of all grace notes for a main note is set equal to 5% of the main note's duration, and the 5% of duration is divided equally amongst the grace notes. The performance was the top-scored automated performance at RenCon 2002—ahead of Kagurame [43], MIS [32] and Ha-Hi-Hun [45]—and it beat one non-automated system.

1.3.5   Statistical Graphical Models

1.3.5.1 Music Plus One

The Music Plus One system [52–54] is able to deal with multiple-instrument polyphonic performances. It has the ability to adjust performances of polyphonic sound files (e.g. orchestral works) to fit as accompaniment for solo performers. This CSEMP contains two modules: the listen and play modules. Listen uses a hidden Markov model (HMM) to track live audio and find the soloist's place in the score in real time. Play uses a Bayesian belief network (BBN) which, at any point in a soloist performance and based on the performance so far, tries to predict the timing of the next note the soloist will play. Music Plus One's BBN is trained by listening to the soloist. As well as timing, the system learns the loudness for each phrase of notes. However, loudness learning is deterministic—it performs the same for each accompaniment of the piece once trained, not changing based on the soloist changing his or her own loudness. Expressive representation is at the note level for timing and phrase level for loudness.

The BBN assumes a smooth changing in tempo, so any large changes in tempo (e.g. a new section of a piece) need to be manually marked up. For playing MIDI files for accompaniment, the score needs to be divided up manually into phrases for dynamics; for using audio files for accompaniment, such a division is not needed. When the system plays back the accompaniment, it can play it back in multiple expressive interpretations depending on how the soloist plays. So it has learned a flexible (almost tempo independent) concept of the soloist's expressive intentions for the piece.

There is no test reported for this system—the author stated the impression that the level of musicality obtained by the system is surprisingly good and asked readers to evaluate the performance themselves by going to the website and listening. Music Plus One is actually being used by composers and for teaching music students. It came in first at RenCon 2003 in the compulsory section with a performance of Chopin's Prelude Number 15, Raindrop, beating Ha-Hi-Hun [45], Kagurame [43] and Widmer's system. To train Music Plus One for this, several performances were recorded played by a human, using a MIDI keyboard. These were used to train the BBN. The model was extended to include velocities for each note, as well as times, with the assumption that the velocity varies smoothly (like a random walk) except at hand-identified phrase boundaries. Then a mean performance was generated from the trained model.

As far as performance creativity goes, the focus on this system is not so much to generate expressive performances as to learn the soloist's expressive behaviour and react accordingly in real time. However, the system has an 'implicit' method of creating new performances of the accompaniment—the soloist can change his or her performance during playback. There is another creative application of this system: multiple pieces have been composed for use specifically with the Music Plus One system—pieces which could not be properly performed without the system. One example contains multiple sections where one musician plays 7 notes whilst the other plays 11. Humans would find it difficult to do this accurately, whereas a soloist and the system can work together properly on this complicated set of polyrhythms.

1.3.5.2 ESP Piano System

Grindlay's ESP piano system [55] is a polyphonic CSEMP designed to simulate expressive playing of pieces of piano music which consist of a largely monophonic melody, with a set of accompanying chords (known as homophony). A hidden Markov model learns expressive performance using music features such as whether the note is the first or last of the piece, the position of the note in its phrase and the note duration relative to its start and the next note's start (called its 'articulation' here). The expressive representation is up to the phrase level. Phrase division is done manually, though automated methods are discussed. The accompaniment is analysed for a separate set of music features, some of which are like the melody music features. Some are unique to chords—for example, the level of consonance/dissonance of the code (based on a method called Euler's solence). Music features are then mapped onto a number of expressive actions such as (for melody) the duration deviation and the velocity of the note compared to the average velocity. For the accompaniment, similar actions are used as well as some chord-only actions, like the relative onset of chord notes (similar to the Kagurame chord time lag). These chordal values are based on the average of the values for the individual notes in the chord.

Despite the focus of this system on homophony, tests were only reported for monophonic melodies, training the HMM on 10 graduate performances of Schumann's Träumerei. Ten out of 14 listeners ranked the expressive ESP output over the inexpressive version. Ten out of 14 ranked the ESP output above that of an undergraduate performance. Four out of seven preferred the ESP output to a graduate student performance.

1.3.6 Other Regression Methods

1.3.6.1 Drumming System

Thus far in this chapter, only pitched instrument systems have been surveyed—mainly piano, saxophone and trumpet. A system for non-pitched (drumming) expression will now be examined. In the introduction, it was mentioned that pop music enthusiastically utilised the 'robotic' aspects of MIDI sequencers. However, eventually pop musicians wanted a more realistic sound to their electronic music, and humanisation systems were developed for drum machines that added random tempo deviations to beats. Later systems also incorporated what are known as grooves—a fixed pattern of tempo deviations which are applied to a drum beat or any part of a MIDI sequence (comparable to a one-level Clynes pulse set discussed earlier). Such groove systems have been applied commercially in mass-market systems like Propellerhead Reason, where it is possible to generate groove templates from a drum track and apply it to any other MIDI track [56]. However, just as some research has suggested limitations in the application of Clynes' composer pulses, so Wright and Berdahl's [82] research shows the limits of groove templates. Their analysis of multi-voiced Brazillian drumming recordings found that groove templates could only account for 30% of expressive timing.

Wright and Berdahl investigated other methods to capture the expressive timing using a system that learns from audio files. The mapping model is based on machine learning regression between audio features and timing deviation (versus a quantized version of the beat). Three different methods of learning the mapping model were tried. This learning approach was found to track the expressive timing of the drums much better than the groove templates. Examples are provided online. Note that the system is not only limited to Brazilian drumming; Wright and Berdahl also tested it on reggae rhythms with similar success.

1.3.6.2 KCCA Piano System

The most recent application of kernel regression methods to expressive performance is the system by [57]. Their main aim is simulatory, to imitate the style of a particular performer and allow new pieces to be automatically performed using the learned characteristics of the performer. A performer is defined based on the 'worm' representation of expressive performance [83]. The worm is a visualisation tool for the dynamics and tempo aspects of expressive performance. It uses a 2-D representation with tempo on the x-axis and loudness on the y-axis. Then, as the piece plays, at fixed periods in the score (e.g. once per bar), an average is calculated for each period and a filled circle plotted on the graph at the average. Past circles remain on the graph, but their colour fades and size decreases as time passes—thus creating the illusion of a wriggling worm whose tail fades off into the distance in time. If the computer played an expressionless MIDI file, then its worm would stand still, not wriggling at all.

The basis of Dorard's approach is to assume that the score and the human performances of the score are two views of the musical semantic content, thus enabling a correlation to be drawn between the worm and the score. The system focuses on homophonic piano music—a continuous upper melody part and an accompaniment—and divides the score into a series of chord and melody pairs. Kernel canonical correlation analysis (KCCA) [84] is then used, a method which looks for a common semantic representation between two views. Its expressive representation is based on the note-group level, since KCCA is looking to find correlations between short groups of notes and the performance worm position. An addition needed to be made to the learning algorithm to prevent extreme expressive changes in tempo and dynamics. This issue is a recurring problem in a number of CSEMPs (e.g. see the systems discussed in this chapter—artificial neural network models and Sibelius).

Testing was performed on Chopin's Etude Op. 10 No. 3—the system was trained on the worm of the first 8 bars and then tried to complete the worm for bars 9–12. The correlation between the original human performance worm for 9–12 and the reconstructed worm was measured to be 0.95, whereas the correlation with a random worm was 0.51. However, the resulting performances were reported (presumably through informal listening tests) to be not very realistic.

1.3.7 Evolutionary Computation

A number of more recent CSEMPs have used evolutionary computation methods, such as genetic algorithms [85] or multi-agent systems [86]. In general (but not always), such systems have opportunities for performance creativity. They often have a parameterisation that is simple to change—for example, a fitness function. They also have an emergent [87] output which can sometimes produce unexpected but coherent results.

1.3.7.1 Genetic Programming Jazz Sax

Some of the first researchers to use EC in computer systems for expressive performance were Ramirez and Hazan. They did not start out using EC, beginning with a regression tree system for jazz saxophone [88] (more detail about their machine learning work—applied to violin—can be found in Chap. 5.) This system will be described before moving on to the genetic programming (GP) approach, as it is the basis of their later GP work. A performance decision tree was first built using a learning algorithm called C4.5. This model was built for musicological purposes—to see what kinds of rules were generated—not to generate any performances. The decision tree system had a 3-note-level expressive representation, and music features used to characterise a note included metrical position and some Narmour IR analysis. These features were mapped onto a number of performance actions from the training performances, such as lengthen/shorten note, play note early/late and play note louder/softer. Monophonic audio was used to build this decision tree using the authors' own spectral analysis techniques and five jazz standards at 11 different tempos. The actual performing system was built as a regression rather than decision tree, thus allowing continuous expressive actions. The continuous performance features simulated were duration, onset and energy variation (i.e. loudness). The learning algorithm used to build the tree was M5Rules, and performances could be generated via MIDI and via audio using the synthesis algorithms. In tests, the resulting correlations with the original performances were 0.72, 0.44 and 0.67 for duration, onset and loudness, respectively. Other modelling methods were tried (linear regression and four different forms of support vector machines) but did not fare as well correlation-wise.

Ramirez and Hazan's next system [58] was also based on regression trees, but these trees were generated using genetic programming (GP), which is ideal for building a population of 'if-then' regression trees. GP was used to search for regression trees that best emulated a set of human audio performance actions. The regression tree models were basically the same as in their previous paper, but in this case a whole series of trees was generated; they were tested for fitness, and then the fittest were used to produce the next generation of trees/programs (with some random mutations added). Fitness was judged based on a distance calculated from a human performance. Creativity and expressive representation are enhanced because, in addition to modelling timing and dynamics, the trees modelled the expressive combining of multiple score notes into a single perfor-mance note (consolidation) and the expressive insertion of one or several short notes to anticipate another performance note (ornamentation). These elements are fairly common in jazz saxophone. It was possible to examine these deviations because the fitness function was implemented using an edit distance to measure score edits.

This evolution was continued until average fitness across the population of trees ceased to increase. The use of GP techniques was deliberately applied to give a range of options for the final performance since, as the authors say, 'perfor-mance is an inexact phenomenon'. Also, because of the mutation element in genetic programming, there is the possibility of unusual performances being generated. So this CSEMP has quite a good potential for performance creativity. No evaluation was reported of the resulting trees' performances—but average fitness stopped increasing after 20 generations.

1.3.7.2 Sequential Covering Algorithm GAs

The sequential covering algorithm genetic algorithm (GA) by Ramirez and Hazan [59] uses sequential covering to learn performance. Each covering rule is learned using a GA, and a series of such rules are built up, covering the whole problem space. In this paper, the authors return to their first (non-EC) paper's level of expressive representation—looking at note-level deviations without orna-mentation or consolidation. However, they make significant improvements over their original non-EC paper. The correlation coefficients for onset, duration and energy/loudness in the original system were 0.72, 0.44 and 0.67—but in this new system, they were 0.75, 0.84 and 0.86—significantly higher. And this system also has the advantage of slightly greater creativity due to its GA approach.

1.3.7.3 Generative Performance GAs

A parallel thread of EC research are Zhang and Miranda's [89] monophonic generative performance GAs which evolve pulse sets [21]. Rather than comparing the generated performances to actual performances, the fitness function here expresses constraints inspired by the generative performance work of Eric Clarke [11]. When a score is presented to the GA system for performance, the system constructs a theoretical timing and dynamics curve for the melody (one advantage of this CSEMP is that this music analysis is automatic). However, this curve is not used directly to generate the actual performance but to influence the evolution. This, together with the GA approach, it increases the performance creativity of the system. The timing curve comes from an algorithm based on Cambouropoulos' [90] local boundary detection model (LBDM)—the inputs to this model are score note timing, pitch and harmonic intervals. The resulting curve is higher for greater boundary strengths. The approximate dynamics curve is calculated from a number of components—the harmonic distance between two notes (based on a measure by Krumhans [91]), the metrical strength of a note (based on the Melisma software [92]) and the pitch height. These values are multiplied for each note to generate a dynamics curve. The expressive representation of this system is the same as the expressive representation of the methodologies used to generate the theoretical curves.

A fitness function is constructed referring to the score representation curves. It has three main elements—fitness is awarded if (1) the pulse set dynamics and timing deviations follow the same direction as the generated dynamics and timing curves; (2) timing deviations are increased at boundaries and (3) timing deviations are not too extreme. Point (1) does not mean that the pulse sets are the same as the dynamics and timing curves, but—all else being equal—that if the dynamics curve moves up between two notes and the pulse set moves up between those two notes, then that pulse set will get a higher fitness than one that moves down there. Regarding point (3), this is reminiscent of the restriction of expression used in the ANN models [38] and the KCCA piano [57] model described earlier. It is designed to preventing the deviations from becoming too extreme.

There has been no formal testing of this GA work, though the authors demonstrate—using an example of part of Schumann's Träumerei and a graphical plot—that the evolved pulse sets are consistent in at least one example with the theoretical timing and dynamics deviation curves. They claim that 'when listening to pieces performed with the evolved pulse sets, we can perceive the expressive dynamics of the piece'. However, more evaluation would be helpful; repeating pulse sets have been shown to not be universally applicable as an expressive action format. Post-Clynes CSEMPs have shown more success using non-cyclic expression.

1.3.7.4 Multi-Agent System with Imitation

Miranda's team [60, 93] developed the above system into a multi-agent system (MAS) with imitation—influenced by Miranda's [94] evolution of music MAS study and inspired by the hypothesis that expressive music performance strategies emerge through interaction and evolution in the performers' society. It is described in more detail in Chap. 4. In this model, each agent listens to other agents' monophonic performances, evaluates them and learns from those whose performances are better than their own. Every agent's evaluation equation is the same as the fitness function used in the previous GA-based system, and performance deviations are modelled as a hierarchical pulse set. So it has the same expressive representation.

This CSEMP has significant performance creativity, one reason being that the pulse sets generated may have no similarity to the hierarchical constraints of human pulse sets. They are generated mathematically and abstractly from agent imitation performances. So entirely novel pulse set types could be produced by agents that a human would never generate. Another element that contributes to creativity is that although a global evaluation function approach was used, a diversity of performances was found to be produced in the population of agents.

1.3.7.5 Ossia

Like the computational music emotion rule system [31], Dahlstedt's [61] Ossia is a CSEMP which incorporates both compositional and performance aspects. However, whereas CMERS was designed to operate on a composition, Ossia is able to generate entirely new and expressively performed compositions. Although it is grouped here as an EC learning system, technically Ossia is not a learning system. It is not using EC to learn how to perform like a human but to generate novel compositions and performances. However, it is included in this section because its issues relate more closely to EC and learning systems than to any of the non-learning systems (the same reason applies for the system *pMIMACS* described in the next section). Ossia generates music through a novel representational structure that encompasses both composition and performance—recursive trees (generated by GAs). These are 'upside-down trees' containing both performance and composition information. The bottom leaves of the tree going from left to right represent actual notes (each with their own pitch, duration and loudness value) in the order they are played. The branches above the notes represent transformations on those notes. To generate music, the tree is flattened—the 'leaves' higher up act upon the leaves lower down when being flattened to produce a performance/composition. So going from left to right in the tree represents music in time. The trees are generated recursively—this means that the lower branches of the tree are transformed copies of higher parts of the tree. Here we have an element we argue is the key to combined performance and composition systems—a common representation—in this case transformations.

This issue of music representation is not something this survey has addressed explicitly, being in itself an issue worthy of its own review, for examples, see [67, 95]. However, a moment will be taken to briefly discuss it now. The representation chosen for a musical system has a significant impact on the functionality—Ossia's representation is what leads to its combined composition and performance generation abilities. The most common music representation mentioned in this chapter has been MIDI, which is not able to encode musical structure directly. As a result, some MIDI-based CSEMPs have to supply multiple files to the CSEMP, a MIDI file together with files describing musical structure. More flexible representations than MIDI include MusicXML, ENP-score-notation [96], WEDELMUSIC XML [97], MusicXML4R [98] and the proprietary representations used by commercial software such as Sibelius, Finale, Notion and Zenph high-resolution MIDI [99] (which was recently used on a released CD of automated Disklavier re-performances of Glenn Gould).

Many of the performance systems described in this chapter so far transform an expressionless MIDI or audio file into an expressive version. Composition is often done in a similar way—motifs are transformed into new motifs, and themes are transformed into new expositions. Ossia uses a novel transformation-based music representation. In Ossia, transformations of note, loudness and duration are possible—the inclusion of note transformations here emphasising the composition aspect of the Ossia. The embedding of these transformations into recursive trees leads to the generation of gradual crescendos, decrescendos and duration curves—which sound like performance strategies to a listener. Because of this, Ossia has a good level of performance creativity. The trees also create a structure of themes and expositions. Ossia uses a GA to generate a population of trees and judges for fitness using such rules as number of notes per second, repetitivity, amount of silence, pitch variation and level of recursion. These fitness rules were developed heuristically by Dahlstedt through analysis-by-synthesis methods.

Ossia's level of expressive representation is equal to its level of compositional representation. Dahlstedt observes 'The general concept of recapitulation is not possible, as in the common ABA form. This does not matter so much in short compositions, but may be limiting.' So Ossia's expressive representation would seem to be within the A's and B's, giving it a note- to section-level expressive representation. In terms of testing, the system has not been formally evaluated, though it was exhibited as an installation at Gaudeamus Music Week in Amsterdam. Examples are also available on Dahlstedt's website, including a composed suite. The author claims that the sound examples 'show that the Ossia system has the potential to generate and perform piano pieces that could be taken for human contemporary compositions'. The examples on the website are impressive in their natural quality. The question of how to test a combined performance and composition, when that system is not designed to simulate but to create, is a sophisticated problem which will not be addressed here. Certainly, listening tests are a possibility, but these may be biased by the preferences of the listener (e.g. preferring pre-1940s classical music or pop music). Another approach is musicological analysis, but the problem then becomes that musicological tools are not available for all genres and all periods—for example, musicology is more developed for pre-1940 than post-1940 art music.

An example score from Ossia is described which contains detailed dynamics and articulations and subtle tempo fluctuations and rubato. This subtlety raises another issue—scores generated by Ossia in common music notation had to be simplified to be simply readable by humans. The specification of exact microfeatures in a score can lead to it being unplayable except by computer or the most skilled concert performer. This has a parallel in a compositional movement which emerged in the 1970s, the 'New Complexity', involving composers such as Brian Ferneyhough and Richard Barrett [100]. In the 'New Complexity', elements of the score are often specified down to the microfeature level, and some scores are described as almost unplayable. Compositions such as this, whether by human or computer, bring into question the whole composition/performance dichotomy. (These issues also recall the end of Ian Pace's quote in the first section of this chapter.) However, technical skill limitations and common music notation scores are not necessary for performance if the piece is being written on and performed by a computer. Microfeatures can be generated as part of the computer (or computer-aided) composition process if desired. In systems such as Ossia and CMERS [31], as in the New Complexity, the composition/performance dichotomy starts to break down—the dichotomy is really between macrofeatures and microfeatures of the music.

1.3.7.6 pMIMACS

Before discussing this final system in the survey, another motivation for bringing composition and performance closer in CSEMPs should be highlighted. A significant amount of CSEMP effort is in analysing the musical structure of the score/audio (using methods like that in Chap. 8). However, many computer composition systems generate a piece based on some structure which can often be made explicitly available. So in computer music it is often inefficient to have separate composition and expressive performance systems—i.e. where a score is generated and the CSEMP sees the score as a black box and performs a structure analysis. Greater efficiency and accuracy would require a protocol allowing the computer composition system to communicate structure information directly to the CSEMP or—like Ossia—simply combine the systems using, for example, a common representation (where microtiming and microdynamics are seen as an actual part of the composition process). A system which was designed to utilise this combination of performance and composition is pMIMACS, developed by the authors of this survey. It is based on a previous system MIMACS (mimetics-inspired multi-agent composition system), which was developed to solve a specific compositional problem: generating a multi-speaker electronic composition.

pMIMACS combines composition and expressive performance—the aim being to generate contemporary compositions on a computer which, when played back on a computer, do not sound too machine-like. In [60] (Chap. 4), the agents imitate each other's expressive performances of the same piece, whereas in pMIMACS, agents can be performing entirely different pieces of music. The agent cycle is a process of singing and assimilation. Initially, all agents are given their own tune—these may be random or chosen by the composer. An agent (A) is chosen to start. A performs its tune, based on its performance skill (explained below). All other agents listen to A, and the agent with the most similar tune, say agent B, adds its interpretation of A's tune to the start or end of its current tune. There may be pitch and timing errors due to its 'mishearing'. Then the cycle begins again but with B performing its extended tune in the place of A.

An agent's initial performing skills are defined by the MIDI pitch average and standard deviation of their initial tune—this could be interpreted as the range they are comfortable performing in or as the tune they are familiar with performing. The further away a note's pitch is from the agent's average learned pitch, the slower the tempo at which the agent will perform. Also, further away pitches will be played more quietly. An agent updates its skill/range as it plays. Every time it plays a note, that note changes the agent's average and standard deviation pitch value. So when an agent adds an interpretation of another agent's tune to its own, then as the agent performs the new extended tune, its average and standard deviation (skill/range) will update accordingly—shifting and perhaps widening—changed by the new notes as it plays them. In pMIMACS, an agent also has a form of performance context, called an excitability state. An excited agent will play its tune with twice the tempo of a non-excited agent, making macro-errors in pitch and rhythm as a result.

The listening agent has no way of knowing whether the pitches, timings and amplitude that it is hearing are due to the performance skills of the performing agent or part of the 'original' composition. So the listening agent attempts to memorise the tune as it hears it, including any performance errors or changes. As the agents perform to each other, they store internally an exponentially growing piece of transforming music. The significant and often smooth deviations in tempo generated by the performance interaction will create a far less robotic-sounding performance than rhythms generated by a quantized palette would do. On the downside, the large-scale rhythmic texture has the potential to become repetitive because of the simplicity of the agents' statistical model of performance skill. Furthermore, the system can generate rests that are so long that the composition effectively comes to a halt for the listener. But overall the MAS is expressing its experience of what it is like to perform the tune, by changing the tempo and dynamics of the tune, and at the same time, this contributes to the composition of the music.

There is also a more subtle form of expression going on relating to the hierarchical structure of the music. The hierarchy develops as agents pass around an ever growing string of phrases. Suppose an agent performs a phrase P and passes it on. Later on, it may receive back a 'super-phrase' containing two other phrases Q and R—in the form QPR. In this case, agent A will perform P faster than Q and R (since it knows P). Now suppose in future A is passed back a super-super-phrase of, say, SQPRTQPRTS, then potentially it will play P fastest, QPR second fastest (since it has played QPR before) and the S and T phrases slowest. So the tempo and amplitude at which an agent performs the parts SQPRTQPRTS are affected by how that phrase was built up hierarchically in the composition/imitation process. Thus, there is an influence on the performance from the hierarchical structure of the music. This effect is only approximate because of the first-order statistical model of performance skill.

No formal listening tests have been completed yet, but examples of an agent's tune memory after a number of cycles are available from the authors by request. Despite the lack of formal listening tests, pMIMACS is reported here as a system designed from the ground up to combine expressive performance and composition.

1.4   Summary

Before reading this summary, another viewing of Table 1.1 at the start of the chapter may be helpful to the reader. Expressive performance is a complex behaviour with many causative conditions—so it is no surprise that in this chapter almost two thirds of the systems produced have been learning CSEMPs, usually learning to map music features onto expressive actions. Expressive performance actions most commonly included timing and loudness adjustments, with some articulation, and the most common non-custom method for analysis of music features was GTTM, followed by IR. Due to its simplicity in modelling performance, the most common instrument simulated was piano—but interestingly this was followed closely by saxophone—possibly because of the popularity of the instrument in the jazz genre. Despite, and probably because, of its simplicity, MIDI is still the most popular representation.

To help structure the chapter, four primary terms of reference were selected: testing status, expressive representation, polyphonic ability and performance creativity. Having applied these, it can be seen that only a subset of the systems have had any formal testing, and for some of them designing formal tests is a challenge in itself. This is not that unexpected—since testing a creative computer system is an unsolved problem and is discussed more in Chap. 7. Also about half of the systems have only been tested on monophonic tunes. Polyphony and homophony introduce problems both in terms of synchronisation and in terms of music feature analysis (see Chap. 6). Further to music feature analysis, most of the CSEMPs had an expressive representation up to one bar/phrase, and over half did not look at the musical hierarchy. However, avoiding musical hierarchy analysis can have the advantage of increasing automation. We have also seen that most CSEMPs are designed for simulation of human expressive performances, general or specific—a valuable research goal and one which has possibly been influenced by the philosophy of human simulation in machine intelligence research.

The results for the primary terms of reference are summarised in Table 1.5. The numerical measures in columns 1, 2 and 4 are an attempt to quantify observations, scaled from 1 to 10. The more sophisticated the expressive representation of music features (levels of the hierarchy, harmony, etc.), the higher the number in column 1. The more extensive the testing (including informal listening, RenCon

Table 1.5 Summary of the four primary terms of reference

CSEMP	Expressive representation	Testing status	Non-monophonic	Performance creativity
Director Musices	6	10	Y	8
Hierarchical parabola model	8	7		3
Composer pulse	6	9	Y	5
Bach fugue	6	4	Y	3
Rubato	7	4	Y	8
Trumpet synthesis	4	1		3
MIS	6	6	Y	3
ANN piano	4	6		3
Music Plus One	4	7	Y	4
SaxEx	5	1		8
CaRo	3	6		7
Emotional flute	4	6		6
Kagurame	8	8	Y	3
Ha-Hi-Hun	6	6	Y	8
PLCG	4	6		3
Phrase-decomposition/PLCG	10	6		3
DISTALL	10	9	Y	3
Pop-E	6	10	Y	8
ESP piano	6	6	Y	3
KCCA piano	4	6	Y	3
Drumming	3	6		3
Genetic programming	7	6		6
Sequential covering GAs	6	6		6
Generative performance GAs	8	4		8
MAS with imitation	8	1		9
Ossia	6	4	Y	10
Music emotionality	6	6	Y	10
pMIMACS	8	1		10

submission, formal listening, correlation and/or successful utilisation in the field), the higher the number in column 2. The greater we perceived the potential of a system to enable the creative generation of novel performances, the higher the number in column 4. Obviously, such measures contain some degree of subjectivity but should be a useful indicator for anyone wanting an overview of the field, based on the four elements discussed at the start of this chapter. Figure 1.4 shows a 3-D plot summary of Table 1.5.

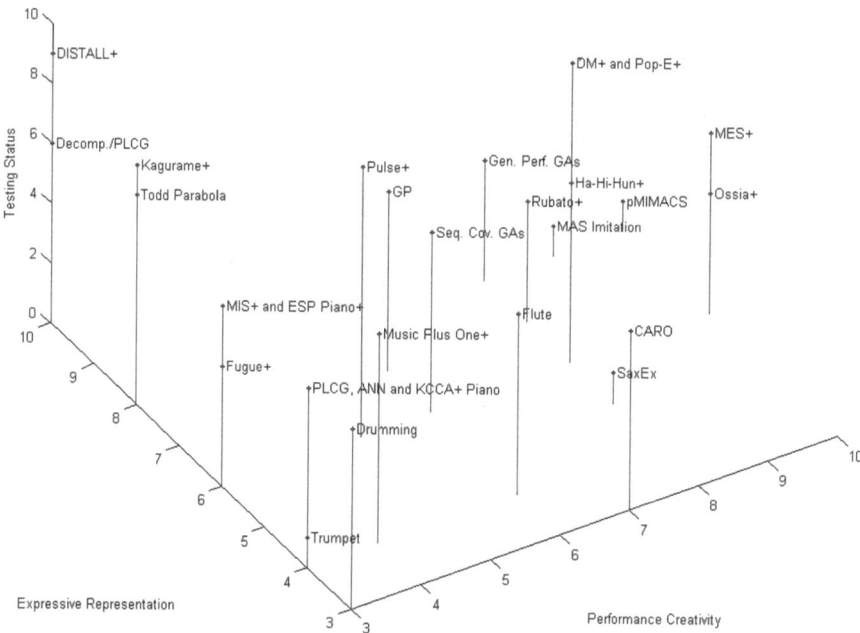

Fig. 1.4 Evaluation of reviewed systems relative to terms of reference ('+' means polyphonic)

1.5   Conclusions

There have been significant achievements in the field of simulating human musical performance in the last 30 years, and there are many opportunities ahead for future improvements in simulation. In fact, one aim of the RenCon competitions is for a computer to win the Chopin competition by 2050. Such an aim begs some philosophical and historical questions but nonetheless captures the level of progress being made in performance simulation. The areas of expressive representation and polyphonic performance appear to be moving forwards. However, the issue of testing and evaluation still requires more work and would be a fruitful area for future CSEMP research.

Another fruitful area for research is around the issue of the automation of the music analysis. Of the eight CSEMPs with the highest expressive representation, almost half of them require some manual input to perform the music analysis. Also, manual marking of the score into phrases is a common requirement. There has been some research into automating musical analysis such as GTTM, as can be seen in Chap. 8. The usage of such techniques, and the investigation of further automation analysis methods specific to expressive performance, would be a useful contribution to the field.

The field could also benefit from a wider understanding of the relationship between performance and composition elements in computer music, for reasons of efficiency, controllability and creativity. This chapter began by developing four terms of reference which were inspired from research into computer composition systems and has been brought to a close with a pair of systems that question the division between expressive performance and composition. Computer composition and computer performance research can cross-fertilise: performance algorithms for expressing structure and emotion/mood can help composition as well as composition providing more creative and controlled computer performance. Such a cross-fertilisation happens to some degree in Chap. 8. The question is also open as to what forms of non-human expression can be developed and provide whole new vistas of the meaning of the phrase 'expressive performance', perhaps even for human players.

One final observation regards the lack of neurological and physical models of performance simulation. The issue was not included as a part of our terms of reference, since it is hard to objectively quantify. But we would like to address this in closing. Neurological and physical modelling of performance should go beyond ANNs and instrument physical modelling. The human/instrument performance process is a complex dynamical system about which there has been some deeper psychological and physical study. However, attempts to use these hypotheses to develop computer performance systems have been rare. More is being learned about the neural correlates of music and emotion [101–103], and Eric Clarke [104] has written on the importance of physical embeddedness of human performance. But although researchers such as Parncutt [105] (in his virtual pianist approach) and Widmer [106] have highlighted the opportunity for deeper models, there has been relatively little published progress in this area of the CSEMP field, though the issues of physically embedded performance are examined further in Chap. 9.

So to conclude, the overarching focus so far means that there are opportunities for some better tested, more creative and neurological and biomechanical models of human performance. These will be systems which help not only to win the Chopin contest but also to utilise the innate efficiencies and power of computer music techniques. Music psychologists and musicologists will be provided with richer models; composers will be able to work more creatively in the micro-specification domain and more easily and accurately generate expressive performances of their work. And the music industry will be able to expand the power of humanisation tools, creating new efficiencies in recording and performance.

Acknowledgements This work was financially supported by the EPSRC-funded project 'Learning the Structure of Music', grant EP/D062934/1. An earlier version of this chapter was published in ACM Computing Surveys Vol. 42, No. 1.

Questions

1. Give two examples of why humans make their performances sound so different to the so-called perfect performance a computer would give.
2. What is the purpose of the 'performance context' module in a generic computer system for expressive music performance?

3. What are two examples of ways in which the performance knowledge system might store its information?
4. Give five reasons that enable computers to perform music expressively.
5. What is the most common form of instrument used in studying computer systems for expressive music performance?
6. What are the two most common forms of expressive performance action?
7. Why is musical structure analysis so significant in computer systems for expressive music performance?
8. In what ways does most Western music usually have a hierarchical structure?
9. What are the potential advantages of combining algorithm composition with expressive performance?
10. Do most of the CSEMPs discussed in this chapter deal with MIDI or audio formats?

References

1. Hiller L, Isaacson L (1959) Experimental music. Composition with an electronic computer. McGraw-Hill, New York
2. Buxton WAS (1977) A composer's introduction to computer music. Interface 6:57–72
3. Roads C (1996) The computer music tutorial. MIT Press, Cambridge
4. Miranda ER (2001) Composing music with computers. Focal Press, Oxford
5. Todd NP (1985) A model of expressive timing in tonal music. Music Percept 3:33–58
6. Friberg A, Sundberg J (1999) Does music performance allude to locomotion? A model of final ritardandi derived from measurements of stopping runners. J Acoust Soc Am 105:1469–1484
7. Pace I (2007) Complexity as imaginative stimulant: issues of rubato, barring, grouping, accentuation and articulation in contemporary music, with examples from Boulez, Carter, Feldman, Kagel, Sciarrino, Finnissy. In: Proceedings of the 5th international Orpheus academy for music, theory, Gent, Belgium, Apr 2007
8. Seashore CE (1938) Psychology of music. McGraw-Hill, New York
9. Palmer C (1997) Music performance. Annu Rev Psychol 48:115–138
10. Gabrielsson A (2003) Music performance research at the millennium. Psychol Music 31:221–272
11. Clarke EF (1998) Generative principles in music performance. In: Sloboda JA (ed) Generative processes in music: the psychology of performance, improvisation, and composition. Clarendon, Oxford, pp 1–26
12. Gabrielsson A, Juslin P (1996) Emotional expression in music performance: between the performer's intention and the listener's experience. Psychol Music 24:68–91
13. Juslin P (2003) Five facets of musical expression: a psychologist's perspective on music performance. Psychol Music 31:273–302
14. Good M (2001) MusicXML for notation and analysis. In: Hewlett WB, Selfridge-Field E (eds) The virtual score: representation, retrieval, restoration. MIT Press, Cambridge, pp 113–124
15. Lerdahl F, Jackendoff R (1938) A generative theory of tonal music. The MIT Press, Cambridge
16. Narmour E (1990) The analysis and cognition of basic melodic structures: the implication-realization model. The University of Chicago Press, Chicago
17. Friberg A, Bresin R, Sundberg J (2006) Overview of the KTH rule system for musical performance. Adv Cognit Psychol 2:145–161

18. Todd NP (1989) A computational model of Rubato. Contemp Music Rev 3:69–88
19. Todd NP (1992) The dynamics of dynamics: a model of musical expression. J Acoust Soc Am 91:3540–3550
20. Todd NP (1995) The kinematics of musical expression. J Acoust Soc Am 97:1940–1949
21. Clynes M (1986) Generative principles of musical thought: integration of microstructure with structure. Commun Cognit 3:185–223
22. Clynes M (1995) Microstructural musical linguistics: composer's pulses are liked best by the musicians. Cognit: Int J Cognit Sci 55:269–310
23. Johnson ML (1991) Toward an expert system for expressive musical performance. Computer 24:30–34
24. Dannenberg RB, Derenyi I (1998) Combining instrument and performance models for high-quality music synthesis. J New Music Res 27:211–238
25. Dannenberg RB, Pellerin H, Derenyi I (1998) A study of trumpet envelopes. In: Proceedings of the 1998 international computer music conference, Ann Arbor, Michigan, October 1998. International Computer Music Association, San Francisco, pp 57–61
26. Mazzola G, Zahorka O (1994) Tempo curves revisited: hierarchies of performance fields. Comput Music J 18(1):40–52
27. Mazzola G (2002) The topos of music – geometric logic of concepts, theory, and performance. Birkhäuser, Basel/Boston
28. Hashida M, Nagata N, Katayose H (2006) Pop-E: a performance rendering system for the ensemble music that considered group expression. In: Baroni M, Addessi R, Caterina R, Costa M (eds) Proceedings of 9th international conference on music perception and cognition, Bologna, Spain, August 2006. ICMPC, pp 526–534
29. Sethares W (2004) Tuning, timbre, spectrum, scale. Springer, London
30. Finn B (2007) Personal communication
31. Livingstone SR, Muhlberger R, Brown AR, Loch A (2007) Controlling musical emotionality: an affective computational architecture for influencing musical emotions. Digit Creat 18:43–53
32. Katayose H, Fukuoka T, Takami K, Inokuchi S (1990) Expression extraction in virtuoso music performances. In: Proceedings of the 10th international conference on pattern recognition, Atlantic City, New Jersey, USA, June 1990. IEEE Press, Los Alamitos, pp 780–784
33. Aono Y, Katayose H, Inokuchi S (1997) Extraction of expression parameters with multiple regression analysis. J Inf Process Soc Jpn 38:1473–1481
34. Ishikawa O, Aono Y, Katayose H, Inokuchi S (2000) Extraction of musical performance rule using a modified algorithm of multiple regression analysis. In: Proceedings of the international computer music conference, Berlin, Germany, August 2000. International Computer Music Association, San Francisco, pp 348–351
35. Canazza S, Drioli C, De Poli G, Roda A, Vidolin A (2000) Audio morphing different expressive intentions for multimedia systems. IEEE Multimed 7:79–83
36. Canazza S, De Poli G, Drioli C, Roda A, Vidolin A (2001) Expressive morphing for interactive performance of musical scores. In: Proceedings of first international conference on WEB delivering of music, Florence, Italy, Nov 2001. IEEE, Los Alamitos, pp 116–122
37. Canazza S, De Poli G, Roda A, Vidolin A (2003) An abstract control space for communication of sensory expressive intentions in music performance. J New Music Res 32:281–294
38. Bresin R (1998) Artificial neural networks based models for automatic performance of musical scores. J New Music Res 27:239–270
39. Camurri A, Dillon R, Saron A (2000) An experiment on analysis and synthesis of musical expressivity. In: Proceedings of 13th colloquium on musical informatics, L'Aquila, Italy, Sept 2000
40. Arcos JL, De Mantaras RL, Serra X (1997) SaxEx: a case-based reasoning system for generating expressive musical performances. In: Cook PR (eds) Proceedings of 1997 international computer music conference, Thessalonikia, Greece, Sept 1997. ICMA, San Francisco, pp 329–336
41. Arcos JL, Lopez De Mantaras R, Serra X (1998) Saxex: a case-based reasoning system for generating expressive musical performance. J New Music Res 27:194–210

42. Arcos JL, Lopez De Mantaras R (2001) An interactive case-based reasoning approach for generating expressive music. J Appl Intell 14:115–129
43. Suzuki T, Tokunaga T, Tanaka H (1999) A case based approach to the generation of musical expression. In: Proceedings of the 16th international joint conference on artificial intelligence, Stockholm, Sweden, Aug 1999. Morgan Kaufmann, San Francisco, pp 642–648
44. Suzuki T (2003) Kagurame phase-II. In: Gottlob G, Walsh T (eds) Proceedings of 2003 international joint conference on artificial intelligence (Working Notes of RenCon Workshop), Acapulco, Mexico, Aug 2003. Morgan Kauffman, Los Altos
45. Hirata K, Hiraga R (2002) Ha-Hi-Hun: performance rendering system of high controllability. In: Proceedings of the ICAD 2002 RenCon workshop on performance rendering systems, Kyoto, Japan, July 2002, pp 40–46
46. Widmer G (2000) Large-scale induction of expressive performance rules: first quantitative results. In: Zannos I (eds) Proceedings of the 2000 international computer music conference, Berlin, Germany, Sept 2000. International Computer Music Association, San Francisco, 344–347
47. Widmer G (2002) Machine discoveries: a few simple, robust local expression principles. J New Music Res 31:37–50
48. Widmer G (2003) Discovering simple rules in complex data: a meta-learning algorithm and some surprising musical discoveries. Artif Intell 146:129–148
49. Widmer G, Tobudic A (2003) Playing Mozart by analogy: learning multi-level timing and dynamics strategies. J New Music Res 32:259–268
50. Tobudic A, Widmer G (2003) Relational ibl in music with a new structural similarity measure. In: Horvath T, Yamamoto A (eds) Proceedings of the 13th international conference on inductive logic programming, Szeged, Hungary, Sept 2003. Springer Verlag, Berlin, pp 365–382
51. Tobudic A, Widmer G (2003) Learning to play Mozart: recent improvements. In: Hirata K (eds) Proceedings of the IJCAI'03 workshop on methods for automatic music performance and their applications in a public rendering contest (RenCon), Acapulco, Mexico, Aug 2003
52. Raphael C (2001) Can the computer learn to play music expressively? In: Jaakkola T, Richardson T (eds) Proceedings of eighth international workshop on artificial intelligence and statistics, 2001. Morgan Kaufmann, San Francisco, pp 113–120
53. Raphael C (2001) A Bayesian network for real-time musical accompaniment. Neural Inf Process Sys 14:1433–1440
54. Raphael C (2003) Orchestra in a box: a system for real-time musical accompaniment. In: Gottlob G, Walsh T (eds) Proceedings of 2003 international joint conference on artificial intelligence (Working Notes of RenCon Workshop), Acapulco, Mexico, Aug 2003. Morgan Kaufmann, San Francisco, pp 5–10
55. Grindlay GC (2005) Modelling expressive musical performance with Hidden Markov Models. PhD thesis, University of Santa Cruz, CA
56. Carlson L, Nordmark A Wikilander R (2003) Reason version 2.5 – getting started. Propellerhead Software
57. Dorard L, Hardoon DR, Shawe-Taylor J (2007) Can style be learned? A machine learning approach towards 'performing' as famous pianists. In: Music, brain and cognition workshop, NIPS 2007, Whistler, Canada
58. Hazan A, Ramirez R (2006) Modelling expressive performance using consistent evolutionary regression trees. In: Brewka G, Coradeschi S, Perini A, Traverso P (eds) Proceedings of 17th European conference on artificial intelligence (Workshop on Evolutionary Computation), Riva del Garda, Italy, Aug 2006. IOS Press, Washington, DC
59. Ramirez R, Hazan A (2007) Inducing a generative expressive performance model using a sequential-covering genetic algorithm. In: Proceedings of 2007 genetic and evolutionary computation conference, London, UK, July 2007. ACM Press, New York
60. Miranda ER, Kirke A, Zhang Q (2010) Artificial evolution of expressive performance of music: an imitative multi-agent systems approach. Comput Music J 34(1):80–96
61. Dahlstedt P (2007) Autonomous evolution of complete piano pieces and performances. In: Proceedings of ECAL 2007 workshop on music and artificial life (MusicAL 2007), Lisbon, Portugal, Sept 2007

62. Papadopoulos G, Wiggins GA (1999) AI methods for algorithmic composition: a survey, a critical view, and future prospects. In: Proceedings of the AISB'99 symposium on musical creativity. AISB, Edinburgh
63. Hiraga R, Bresin R, Hirata K, RenCon KH (2004) Turing test for musical expression proceedings of international conference on new interfaces for musical expression. In: Nagashima Y, Lyons M (eds) Proceedings of 2004 new interfaces for musical expression conference, Hamatsu, Japan, June 2004. Shizuoka University of Art and Culture, ACM Press, New York pp 120–123
64. Arcos JL, De Mantaras RL (2001) The SaxEx system for expressive music synthesis: a progress report. In: Lomeli C, Loureiro R (eds) Proceedings of the workshop on current research directions in computer music, Barcelona, Spain, Nov 2001. Pompeu Fabra University, Barcelona, pp 17–22
65. Church M (2004) The mystery of Glenn Gould. Independent Newspaper, Published by Independent Print Ltd, London, UK
66. Kirke A, Miranda ER (2007) Capturing the aesthetic: radial mappings for cellular automata music. J ITC Sangeet Res Acad 21:15–23
67. Anders T (2007) Composing music by composing rules: design and usage of a generic music constraint system. PhD thesis, University of Belfast
68. Tobudic A, Widmer G (2006) Relational IBL in classical music. Mach Learn 64:5–24
69. Sundberg J, Askenfelt A, Fryden L (1983) Musical performance. A synthesis-by-rule approach. Comput Music J 7:37–43
70. Bresin R, Friberg A (2000) Emotional coloring of computer-controlled music performances. Comput Music J 24:44–63
71. Friberg A (2006) pDM: an expressive sequencer with real-time control of the KTH music-performance rules. Comput Music J 30:37–48
72. Desain P, Honing H (1993) Tempo curves considered harmful. Contemp Music Rev 7:123–138
73. Thompson WF (1989) Composer-specific aspects of musical performance: an evaluation of Clynes's theory of pulse for performances of Mozart and Beethoven. Music Percept 7:15–42
74. Repp BH (1990) Composer's pulses: science or art. Music Percept 7:423–434
75. Hashida M, Nagata N, Katayose H (2007) jPop-E: an assistant system for performance rendering of ensemble music. In: Crawford L (eds) Proceedings of 2007 conference on new interfaces for musical expression (NIME07), New York, NY, pp 313–316
76. Meyer LB (1957) Meaning in music and information theory. J Aesthet Art Crit 15:412–424
77. Canazza S, De Poli G, Drioli C, Roda A, Vidolin A (2004) Modeling and control of expressiveness in music performance. Proc IEEE 92:686–701
78. De Poli G (2004) Methodologies for expressiveness modeling of and for music performance. J New Music Res 33:189–202
79. Lopez De Mantaras R, Arcos JL (2002) AI and music: from composition to expressive performances. AI Mag 23:43–57
80. Mitchell T (1997) Machine learning. McGraw-Hill, New York
81. Emde W, Wettschereck D (1996) Relational instance based learning. In: Saitta L (eds) Proceedings of 13th international conference on machine learning, Bari, Italy, July 1996. Morgan Kaufmann, San Francisco, pp 122–130
82. Wright M, Berdahl E (2006) Towards machine learning of expressive microtiming in Brazilian drumming. In: Zannos I (eds) Proceedings of the 2006 international computer music conference, New Orleans, USA, Nov 2006. ICMA, San Francisco, pp 572–575
83. Dixon S, Goebl W, Widmer G (2002) The performance worm: real time visualisation of expression based on Langrer's tempo-loudness animation. In: Proceedings of the international computer music conference, Goteborg, Sweden, Sept, pp 361–364
84. Sholkopf B, Smola A, Muller K (1998) Nonlinear component analysis as a kernel eigenvalue problem, Neural computation 10. MIT Press, Cambridge, MA, pp 1299–1319
85. Mitchell M (1998) Introduction to genetic algorithms. The MIT Press, Cambridge
86. Kirke A (1997) Learning and co-operation in mobile multi-robot systems. PhD thesis, University of Plymouth

87. Chalmers D (2006) Strong and weak emergence. In: Clayton P, Davies P (eds) The re-emergence of emergence. Oxford University Press, Oxford
88. Ramirez R, Hazan A (2005) Modeling expressive performance in Jazz. In: Proceedings of 18th international Florida Artificial Intelligence Research Society conference (AI in Music and Art), Clearwater Beach, FL, USA, May 2005. AAAI Press, Menlo Park, pp 86–91
89. Zhang Q, Miranda ER (2006) Towards an interaction and evolution model of expressive music performance. In: Chen Y, Abraham A (eds) Proceedings of the 6th international conference on intelligent systems design and applications, Jinan, China, Oct 2006. IEEE Computer Society, Washington, DC, pp 1189–1194
90. Cambouropoulos E (2001) The local boundary detection model (LBDM) and its application in the study of expressive timing. In: Schloss R, Dannenberg R (eds) Proceedings of the 2001 international computer music conference, Havana, Cuba, Sept 2001. International Computer Music Association, San Francisco
91. Krumhansl C (1991) Cognitive foundations of musical pitch. Oxford University Press, Oxford
92. Temperley D, Sleator D (1999) Modeling meter and harmony: a preference rule approach. Comput Music J 23:10–27
93. Zhang Q, Miranda ER (2007) Evolving expressive music performance through interaction of artificial agent performers. In: Proceedings of ECAL 2007 workshop on music and artificial life (MusicAL 2007), Lisbon, Portugal, Sept
94. Miranda ER (2002) Emergent sound repertoires in virtual societies. Comput Music J 26(2):77–90
95. Dannenberg RB (1993) A brief survey of music representation issues, techniques, and systems. Comput Music J 17:20–30
96. Laurson M, Kuuskankare M (2003) From RTM-notation to ENP-score-notation. In: Proceedings of Journées d'Informatique Musicale 2003, Montbéliard, France
97. Bellini P, Nesi P (2001) WEDELMUSIC format: an XML music notation format for emerging applications. In: Proceedings of first international conference on web delivering of music, Florence, Nov 2001. IEEE Press, Los Alamitos, pp 79–86
98. Good M (2006) MusicXML in commercial applications. In: Hewlett WB, Selfridge-Field E (eds) Music analysis east and west. MIT Press, Cambridge, MA, pp 9–20
99. Atkinson JJS (2007) Bach: the Goldberg variations. Stereophile, Sept 2007
100. Toop R (1988) Four facets of the new complexity. Contact 32:4–50
101. Koelsch S, Siebel WA (2005) Towards a neural basis of music perception. Trends Cogn Sci 9:579–584
102. Britton JC, Phan KL, Taylor SF, Welsch RC, Berridge KC, Liberzon I (2006) Neural correlates of social and nonsocial emotions: an fMRI study. Neuroimage 31:397–409
103. Durrant S, Miranda ER, Hardoon D, Shawe-Taylor J, Brechmann A, Scheich H (2007) Neural correlates of tonality in music. In: Proceedings of music, brain, cognition workshop – NIPS Conference, Whistler, Canada
104. Clarke EF (1993) Generativity, mimesis and the human body in music performance. Contemp Music Rev 9:207–219
105. Parncutt R (1997) Modeling piano performance: physics and cognition of a virtual pianist. In: Cook PR (eds) Proceedings of 1997 international computer music conference, Thessalonikia, Greece, Sept 1997. ICMA, San Francisco, pp 15–18
106. Widmer G, Goebl W (2004) Computational models of expressive music performance: the state of the art. J New Music Res 33:203–216

Systems for Interactive Control of Computer Generated Music Performance

2

Marco Fabiani, Anders Friberg, and Roberto Bresin

Abstract

This chapter is a literature survey of systems for real-time interactive control of automatic expressive music performance. A classification is proposed based on two initial design choices: the music material to interact with (i.e., MIDI or audio recordings) and the type of control (i.e., direct control of the low-level parameters such as tempo, intensity, and instrument balance or mapping from high-level parameters, such as emotions, to low-level parameters). Their pros and cons are briefly discussed. Then, a generic approach to interactive control is presented, comprising four steps: control data collection and analysis, mapping from control data to performance parameters, modification of the music material, and audiovisual feedback synthesis. Several systems are then described, focusing on different technical and expressive aspects. For many of the surveyed systems, a formal evaluation is missing. Possible methods for the evaluation of such systems are finally discussed.

2.1 Introduction

Acquiring the skills to perform a piece of music requires countless hours of practice and hard work, something not everyone can afford, in terms of both time and money. Nevertheless, many people are passionate about music, even if they do not play any instrument: they love to listen to it, move with it, and perhaps conduct it in the privacy of their living rooms. Although one can always choose a piece of music that

M. Fabiani • A. Friberg (✉) • R. Bresin
Department of Speech, Music & Hearing, KTH Royal Institute of Technology,
Lindstedtsvägen 24, 100 44 Stockholm, Sweden
e-mail: himork@kth.se; roberto@kth.se

A. Kirke and E.R. Miranda (eds.), *Guide to Computing for Expressive Music Performance*, 49
DOI 10.1007/978-1-4471-4123-5_2, © Springer-Verlag London 2013

suits her mood or taste in that moment, listening to recorded music is a passive process, in the sense that we do not have any control over the way the recorded music is performed. The emotions we feel and the movements we make (e.g., tapping our foot, dancing, conducting) are driven by the music, and not vice versa.

Systems for the interactive control of computer-generated music performance are a possible solution for addressing all these problems. Such systems have many fields of application, which can be grouped into three main areas: music therapy, music education, and entertainment.

Active music therapy is a form of music therapy based on musical improvisation between patient and therapist. Since patients can have different degrees of cognitive and motor abilities, they could benefit from technology that allows for the control of expression in music performance without the need for controlling a musical instrument [1, 2].

Music education can definitely benefit from systems for interactive control of music performance, for example, for building an inexpensive system for students to practice their conducting skills [3, 4] or for conductors to test different performance styles before meeting with the actual orchestra [5]. Max Mathews proposed his *Conductor Program* [6] in 1975, in which two batons are used for controlling a MIDI file playback (one baton for controlling tempo and the other for sound level). Such system can be used for the accompaniment of soloist musicians like singers or pianists. In this approach, the orchestra follows the soloist, as opposed to the *Music Minus One* accompaniment recordings, where it is the soloist that has to follow the orchestra.

Entertainment is one of the main reasons for playing music. Conducting systems allow all music lovers to enjoy the experience of conducting an orchestra, even if a virtual one, in an active way, that is, by taking control of the musical expression. *Active music listening* [7–9] is a relatively new trend in sound and music computing research that aims at allowing the listener to be in control of how the music is played back. The success in recent years of music video games such as *Guitar Hero* (2005), *Rock Band* (2007), and *Wii Music* (2008) has shown a strong interest from the general public with the concept of being able to control a music performance without really playing an instrument. Of course, the way in which it is implemented in these video games is rather naïve and constrained. The player, to score points, has to perform the right action at the right moment, which means the experience is still strongly driven by the music. Nevertheless, we can consider this a first step toward an active interaction with music.

The introduction to the market of such video games is quite recent; however, research in the field of interactive control of computer-generated music performance dates back many years. One of the first examples of such a system is the abovementioned Mathews' *Conductor Program*. Several systems emerged in the following 20 years, described in various publications, and sometimes presented to the general public in museums and expositions. The creation of a system for active music listening is a highly complex and multidisciplinary task, spanning music theory and computer vision, psychology and perception, signal processing and machine learning, as well as artificial intelligence. For this reason, the various systems developed over the years have focused on different aspects of the problem, depending on the authors' area of expertise. At the same time, the complexity and multidisciplinarity of such systems make them a perfect environment for testing different methods, algorithms, and technology [10–12] which can be exported to other areas outside of music.

The prototypical task which interactive systems for music performance are typically designed for is conducting a virtual orchestra. It is possible to group the attempts to create such a system on the basis of its characteristics, such as the type of controller used, which musical parameters can be modified, how the music is reproduced, and if the conductor has some visual representation of the "musicians" she is conducting. All these aspects present technical as well as musical challenges (i.e., concerning the artistic quality of the musical performance).

A general approach to the construction of a virtual conducting system is presented in the next section. The abovementioned grouping is discussed, and several examples are given that illustrate different approaches to the solution of various technical problems. In Sect. 2.3, a selection of the systems found in the literature is presented in detail as case studies. A discussion about possible methods for evaluating such systems is presented in Sect. 2.4. Finally, possible technical as well as artistic issues are highlighted in Sect. 2.5.

2.2   General Design Approach

As previously mentioned, orchestra conducting is the most common model for systems for the interactive control of a computer-generated music performance. Figure 2.1 shows a general scheme of such a conducting system. The movements of the conductor (i.e., user) are detected using different sensors and subsequently analyzed. Several parameters extracted from gesture data are mapped to performance parameters of different levels of abstraction (e.g., note level, phrase level, overall level). The modifications to the nominal performance are applied in real time, and feedback (audio and eventually visual) is provided to the user.

The various parts of the general system will now be discussed with the help of examples from literature, roughly following the block division in Fig. 2.1.

2.2.1   Sensors for Gesture Capture

Several options are available to convey the intentions of the user to the system. Control methods can be anything from physical sliders with which the user changes the values of single performance parameters to batons fitted with sensors and from simple video cameras to more complex devices such as motion capture systems or biometric devices.

Probably the first system for interactive control of a music performance was the *Conduct* system [13]. It did not try to simulate an orchestra conductor experience but nevertheless allowed the control of several parameters of a specially designed

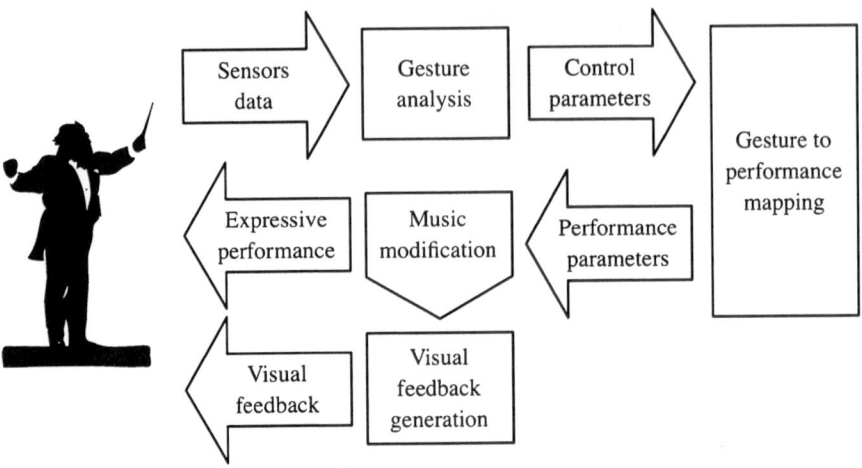

Fig. 2.1 Block diagram of a generic virtual conducting system

score, at playback time. The control transducers for this system were a computer keyboard, a slider box, and a "tablet" (i.e., a computer mouse).

Because of the real-time multimodal nature of such an interactive system, the classic point-and-click interaction paradigm (which imposes significant limitations on the control of multiple parameters) was replaced with alternative methods, based on a number of sensor types. The concept of orchestra conducting naturally led to the adoption of the standard conductor's instrument, the baton. The movements of the baton – and in general of the conductor's hands – are tracked using various methods.

A mechanical baton, the *Daton*, was first adopted by Mathews [6] to control the *Conductor Program* (see Sect. 2.3.1 for a description of the system). Later, Mathews also designed the *Radio Baton* (Fig. 2.2) to control the same program [14]. The *Radio Baton* is a device that tracks the motion of the tips of two batons in three-dimensional space. The main components of the system are the two batons and a base unit called the "antenna." The tips of each of the batons are shrouded in copper, and five copper plates are housed in the base unit. By measuring the electrical capacitance between the tip of the baton and each one of the five plates, the system is able to localize the tip of each baton.

A more recent solution to track the movement of batons has been to fit them with movement sensors, for example, accelerometers [3, 15]. Other more readily available devices equipped with accelerometers which are sturdier but much heavier than a baton have also been employed, for example, the Wiimote [4, 16, 17] and mobile phones [18]. Although the accelerometer data can be low-pass filtered to remove the constant component due to the gravitational force, it has been pointed out by several authors that it tends to be imprecise, especially if position tracking is required. Furthermore, the sampling frequency of the accelerometers used in the past has been below the 100 Hz required to accurately track a conductor's movements (as pointed out in [19]).

Fig. 2.2 Max Mathews with
the Radio Baton

One method for obtaining more precise position tracking has been to attach a modulated infrared light emitter to the tip of the baton [20–25] and track using infrared light sensors or cameras. Infrared light sensors have the advantage of being robust to changes in the background and lightning. However, the range can be limited due to their small angle of view.

In more recent years, the availability of video analysis frameworks such as EyesWeb [26, 27], or Jitter within the MAX/MSP platform [28], has encouraged the use of computer vision algorithms such as those provided by the OpenCV library [29]. These can analyze the video streams obtained from multiple cameras [12, 30–34] or a single camera. This allows other features to be extracted from video data as well as the baton position in 2D or 3D. Often, the first step in such a process is to perform background separation, that is, to identify and isolate the person/actor in the video stream. This can be performed by computing the difference between two adjacent frames, thus identifying only moving parts of the picture (or by subtracting a still picture of the background). Different gesture features can then be extracted. Using differentiation in color or enhanced colored gloves allows the position of the hands to be tracked [32]. Other more general features can be extracted, for example, overall quantity of motion or an expansion index. Cameras have the additional advantage of making the batons lighter, due to a lack of attached sensor weight. This can be important because – as pointed out in [19] – this additional weight could cause discomfort or lead to less natural gestures.

Baton and hand position tracking can also be done using magnetic field trackers [11, 35], the theremin [20, 36], capacity transducers [37], and gyroscopes [38, 39]. Due to commercial interest in interactive games, new interfaces appear on the market regularly. The *Kinect* interface [40] from Microsoft is based on video techniques and can accurately track the hands of the user in three dimensions. It could thus serve as a good sensor front end for conducting systems.

Aside from tracking the position of the baton's tip, other control signals have been employed over the years, though less commonly, for example, attaching movement sensors directly to the conductor's hands [20, 25, 41] and body [42]. Of particular interest in this respect is the *Conductor's Jacket* by Marrin Nakra [19], a wearable interface containing several physiological sensors that sense body parameters such as muscle tension, respiration rate, heart rate, skin conductivity, and temperature. Other sensors implemented over the years include breath and gaze tracking sensors[3] and even a video game steering wheel and pedals to "drive" a performance [43].

2.2.2   Mapping Gesture Data to Performance Parameters

As discussed in the previous section, a variety of sensors can be used to record data expressing the intentions of the conductor. These intentions need to be recognized and mapped from the sensors' data to performance parameters. Several studies specifically address the analysis of conductor's gestures, though without employing the results in any interactive system. Because of their importance for such systems, these studies are summarized here, in addition to the methods designed explicitly for virtual conducting.

The role of the user in an interactive system for music performance is similar to the role of the conductor in a traditional orchestra. The conductor controls the overall interpretation of the piece but leaves the execution of the notes to the musicians (and in the case of interactive performance, the computer). Three criteria for comparing interactive performance systems were proposed by Buxton [13] in 1980, based on the relationship between the user and the virtual orchestra. These criteria were the following: (1) what is the overall amount of decision-making required by the system (e.g., playback of recorded music requires none, whereas improvisation requires full control), (2) what is the level of decision-making (from the note-level to high-level structures), and (3) what is the distribution of decision-making (i.e., what is controlled by the user-conductor and what by the computer-musician)?

The types of interactive systems considered in this chapter all have similar amounts of decision-making. They usually provide a score (fixed) that is performed based on the intentions of the user. The level of decision-making however varies substantially – from note-by-note modifications of length, intensity, and timbre to solely tempo and sound level modulations. Note that the type of musical material used in the system strongly influences the level of control utilized (see Sect. 2.2.3.1). It is much easier to change the parameters of a MIDI note than to modify a tone in an audio recording.

In this section, the third criterion – the distribution of decision-making – will be utilized to group systems. The systems will be divided into three groups: systems where the user has direct control of the performance parameters (e.g., tempo, dynamics, articulation, instrument section balance), systems where the user has control of mid-level parameters (e.g., performance model parameters), and systems where the user has control of high-level parameters defined by semantic descriptors, for instance, basic emotions. It should be noted that the distinction between these groups is necessarily fuzzy; many use combinations of the three levels.

2.2.2.1 Direct Control

When thinking of a conductor, the first image that comes to mind is the movement of the baton that dictates the tempo to the orchestra. All the available systems allow more or less direct control of tempo. The most common method to extract tempo information from gesture data is to detect sudden changes in the direction of the baton. Beats extracted this way can be directly coupled to beats in the score, giving the user a strict control over the timing [6]. Also, the tempo estimate can be used to control playback speed in a more flexible way [17, 22]. Measurements have shown (e.g., [41]) that in real orchestras the musicians do not exactly follow the conductor and that there is a variable amount of delay between the conductor's beats and the musicians', depending – among other things – on the current tempo. Such delays in the response of the orchestra, based on more or less complex models, have been incorporated into several systems to create a more realistic conducting experience (e.g., [20, 41]).

Another way to achieve direct tempo control is to predefine sets of movements that are taken from, for example, manuals for conductors [44]. Hidden Markov models (HMMs) [3, 32, 34, 35, 45], artificial neural networks (ANNs) [12, 38, 42], and simple rule heuristics [25, 42] have all been used for this purpose. Matching predefined features or gestures can also be used to additional information, such as the beat pattern, articulation (staccato-legato), crescendo-decrescendo, accents, vibrato, portamento, and fermatas [3, 25, 32, 34, 35]. A framework for simplifying systems for adaptive conducting gesture analysis is described in [46]. In many systems, the movements of both hands are tracked. Usually, the right hand (holding the baton) is mapped to tempo, with left-hand gestures being utilized for other expressive purposes.

The method of using predefined sets of movements has some issues, two of which have particularly been highlighted (e.g., see [12]). The first is that the expressive possibilities of the system are limited to the predefined gestures. The second is that detection accuracy can be compromised by different users performing the same gesture in varying ways. Two partial solutions to these problems are training HMMs or ANNs for a specific user and letting that user define their own gestures [47].

Another control parameter found in all systems is that of intensity, and it is normally coupled directly to the energy with which the user makes their gesture. Other, less common, performance parameters described in the control literature include breathing, mapped in [3] and [48] to phrasing, and sliders [6], gaze direction [3], and the direction of the baton [10, 25] are all used to emphasize certain sections of the orchestra.

2.2.2.2 Model-Based Performance Control

It can require a lot of practice to control several performance parameters in real time and obtain a performance that sounds pleasant and that corresponds to one's intentions. For nonmusicians and children, even the task of keeping a constant beat with the baton can be challenging. Furthermore, the conductor does not in reality have full control over every single person in the orchestra [20]. Musicians are significantly autonomous in their performances, loosely following the direction of the conductor. The actual specific performance may be decided a priori by the conductor and learned after multiple rehearsals. As a solution to these two issues, the interactive control of performance models has been introduced. The use of performance models involves delegating control of low-level performance parameters to the underlying system (cf. the musicians in the orchestra) while leaving higher-level control to the user (the conductor). Performance models are obtained using a variety of techniques (for an overview, see [49]).

As an example, consider the commonly used performance technique of phrasing. A key phrasing method is to play a crescendo-decrescendo and accelerando-ritardando arch pattern over the desired phrase. For *direct* control of tempo and intensity, the user has to identify the beginning and end of a phrase as well as create the arch themselves. With a phrasing model implemented, for example, the phrase-arch rule in the KTH rule system for music performance [50], the user can focus on how much emphasis to put on this phrasing. The arch will be applied to the music automatically by the system. Using such performance models requires more complex mappings between control data and performance parameters.

As has been mentioned, the boundaries between control categories are not strictly defined. For example, the flexible control of tempo obtained by introducing variable delays in the orchestra's response (Sect. 2.2.2) could be viewed as a form of simple performance model. Flexible control of tempo is important because of potentially large variations in the beat extracted from baton gestures, thus leading to sudden and unnatural-sounding tempo changes. Moving averages [31] and heuristic rules [42] have been used to smooth such tempo issues. In [20], heuristic rules that take into account musical genre are used to adjust tempo.

Tempo predictors have also been used, in which the current tempo estimate obtained from the baton beats is combined with the tempo expected from the performance model. This has been done using various mathematical methods [20, 25, 37] including fuzzy logic [3]. Predictors have also been used to control dynamics as well as other parameters describable by performance models [37]. When it comes to parameter manipulation, there is always a trade-off between stability and sensitivity. If more weight is put on the model, sudden changes in a parameter desired by the user, for example, a large *ritardando* or a fermata, might be smoothed out (unless a specialized detection protocol is included to handle it). On the other hand, if too much weight is put on the live control data from the user, this may result in an unnatural-sounding performance.

To combine control and model parameter values, a performance template is required. This template can be based on a database of performances (e.g., [51]) or created by the user for the live performance (e.g., [5, 52]). The template may be very specific, particularly if derived strongly from analysis of actual performance data. A wider range of performance is possible through the use of generic performance rules such as in the KTH rule system [50]. Rule parameters can be controlled in real time [18, 33, 53] using, for example, virtual or physical sliders [54]. However, it is impractical for one individual to control multiple rules at the same time. To simplify usage of such performance models, high-level semantic descriptors can be used where several model's parameters are combined and mapped to a few intuitive values. These, in turn, are mapped to sensor data.

2.2.2.3 Semantic Descriptors

Examples of higher-level descriptors include emotional expressions such as aggressive, dreamy, and melancholic. Others are typical performance instructions – often referring to motion – such as andante or allegretto. The use of high-level semantic descriptors makes control more intuitive, particularly useful for less-skilled users, such as children. The *You're the Conductor* installation, by Lee et al. [1], introduces a control modality specifically designed for children, one which can accommodate irregular conducting gestures.

An emotional descriptor is an example of semantic descriptor. Emotional expression in music performance can be characterized by a set of acoustic features. Juslin [55] summarizes the use of acoustic features in the communication of emotion. The study is an overview which associates a set of acoustic parameters and their qualitative values with a position of an emotion in the two-dimensional activity-valence space [56]. For example, they characterize a happy performance by fast average tempo, high sound level, staccato articulation, bright timbre, and fast tone attack, while a sad one is characterized by slow average tempo, low sound level, legato articulation, dull timbre, and slow tone attacks. Another way of representing emotion in music performance is to associate a set of performance rules parameterized in specific ways to each position in the activity-valence space. For example, the Director Musices and pDM programs [33, 57, 58] allow a rule palette to be defined for a specific emotion [59]. This rule palette is a set of performance rules with control parameter setting which enable the communication of a specific emotion. Through this, it is possible – through changing the control parameters of the rules in real time – to control the emotional expression of a music performance in real time.

So an emotional descriptor can be represented either as a set of acoustic features and their qualitative values or a set of performance rules and the values of their control parameters.

2.2.3 Feedback to the User

2.2.3.1 Audio Feedback

A crucial choice in the design of interactive music performance systems is the format of music material to use in audio feedback. The two available options are a synthesizer controlled by a score file (e.g., MIDI or MusicXML) or audio recordings of actual performances.

Symbolic representations have the advantage of being easy to modify and require less computing power to process. Any available score can in principle be manipulated. However, some systems (e.g., [6, 13, 33, 37]) require specific score formats in which extra information, such as performance model parameters, is added to the standard notation. One advantage of score files is they allow a high degree of control with every single note (e.g., note duration, pitch, intensity, timbre). A key disadvantage of the symbolic music approach is the quality and naturalness of the resulting sound, which depend on the synthesizer. Good synthesizers tend to be very expensive, while standard ones usually sound very unconvincing. Systems based on symbolic file formats are detailed in [3, 6, 11, 13, 18, 20, 21, 25, 30, 33, 37, 38, 42, 43, 48].

Real audio recordings, on the other hand, have the advantage of sounding more natural, for example, with more nuanced variations between tones and various instrument and ambient sounds. However, using audio files involves a number of complex technical issues, even when doing basic modification of tempo, dynamics, and articulation. (These three factors alone, according to previous research, account for about 95% of the communication of emotion in expressive music performance.)

Tempo can be modified using time scaling algorithms that change the speed of reproduction while maintaining the original pitch. The most common algorithms are those based on the phase vocoder [60], though there are other methods. Time scaling by phase vocoder introduces audio artifacts, especially at extreme scaling factors, for example, transient smearing and "phasiness."

Dynamics are normally handled by a simple change of loudness, although to obtain a more natural effect the timbre of the acoustic instruments also needs to be modified [61]. Acoustic instruments have different timbres when played at different intensities [62] (usually, the louder the tone, the brighter the timbre). In terms of instrument section balance, the majority of the systems [10, 12, 17] use ad hoc recordings in which each section has been recorded separately. Any recording can be used when no control over section balance is required [31] or if the sections are isolated using source separation techniques.

Note-level modifications of audio recordings, for example, articulation and timbre manipulations, can be highly complex, especially in the case of polyphonic music. A complete analysis of the signal, using, for example, analysis-synthesis techniques [63], is required in order to isolate and separately modify each tone. For example, the *SaxEx* system [64] allows for offline, expressive modifications of monophonic saxophone recordings. More recently, an attempt to apply the KTH rule system for music performance in real time to audio recordings has been described in [53] (see also Sect. 2.3.3).

2.2.3.2 Visual Feedback

Some of the interactive systems found in the literature provide a visual feedback in addition to the sound output. For example, systems using ad hoc audio recordings [10, 17] can have a screen or projector showing the video of the recording session, synchronized with the sound. To this end, a framework for integrating real-time control of audio and video is proposed in [65]. The orchestra image, as discussed in Sect. 2.2.1, is crucial for mapping the baton or conductor's gaze direction to the different sections of the orchestra, for controlling section prominence in a sound mix.

When no video recordings are available – for example, when symbolic music files are used – an alternative is the creation of virtual spaces populated by virtual musicians [11, 66]. Changing the shape of the virtual space and the position of the musicians allows different acoustic effects to be obtained. A combination of the two approaches – that is, a virtual space with videos of real musicians – has been used [12]. In [30], virtual dancers instead of musicians are synchronized with the performance.

An entirely different approach to visual feedback is the use of graphical models to visualize the character of a performance. For example, tempo and dynamics in a 2D representation called the "Air Worm" are used in [36]. A third performance dimension (expressivity) is added to tempo and dynamics in [37]. In [67], a virtual ball in a 3D space changes not only its position but also its shape and color according to both basic performance parameters (i.e., tempo and dynamics) and its emotional expression. The emotional content of the performance has also been visualized by the facial expression of an embodied conversational agent (ECA) [68].

2.3   Case Studies

Three systems will now be described in detail: Mathews' *Conductor Program* [6] (reviewed for a historical perspective), the *Personal Orchestra* series by Borchers et al. [10] (the first system to use audio with video recordings), and the three systems which use the KTH rule system for music performance, *pDM* [33], *Permorfer* [53], and *MoodifierLive* [18] (they exemplify the high-level performance control mapping discussed in Sect. 2.2.2).

2.3.1   The Conductor Program

Designed by Mathews [6], the *Conductor Program* is one of the first systems to have allowed real-time control of a music performance through the orchestral conductor paradigm. It uses a custom-designed score file. The different instrument tracks are defined in a header, with one track containing trigger points (which can represent, e.g., the beat position or a single note onset). Notes are defined by duration and pitch and can be grouped into chords. The *Conductor Program* acts as a sequencer, controlling a MIDI synthesizer.

The user has control over the tempo, loudness, and balance of the various voices/tracks using three different control devices. To set the tempo, a mechanical baton called *Daton* is used. It is a plate mounted on gauges, each generating an electrical pulse when struck using a soft drumstick. The pulses are sent as triggers to the *Conductor Program*. If the trigger defined in the score track comes before the *Daton* struck, the playback stops; if it comes later, the playback skips to the next trigger position. This enables highly accurate control of tempo but requires practice (even for an experienced conductor) in order not to miss any notes/triggers. A joystick that stays in position when released is used to control continuous factors, for example, loudness and violin vibrato. A set of ten rotary controllers control the sound level balance among tracks.

Mathews also developed the famous *Radio Baton* (see Sect. 2.2.1), which can be used to control the *Conductor Program* [14]. The *Radio Baton* involves two sticks whose 3D position in the space above a plate is measured by an antenna array, contained in the plate itself. Typically, one stick beats tempo, while the other controls dynamics. As described in [69], the KTH rule system for music performance [50] was used to preprocess the score for the *Conductor Program* in order to obtain a more realistic and natural automatic performance.

2.3.2   The Personal Orchestra Series

The *Personal Orchestra* series consists of installations by Borchers et al.
(*Virtual Conductor* [70], *You're the Conductor* [71], *Maestro!/iSymphony* [72],
and *Virtual Conductor Reloaded* [10]). The development started with the observation that when people listen to a CD of classical music, they enjoy acting as if they
are conducting. This is a passive activity since the listener only follows a fixed
recording. A more realistic and active experience would be to control a virtual
orchestra. The project has several goals [10]: the creation of innovative interfaces
for musical expression, the creation of a framework for time design of multimedia,
gesture recognition and modeling, and real-time audio and video time stretching.

All the instances of the *Personal Orchestra* share some basic features: (1) a baton
controls the performance, (2) they are based on ad hoc multitrack audio recordings,
and (3) the sound is coupled with the video of the orchestra that performed it.

The *Virtual Conductor* [70] was the first system that allowed users to conduct an
audio and video recording of an orchestra, in this case the Vienna Philharmonic.
It has been the main attraction of the House of Music in Vienna since its opening
in June 2000. The baton, a Buchla Lightning II [23], is equipped with an
infrared emitter. A receiver – placed under the screen – translates the position of
the baton into 2D Cartesian coordinates. From these coordinates, the system detects
downward-turning points – interpreted as a *downbeat* – corresponding to a series of
positions in the movie. These positions were previously marked manually as beats.
The tempo values are low-pass filtered to avoid over-fast change, and an algorithm
is used to maintain the synchronization of music beats with user beats. The amplitude of gestures controls the volume. Directing the baton toward a specific instrument group emphasizes its presence in the audio mix (this is possible because of
the ad hoc multitrack recordings). The tempo of audio tracks is modified by a
time-stretching algorithm, which changes the speed while maintaining pitch. At the
time of development (1999–2000), no real-time high-quality time-stretching algorithms were available, so each track had been previously time-scaled at various
speeds, and changes were made by cross-fading between different speed tracks
while simultaneously changing the reproduction speed of the video.

You're the Conductor [71] is an interactive conducting system for children.
The baton again uses an infrared emitter. Its position is tracked via an infrared
sensor. Interaction is adapted for easy use by children. Thus, synchronization is
decoupled from beat positions, as it is too difficult for children to follow beats.
Instead, the tempo is controlled by the speed of the gestures. In this iteration of the
Personal Orchestra, a real-time time-stretching system was introduced, based on
the phase-locked phase vocoder [60], which allows fine-tuning tempo changes.
You're the Conductor was exhibited at the Children's Museum of Boston and
featured *Stars and Stripes Forever* performed by the Boston Symphony Orchestra.

In *Maestro!* [10] (an interactive music exhibit for the Betty Brinn Children's
Museum in Milwaukee, USA) and later in *iSymphony* [72], the gesture recognition
and interpretation is improved through a framework for motion feature detection,
CONGA (Conducting Gesture Analysis framework [46]). Three profiles with three

Fig. 2.3 The personal orchestra reloaded at the House of Music in Vienna (Photo: © AnnaRauchenberg/fotodienst.at)

conducting styles are available. These are selected using the system: four-beat, up and down (as in *Virtual Conductor*), and random (as in *You're the Conductor*). An improved audio-video time stretching [65] is also utilized.

In 2009, the *Virtual Conductor Reloaded* (Fig. 2.3) – an updated version of the first version of the *Virtual Conductor* – was installed at the House of Music in Vienna. New audio-video recordings with the Vienna Philharmonic were realized in high definition. This new installation also features several improvements, for example, an electronic music stand [73], high-quality time stretching [74], and new control strategies such as fermatas.

2.3.3   KTH Rule-Based Systems

Limiting conductor systems to more or less directly controlling tempo and dynamics has two consequences. Firstly, finer details – such as articulation or phrasing – are precomputed (or prerecorded) and therefore are static. Articulation is important for setting the gestural and motional quality of the performance but cannot be applied on an average basis. Staccato, an articulation, is set on a note-by-note basis depending on melodic lines and grouping (see [59, 75]). This cannot be controlled directly in a conductor system. The second consequence is that the user must have a precise idea of how the performance should sound, for example, in terms of phrasing like *accelerando* and *ritardando*. They also need to be rather skillful to obtain it, very difficult in the case of naïve users. Decoupling the beat from the gestures – as, for example, in [71] – is a first step toward making an interactive system easier to use. It is possible to move one step further using higher-level parameters to control a computer-generated performance (as explained in Sect. 2.2.2).

Most listeners find the recognition of emotional expression in music an easy task, including children from about 6 years of age, even without any musical training [76]. Therefore, an interactive system that uses simple high-level emotion descriptions such as happy, sad, or angry has the potential of being intuitive and easily understood by most users (including children).

In the systems based on the KTH rule system for music performance [50] (i.e., *pDM* [33], *Permorfer* [53], and *MoodifierLive* [18]), the musical parameters can be controlled both directly and indirectly, using a set of performance rules that are mapped to high-level expressive control parameters. This set of abstractions and tools allow user control of finer performance details at a higher level, without the need to shape each individual note. It is important to design intuitive, easy-to-use mappings of gesture parameters to music parameters, because the rule system is quite complex and is built on a large number of parameters.

We will now describe the KTH rule system, which is common to all three systems (this has been done to some degree in Chap. 1). Then, each application is presented, pointing out the type of sensors used, the gesture analysis performed, and the mapping for the performance rules.

2.3.3.1 KTH Rule System

The KTH rule system is the result of an ongoing long-term research project about music performance initiated by Johan Sundberg (e.g., [67, 77–79]). A recent overview is given in [50]. The idea of the rule system is to model the variations introduced by the musician when playing a score. It contains currently about 30 rules modeling many performance aspects such as different types of phrasing, accents, timing patterns, and intonation. Each rule introduces variations in one or several of the performance variables: IOI (interonset interval), articulation, tempo, sound level, vibrato rate, vibrato extent, as well as modifications of sound level and vibrato envelopes. Most rules operate on the "raw" score using only note values as input. However, some of the rules, for phrasing as well as for harmonic and melodic charge, need a phrase analysis and a harmonic analysis provided in the score. This has to be done manually, because the rule system does not in general contain analysis models. This is a separate and complex research issue which is discussed in Chaps. 1 and 8. One exception is the punctuation rule, which includes a melodic grouping analysis [80].

For each rule, there is one main parameter k that controls the overall rule amount. When $k = 0$, there is no effect of the rule, and when $k = 1$, the effect of the rule is considered normal. However, this "normal" value is selected arbitrarily by researchers and should be used only for the guidance of parameter selection. By making a selection of rules and k values, different performance styles and performer variations can be simulated. Therefore, the rule system should be considered as a musician's toolbox rather than providing a fixed interpretation.

Performances of emotional expressions can easily be modeled using different selections of rules and rule parameters as demonstrated by [81]. *Director Musices* (*DM*) is the main implementation of the rule system and is a stand-alone program available for Windows, documented in [57, 58].

2.3.3.2 Real-Time Control of Rules in *pDM*

In the original *Director Musices*, there is no support for real-time music processing. To solve this, the *pDM* program [33] was implemented in *Pure Data* [82]. *pDM* functions as an expressive player in which each rule weighting (k value) can be controlled in real time. It uses a score that has been preprocessed in DM containing all possible rule-induced variations of all performance parameters.

pDM also contains a set of maps that translate high-level expression descriptions into rule parameters. Basic emotion descriptions are usually used (happy, sad, angry, tender), but also other descriptions such as hard, light, heavy, or soft have been implemented. The emotion descriptions are based on extensive research concerning the relationship between emotions and musical parameters [55, 59].

There is usually a need for mapping interpolations between these high-level descriptors to obtain low-level parameters. One option, implemented in *pDM*, is to use a 2D plane in which each corner is specified in terms of a set of rule weightings corresponding to a certain descriptor. In this way, the well-known activity-valence space (elsewhere in this book also described as arousal-valence space) for describing emotional expression can be implemented [55]. Activity is related to high or low energy, and valence is related to positive or negative emotions. The quadrants of the space can be characterized as happy (high activity, positive valence), angry (high activity, negative valence), tender (low activity, positive valence), and sad (low activity, negative valence). When moving in the plane, using, for example, the mouse pointer, the rule weightings are interpolated in a semilinear fashion.

2.3.3.3 Home Conducting

The home conducting system is designed for gesture-based control of music performance using the KTH rule system [33, 83]. The system is intended to be used by the listeners in their homes rather than by performers on a stage, thus functioning as an add-on for extended or active listening. A design goal is a system that is easy and fun to use, both for novices and experts, and one that is realized on standard equipment utilizing modest computer power. The system consists of a gesture analysis module followed by different mapping modules that control the rules in *pDM*, using both low- and high-level parameters.

Gestures are captured via a webcam and analyzed through a simple motion detection algorithm implemented in *EyesWeb* [26, 27]. The first step in the motion detection is computing the difference signal between video frames. This is a convenient way of removing all background (static) information in the picture. Thus, there is no need to worry about special lightning, clothes, or background content. Then, a limited set of parameters are used for detection: the overall quantity of motion (QoM), horizontal and vertical position of the overall motion, and size and velocity of horizontal and vertical gestures.

The mapping strategies can be divided in three categories, depending on the desired application and user ability:

- Level 1 (active listener level). The musical expression is controlled via basic emotions (happy, sad, angry). This gives intuitive and simple music feedback without the need for any particular musical knowledge.
- Level 2 (basic conductor level). Basic broad music features are controlled using, for example, the energy-kinematics space found relevant for describing musical expression [84].
- Level 3 (advanced conductor level). Overall expressive musical features and emotional expressions in level 1 and 2 are combined with the explicit control of each beat, as in the Radio Baton system (see Sect. 2.3.1).

Having several interaction levels makes the system suitable for novices, children, and expert users. Unlike traditional instruments, this system can "sound good" even with a beginner using a lower interaction level. It can also encourage and challenge the user to practice in order to master higher levels of ability, similar to the challenge provided in computer gaming.

A number of complete prototypes for level 1 and 2 have been assembled and tested using a variety of mappings. One basic level 1 mapping strategy is to analyze emotional expression in a gesture using a fuzzy analyzer [85] and then feed that to the emotion control of *pDM*. However, the most used mapping is a simple but effective gesture interface that merely utilizes two video analysis parameters: (1) overall quantity of motion (QoM) computed as the total number of visible pixels in the difference image and (2) the vertical position computed as the center of gravity for the visible pixels in the difference image. These are directly mapped to the activity-valence emotion dimensions. QoM is mapped to activity (high QoM corresponds to high activity) and vertical position mapped to valence (high position corresponds to positive valence). Additionally, visual feedback is provided for the user's gesture analysis as well as color feedback reflecting the expressed emotion. This interface has been demonstrated numerous times and received highly positive responses. However, no formal testing – in form of usability studies – has been performed. In Fig. 2.4, an example is shown with the home conducting system connected to a Yamaha Disklavier piano.

2.3.3.4 Permorfer

Permorfer [53] is an evolution of *pDM* written in Python for portability reasons. It can process *pDM* score files (MIDI) and provides the same basic performance controls as *pDM* such as the rule sliders and the activity-valence space. In Permorfer, a colored ball is used to navigate in a 2D plane: the color and size of the ball change according to the expressed emotion, based on the results of a study where participants were asked to assign colors to expressive music performances [86]. The program can be controlled using OSC (Open Sound Control) messages, allowing it to be easily connected to other software for video analysis, for example, EyesWeb.

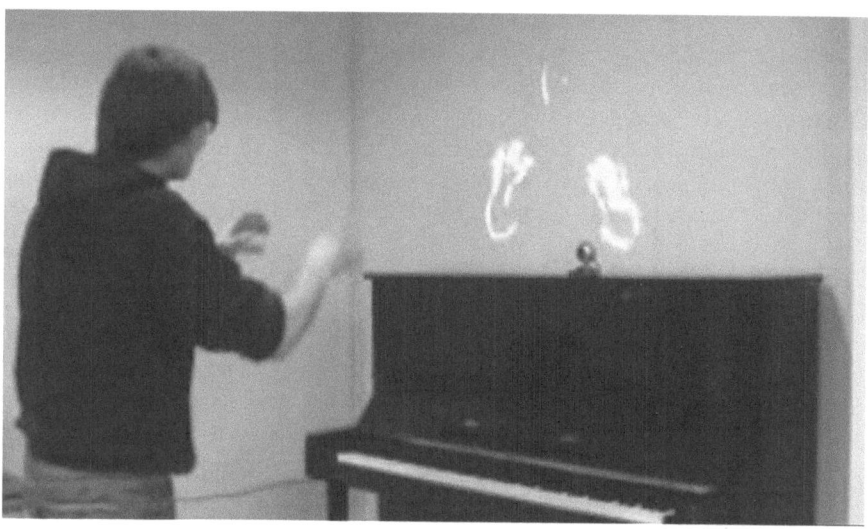

Fig. 2.4 The home conducting system connected to a Yamaha Disklavier piano. The webcam on *top* of the piano is picking up the user's movements, and the *display above* gives color feedback related to the expressed emotion

What differentiates the two programs is the possibility, in *Permorfer*, to apply the KTH rules to audio recordings. A corresponding *pDM* score file is required, and the audio is aligned with the score file, to obtain default rule values. The spectrogram of the audio signal is then computed and analyzed in order to detect and separate the parts of the spectrum corresponding to the different tones. The availability of a score eases the analysis, since the system knows approximately which fundamental frequencies and partials to look for. The analysis is only performed once, and the discovered notes are saved in a database. A residual spectrogram is obtained by subtracting these from the original one.

During playback, *Permorfer* builds a new spectrogram by adding to the residual the required pitches from the database, after modifying their intensity, timbre, and length in relation to the performance rule values (just as the MIDI note parameters are modified in *pDM*). Global tempo is modified using an approach similar to that found in the phase vocoder [60], that is, changing the amount of overlap between analysis frames. To obtain higher stretching ratios, some frames are discarded or repeated. The time signal corresponding to the new spectrogram is obtained using a modified version of the Real-Time Iterative Spectrogram Inversion with Look-Ahead (RTISI-LA [87]).

Working directly with audio recording presents some complex problems. Firstly, in the analysis, it is important to accurately detect *all* the partials. This is particularly difficult with reverberant monophonic signals and polyphonic signals because of the presence of overlapping partials. The availability of the score and the use of a method to separate two overlapping partials [88] help to improve the analysis accuracy. Secondly, as pointed out in Sect. 2.2.3.1, a natural-sounding change in the dynamic level of a tone requires both volume and timbre modifications. To achieve this, *Permorfer* uses filters with specific spectral envelopes from several instruments and dynamic levels and adds high-frequency partials to enhance brightness when needed [61]. Thirdly, *staccato* and *legato* articulation can be implemented through removing or duplicating parts of the tone during the sustain while preserving the attack and release of the tone. For best results, vibrato rate and amplitude envelopes should also be estimated and interpolated.

2.3.3.5 MoodifierLive

Large parts of the Python code in *Permorfer* have been ported to Nokia S60 mobile phones (for which a Python interpreter is available [89]). The resulting mobile application, called *MoodifierLive* [18], which supports only MIDI file reproduction, differentiates itself from *Permorfer* in the way the user can interact with the performance. The phone's built-in accelerometer is exploited to create various interaction modes based on expressive gesture recognition.

Four interaction modes are available. The *Sliders* mode allows the control of four basic parameters (tempo, dynamics, articulation, and phrasing) using virtual sliders. The *Navigate the Performance* mode is based on the activity-valence space, as in *pDM* and *Permorfer*. A virtual ball, controlled by the tilt of the phone, moves in a 2D space, changing color and size according to the expressed emotion. Another mode based on the activity-valence model is called *Marbles in a Box*. An imaginary box of marbles can be moved and shaken to express different emotions. The activity is mapped directly to the energy of the shaking, while the valence is mapped to the tilt (up for positive emotions, down for negative ones). Finally, the *Free Movement* mode uses a simple gesture recognition algorithm to identify four expressive gestures (happy, angry, sad, and tender) and applies the corresponding performance rule template, obtained from a previous study with professional musicians investigating the relation between emotions and performance rule values [54].

2.4   How to Evaluate

The general issue of evaluation is discussed in Chap. 7. This section focuses on evaluation of interactive systems. As previously pointed out, interactive conducting systems involve highly complex methodologies that touch upon several issues. For evaluation, one first has to define exactly what part of the system is the objective of the evaluation – different objectives require different methods. One option is to objectively evaluate how well individual parts of the system work. In the analysis of control data, for example, extraction of beats from hand gestures or gesture recognition using HMMs, a group of subjects can be instructed to perform different specific gestures. Then, the percentage of correct classification responses is easily obtained (see, e.g., [3, 32, 34, 35, 39, 46]). Latency between the gesture and the response from the system can also be measured, as was done in [46].

Another aspect that can be evaluated, using psychoacoustic tests [90], is the quality of the audio feedback, when audio recordings are directly manipulated.

Looking at more general evaluations, the performance success in terms of expressivity and artistic quality can be measured by recording different performances, designing targeted listening tests, and analyzing the results statistically. For example, this methodology has been used to evaluate the KTH rules' efficacy at producing performances with different expressive aims [81], as well as differences in expressivity and controllability between two control mappings [37], and also how well different control modes can translate expressive gestures into corresponding music performances [91].

Looking even more generally, conducting systems can be regarded as a subgroup of Human-Computer Interaction (HCI) interfaces. Thus, the HCI research field [92] can be used to source ideas and methods for the evaluation of conducting systems, for example, the so-called heuristic evaluation, which utilizes a selection of the ten heuristics suggested by Nielsen [93]. This is a rather simple and rapid method for identifying problems associated with the design of user interfaces. Such testing, which in the case of heuristic evaluation can be done using only one expert, can easily be performed during the development of any new interface. This approach was used, for example, in [20], interviewing a professional conductor.

Another standard procedure to evaluate more general aspects of interactive systems is testing them with large groups of users using scorings based on usability and level of engagement. In this approach, the user usually trials the system autonomously for a significant period of time and then answers a questionnaire [94] or is interviewed [12, 17, 20, 25, 71]. This approach is often used when the system is presented at exhibitions and museums because of a significant availability of participants. This scenario does have drawbacks, because subjects often do not have time to focus on the task and might get only a superficial idea of the system. Furthermore, they may not give much time to answering questionnaires. Hence, the usual approach in these cases is to observe the participants interacting with the system and then briefly interview them. Interviews do not provide quantitative data for statistical analysis but can give a general idea about what people liked or did not like about the system and possible problems that need to be addressed.

2.5   Conclusions

In this chapter, we have discussed some of the technical aspects involved in the design of interactive control of computer-generated expressive music performances. Since this is a very broad area of research, we decided to focus our attention on the so-called virtual conducting systems. Virtual conducting systems allow a human agent to control the performance parameters (usually tempo and dynamics) of a predefined score in real time. In the broader sense, interactive control of musical performance includes score-following systems [95, 96] as well as systems in which the sound and music are automatically generated through specific rules that map gestures to synthesis parameters. Several systems of dancers' movements to sound have been designed and used in live shows [26].

There are several trade-offs that arise in the design of such systems, which have been discussed. For example, the use of symbolic scores (e.g., MIDI) facilitates the generation of expressive performances; however, the sound quality and naturalness do not match that of audio recordings. Also, the use of more accurate but more intrusive sensors can have a negative effect on the naturalness of the expressive control. These are technical trade-offs that will hopefully be overcome as technology advances.

A different kind of trade-off involves the level of abstraction at which the user controls performance parameters. According to theories of flow [97], a successful system for the control of expressivity should include different levels of abstraction that allow the user to keep themselves in a flow condition where the system's level of challenge grows in parallel with user's skills. Typically, such a system would allow the user to move from a simple but engaging higher-level control mediated by semantic descriptors and performance models ("amateur" level) to a more direct control of low-level musical parameters ("expert" level). In light of the orchestra paradigm, where musicians play under the supervision of the conductor, we might say that the "amateur" level is closer to a real conducting experience. However, the choice depends on the application the system is designed for, and ultimately, it is also a matter of personal taste.

Questions

1. What is the difference between an interactive and noninteractive system for expressive music performance?
2. Describe three uses for these systems for interactive control of computer-generated music performance.
3. What is the prototypical task for interactive systems for music performance?
4. What are two examples of sensors used for gesture capture?
5. What is the difference between direct control and model-based performance control?
6. How many rules does the KTH rule system contain?
7. What form of emotional space is used in pDM?
8. What field of computer science can help to contribute to the evaluation of interactive performance systems?
9. Why is using audio recordings more difficult than using MIDI representations?
10. What are two of the key trade-offs in the interactive music systems discussed?

References

1. Hunt A, Kirk R, Neighbour M (2004) Multiple media interfaces for music therapy. IEEE Multimed 11(3):50–58
2. Dravins C, van Besouw R, Hansen KF, Kuske S (2010) Exploring and enjoying non-speech sounds through a cochlear implant: the therapy of music. In: 11th international conference on cochlear implants and other implantable technologies, Stockholm, Sweden, p 356
3. Usa S, Mochida Y (1998) A multi-modal conducting simulator. In: Proceedings of international computer music conference (ICMC1998), Ann Arbor, MI, USA, pp 25–32

4. Peng L, Gerhard D (2009) A gestural interface for orchestral conducting education. In: Proceedings of 1st international conference on computer supported education (CSEDU), Lisboa, Portugal, pp 406–409
5. Hashida M, Tanaka S, Katayose H (2009) Mixtract: a directable musical expression system. In: Proceedings of 3rd international conference on affective computing and intelligent interaction (ACII2009), Amsterdam, the Netherlands
6. Mathews MV (1989) The conductor program and mechanical baton. In: Current directions in computer music research. MIT Press, Cambridge, MA
7. Goto M (2007) Active music listening interfaces based on sound source separation and F0 estimation. J Acoust Soc Am 122(5):2988
8. Goto M (2007) Active music listening interfaces based on signal processing. In: IEEE international conference on acoustics, speech and signal processing (ICASSP2007), Honolulu, Hawaii, pp 1441–1444
9. Camurri A (2009) Non-verbal full body emotional and social interaction: a case study on multimedia systems for active music listening. In: Niholt A, Reidsma D, Hondorp H (eds) Intelligent technologies for interactive entertainment, LNCST. Springer, Berlin/Heidelberg/New York, pp 9–18
10. Personal Orchestra. http://hci.rwth-aachen.de/po. Accessed 15 Nov 2010
11. Schertenleib S, Gutierrez M, Vexo F, Thalmann D (2004) Conducting a virtual orchestra. IEEE Multimed 11(3):40–49
12. Bruegge B, Teschner C, Lachenmaier P, Fenzl E, Schmidt D, Bierbaum S (2007) Pinocchio: conducting a virtual symphony orchestra. In: Proceedings of international conference on advances in computer entertainment technology (ACE2007), Salzburg, Austria
13. Buxton W, Reeves W, Fedorkow G, Smith KC, Baecker R (1980) A microcomputer-based conducting system. Comput Music J 4(1):8–21
14. Mathews MV (1991) The Radio Baton and conductor program, or: pitch, the most important and least expressive part of music. Comput Music J 15(4):37–46
15. Marrin T (1997) Possibilities for the digital baton as a general-purpose gestural interface. In: Extended abstracts conference on human factors in computing systems (CHI97), Atlanta, GA, USA, pp 311–312
16. Wii Remote. http://en.wikipedia.org/wiki/Wii_Remote/. Accessed 16 Feb 2011
17. Marrin Nakra T, Ivanov Y, Smaragdis P, Adult C (2009) The UBS virtual maestro: an interactive conducting system. In: Proceedings of conference on new interfaces for musical expression (NIME09), Pittsburgh, PA, USA
18. Fabiani M, Dubus G, Bresin R (2011) MoodifierLive: interactive and collaborative music performance on mobile devices. In Proceedings of the International Conference on New Interfaces for Musical Expression (NIME11) (pp. 116–119). Oslo, Norway: University of Oslo and Norwegian Academy of Music.
19. Marrin Nakra T (2000) Inside the conductor's jacket: analysis, interpretation and musical synthesis of expressive gesture. PhD dissertation, MIT Massachusetts Institute of Technology
20. Baba T, Hashida M, Katayose H (2010) "VirtualPhilharmony": a conducting system with heuristics of conducting an orchestra. In: Proceedings of conference on new interfaces for musical expression (NIME10), Sydney, Australia, pp 263–270
21. Bertini G, Carosi P (1992) Light baton: a system for conducting computer music performance. In: Proceedings of international computer music conference (ICMC1992), San Jose, CA, USA, pp 73–76
22. Borchers J, Lee E, Samminger W (2004) Personal orchestra: a real-time audio/video system for interactive conducting. Multimed Sys 9(5):458–465
23. Lightning II. http://www.buchla.com/lightning/descript.html. Accessed 4 Feb 2011
24. Lightning III MIDI Controller. http://www.buchla.com/lightning3.html. Accessed 2 Feb 2011
25. Morita H, Hashimoto S, Otheru S (1991) A computer music system that follows a human conductor. IEEE Comput 24(7):44–53
26. Camurri A, Hashimoto S, Ricchetti M, Trocca R, Suzuki K, Volpe G (2000) EyesWeb: toward gesture and affect recognition in interactive dance and music systems. Comput Music J 24(1):941–952

27. Camurri A, Mazzarino B, Volpe G (2004) Analysis of expressive gesture: the EyesWeb expressive gesture processing library. In: Camurri A, Volpe G (eds) Gesture-based communication in human-computer interaction, vol 2915, LNAI. Springer, Heidelberg, pp 460–467
28. Max – Interactive Visual Programming Environment for Music, Audio, and Media. http://cycling74.com/products/maxmspjitter/. Accessed Feb 16 2011
29. OpenCV. http://opencv.willowgarage.com/wiki/. Accessed 16 Feb 2011
30. Segen J, Gluckman J, Kumar S (2000) Visual interface for conducting virtual orchestra. In: Proceedings of 15th international conference on pattern recognition (ICPR), Barcelona, Spain, pp 276–279
31. Murphy D, Andersen TH, Jensen K (2004) Conducting audio files via computer vision. In: Camurri A, Volpe G (eds) Gesture-based communication in human-computer interaction, vol 2915, LNAI. Springer, Heidelberg, pp 529–540
32. Kolesnik P, Wanderley M (2004) Recognition, analysis and performance with expressive conducting gestures. In: Proceedings of international computer music conference (ICMC2004), Miami, FL, USA, pp 572–575
33. Friberg A (2006) pDM: an expressive sequencer with real-time control of the KTH music-performance rules. Comput Music J 30(1):37–48
34. Modler P, Myatt T, Saup M (2003) An experimental set of hand gestures for expressive control of musical parameters in realtime. In: Proceedings of conference on new interfaces for musical expression (NIME03), Montreal, Canada, pp 146–150
35. Garnett GE, Jonnalagadda M, Elezovic I, Johnson T, Small K (2001) Technological advances for conducting a virtual ensemble. In: Proceedings of international computer Music Conference (ICMC2001), Havana, Cuba, pp 167–169
36. Dixon S (2005) Live tracking of musical performances using on-line time warping. In: Proceedings of 8th international conference on digital audio effects (DAFx05), Madrid, Spain
37. Katayose H, Okudaira K (2004) iFP: a music interface using an expressive performance template. In: Rauterberg M (ed) Proceedings of 3 rd international conference on entertainment computing (ICEC2004), vol 3166, LNCS. Springer, Eindhoven, pp 225–251
38. Dillon R, Wong G, Ang R (2006) Virtual orchestra: an immersive computer game for fun and education. In: Proceedings of international conference on game research and development (CyberGames '06), Perth, Australia, pp 215–218
39. Höfer A, Hadjakos A, Mühlhäuser M (2009) Gyroscope-based conducting gesture recognition. In: Proceedings of conference on new interfaces for musical expression (NIME09), Pittsburgh, PA, USA, pp 175–176
40. Kinect. http://en.wikipedia.org/wiki/Kinect/. Accessed 16 Feb 2011
41. Baird B, Izmirli O (2001) Modeling the tempo coupling between an ensemble and the conductor. In: Proceedings of international computer music conference (ICMC2001), Havana, Cuba
42. Ilmonen T, Takala T (2000) The virtual orchestra performance. In: Proceedings of conference on human factors in computing systems (CHI2000), Springer, Haag, the Netherlands, pp 203–204
43. Chew E, Francois A, Liu J, Yang A (2005) ESP: a driving interface for musical expression synthesis. In: Proceedings of conference on new interfaces for musical expression (NIME05), Vancouver, B.C., Canada
44. Rudolf M (1995) The grammar of conducting: a comprehensive guide to baton technique and interpretation. Schirmer Books, New York
45. Usa S, Machida Y (1998) A conducting recognition system on the model of musicians' process. J Acoust Soc Jpn 19(4):275–288
46. Lee E, Gruell I, Kiel H, Borchers J (2006) conga: a framework for adaptive conducting gesture analysis. In: Proceedings of conference on new interfaces for musical expression (NIME06), Paris, France
47. Bevilacqua F, Zamborlin B, Sypniewski A, Schnell N, Guédy F, Rasamimanana N (2010) Continuous realtime gesture following and recognition. In: Kopp S, Wachsmuth I (eds) Gesture

in embodied communication and human-computer interaction, vol 5934, LNAI. Springer, Heidelberg, pp 73–84

48. Marrin Nakra T (2001) Synthesizing expressive music through the language of conducting. J New Music Res 31(1):11–26

49. Widmer G, Goebl W (2004) Computational models of expressive music performance: the state of the art. J New Music Res 33(3):203–216

50. Friberg A, Bresin R, Sundberg J (2006) Overview of the KTH rule system for musical performance. Adv Cognit Psychol Spec Issue Music Perform 2(2–3):145–161

51. Hashida M, Matsui T, Katayose H (2008) A new music database describing deviation information of performance expressions. In: Proceedings of 9th international conference music information retrieval (ISMIR2008), Philadelphia, PA, USA, pp 489–494

52. Hashida M, Nagata N, Katayose H (2007) jPop-E: an assistant system for performance rendering of ensemble music. In: Proceedings of conference on new interfaces for musical expression (NIME07), New York, NY, USA, pp 313–316

53. Fabiani M (2011) Interactive computer-aided expressive music performance – Analysis, control, modification, and synthesis methods. Doctoral dissertation, KTH Royal Institute of Technology.

54. Bresin R, Friberg A (2011) Emotion rendering in music: Range and characteristic values of seven musical variables. Cortex 47(9):1068–1081.

55. Juslin PN (2001) Communicating emotion in music performance: a review and a theoretical framework. In: Juslin PN, Sloboda JA (eds) Music and emotion: theory and research. Oxford University Press, New York, pp 305–333.

56. Russell JA (1980) A circumplex model of affect. J Personal Soc Psychol 39:1161–1178

57. Friberg A, Colombo V, Fryden L, Sundberg J (2000) Generating musical performances with director musices. Comput Music J 24:23–29

58. Bresin R, Friberg A, Sundberg J (2002) Director musices: the KTH performance rules system. In: Proceedings of SIGMUS-46, Kyoto, Japan, pp 43–48

59. Bresin R, Battel GU (2000) Articulation strategies in expressive piano performance. Analysis of legato, staccato, and repeated notes in performances of the andante movement of Mozart's sonata in G major (K 545). J New Music Res 29(3):211–224

60. Laroche J, Dolson M (1999) Improved phase vocoder time-scale modification of audio. IEEE Trans Speech Audio Process 7(3):323–332

61. Fabiani M (2009) A method for the modification of acoustic instrument tone dynamics. In: Proceedings of 12th international conference on digital audio effects (DAFx-09), Como, Italy

62. Luce DA (1975) Dynamic spectrum changes of orchestral instruments. J Audio Eng Soc 23 (7):565–568

63. Wright M, Beauchamp J, Fitz K, Rodet X, Robel A, Serra X, Wakefield G (2000) Analysis/ synthesis comparison. Organ Sound 5(3):173–189

64. Arcos JL, Lopez de antaras R, Serra X (1997) Saxex: a case-based reasoning system for generating expressive musical performances. J New Music Res 27:194–210

65. Lee E, Karrer T, Borchers J (2006) Toward a framework for interactive systems to conduct digital audio and video streams. Comput Music J 30(1):21–36

66. Lokki T, Savioja L, Huopaniemi J, Hänninen R, Ilmonen T, Hiipakka J, Pulkki V, Väänänen R, Takala T (1999) Virtual concerts in virtual spaces – in real time. In: Joint ASA/EAA meeting – special session on auditory display, Berlin, Germany

67. Friberg A, Battel GU (2002) Structural communication. In: Parncutt R, McPherson GE (eds) The science and psychology of music performance: creative strategies for teaching and learning. Oxford University Press, New York/Oxford, pp 199–218

68. Mancini M, Bresin R, Pelachaud C (2007) A virtual head driven by music expressivity. IEEE Trans Audio Speech Lang Process 15(6):1833–1841

69. Mathews MV, Friberg A, Bennett G, Sapp C, Sundberg J (2003) A marriage of the director musices program and the conductor program. In: Proceedings of Stockholm music acoustics conference (SMAC03), Stockholm, Sweden, pp 13–16

70. Borchers JO, Samminger W, Muhlhauser M (2002) Engineering a realistic real-time conducting system for the audio/video rendering of a real orchestra. In: IEEE 4th international symposium on multimedia software engineering (MSE2002), Newport Beach, CA, USA

71. Lee E, Nakra TM, Borchers J (2004) You're the conductor: a realistic interactive conducting system for children. In: Proceedings of conference on new interfaces for musical expression (NIME04), Hamamatsu, Japan

72. Lee E, Kiel H, Dedenbach S, Gruell I, Karrer T, Wolf M, Borchers J (2006) iSymphony: an adaptive interactive orchestral conducting system for conducting digital audio and video streams. In: Extended abstracts conference on human factors in computing systems (CHI06), Montreal, Canada

73. Borchers J, Hadjakos A, Muhlhauser M (2006) MICON: a music stand for interactive conducting. In: Proceedings of conference on new interfaces for musical expression (NIME06), Paris, France, pp 254–259

74. Karrer T, Lee E, Borchers J (2006) PhaVoRIT: a phase vocoder for real-time interactive time-stretching. In: Proceedings of international computer music conference (ICMC2006), New Orleans, LA, USA, pp 708–715

75. Bresin R, Widmer G (2000) Production of staccato articulation in Mozart sonatas played on a grand piano. Preliminary results. TMH-QPSR, 4/2000. KTH Royal Institute of Technology, Stockholm

76. Peretz I (2001) Listen to the brain: a biological perspective on musical emotions. In: Juslin PN, Sloboda JA (eds) Music and emotion: theory and research. Oxford University Press, New York, pp 105–134

77. Sundberg J, Askenfelt A, Frydén L (1983) Musical performance: a synthesis-by-rule approach. Comput Music J 7(1):37–43

78. Sundberg J (1993) How can music be expressive? Speech Commun 13:239–253

79. Friberg A (1991) Generative rules for music performance: a formal description of a rule system. Comput Music J 15(2):56–71

80. Friberg A, Bresin R, Frydén L, Sundberg J (1998) Musical punctuation on the microlevel: automatic identification and performance of small melodic units. J New Music Res 27(3):271–292

81. Bresin R, Friberg A (2000) Emotional coloring of computer-controlled music performances. Comput Music J 24(4):44–63

82. Pure Data. http://puredata.info/. Accessed 16 Feb 2011

83. Friberg A (2005) Home conducting: control the overall musical expression with gestures. In: Proceedings of international computer music conference (ICMC2005), Barcelona, Spain, pp 479–482

84. Canazza S, De Poli G, Rodà A, Vidolin A (2003) An abstract control space for communication of sensory expressive intentions in music performance. Comput Music J 32(3):281–294

85. Friberg A (2005) A fuzzy analyzer of emotional expression in music performance and body motion. In: Proceedings of music and music science, Stockholm, Sweden

86. Bresin R (2005) What is the color of that music performance? In: Proceedings of international computer music conference (ICMC2005), Barcelona, Spain, pp 367–370

87. Zhu X, Beauregard GT, Wyse L (2007) Real-time signal estimation from modified short-time Fourier transform magnitude spectra. IEEE Trans Audio Speech Lang Process 15(5):1645–1653

88. Fabiani M (2010) Frequency, phase and amplitude estimation of overlapping partials in monaural musical signals. In: Proceedings of 13th international conference on digital audio effects (DAFx-10), Graz, Austria

89. pys60. https://garage.maemo.org/projects/pys60/. Accessed 16 Feb 2011

90. Bech S, Zacharov N (2006) Perceptual audio evaluation – theory, method and application. Wiley, New York

91. Fabiani M, Bresin R, Dubus G (2011) Interactive sonification of expressive hand gestures on a handheld device. Journal on Multimodal User Interfaces, 1–9

92. Rubin J, Chisnell D (2008) Handbook of usability testing – how to plan and conduct effective tests. Wiley, New York

93. Nielsen J (1994) Heuristic evaluation. In: Nielsen J, Mack RL (eds) Usability inspection methods. Wiley, New York

94. Borchers J, Samminger W, Muhlhausen M (2001) Conducting a realistic electronic orchestra. In: Proceedings of 14th annual ACM symposium on user interface software and technology (UIST2001), Orlando, FL, USA

95. Dannenberg R (1984) An on-line algorithm for real-time accompaniment. In: Proceedings of international computer music conference (ICMC'84), Paris, France
96. Vercoe BL (1984) The synthetic performer in the context of live performance. In: Proceedings of international computer music conference (ICMC'84), Paris, France, pp 199–200
97. Csikszentmihalyi M (1998) Finding flow: The psychology of engagement with everyday life. Basic Books, New York

Expressive Performance Rendering with Probabilistic Models

3

Sebastian Flossmann, Maarten Grachten, and Gerhard Widmer

Abstract

We present YQX, a probabilistic performance rendering system based on Bayesian network theory. It models dependencies between score and performance and predicts performance characteristics using information extracted from the score. We discuss the basic system that won the Rendering Contest RENCON 2008 and then present several extensions, two of which aim to incorporate the current performance context into the prediction, resulting in more stable and consistent predictions. Furthermore, we describe the first steps towards a multilevel prediction model: Segmentation of the work, decomposition of tempo trajectories, and combination of different prediction models form the basis for a hierarchical prediction system. The algorithms are evaluated and compared using two very large data sets of human piano performances: 13 complete Mozart sonatas and the complete works for solo piano by Chopin.

S. Flossmann (✉)
Department of Computational Perception, Johannes Kepler Universitat,
Altenbergerstr 69, 4040 Linz, AT, Austria
e-mail: sebastian.flossmann@jku.at

M. Grachten
Post Doctoral Researcher at the Department of Computational Perception,
Johannes Kepler University, Linz, Austria

G. Widmer
Department of Computational Perception,
Johannes Kepler University (JKU), Linz, Austria

The Austrian Research Institute for Artificial Intelligence (OFAI),
Freyung 6/6, A-1010 Vienna, Austria

A. Kirke and E.R. Miranda (eds.), *Guide to Computing for Expressive Music Performance*, 75
DOI 10.1007/978-1-4471-4123-5_3, © Springer-Verlag London 2013

3.1   Introduction

Expressive performance modelling is the task of automatically generating an expressive rendering of a music score such that the performance produced sounds both musical and natural. This is done by first modelling the score or certain structural and musical characteristics of it. Then the score model is projected onto performance trajectories (for timing, dynamics, etc.) by a predictive model typically learned from a large set of example performances.

Unlike models in, for instance, rule-based or case-based approaches, the probabilistic performance model is regarded as a conditional multivariate probability distribution. The models differ in the way the mapping between score and performance model is achieved. Gaussian processes [31], hierarchical hidden Markov models [10], and Bayesian networks [38] are some of the techniques used.

Aside from the central problem of mapping the score to the performance, the main challenges in the process are acquisition and annotation of suitable example performances and the evaluation of the results. The data must encompass both precise performance data and score information and must be sufficiently large to be statistically representative. The level of precision required cannot yet be achieved through analysis of audio data, which leaves computer-controlled pianos, such as the Bösendorfer CEUS or the Yamaha Disklavier, as the main data source. For the training of our system, we have available two datasets recorded on such a device: 13 complete Mozart sonatas, performed by the Viennese pianist R. Batik in 1990, and the complete works for solo piano by Chopin, performed by the Russian pianist N. Magaloff in several live performances at the Vienna Konzerthaus in 1989.

Judging expressivity in terms of "humanness" and "naturalness" is a highly subjective task. The only scientific environment for comparing models according to such criteria is the annual Performance Rendering Contest RENCON [11], which offers a platform for presenting and evaluating, via listener ratings, state-of-the-art performance modelling systems. Alternatively, rendering systems can be evaluated automatically by measuring the similarity between rendered and real performances of a piece. This, however, is problematic: In some situations, small differences may make the result sound unintuitive and completely unmusical, whereas in other situations, a rendering may be reasonable despite huge differences.

In this chapter, we discuss a prototypical performance rendering system and its different stages: The basic system was entered successfully into the RENCON 2008 rendering contest. Several extensions have been developed that shed light on the problems and difficulties of probabilistic performance rendering.

3.2   Related Work

Systems can be compared in terms of two main components: the score representation and the learning and prediction model. The way expressive directives given in the score are rendered also makes a considerable difference in rendered performances, but this is beyond the scope of this chapter.

Score models – i.e., representations of the music and its structure – may be based either (1) on a sophisticated music theory such as Lerdahl and Jackendoff's

Generative Theory of Tonal Music (GTTM) [15] and Narmour's Implication–Realization (IR) model [22] or (2) simply on basic features capturing some local score characteristics (see, e.g., [7, 9, 10, 31, 35]). Many current models work with a combination of computationally inexpensive descriptive score features and particular structural aspects – mainly phrasal information or simplifications thereof – that are calculated via musicological models. Examples are the models of Arcos and de Mántaras [1], who partially apply the GTTM, and our system [4, 38], which implements parts of the IR model to approximate the phrasal structure of the score.

Regarding the learning and prediction models used, three different categories can be distinguished [36]: case-based reasoning (CBR), rule extraction, and probabilistic approaches. Case-based approaches use a database of example performances of music segments. New segments are played imitating stored ones on the basis of a distance metric between score models. Prototypical case-based performance models are *SaxEx* [1] and *Kagurame Phase II* [29]. In [32, 37], a structurally similar system is described that is based on a hierarchical phrase segmentation of the music score. The results are exceedingly good, but the approach is limited to small-scale experiments, as the problem of algorithmic phrase detection is still not solved in a satisfactory way. Dorard et al. [2] used Kernel methods to connect their score model to a corpus of performance worms, aiming to reproduce the style of certain performers.

Rule-based systems use a matching process to map score features directly to performance modifications. Widmer [35] developed an inductive rule learning algorithm that automatically extracts performance rules from piano performances; it discovered a small set of rules that cover a surprisingly large amount of expressivity in the data. Our YQX system uses some of these rules in combination with a probabilistic approach. Ramirez et al. [25] followed a similar approach using inductive logic programming to learn performance rules for jazz saxophone from audio recordings. Perez et al. [24] used a similar technique on violin recordings. The well-known KTH rule system was first introduced in [28] and has been extended in more than 20 years of research. A comprehensive description is given in [7]. The *Director Musices* system is an implementation of the KTH system that allows for expressive performance rendering of musical scores. The rules in the system refer to low-level musical situations and theoretical concepts and relate them to predictions of timing, dynamics, and articulation.

The performance model in probabilistic approaches is regarded as a multivariate probability distribution onto which the score model is mapped. The approaches differ in how the mapping is achieved. The Naist model [31] applies Gaussian processes to fit a parametric output function to the training performances. YQX [4] uses Bayesian network theory to model the interaction between score and performance. In addition, a small set of note-level rules adapted from Widmer's rule-based system are applied to further enhance musical quality. Grindlay and Helmbold first proposed a hidden Markov model (HMM) [9], which was later extended to form a hierarchical HMM [10], the advantage of which is that phrase information is coded into the structure of the model. All approaches mentioned above learn a monophonic performance model, predict the melody voice of the piece, and, in the rendering, synchronize the accompaniment according to the expressivity in the lead voice. Kim et al. [13] proposed a model of three sub-models: local expressivity models for the two outer voices (highest and lowest pitch of any given onset) and a harmony model for the inner voices.

Mazzola follows a different concept, building on a complex mathematical theory of musical structure [16]. The *Rubato* system [17, 19] is an implementation of this model.

3.3   The Data

Probabilistic models are usually learned from large sets of example data. For expressive performance modelling, the data must provide information on what was played (score information) and how it was played (performance information). The richness of available score information limits the level of sophistication of the score model: The more score information is provided, the more detailed a score model can be calculated. Piano performances can be described adequately by three dimensions: tempo, loudness, and articulation (our current model ignores pedalling). However, the information cannot be extracted from audio recordings at the necessary level of precision. This leaves a computer-controlled piano, such as the Bösendorfer CEUS (or the earlier version, the Bösendorfer SE) or a Yamaha Disklavier, as the only possible data source. This, of course, poses further problems. The number of recordings made on such devices is very small. Since such instruments are not normally used in recording studios or in public performances, the majority of available recordings stem from a scientific environment and do not feature world-class artists.

For our experiments, we use two unique data collections: the *Magaloff Corpus* and a collection of Mozart piano sonatas. In Spring 1989, Nikita Magaloff, a Russian–Georgian pianist famous for his Chopin interpretations, performed the entire work of Chopin for solo piano that was published during Chopin's lifetime (op. 1–64) in six public appearances at the Vienna Konzerthaus. Although the technology was fairly new at the time (first prototype in 1983, official release 1985 [20]), all six concerts were played and recorded on a Bösendorfer SE, precisely capturing every single keystroke and pedal movement. This was probably the first time the Bösendorfer SE was used to such an extent. The collected data is presumably the most comprehensive single-performer corpus ever recorded. The data set comprises more than 150 pieces with over 320,000 performed notes. We scanned the sheet music of all pieces and transformed it into machine-readable, symbolic scores in musicXML [27] format using the optical music recognition software SharpEye.[1] The MIDI data from the recordings were then matched semi-automatically to the symbolic scores. The result is a completely annotated corpus containing precisely measured performance data for almost all notes Chopin has ever written for solo piano.[2] Flossmann et al. [5] provided a comprehensive overview of the corpus, its construction, and results of initial exploratory studies of aspects of Magaloff's performance style.

The second data collection we use for the evaluation of our models is the 13 complete Mozart piano sonatas played by the Viennese pianist R. Batik, likewise

---

[1] see http://www.visiv.co.uk

[2] Some of the posthumously published works were played as encores but have not yet been included in the dataset.

Table 3.1 Overview of the data corpora

	Magaloff corpus	Mozart corpus
Pieces/movements	155	39
Score notes	328,800	100,689
Performed notes	335,542	104,497
Playing time	10 h 7 m 52 s	3 h 57 m 40 s

recorded on a Bösendorfer computer piano and matched to symbolic scores. This data set contains roughly 104,000 performed notes. Table 3.1 shows an overview of the two corpora.

3.4   Score and Performance Model

As indicated above, our rendering system is based on a score model comprising simple score descriptors (the *features*) and a musicological model – the Implication – Realization model by Narmour. Performances are characterized in three dimensions: tempo, loudness, and articulation. The way the performance characteristics (the *targets*) are defined has a large impact on the quality of the rendered pieces.

The prediction is done note by note for the melody voice of the piece only. In the Mozart sonatas, we manually annotated the melody voice in all pieces. In the case of the Chopin data, we assume that the highest pitch at any given time is the melody voice of the piece. Clearly, this very simple heuristic does not always hold true, but in the case of Chopin, it is correct often enough to be justifiable.

3.4.1   Performance Targets

Tempo in musical performances usually refers to a combination of two aspects: (1) the current tempo of a performance that evolves slowly and changes according to ritardandi or accelerandi; (2) the tempo of individual notes, often referred to as *local timing*, i.e., local deviations from the current tempo, used to emphasize single notes through delay or anticipation. Tempo is often measured in absolute beats per minute. We define the tempo relative to interonset intervals (IOI), i.e., the time between two successive notes. A performed IOI that is longer than prescribed by the score and the current tempo implies a slowing down, while a shorter IOI implies a speeding up. Thus, the description is independent of the absolute tempo and focuses on changes.

Loudness is not measured in absolute terms but relative to the overall loudness of the performance. Articulation describes the amount of legato between two successive notes: The smaller the audible gap between two successive notes, the more legato the first one becomes; the larger the gap, the more staccato.

Formally, we define the following performance targets:

Timing: The timing of a performance is measured in *interonset intervals* (IOIs), i.e., the time between two successive notes. The *IOI ratio* of a note relates the nominal score IOI and the performance IOI to the subsequent note. This indicates whether the next onset occurred earlier or later than prescribed by the score and thus also whether the previous note was shortened or lengthened. Let s_i and s_{i+1} be the two successive score notes, p_i and p_{i+1} the corresponding notes in the performance, $ioi_{i,i+1}{}^s$ the score IOI, $ioi_{i,i+1}{}^p$ the performance IOI of the two notes,[3] l_s the duration of the complete piece in beats, and l_p the length of the performance. The IOI ratio $ioiR_i$ of s_i is then defined as

$$ioiR_i = \log \frac{ioi^p_{i,i+1} * l_s}{ioi^s_{i,i+1} * l_p}.$$

Normalizing both score and performance IOIs to fractions of the complete score and performance makes this measure independent of the actual tempo. The logarithm is used to scale the values to a range symmetrical around zero, where $ioiR_i > 0$ indicates a prolonged IOI, i.e., a tempo slower than notated, and $ioiR_i < 0$ indicates a shortened IOI, i.e., a tempo faster than notated.

Split tempo and timing: It can be beneficial to divide the combined tempo into current tempo and local timing. The current tempo is defined as the lower-frequency components of the IOI ratio time series. A simple way of calculating the low-frequency component is to apply a windowed moving average function to the curve. The residual is considered the local timing. Let $ioiR_i$ be the IOI ratio of note s_i and $n \in \mathbb{N}$ (usually $5 \leq n \leq 10$), then the current tempo ct_i of the note s_i is calculated by

$$ct_i = \frac{1}{n} \sum_{j=i-\frac{(n-1)}{2}}^{i+\frac{(n-1)}{2}} ioiR_j.$$

The residual high-frequency content can be considered as the local timing lt_i and, in relation to the current tempo, indicates that a note is either played faster or slower with respect to the current tempo:

$$lt_i = \frac{ioiR_j - ct_i}{ct_i}.$$

Loudness: The loudness, also referred to as velocity,[4] of a performance is described as the ratio between the loudness of a note and the mean loudness of the performance. Again, the logarithm is used to scale the values to a range symmetrical around zero, with values above 0 being louder than average and those below 0 softer

---

[3] The unit of the duration does not matter in this case, as it cancels out with the unit of the complete duration of the performance.

[4] Computer-controlled pianos measure loudness by measuring the velocity at which a hammer strikes a string.

than average. Let $mvel_i$ be the midi velocity of note s_i. The loudness vel_i is then calculated by

$$vel_i = \log \frac{mvel_i}{\sum_j mvel_j}.$$

Articulation: Articulation measures the amount of legato between two notes, i.e., the ratio of the gap between them in a performance and the gap between them in the score. Let $ioi^s_{i, i+1}$ and $ioi^p_{i, i+1}$ be the score and performance IOIs between the successive notes s_i and s_{i+1}, and dur_i^s and dur_i^p the nominal score duration and the played duration of s_i, respectively. The articulation art_i of a note s_i is defined as

$$art_i = \frac{ioi^s_{i,i+1} * dur^p_i}{dur^s_i * ioi^p_{i,i+1}}.$$

3.4.2 Score Features

As briefly mentioned above, there are basically two ways of modelling a musical score: using (1) sophisticated musicological models, such as implementations of the GTTM [15] or Narmour's Implication–Realization model [22], and (2) feature-based descriptors of the musical content. We use a combination of both approaches.

Features fall into different categories, according to the musical content they describe: rhythmic, melodic, and harmonic descriptors.

Rhythmic features describe the relations of score durations of successive notes and their rhythmic context. In our system, we use:

Duration ratio: Let dur_i be the score duration of note s_i measured in beats; the duration ratio $durR_i$ is then defined by

$$durR_i = \frac{dur_i}{dur_{i+1}}.$$

Rhythmic context: The score durations of notes s_{i-1}, s_i, and s_{i+1} are sorted and assigned three different labels: short (s), neutral (n), and long (l). When a rest immediately before (and/or after) s_i is longer than half the duration of s_{i-1} (and/or s_{i+1}), the respective labels are replaced with (−). The rhythmic context $rhyC_i$ of s_i is then one of the 20 possible label triplets.[5]

---

[5] In the case of two equally long durations, we only discriminate between long and neutral. Hence, there are no situations labelled *lsl*, *sls*, *ssl*, etc., only *lnl*, *nln*, *nnl*, etc., which reduces the number of combinations used.

Melodic features: Melodic features describe the melodic content of the score, mainly pitch intervals and contours.

Pitch interval: The interval to the next score note, measured in semitones. The values are cut off at -13 and $+13$ so that all intervals greater than one octave are treated identically.

Pitch contour: The series of pitch intervals is smoothed to determine the distance of a score note to the next maximum or minimum pitch in the melody. The smoothing is needed to avoid choosing a local minimum/maximum.

IR features: One category of features is based on Narmour's Implication–Realization model of melodic expectation [22]. The theory constitutes an alternative to Schenkerian analysis and is focused more on cognitive aspects than on musical analysis. A short overview is given in Sect. 3.4.3. We use the labels assigned to each melody note and the distance of a melody note to the nearest point of closure as score features.

Harmonic consonance: Harmonic features describe perceptual aspects related to melodic consonance. Using Temperley's key profiles [30], we automatically determine the most likely local harmony given the pitches at a particular onset. The consonance of a note within an estimated harmony is judged using the key profiles proposed by Krumhansl and Kessler [14].

3.4.3 Narmour's Implication–Realization (IR) Model

The Implication-Realization (IR) model proposed by Narmour [22, 23] is a cognitively motivated model of musical structure. It tries to describe explicitly the patterns of listener expectation with respect to the continuation of the melody. It applies the principles of Gestalt theory to melody perception, an approach introduced by Meyer [18]. The model describes both the continuation implied by particular melodic intervals and the extent to which this (expected) continuation is actually realized by the following interval. Grachten [8] provides a short introduction to the processes involved.

Two main principles of the theory concern the direction and size of melodic intervals. (1) Small intervals imply an interval in the same registral direction, and large intervals imply a change in registral direction. (2) A small interval implies a following similarly sized interval, and a large interval implies a smaller interval. Based on these two principles, melodic patterns, or *structures*, can be identified that either satisfy or violate the implications predicted by the principles. Figure 3.1 shows eight such structures: process (P), duplication(D), intervallic duplication (ID), intervallic process (IP), registral process (VP), reversal (R), intervallic reversal (VR), and registral reversal (VR). The Process structure, for instance, sastisfies both registral and intervallic implications. Intervallic Process satisfies the intervallic difference principle but violates the registral implication.

Another notion derived from the concept of implied expectations is *closure*, which refers to situations in which listeners might expect a caesura. In the IR model, closure can be evoked in several dimensions of the music: intervallic progression,

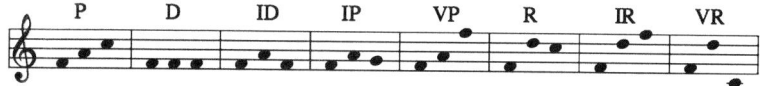

Fig. 3.1 Examples of eight IR structures

metrical position, rhythm, and harmony. The accumulated degrees of closure in each dimension constitute the perceived overall closure at any point in the score. Occurrences of strong closure may coincide with a more commonly used concept of closure in music theory that refers to the completion of a musical entity, for example, a phrase. Hence, calculating the distance of each note to the nearest point of closure can provide a segmentation of a piece similar to phrasal analysis.

3.5 YQX: The Simple Model

Our performance rendering system, called YQX, models the dependencies between score features and performance targets by means of a probabilistic network. The network consists of several interacting nodes representing different features and targets. Each node is associated with a probability distribution over the values of the corresponding feature or target. A connection between two nodes in the graph implies a conditioning of one feature or target distribution on the other. Discrete score features (the set of which we call **Q**) are associated with discrete probability tables, while continuous score features (**X**) are modelled by Gaussian distributions. The predicted performance characteristics, the targets (**Y**), are continuously valued and conditioned on the set of discrete and continuous features. Figure 3.2 shows the general layout. The semantics is that of a linear Gaussian model [21]. This implies that the case of a continuous distribution parenting a continuous distribution is implemented by making the mean of the child distribution linearly dependant on the value of the condition. Sets are hereafter denoted by bold letters, and vectors are indicated by variables with superscribed arrows.

Mathematically speaking, a target y is modelled as a conditional distribution $P(y|\mathbf{Q},\mathbf{X})$. Following the linear Gaussian model, this is a Gaussian distribution $\mathcal{N}(y; \mu, \sigma^2)$ with the mean μ varying linearly with **X**. Given specific values, $\mathbf{Q} = \mathbf{q}$ and $\mathbf{X} = \vec{x}$ (treating the real-valued set of continuous score features as a vector):

$$\mu = d_{\mathbf{q}} + \vec{k}_{\mathbf{q}} \cdot \vec{x},$$

where $d_{\mathbf{q}}$ and $\vec{k}_{\mathbf{q}}$ are estimated from the data by least-squares linear regression. The average residual error of the regression is the variance σ^2 of the distribution. Thus, we collect all instances in the data that share the same combination of discrete feature values and build a joint probability distribution of the continuous features and targets of these instances. This implements the conditioning on the discrete features **Q**. The linear dependency of the mean of the target distribution on the

Fig. 3.2 The probabilistic
network forming the YQX
system

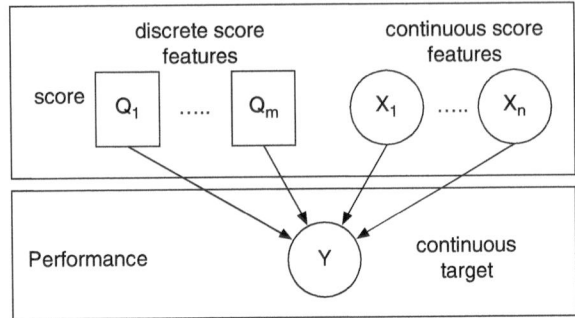

values of the continuous features introduces the conditioning on **X**. This constitutes
the training phase of the model.

Performance prediction is done note by note. The score features of a note are
entered into the network as evidence $\vec{x}$ and **q**. The instantiation of the discrete
features determines the appropriate probability table and the parameterization
$d_\mathbf{q}$ and $\vec{k}_\mathbf{q}$, and the continuous features are used to calculate the mean of the target
distribution μ. This value is used as the prediction for the specific note. As the targets
are independent, we create models and predictions for each target separately.

3.5.1 Quantitative Evaluation of YQX

We evaluated the model using the datasets described in Sect. 3.3: the complete
Chopin piano works played by N. Magaloff and the 13 complete Mozart piano
sonatas played by R. Batik. The Mozart data were split into two different datasets –
fast movements and slow movements – as they might reflect different interpretational concepts that would also be reproduced in the predictions. Thus, we also show
the results for the Chopin data for different categories (ballades, nocturnes, etc.[6])
The quality of a predicted performance is measured by Pearson's correlation coefficient between the predicted curve and the curve calculated from the training data.

Table 3.2 shows the averaged results of threefold cross-validations over the
datasets. For each result, we chose the combination of score features with the best
generalization on the test set. On the basis of predictions of local timing and current
tempo, the complete IOI curve can be reassembled by reversing the splitting
process described in Sect. 3.4.1. The column marked *ioi (r)* shows the best combined predictions for the each dataset.

The first observation is that the Chopin data generally show lower prediction
quality, which implies that these data are much harder to predict than the Mozart

---

[6] The category *Pieces* comprises Rondos (op. 1, op. 5, op. 16), Variations op. 12, Bolero op. 19,
Impromptus (op. 36, op. 51), Tarantelle op. 43, Allegro de Concert op. 46, Fantaisie op. 49,
Berceuse op. 57, and Barcarolle op. 61.

Table 3.2 Correlations between predicted and real performance for YQX. The targets shown are IOI ratio (*IOI*), loudness (*vel*), articulation (*art*), local timing (*timing*), current tempo (*tempo*), and reassembled IOI ratio (*IOI (r)*)

	IOI	Vel	Art	Timing	Tempo	IOI (r)
Mozart fast	0.46	0.42	0.49	0.43	0.39	0.46
Mozart slow	0.48	0.41	0.39	0.48	0.35	0.48
Chopin	0.22	0.16	0.33	0.15	0.18	0.22
Ballades	0.33	0.17	0.40	0.12	0.37	0.33
Etudes	0.17	0.15	0.17	0.09	0.20	0.16
Mazurkas	0.23	0.14	0.29	0.20	0.13	0.23
Nocturnes	0.17	0.17	0.33	0.14	0.11	0.17
Pieces	0.20	0.15	0.35	0.17	0.14	0.19
Polonaises	0.20	0.16	0.32	0.13	0.14	0.20
Preludes	0.20	0.15	0.33	0.15	0.16	0.21
Scherzi	0.33	0.23	0.26	0.16	0.30	0.33
Sonatas	0.16	0.14	0.32	0.12	0.20	0.16
Waltzes	0.35	0.16	0.29	0.22	0.35	0.35

pieces. This is probably due to the much higher variation in the performance characteristics for which the score features must account. Second, the loudness curves seem harder to predict than the tempo curves, a problem also observed in previous experiments with the model (see [4] and [37]). Third, articulation seems to be easier to predict than tempo (with the exception of the slow Mozart movements and the Chopin scherzi, mazurkas, and waltzes, for which articulation was harder to predict than tempo). The Chopin categories show huge differences in the prediction quality for tempo (the scherzi being the hardest to predict and the waltzes the easiest), suggesting that there are indeed common interpretational characteristics within each category.

Predicting the IOI ratio by combining the predictions for local timing and current tempo seems moderately successful. Only in some cases is the best combined prediction better than the best prediction for the separate components. It must be noted though that the combined predictions used the same set of features for both local timing and current tempo. Due to the extremely high number of possible combinations involved, experiments to find the two feature sets that lead to the best combined prediction have not yet been conducted.

3.5.2 Qualitative Evaluation of YQX

All quantitative evaluations of performances face the same problem: Although similarities between the predicted and the original curves can be measured to a certain degree, there is no computational way of judging the aesthetic qualities, or the degree of naturalness of expression, of a performance. The only adequate measure of quality is human judgement. The annual rendering contest RENCON [11] offers a scientific platform on which performance rendering systems can be compared and rated by the audience.

The system YQX participated in RENCON08, which was hosted alongside the ICMPC10 in Sapporo. Entrants to the "autonomous section" were required to render two previously unknown pieces (composed specifically for the competition) without any audio feedback from the system and within the time frame of 1 h. Four contestants entered the autonomous section and competed for three awards: The Rencon award was to be given to a winner selected by audience vote (both through web and on-site voting), the Rencon technical award was to be given to the entrant judged most interesting from a technical point of view, and finally the Rencon Murao Award was to be given to the entrant that most impressed the composer Prof. T. Murao. YQX won all three prizes. While this is no proof of the absolute quality of the model, it does give some evidence that the model is able to capture and reproduce certain aesthetic qualities of music performance. A video of YQX performing at RENCON08 can be seen at http://www.cp.jku.at/projects/yqx/yqx_cvideo2.flv.[7]

3.6   YQX: The Enhanced Dynamic Model

The predictions of the basic YQX system are note-wise; each prediction depends only on the score features at that particular score onset. In a real performance, this is of course not the case: Typically, changes in dynamics or tempo evolve gradually. Clearly, this necessitates awareness of the surrounding expressive context.

In this section, we present two extensions to the system that both introduce a dynamic component by incorporating the prediction made for the preceding score note into the prediction of the current score note. Graphically, this corresponds to first unfolding the network in time and then adding an arc from the target in time-step $t - 1$ to the target in time-step t. Figure 3.3 shows the unfolded network. This should lead to smoother and more consistent performances with less abrupt changes and, ideally, to an increase in the overall prediction quality.

The context-aware prediction can be done in two different ways: (1) Using the previous target simply as an additional parent probability distribution to the current target allows optimization with respect to one preceding prediction. Minimal adaptation has to be made to the algorithm (see Sect. 3.6.1). (2) Using an adaptation of the Viterbi decoding in hidden Markov models results in a predicted series that is optimal with respect to the complete piece (see Sect. 3.6.2).

---

[7] The performed piece "My Nocturne," a piano piece in a Chopin-like style, was composed by Prof. Tadahiro Murao specifically for the competition.

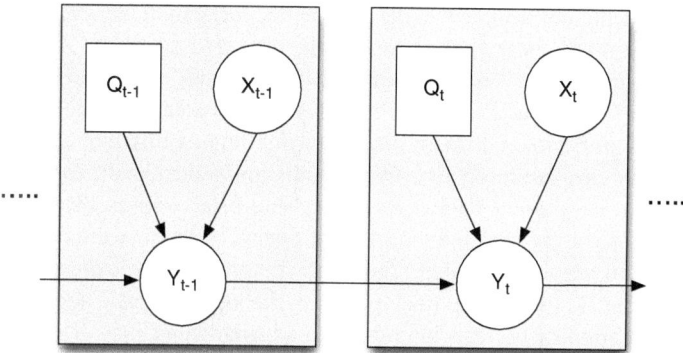

Fig. 3.3 The network unfolded in time

3.6.1 YQX with Local Maximisation

The first method is rather straightforward: We use the linear Gaussian model and treat the additional parent (the target y_{t-1}) to the target y_t as an additional feature that we calculate from the performance data. In the training process, the joint distribution of the continuous features, the target y_t, and the target in the previous time-step y_{t-1} given the discrete score features – in mathematical terms $P(y_{t-1}, y_t, \overrightarrow{x}_t | \mathbf{q}_t)$ – is estimated. This alters the conditional distribution of the target y_t to $P(y_t | \mathbf{Q}, \mathbf{X}, y_{t-1}) = \mathcal{N}(y; \mu, \sigma^2)$ with[8]

$$\mu = d_{\mathbf{q}, y_{t-1}} + \overrightarrow{k}_{\mathbf{q}, y_{t-1}} \cdot (\overrightarrow{x}, y_{t-1}).$$

The prediction phase is equally straightforward. As in the simple model, the mean of $P(y_t | \mathbf{q}_t, \overrightarrow{x}_t, y_{t-1})$ is used as the prediction for the score note in time-step t. This is the value with the highest local probability.

3.6.2 YQX with Global Maximisation

The second approach drops the concept of a linear Gaussian model completely. In the training phase, the joint conditional distributions $P(y_{t-1}, y_t, \overrightarrow{x}_t | \mathbf{q}_t)$ are estimated as before, but no linear regression parameters need to be calculated. The aim is to construct a sequence of predictions that maximizes the conditional probability of the performance given the score features with respect to the complete history of predictions made up to that point.

---

[8] The construct $(\overrightarrow{x}, y_{t-1})$ is a concatenation of the vector $\overrightarrow{x}$ and the value y_{t-1} leading to a new vector of dimension $dim(\overrightarrow{x}) + 1$.

This is calculated in similarly to the Viterbi decoding in hidden Markov models, which tries to find the best explanation for the observed data [12]. Aside from the fact that the roles of evidence nodes and query nodes are switched, the main conceptual difference is that − unlike the HMM setup, which uses tabular distributions − our approach must deal with continuous distributions. This rules out the dynamic programming algorithm usually applied and calls for an analytical solution, which we present below. As in the Viterbi algorithm, the calculation is done in two steps: a forward and a backward sweep. In the forward movement, the most probable target is calculated relative to the previous time-step. In the backward movement, knowing the final point of the optimal path, the sequence of predictions is found by backtracking through all time-steps.

The Forward Calculation Let $\vec{x}_t, \mathbf{q}_t$ be the sets of continuous and discrete features at time t, and N be the number of data points in a piece. Further, let α_t be the probability distribution over the target values y_t to conclude the optimal path from time-steps 1 to t. By means of a recursive formula, $\alpha(y_t)$ can be calculated for all time-steps of the unfolded network[9]:

$$\alpha(y_1) = p(y_1 | \mathbf{x}_1, \mathbf{q}_1) \tag{3.1}$$

$$\alpha(y_t) = \max_{y_{t-1} \in \mathbb{R}} \left[p(y_t, y_{t-1} | \vec{x}_t, \mathbf{q}_t) \cdot \alpha(y_{t-1}) \right] \tag{3.2}$$

This formula can be interpreted as follows: Assume that we know for all the target values y_{t-1} in time-step $t-1$ the probability of being part of the optimal path. Then we can calculate for each target value y_t in time-step t the predecessor that yields the highest probability for each specific y_t of being on the optimal path. In the backward movement, we start with the most probable final point of the path (the mean of the last α) and then backtrack to the beginning by choosing the best predecessors. As we cannot calculate the maximum over all $y_{t-1} \in \mathbb{R}$ directly, we need an analytical way of calculating $\alpha(y_t)$ from $\alpha(y_{t-1})$, which we derive below. We will also show that $\alpha(y_t)$ remains Gaussian through all time-steps. This is particularly important because we rely on the parametric representation using mean and variance.

We hereafter use the distribution $p(y_{t-1} | y_t, \vec{x}_t, \mathbf{q}_t) \propto \mathcal{N}(y_{t-1}; \mu_{t-1}, \sigma_{t-1}^2)$ that can be calculated via conditioning from the joint conditional distribution $p(y_{t-1}, y_t, \vec{x}_t | \mathbf{q}_t)$ that is estimated in the training of the model. For details as to how this is done see, for instance, [26]. Anticipating our proof that the $\alpha(y_t)$ are Gaussian, we refer to the mean and variance as $\mu_{\alpha, t}$ and $\sigma^2_{\alpha, t}$.

The inductive definition of α (Eq. 3.2) can be rewritten (the conditioning on $\mathbf{q}_t, \vec{x}_t$ is omitted for simplicity) as

$$\alpha(y_t) = \max_{y_{t-1} \in \mathbb{R}} [p(y_{t-1} | y_t) \cdot \alpha(y_{t-1})] \cdot p(y_t). \tag{3.3}$$

---

[9] We use $\alpha(y_t)$ and $p(y_t)$ as abbreviations of $\alpha(Y_t = y_t)$ and $p(Y_t = y_t)$, respectively.

Assuming that $\alpha(y_{t-1})$ is Gaussian, the result of the product in brackets is Gaussian $\mathcal{N}(y_{t-1}; \mu_*, \sigma_*^2)$ with a normalizing constant z, that is Gaussian in both means of the factors:

$$\sigma_*^2 = \frac{\sigma_{t-1}^2 * \sigma_{\alpha,t-1}^2}{\sigma_{t-1}^2 + \sigma_{\alpha,t-1}} \tag{3.4}$$

$$\mu_* = \sigma_*^2 \left(\frac{\mu_{t-1}}{\sigma_{t-1}^2} + \frac{\mu_{\alpha,t-1}}{\sigma_{\alpha,t-1}^2} \right) \tag{3.5}$$

$$z = \frac{1}{\sqrt{2\pi|\sigma_{1-1}^2 + \sigma_{\alpha,t-1}^2|}} e^{\left(\frac{-(\mu_{t-1} - \mu_{\alpha,t-1})^2}{2(\sigma_{t-1}^2 + \sigma_{\alpha,t-1}^2)} \right)} \tag{3.6}$$

Later, z is to be multiplied with a Gaussian distribution over y_t. Hence, z must be transformed into a distribution over the same variable. By finding a y_t such that the exponent in Eq. 3.6 equals 0, we can construct the mean μ_z and variance σ_z^2 of z. Note that the variable μ_{t-1} is dependent on y_t due to the conditioning of $p(y_{t-1}|y_t)$ on y_t.

$$z \propto \mathcal{N}(y_t; \mu_z, \sigma_z^2) \tag{3.7}$$

$$\mu_z = -\frac{\sigma_t^2 \cdot (\mu_{t-1} + \mu_{\alpha,t-1}) + \mu_t \cdot \sigma_{t,t-1}^2}{\sigma_{t,t-1}^2} \tag{3.8}$$

$$\sigma_z^2 = \sigma_{t-1}^2 + \sigma_{\alpha,t-1}^2 \tag{3.9}$$

As z is independent of y_{t-1}, it is not affected by the calculation of the maximum:

$$\alpha(y_t) \propto \max_{y_{t-1} \in \mathbf{R}} [\mathcal{N}(y_{t-1}; \mu_*, \sigma_*^2)] \cdot$$
$$\mathcal{N}(y_t; \mu_z, \sigma_z^2) \cdot p(y_t) \tag{3.10}$$

$$= \frac{1}{\sqrt{2\pi\sigma^2}} \cdot \mathcal{N}(y_t; \mu_z, \sigma_z^2) \cdot p(y_t). \tag{3.11}$$

The factor $\frac{1}{\sqrt{2\pi\sigma^2}}$ can be neglected, as it does not affect the parameters of the final distribution of $\alpha(y_t)$. The distribution $P(y_t)$ is Gaussian by design, and hence, the remaining product again results in a Gaussian and a normalizing constant. As the means of both factors are fixed, the normalizing constant in this case is a single factor. The mean $\mu_{\alpha,t}$ and variance $\sigma_{\alpha,t}^2$ of $\alpha(y_t)$ follow:

$$\alpha(y_t) \propto \mathcal{N}(y_t; \mu_{\alpha,t}, \sigma_{\alpha,t}^2) \tag{3.12}$$

$$\sigma_{\alpha,t} = \frac{\sigma_t^2 \cdot \sigma_z^2}{\sigma_t^2 + \sigma_z^2} \tag{3.13}$$

$$\mu_{\alpha,t} = \sigma_{\alpha,t}\left(\frac{\mu_z}{\sigma_z^2} + \frac{\mu_t}{\sigma_t^2}\right). \tag{3.14}$$

Thus, $\alpha(y_t)$ is Gaussian in y_t, assuming that $\alpha(y_{t-1})$ is Gaussian. Since $\alpha(y_1)$ is Gaussian, it follows that $\alpha(y_t)$ is Gaussian for $1 \le t \le N$. This equation shows that the mean and variance of $\alpha(y_t)$ can be computed recursively using the mean $\mu_{\alpha,t-1}$ and variance $\sigma^2_{\alpha,t-1}$ of $\alpha(y_{t-1})$. The parameters of α_{y_1} are equal to μ_{y_1} and $\sigma_{y_1}^2$, which are the mean and the variance of the distribution $p(y_1|\overrightarrow{x}_1, \mathbf{q}_1)$, and are estimated from the data.

The Backward Calculation Once the mean and variance μ_t, σ_t^2 of $\alpha(y_t)$ are known for $1 \le t \le N$, the optimal sequence $y_1, \ldots, y_N$ can be calculated:

$$y_N = \mu_{\alpha,N} \tag{3.15}$$

$$y_{t-1} = \arg\max_{y_{t-1}} \left[\mathcal{N}(y_{t-1}; \mu_*, \sigma_*^2\right] \tag{3.16}$$

$$= \mu_*. \tag{3.17}$$

3.6.3 Quantitative Evaluation

We evaluated the enhanced algorithms using the same datasets as for the original YQX model. As before, the correlation between predicted and human performance serves as a measure of quality. Table 3.3 shows the results. For comparison, we also included the results for the original YQX model as presented in Sect. 3.5.1.

For the Chopin data (both complete set and individual categories), the prediction quality for tempo increases in all cases and for loudness in some cases. Prediction quality for articulation decreases compared to the original model for both local and global optimization. This is not surprising because articulation is a local phenomenon that does not benefit from long-term modelling. This also holds for the timing, i.e., the local tempo component: In most cases, local or global optimization does not improve the prediction quality. However, the current tempo – the low-frequency component of the IOI ratio – on the other hand, does benefit from optimizing the prediction globally with respect to the performance context: The prediction quality is increased in all cases (the biggest gain, almost 80%, is registered in the mazurkas).

Surprisingly, the Mozart data paint a different picture: None of the performance targets (with the exception of the current tempo prediction for the fast movements)

Table 3.3 Correlations between predicted and real performance for the basic YQX and the locally and globally optimized models. The targets shown are IOI ratio (*IOI*), loudness (*vel*), articulation (*art*), local timing (*timing*), current tempo (*tempo*), and reassembled IOI ratio (*IOI (r)*)

		IOI	Vel	Art	Timing	Tempo	IOI (r)
Mozart fast	YQX	0.46	0.42	0.49	0.43	0.39	0.46
	Local	0.44	0.41	0.48	0.42	0.43	0.44
	Global	0.39	0.37	0.37	0.32	0.43	0.39
Mozart slow	YQX	0.48	0.41	0.39	0.48	0.35	0.48
	Local	0.46	0.39	0.38	0.48	0.42	0.47
	Global	0.46	0.35	0.23	0.44	0.34	0.46
Chopin	YQX	0.22	0.16	0.33	0.15	0.18	0.22
	Local	0.21	0.14	0.14	0.15	0.16	0.20
	Global	0.23	0.15	0.14	0.16	0.22	0.23
Ballades	YQX	0.33	0.17	0.40	0.12	0.37	0.33
	Local	0.36	0.17	0.39	0.12	0.30	0.25
	Global	0.38	0.19	0.36	0.12	0.46	0.38
Etudes	YQX	0.17	0.15	0.17	0.09	0.20	0.16
	Local	0.14	0.14	0.16	0.09	0.17	0.14
	Global	0.22	0.15	0.15	0.13	0.26	0.23
Mazurkas	YQX	0.23	0.14	0.29	0.20	0.13	0.23
	Local	0.22	0.14	0.28	0.22	0.13	0.21
	Global	0.23	0.13	0.27	0.20	0.19	0.24
Nocturnes	YQX	0.17	0.17	0.33	0.14	0.11	0.17
	Local	0.17	0.11	0.32	0.14	0.17	0.16
	Global	0.20	0.18	0.31	0.15	0.14	0.18
Pieces	YQX	0.20	0.15	0.35	0.17	0.14	0.19
	Local	0.22	0.12	0.33	0.12	0.16	0.18
	Global	0.23	0.14	0.33	0.17	0.25	0.26
Polonaises	YQX	0.20	0.16	0.32	0.13	0.14	0.20
	Local	0.18	0.19	0.32	0.13	0.15	0.16
	Global	0.22	0.19	0.31	0.14	0.20	0.23
Preludes	YQX	0.20	0.15	0.33	0.15	0.16	0.21
	Local	0.19	0.11	0.31	0.15	0.22	0.18
	Global	0.22	0.14	0.28	0.14	0.23	0.22
Scherzi	YQX	0.33	0.23	0.26	0.16	0.30	0.33
	Local	0.34	0.18	0.26	0.15	0.32	0.31
	Global	0.34	0.18	0.25	0.13	0.36	0.34
Sonatas	YQX	0.16	0.14	0.32	0.12	0.20	0.16
	Local	0.17	0.12	0.32	0.12	0.18	0.15
	Global	0.21	0.15	0.32	0.09	0.28	0.22
Waltzes	YQX	0.35	0.16	0.29	0.22	0.35	0.35
	Local	0.37	0.18	0.28	0.23	0.31	0.14
	Global	0.38	0.24	0.29	0.22	0.44	0.38

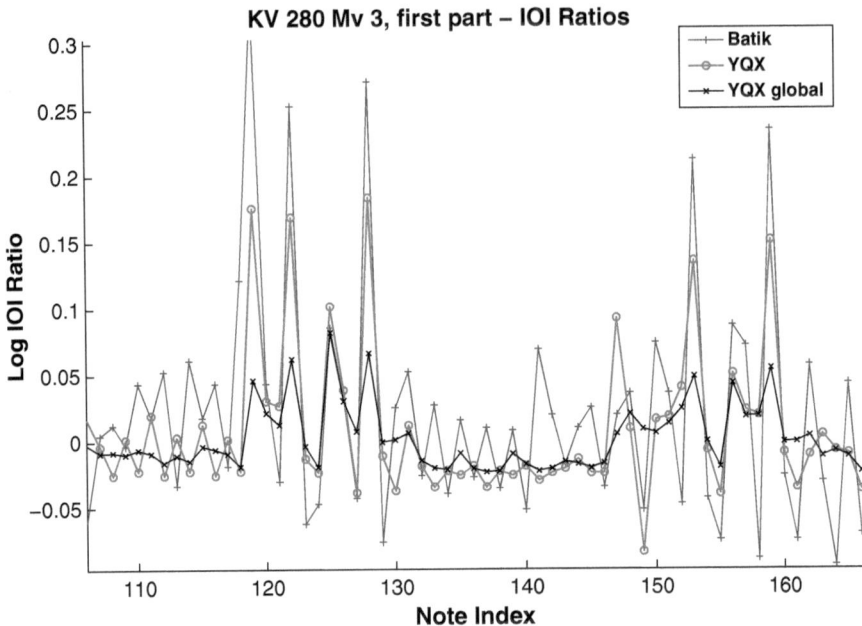

Fig. 3.4 IOI ratios predicted for bars 31–54 of *K*. 280, Mv.3

benefits from including the performance context into the predictions. Previous experiments [4] showed that, given a specific, fixed set of features, local or global optimization improves the prediction quality. However, given the freedom of choosing the best set of features for each particular target (which is the evaluation setup we chose here), feature sets exist with which the original, simple model outperforms the enhanced versions in terms of average correlation.

3.6.4 Qualitative Evaluation

Figure 3.4 shows the IOI ratio predictions for bars 31–54 in the third movement of Mozart Sonata *K*. 280. The original YQX algorithm exhibits small fluctuations that are largely uncorrelated with the human performance. This results in small but noticeable irregularities in the rendered performance. In contrast to the human performance, which is far from yielding a flat curve, these make the result sound inconsistent instead of lively and natural. The globally optimized YQX eliminates them at the expense of flattening out some of the (musically meaningful) spikes. The correlation for the movement was improved by 57. 2% from 0. 29 (YQX) to 0. 456 (YQX global).

3.7   Further Extensions

3.7.1   Note-Level Rules

In 2003, Widmer developed a rule extraction algorithm for musical expression [35]. Applied to the Mozart sonatas, this resulted in a number of simple rules suggesting expressive change under certain melodic or rhythmic circumstances. Some of them were used with surprising consistency [34]. We use two of the rules to further enhance the aesthetic qualities of the rendered preformances:

Staccato rule: If two successive notes (not exceeding a certain duration) have the same pitch, and the second of the two is longer, then the first note is played staccato. In our implementation, the predicted articulation is substituted with a fixed small value, usually around 0. 15, which amounts to 15% of the duration in the score in terms of the current performance tempo.

Delay next rule: If two notes of the same length are followed by a longer note, the last note is played with a slight delay. The IOI ratio of the middle note of a triplet satisfying the condition is calculated by taking the average of the two preceding notes and adding a fixed amount.

Figure 3.5 shows the effect of the delay next rule on the IOI ratios predicted for Chopin prelude op. 28 no. 18, bars 12–17. Instances of the delay next rule occur at beats 24, 24. 5, 26. 5, 28. 5, and 29. 5, all of which coincide with local delays in Magaloff's performance.

3.7.2   Combined Tempo and Timing Model

As discussed briefly in Sect. 3.5.1, it seems reasonable to split the tempo curve into a high- and a low-frequency component (the local and global tempo), predict the two separately, and reassemble a tempo prediction from the two curves. Considering the effect of global optimization, as discussed in Sect. 3.6.3, it also seems appropriate to use the basic model for the local timing predictions and the global optimization algorithm for the current tempo predictions.

An obvious extension to the experiments already presented would be to use different feature sets for the two components. In previous studies [3], we have discovered a relation between the size of the context a feature describes and its prediction quality for global and local tempo changes. The low-frequency components of certain features that are calculated, for instance, via a windowed moving average, are more suitable for global tempo prediction than are the high-frequency components, and vice versa for local tempo changes. Preliminary experiments that integrate this concept in the YQX algorithms show a slight quality increase (around 5%) for the current tempo and, consequently, for the combined IOI ratio target.

Also, global tempo trends in classical music are highly correlated with the phrase structure of a piece. This fact is often discussed in research on models of expressivity, such as the kinematic models introduced by Friberg and Sundberg [6] and by Todd [33]. Instead of training a model on the tempo curve of a complete piece,

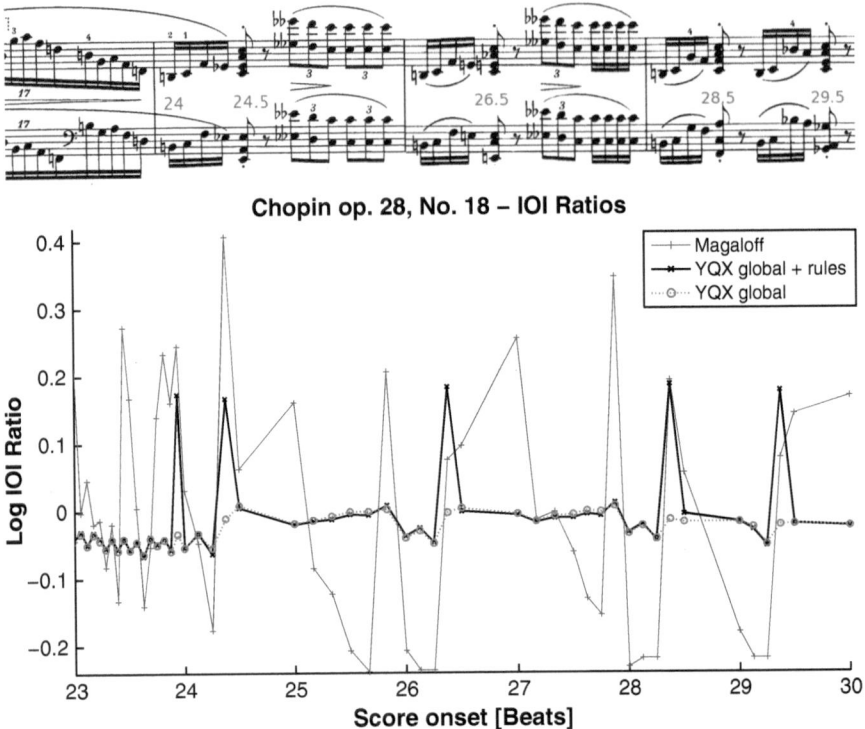

Fig. 3.5 *Upper panel*: score of Chopin prelude op. 28 no. 18, bars 13–15, the onsets in questions are marked; *lower panel*: effect of the delay next rule applied to the YQX prediction for Chopin prelude op. 28 no. 18, beats 22–32

a promising approach would thus be to train and predict phrases or phrase-like segments of the score. A possible, albeit simplistic, implementation would assume that tempo and loudness follow a n approximately parabolic trend – soft and slow at the beginning and end of a phrase, faster and louder in the middle. A performance would then be created by combining the local tempo predictions made by a probabilistic model with a segment-wise parabolic global tempo. To refine the segment-wise predictions of global tempo, any kind of more sophisticated model could be used – a probabilistic system, a parametric model, or a case-based one (as in [37]).

3.7.3 Dynamic Bayesian Networks

Both models presented above, the Bayesian reasoning of YQX and the context-aware dynamic YQX, are subclasses of the general complex of Bayesian networks. The obvious generalization of the models is towards a dynamic Bayesian network (DBN). The main differences lie in (1) the network layout and (2) the way the model is trained.

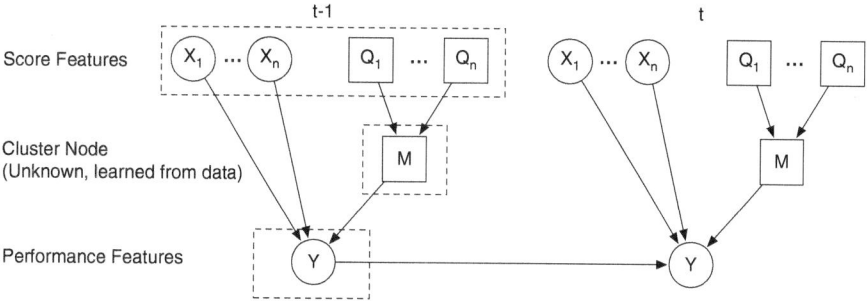

Fig. 3.6 Possible extension of YQX to a dynamic Bayesian network

We restricted our system to connections from score features to the performance targets within one time-step. For the training of the model, all features and targets had to be known in advance. Figure 3.6 shows what a DBN could look like for expressive performance rendering. The basic idea is the same: The performance targets are statistically dependent on the score features and the previously predicted target value. In addition, an intermediate layer (the discrete node M in Fig. 3.6) can be added that does not represent any particular score characteristic but instead functions as a clustering element for the discrete score features $Q_1, \ldots, Q_n$. This mitigates the sparsity problem caused by the huge number of possible combinations of values for the discrete features. The values of M are not known in advance, only the number of discrete states that the node can be in is fixed. The conditional probability distribution of M given the parenting nodes $Q_1, \ldots, Q_n$ is estimated in the training process of the model. The training itself is done by maximizing the log likelihood of the predicted values with an expectation-maximization algorithm [21].

However, the most significant difference is that instead of feeding the complete piece into the model at once, DBNs work on short segments. In theory, any trend common to all or most of the segments should also be recognizable in the predicted curves. Given a segmentation of musical works into musically meaningful fragments – ideally phrases – the network should be able to reproduce patterns of tempo or loudness that are common across phrases.

3.8   Conclusion

Automatic synthesis of expressive music is a very challenging task. Of particular difficulty is the evaluation of a system, as one cannot judge the aesthetic quality of a performance by numbers. The only adequate measure of quality is human judgement. The rendering system presented passed this test in the RENCON08 and therefore constitutes a baseline for our current research. The two extensions we devised incorporate the current performance context into predictions. This proved useful for reproducing longer-term trends in the data at the expense of local expressivity.

We consider this a work in progress. There is still a long way to go to a machine-generated performance that sounds profoundly musical. The main goal in the near future will be to further develop the idea of a multilevel system comprising several sub-models, each specialized on a different aspect of perfor-mance – global trends and local events. Segmentation of the input pieces will also play a significant role, as this reflects the inherently hierarchical structure of music performance.

Acknowledgements We express our gratitude to Mme Irène Magaloff for her generous permis-sion to use the unique resource that is the Magaloff Corpus for our research. This work is funded by the Austrian National Research Fund FWF via grants TRP 109-N23 and Z159 ("Wittgenstein Award"). The Austrian Research Institute for Artificial Intelligence acknowledges financial support from the Austrian Federal Ministries BMWF and BMVIT.

Questions

1. Aside from the central problem of mapping the score to the performance, what are the other main challenges in the process of generating a computer performance?
2. Why is evaluating automatically by measuring the similarity between rendered and real performances of a piece problematic?
3. What are the two methods on which score models (i.e., representations of the music and its structure) may be based?
4. What three different categories can be distinguished regarding the learning and prediction models used in CSEMPs?
5. In probabilistic approaches, how is the performance model regarded?
6. For data used in developing an expressive performance statistical model, the data must provide information on what two elements?
7. What musicological model was selected for the YQX system?
8. In what three dimensions are performances characterized in YQX?
9. What is the difference in implementation between the local and the global maximization approaches in YQX?
10. What is the difference in results between the local and the global maximization approaches in YQX?

References

1. Arcos J, de Mántaras R (2001) An interactive CBR approach for generating expressive music. J Appl Intell 27(1):115–129
2. Dorard L, Hardoon D, Shawe-Taylor J (2007) Can style be learned? A machine learning approach towards "performing" as famous pianists. In: Proceedings of music, brain & cogni-tion workshop – the neural information processing systems 2007 (NIPS 2007), Whistler
3. Flossmann S, Grachten M, Widmer G (2008) Experimentally investigating the use of score features for computational models of expressive timing. In: Proceedings of the 10th interna-tional conference on music perception and cognition 2008 (ICMPC '08), Sapporo

4. Flossmann S, Grachten M, Widmer G (2009) Expressive performance rendering: introducing performance context. In: Proceedings of the 6th sound and music computing conference 2009 (SMC '09), Porto, pp 155–160
5. Flossmann S, Goebl W, Grachten M, Niedermayer B, Widmer G (2010) The magaloff project: an interim report. J New Music Res 39(4):363–377
6. Friberg A, Sundberg J (1999) Does music performance allude to locomotion? A model of final ritardandi derived from measurements of stopping runners. J Acoust Soc Am 105 (3):1469–1484
7. Friberg A, Bresin R, Sundberg J (2006) Overview of the KTH rule system for musical performance. Adv Cognit Psychol 2(2–3):145–161
8. Grachten M (2006) Expressivity-aware tempo transformations of music performances using case based reasoning. Ph.D. thesis, Pompeu Fabra University, Barcelona
9. Grindlay GC (2005) Modeling expressive musical performance with Hidden Markov models. Master's thesis, University of California, Santa Cruz
10. Grindlay G, Helmbold D (2006) Modeling, analyzing, and synthesizing expressive piano performance with graphical models. Mach Learn 65(2–3):361–387
11. Hashida M (2008) RENCON – Performance Rendering Contest for computer systems. http://www.renconmusic.org/. Accessed Sep 2008
12. Juang BH, Rabiner LR (1991) Hidden Markov Models for speech recognition. Technometrics 33(3):251–272
13. Kim TH, Fukayama S, Nishimoto T, Sagayama S (2010) Performance rendering for polyphonic piano music with a combination of probabilistic models for melody and harmony. In: Proceedings of the 7th sound and music computing conference 2010 (SMC '10), Barcelona
14. Krumhansl CL, Kessler EJ (1982) Tracing the dynamic changes in perceived tonal organization in a spatioal representation of musical keys. Psychol Rev 89:334–368
15. Lerdahl F, Jackendoff R (1983) A generative theory of tonal music. The MIT Press, Cambridge
16. Mazzola G (2002) The topos of music – geometric logic of concepts, theory, and performance. Birkhäuser Verlag, Basel
17. Mazzola G (2006) Rubato software. http://www.rubato.org
18. Meyer L (1956) Emotion and meaning in music. University of Chicago Press, Chicago
19. Milmeister G (2006) The Rubato composer music software: component-based implementation of a functorial concept architecture. Ph.D. thesis, Universität Zürich, Zürich
20. Moog RA, Rhea TL (1990) Evolution of the keyboard interface: the Boesendorfer 290 SE recording piano and the moog multiply-touch-sensitive keyboards. Comput Music J 14 (2):52–60
21. Murphy K (2002) Dynamic Bayesian networks: presentation, inference and learning. Ph.D. thesis, University of California, Berkeley
22. Narmour E (1990) The analysis and cognition of basic melodic structures: the implication--realization model. University of Chicago Press, Chicago
23. Narmour E (1992) The analysis and cognition of melodic complexity: the implication–realization model. University of Chicago Press, Chicago
24. Perez A, Maestre E, Ramirez R, Kersten S (2008) Expressive irish fiddle performance model informed with bowing. In: Proceedings of the international computer music conference 2008 (ICMC '08), Belfast
25. Ramirez R, Hazan A, Gòmez E, Maestre E (2004) Understanding expressive transformations in saxophone Jazz performances using inductive machine learning in saxophone jazz performances using inductive machine learning. In: Proceedings of the sound and music computing international conference 2004 (SMC '04), Paris
26. Rasmussen CE, Williams CKI (2006) Gaussian processes for machine learning. The MIT Press, Cambridge. www.GaussianProcess.org/gpml
27. Recordare (2003) MusicXML definition. http://www.recordare.com/xml.html
28. Sundberg J, Askenfelt A, Frydén L (1983) Musical performance: a synthesis-by-rule approach. Comput Music J 7:37–43

29. Suzuki T (2003) The second phase development of case based performance rendering system "Kagurame". In: Working notes of the IJCAI-03 rencon workshop, Acapulco, pp 23–31
30. Temperley D (2007) Music and probability. MIT Press, Cambridge
31. Teramura K, Okuma H, et al (2008) Gaussian process regression for rendering music performance. In: Proceedings of the 10th international conference on music perception and cognition 2008 (ICMPC '08), Sapporo
32. Tobudic A, Widmer G (2006) Relational IBL in classical music. Mach Learn 64(1–3):5–24
33. Todd NPM (1992) The dynamics of dynamics: a model of musical expression. J Acoust Soc Am 91:3450–3550
34. Widmer G (2002) Machine discoveries: a few simple, robust local expression principles. J New Music Res 31(1):37–50
35. Widmer G (2003) Discovering simple rules in complex data: a meta-learning algorithm and some surprising musical discoveries. Artif Intell 146(2):129–148
36. Widmer G, Goebl W (2004) Computational models of expressive music performance: the state of the art. J New Music Res 33(3):203–216
37. Widmer G, Tobudic A (2003) Playing Mozart by analogy: learning multi-level timing and dynamics strategies. J New Music Res 32(3):259–268
38. Widmer G, Flossmann S, Grachten M (2009) YQX plays Chopin. AI Mag 30(3):35–48

Artificial Evolution of Expressive Performance of Music: An Imitative Multi-Agent Systems Approach

Eduardo R. Miranda, Alexis Kirke, and Qijun Zhang

Abstract

This chapter introduces an imitative multi-agent system approach to generate expressive performances of music, based on agents' individual parameterized musical rules. We have developed a system called IMAP (imitative multi-agent performer). Aside from investigating the usefulness of such an application of the imitative multi-agent paradigm, there is also a desire to investigate the inherent feature of diversity and control of diversity in this methodology: a desirable feature for a creative application, such as musical performance. To aid this control of diversity, parameterized rules are utilized based on previous expressive performance research. These are implemented in the agents using previously developed musical analysis algorithms. When experiments are run, it is found that agents are expressing their preferences through their music performances and that diversity can be generated and controlled.

4.1   Introduction

As early as the 1950s and early 1960s, pioneers such as Lejaren Hiller, Gottfried Michael Koenig, Iannis Xenakis, and Pietro Grossi, among a few others, started to gain access to computers to make music. It soon became clear that in order to render music with the so-called human feel, computers needed to process information about performance (e.g., deviations in tempo and loudness), in addition to the

E.R. Miranda (✉) • A. Kirke • Q. Zhang
Interdisciplinary Centre for Computer Music Research, Plymouth University, Faculty of Arts, Drake Circus, PL4 8AA Plymouth, UK
e-mail: eduardo.miranda@plymouth.ac.uk; alexis.kirke@plymouth.ac.uk; qijun.zhang@plymouth.ac.uk;

A. Kirke and E.R. Miranda (eds.), *Guide to Computing for Expressive Music Performance*, 99
DOI 10.1007/978-1-4471-4123-5_4, © Springer-Verlag London 2013

symbols that are normally found in a traditional musical score (e.g., pitch and rhythm). This was especially relevant for those interested in using the computer to playback scores.

Indeed, the first ever attempt at creating a computer music programming language by Max Mathews at Bell Telephone Laboratories in 1957 was motivated by his wish to "write a program to perform music on the computer" [1] (p. 10). It appears that this development began after Mathews and John Pierce went to a piano concert together. During the intermission, Pierce suggested that perhaps a computer could perform as well as the pianist. Mathews took up the challenge, which resulted in Music I: the ancestor of music programming languages such as Csound [2].

Research into computational models of expressive performance of music [3] is still booming with activity nowadays, especially research into devising increasingly more sophisticated automated and semiautomated computer system for expressive music performance, hereinafter referred to as CSEMP.

A CSEMP is a system able to generate expressive performances of music. For example, software for music typesetting is often used to write a piece of music, but most packages play back the music in a "robotic" way, without expressive performance. The provision of a CSEMP engine would enable such systems to produce more realistic playbacks.

A variety of techniques have been used to implement CSEMPs [3, 4]. These are discussed in Chap. 1 and include:

(a) Rule- and grammar-based approaches [5–8] including expert systems [9]
(b) Linear and nonlinear regression systems [10, 11] including artificial neural networks [12, 13], hidden Markov models [14], Bayesian belief networks [15], sequential covering methods [16], and regression trees [17]
(c) Evolutionary computing (EC) methods [18, 19]

An introduction to expressive music performance [21–25] can be found in the first chapter of this book. In this chapter, we will introduce a new approach using the imitative multi-agents paradigm.

4.1.1 Evolutionary Computation

Evolutionary computation (EC) methods have been successfully applied to algorithmic composition; please refer to [26] for an introduction to a number of such systems. The great majority of these systems use genetic algorithms [27], or GA, to produce melodies and rhythms. In these systems, music parameters are represented as "genes" of software agents, and GA operators are applied to "evolve" music according to given fitness criteria.

More recently, progress in applying EC to CSEMP has been reported [17–19]. EC-based CSEMPs have all applied the neo-Darwinian approach of selecting the musically fittest genes to be carried into the next generation. We are interested, however, in investigating the application of an alternative EC approach to expressive performance, one which is based on cultural transmission rather than genetic transmission.

Musical behavior in human beings is based both in our genetic heritage and also our cultural heritage [28]. One way of achieving a cultural, as opposed to genetic, transmission is through imitation of behavior [29, 30]. Work on the application of this imitative cultural approach to algorithmic composition has been initiated by Miranda [31]. In this chapter, we follow up the cultural transmission methodology with an application of an imitative multi-agent systems approach to expressive music performance. We have developed a system referred to as imitative multi-agent performer, or IMAP, which is introduced below.

In the genetic algorithm (GA) model of transmission of behavior, a population of agents is generated having its own behavior defined by their "genetic" code. The desirability of the behavior is evaluated by a global fitness function, and agents with low fitness are often discarded, depending on which version of the algorithm is adopted [27]. Then, a new population of agents is generated by combination, and deterministic or nondeterministic transformation, of the genes of the highest-scoring agents. Conversely, in the imitation model of transmission of behavior, an agent interacts with one or more other agents using a protocol that communicates to the other agents the behavior the first agent has. The other agent evaluates the first agent's behavior based on some evaluation function, and if the evaluation scores are high enough, one or more of the other agents will change their own behaviors based on the first agent's behavior. The evaluation function in the imitation model plays a similar role to the fitness function in the GA model. However, in imitative multi-agent systems, the evaluation function is particularly suited for the design of EC systems using a nonglobal fitness function, for example, by giving each agent their own evaluation function.

The potential for diversity is a desirable trait for a system for generating novel expressive music performances – as opposed to replicating existing ones – because there is no objectively defined optimal performance for a musical score [6, 19]. Performance is a subjective creative act, as discussed in Chap. 1. Previous work on genetic transmission in generating expressive music performance has been significantly motivated by the desire to generate a variety of performances. As will be demonstrated below, there is even more scope for such variety in IMAP because a multiplicity of evaluation functions is used. Furthermore, there is scope for easily controlling the level of diversity in IMAP.

It is not our intention to compare the imitative approach with the GA approach because both approaches have their own merits and should be considered as complementary approaches. Ramirez et al. [19] have demonstrated the validity of a GA model, and the experiments later in this article demonstrate the validity of our imitative approach.

One obvious measure of validity will be whether the system generates performances that are expressive. The other two measures of validity will relate to those elements of the imitative approach, which differentiate it from the standard GA approach, in particular, the ability to easily provide the system with a number of parallel interacting fitness functions. Hence, IMAP will be evaluated in terms of:
(a) The expressiveness of IMAP-generated performances. (Note, however, that this is not assessed by means of experiments with human subjects. What is assessed is

how well the agents can generate performances that embody their preference weights)

(b) Performance diversity generation and control of the level of diversity
(c) The ability to control diversity when it is being affected by multiple musical elements simultaneously

Imitative learning has been frequently used in other multi-agent systems research [32, 33]. However, to the best of our knowledge, IMAP is the first application of such methods to the generation of expressive musical performances.

4.2 Imitative Multi-Agent Performer: IMAP

4.2.1 Overview

IMAP is a multi-agent system. Here, the agents are considered as performers who evolve their own expressive performance actions to perform a given melody. Each agent has two communication functions: (a) it can listen to the performance of another agent, and (b) it can perform to another agent. All agents are provided with the same monophonic melody, the melody from which expressive performances will be generated. In all interactions, all agents perform the same melody, usually with different expressive actions. Agents in IMAP have two types of expressive actions: (a) changes in tempo and (b) changes in note loudness. Each agent also has a musical evaluation function based on a collection of rules, where different agents give different weightings to the rules and use the combination to evaluate the performances they hear. Initially, agents will perform with random expressive actions. If they evaluate another agent's expressive performance highly enough through their evaluation function, then they will adjust their own future performances towards the other agent's expressive actions. As this process continues, a repertoire of different expressive performances evolves across the population.

4.2.2 Agent Evaluation Functions

The agents' evaluation functions could be generated in a number of ways. One of the most common methods used in CSEMPs is learning from human examples using machine-learning techniques [12, 14, 16]. A second common method is providing agents with rules describing what features an expressive performance should have [5, 8, 34, 35]. The second approach was chosen for IMAP because we wanted to provide the means to explicitly change the influence of various musical factors on the final expressive performance. Machine-learning approaches, such as those based on artificial neural networks, tend to develop a more implicit reasoning system [36]. An explicitly described rule set allows for simpler controllability of a multi-agent system. However, unlike many rule-based CSEMPs, the agents in IMAP do not use their rules to generate their performances. Rather, they use them to evaluate performances (their own and those of other agents) and therefore choose which other agents to imitate. This will become clearer as we introduce the system below. In short, the more highly another agent's performance is scored by the parameterized evaluation function of a listening agent, the more highly the listening agent will regard the performing agent.

An agent's evaluation function is defined at two stages: the rule level and the analytics level. The first stage – the rule level – involves a series of five rules derived from previous work on generative performance. The second stage – the analytics level – involves a group of musical analysis functions, which the agent uses to represent the structure of the musical score. The rule level and the analytics level are both parameterized in order to allow the user to control which elements have most influence on the resulting performances.

For the rule level, we could have selected a large number of rules available from previous research into CSEMP. In order to keep the rule list of IMAP manageable, only five rules were selected, bearing in mind the application and controllability of the imitative approach. One should note, however, that these rules are not absolute. As it will be demonstrated later, the agents often create performances that do not fully conform to all rules. For this reason, we refer to these rules as preference rules.

The five preferences rules of the rule level relate to performance curves, note punctuation, loudness emphasis, accentuation, and boundary notes. Each preference rule is based on previous research into music performance, as follows:

1. Performance curves: performance deviations for tempo between note-group boundaries (e.g., motif and phrase boundaries) should increase for the beginning part of the group and decrease for the second part of the group; how these "parts" are defined is explained later. This is consistent with the expressive shapes, which are well established in the field of CSEMP [8, 34, 35, 37]. This shape should also occur for the loudness deviations [38].
2. Note punctuation: the ending note of a group of notes should be lengthened [37].
3. Loudness emphasis: performance deviations for loudness should emphasize the metrical, melodic, and harmonic structure [39, 40].
4. Boundary notes: the last note in a note grouping should have an expressive tempo, which is either a local minimum or local maximum [39].
5. Accentuation: any note at a significantly accentuated position (as defined later) must either have a lengthened duration value or a local loudness maximum [39, 41].

These five preference rules of the rule level were implemented as a set of evaluation equations, which are detailed below. The user can change the influence of a preference rule in the final evaluation through the setting of weights. The rules take as input the result of a musical score analysis done by four analysis functions in the analytics level, namely, Local Boundary Detection Model (LBDM), metric hierarchy, melodic accent, and key change. A detailed explanation of these analysis functions is beyond the scope of this chapter; the reader is invited to consult the given references.

4.2.2.1 Local Boundary Detection Model (LBDM)

The first of these, LBDM, takes as input a monophonic melody and returns a curve that estimates the grouping structure of the music, that is, where the note-group boundaries are and how important each boundary is [41]. Each adjacent note pair is given an LBDM value. The higher the value, the more likely that the interval is at a grouping boundary; the higher the value at a boundary, the more important the boundary is. This function allows an agent to express aspects of the grouping structure of the music.

4.2.2.2 Metric Hierarchy

The second function is the metric hierarchy function, which uses the Lerdahl and Jackendoff [42] method of assigning notes a position in a metric hierarchy. In most Western European classical music, each note has a position in a metric hierarchy. For example, a piece in 4/4 time might have a note with a strong beat at the start of every bar and a weaker beat halfway through each bar. The metric hierarchy function is implemented in IMAP as a function that takes as input a melody and returns the strength of each beat. (Detailed explanation of the implementation is beyond the scope of this chapter; it suffices to say that the representation does not explicitly include information about bar lines and time signatures.) Thus, it allows an agent to express aspects of the metric structure in its performance.

4.2.2.3 Melodic Accent

Another form of accent analysis used in the analysis level is the melodic accent. Thomassen [43] proposes a methodology for analyzing the importance of each note in a melody; each note is assigned an importance value. This allows an agent to express aspects of the melodic structure in its performance.

4.2.2.4 Key Change

The fourth function in the analysis level is the key change analysis. Krumhansl [44] introduces an algorithm, based on perceptual experiments, for analyzing changes of key in a melody. This algorithm allows an agent to express aspects of the harmonic structure in its performance.

Therefore, an agent will represent the score by its note groupings, metric hierarchy, melodic accents, and key changes, although different agents may see the music score differently depending on how they parameterize the functions in the analytics level. Then, based on the preference rules 1, 2, 3, 4, and 5, the agents will prefer certain expression deviations for different parts of the musical score, with the types of expressive deviations preferred depending on an agent's parameterization of the preference rules in the rules level.

4.2.3 Agent Function Definitions

The evaluation function $E(P)$ of an agent evaluating a performance P is defined in Eq. 4.1:

$$E(P) = w_{Tem} * E_{Tem}(P) + w_{Lou} * E_{Lou}(P) \qquad (4.1)$$

E_{Tem} and E_{Lou} are the agent's evaluation of how well a performance fits with its preference for expressive deviations in tempo and loudness, respectively. (Although the weights in this two-parameter equation are designed to add up to 1 and could therefore be rewritten in a single weight form with multipliers of w and $(1 - w)$, both weights are explicitly written for reasons of clarity and for conformity with the format of the other equations below.) The preference weights w_{Tem} and w_{Lou} define how much an agent focuses on timing elements of expression in relation to loudness elements of expression. The evaluation functions for tempo and loudness are defined using evaluation subfunctions E_{iTem} and E_{iLou}, which evaluate all five preference rules discussed earlier. Indices 1–5 relate to preference rules 1–5, respectively:

$$E_{Tem} = w_{1Tem} * E_{1Tem} + w_{2Tem} * E_2 + w_{4Tem} * E_{4Tem} + w_{5Tem} * E_5 \qquad (4.2)$$

$$E_{Lou} = w_{1Lou} * E_{1Lou} + w_{3Lou} * E_3 + w_{4Lou} * E_{4Lou} \qquad (4.3)$$

The E_{1Tem} and E_{1Lou} functions refer to preference rule 1 and affect both tempo and loudness, respectively. Function E_2 refers to preference rule 2 and affects only tempo. Similarly, function E_3 refers to preference rule 3 and only affects loudness. Functions E_{4Tem} and E_{4Lou} refer to preference rule 4 and affect both loudness and tempo, and function E_5 refers to rule 5 and only affects tempo.

The weights w_{iTem}, and w_{iLou} allow the setting of agent preferences for each of the five rules, though not all rules need to be part of both functions because some apply only to tempo or only to loudness. The subfunctions are defined in terms of the deviations of tempo and loudness from the nominal score values found in a performance. The subfunctions are given in Eqs. 4.4, 4.5, 4.6, 4.7, 4.8, 4.9, and 4.10. Equations 4.4 and 4.5 implement the preference rule 1:

$$E_{1Tem} = \sum_1^n \left(\sum_{i=S_{start}}^{S_{turn}-1} \left\{ \begin{array}{l} 1(dev_{Tem}(i+1) > dev_{Tem}(i)) \\ 0(dev_{Tem}(i+1) \leq dev_{Tem}(i)) \end{array} \right. \right.$$
$$\left. + \sum_{i=S_{turn}}^{S_{end}-1} \left\{ \begin{array}{l} 1(dev_{Tem}(i+1) < dev_{Tem}(i)) \\ 0(dev_{Tem}(i+1) \geq dev_{Tem}(i)) \end{array} \right. \right) \qquad (4.4)$$

$$E_{1Lou} = \sum_1^n \left(\sum_{i=S_{start}}^{S_{turn}-1} \left\{ \begin{array}{l} 1(dev_{Lou}(i+1) > dev_{Lou}(i)) \\ 0(dev_{Lou}(i+1) \leq dev_{Lou}(i)) \end{array} \right. \right.$$
$$\left. + \sum_{i=S_{turn}}^{S_{end}-1} \left\{ \begin{array}{l} 1(dev_{Lou}(i+1) < dev_{Lou}(i)) \\ 0(dev_{Lou}(i+1) \geq dev_{Lou}(i)) \end{array} \right. \right) \qquad (4.5)$$

The i-th note's tempo and loudness expressive deviations are written as $dev_{Tem}(i)$ and $dev_{Lou}(i)$ in the subfunctions. By virtue of the first (outer) summation in each equation, the calculations are applied to each note grouping separately and the scores summed across the whole performance. The index values s_{start} and s_{end} are the note indices at which a note grouping starts and ends, and s_{turn} is its *turning point*. There is no fixed threshold for defining boundaries using the LBDM method. We opted for one, which was found sufficient for the purposes of IMAP: for a note to be a boundary note, its LBDM value must be greater than the average LBDM value of the whole melody. The turning point of a grouping is the point at which the expressive tempo defined by the preference rule 1 peaks before dropping; it is not defined explicitly by LBDM either. In IMAP, the "third most important note" in the group is selected as representing a boundary between the first part of the group and the last part. So the turning point is defined as the note having the third highest LBDM in the group: the start and end notes will be the two highest LBDM values. This definition of turning point was found to be more musically meaningful than simply taking the midpoint between the start and end notes. In order to ensure that every note grouping has at least one potential turning point, another constraint is placed on note groupings: they must contain at least four notes, that is, three intervals.

Equation 4.6 is summed over all note groups in the melody. This subfunction implements the preference rule 2. A tempo deviation value equal to 1 means the performance is the same as the nominal value in the score; a value greater than one means louder or faster than the score. This is applied to each note group in the melody:

$$E_2 = \sum_1^n \begin{cases} 1 & (dev_{Tem}(S_{end})<1) \\ 0 & (dev_{Tem}(S_{end}) \geq 1) \end{cases} \qquad (4.6)$$

Equation 4.7 implements the preference rule 3. The curve $s_A(i)$ used in this equation is the *accentuation curve*, which is generated by a weighted sum of three other curves: *melodic accent, metrical hierarchy,* and the *key change,* thus representing multiple musical elements. (Note: the notion of "curve" here is broadly metaphorical; it is not a mathematical curve in the strict sense of the term.)

$$E_3 = \sum_{i=1}^{q-1} \begin{cases} 1 & (\Delta d * \Delta dev_{Lou}>0) \\ 0 & (\Delta d * \Delta dev_{Lou} \leq 0) \end{cases}$$

$$\text{where} \quad \begin{aligned} \Delta d &= s_{A(i+1)} - s_{A(i)} \\ \Delta dev_{Lou} &= dev_{Lou}(i+1) - dev_{Lou}(i) \end{aligned} \qquad (4.7)$$

The melodic accent curve moves higher for more important melodic notes [43], whereas the metrical hierarchy curve moves higher for notes that are more important in the metrical hierarchy [42]. The higher the key change curve moves, the further away the melody moves from the estimated key [44] of the previous N bars, the default being two bars. These three curves are normalized, and then weighted based on an agent's preferences, and added to generate the accentuation curve $s_A(i)$. Equation 4.7 will evaluate more highly if the loudness deviation curve of a performance follows the same direction as this accentuation curve, encouraging the emphasis of the parts of the performance based on elements of their melodic, metrical, and harmonic properties.

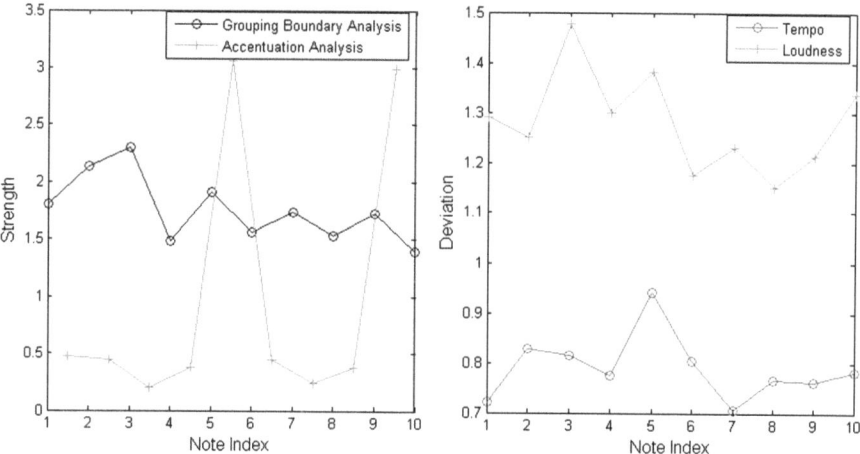

Fig. 4.1 Example characteristics of a single agent with respect to a given sequence of ten notes (see text)

Figure 4.1 shows examples of accentuation and loudness curves (as well as the LBDM and tempo deviation curves) for a single agent, given a sequence of ten notes. This sort of analysis is done once per agent.

In Fig. 4.1, both x-axes refer to note index, where 1 is the first note in the score, 2 the second note, etc. The left side of Fig. 4.1 shows part of an example LBDM curve (circled points) used to define grouping boundaries and an accentuation curve (crossed points) used for expressive loudness. The y-axis is the normalized strengths of the curves. It is not the absolute strength that is important but the relative values. The right side of Fig. 4.1 shows the resulting deviation curves for tempo (circles) and loudness (crosses) after a number of iterations. A deviation greater than 1 implies an increase in tempo or an increase in loudness; a deviation less than 1 implies tempo decrease or loudness decrease.

Equations 4.8 and 4.9 implement the preference rule 4. The rule is only applied to accentuated notes $\{a_1, \ldots, a_m\}$, which are defined as those notes i whose value on the accentuation curve $s_A(i)$ is a local maximum on the s_A curve. This definition chooses notes whose metric, melodic, or harmonic properties make them more significant than the notes surrounding them. The values of Eqs. 4.8 and 4.9 are higher if an accentuated note is respectively (i) reduced in tempo more than its neighbor notes or (ii) played with a higher loudness:

$$E_{4Tem} = \sum_{j=a_1}^{a_m} \begin{cases} 1 & (dev_{Tem}(j) < dev_{Tem}(j-1) \text{ and } dev_{Tem}(j) < dev_{Tem}(j+1)) \\ 0 & (otherwise) \end{cases} \quad (4.8)$$

$$E_{4Lou} = \sum_{j=a_1}^{a_m} \begin{cases} 1 & (dev_{Lou}(j) \geq dev_{Lou}(j-1) \text{ and } dev_{Lou}(j) \geq dev_{Lou}(j+1)) \\ 0 & (otherwise) \end{cases}$$

$$(4.9)$$

Equation 4.10 implements the preference rule 5, checking that notes at the end of a group have a higher or lower tempo deviation, compared to the notes on either side:

$$E_5 \sum_1^n \begin{cases} 1 & (dev_{Tem}(s_{end}) - dev_{Tem}(s_{end} - 1)) * (dev_{Tem}(s_{end}) - dev_{Tem}(s_{end} + 1)) > 0 \\ 0 & (\text{otherwise}) \end{cases}$$

$$(4.10)$$

With the above Eqs. 4.1, 4.2, 4.3, 4.4, 4.5, 4.6, 4.7, 4.8, 4.9, and 4.10, a user can set weights to control how an agent represents or, speaking metaphorically, "sees" the score and also how the agent prefers such a "seen" score to be performed.

4.2.4 Agent Cycle

Agents are initialized with evaluation weights for their evaluation functions, and with a common monophonic score in MIDI form, which they will perform. Agents are also initialized with an initial performance. This will be a set of expressive deviations from the score in loudness and tempo, which are implemented when the agent plays to another agent. These initial deviations are usually set randomly but they can be set by the user should one wish to do so. Default minimum and maximum values used are the following: for tempo 55% and 130% of nominal and for loudness 75% and 125%. These values were established intuitively after experimenting with different ranges. Agents have a learning rate between 0% and 100%. If an agent with a learning rate $L\%$ hears a performance P, which it prefers to its own, then it will move its own performance deviations linearly towards P by $L\%$. An agent with a learning rate of 100% will allow another agent's performance to influence 100% of its own performance. That is, the agent will replace its performance entirely with any it hears, which it prefers to its own. An agent with a learning rate of 0% will ignore all other performances it hears.

The core algorithm of the agents' interaction cycle is given in Fig. 4.2. Note that the algorithm shown here is sequential, but in reality the agents are asynchronous in the sense that all agents are operating simultaneously in separate threads.

4.2.5 User-Generated Performances with IMAP

Before describing how to generate expressive performances with IMAP we would like to discuss some of the issues with practical performance generation. Kirke and the term "performance creativity" are introduced in Chap. 1 to refer to the ability of a CSEMP to generate novel and original performances, as opposed to simulating previous human strategies. Such creative and novel performance is often applauded in human performers. For example, Glenn Gould created highly novel expressive performances of pieces of music and has been described as having a vivid musical imagination. Expressive computer performance provides possibilities for even

---

Beginning of Cycle 1
An agent is selected to perform, say agent **A1**.
Agent **A1** performs·
All agents **Aj** apart from **A1** evaluate **A1**'s performance, to get **Ej1**.
If an agent **Aj**'s evaluation **Ej1** is greater than its evaluation of its own performance,
> then **Aj** moves its own expressive performance deviations closer to
> > **A1**'s performance by an amount defined by the learning rate.

An agent is selected to perform, say agent **A2** .
Agent **A2** performs
All agents **Aj** apart from **A2** evaluate **A2**'s performance, to get **Ej2**
If an agent **Aj**'s evaluation **Ej2** is greater than its evaluation of its own performance,
> then **Aj** moves its own expressive performance deviations closer to
> > **A2**'s performance by an amount defined by the learning rate.

. . .
Continue this process until all agents have performed, then Cycle 1 is complete
End of Cycle 1
Repeat cycles until some user-defined stopping condition is met.

Fig. 4.2   The core algorithm of the agents' interaction cycle

more imaginative experimentation with performance strategies. Many CSEMP, for example, the artificial neural network piano system [12, 45], are designed to simulate human performances, an important research goal, but not to create novel performances. IMAP is less constrained in the generation of performances than a number of systems that learn from human examples. It also has a parameterization ability, which can be manipulated creatively to generate entirely novel performances.

For performance creativity, a balance needs to exist between automation and creative flexibility. As described earlier, in IMAP there are a number of weights, which need to be defined for an agent's evaluation function. Table 4.1 lists all the weights that need to be set in IMAP. Although a set of nine weights may seem too large for practical performance creativity, in reality many of these weights can be fitted to default values, and the remaining weights would still provide a wide scope for creativity. For example, users could simply adjust the top two weights of the equation hierarchy (w_{Tem} and w_{Lou}) for Eq. 4.1, fixing all other weights to their default values. This two-weight set could be simply extended by also allowing the user to adjust the weights w_{4Tem} and w_{4Lou} – in Eqs. 4.2 and 4.3 – to change the amount of tempo and loudness emphasis, respectively, of accentuated notes. It is worth noting that the parameters in the analytics level can also be made available to users; for example, the user could set weights that would indirectly change the shape of the accentuation curve shown in Fig. 4.1.

Another key element of IMAP is how agents can have different "views" on what makes a good expressive performance. This provides an ability, which will be demonstrated later in the chapter, for generating and controlling diversity in the results of the population learning. For example, a population whose initial preference weights are all very close will tend to learn a group of far more similar performances than a population whose initial weight values differ widely.

Table 4.1 IMAP weights that can be set in Eqs. 4.1, 4.2, and 4.3 by the user to influence the final expressive performance. These nine weights define the effects of the five preference rules in the rules level

Preference rule	Weight	Equation
All tempo-based effects	w_{Tem}	Equation 4.1
All loudness-based effects	W_{Lou}	Equation 4.1
Rule (I) tempo effects	w_{1Tem}	Equation 4.2, tempo
Rule (II) tempo effects	w_{2Tem}	Equation 4.2, tempo
Rule (IV) tempo effects	w_{4Tem}	Equation 4.2, tempo
Rule (V) tempo effects	w_{5Tem}	Equation 4.2, tempo
Rule (I) loudness effects	w_{1Lou}	Equation 4.3, loudness
Rule (III) loudness effects	w_{3Lou}	Equation 4.3, loudness
Rule (IV) loudness effects	w_{4Lou}	Equation 4.3, loudness

We will now describe how to generate expressive performances with IMAP. Before the first cycle of IMAP, a population size is defined, for example, 3, 10, or 50 agents. Larger populations may have the advantage of greater statistical stability and a larger choice of performances. Then, a learning rate needs to be set. In this chapter a global learning rate is used: all agents have the same learning rate, a default of 10%. A low learning rate was desired so as to allow agents to build up a good combination of performances through imitation. A learning rate closer to 100% would turn the system into more of a performance-swapping population rather than one for performance-combining. However, too low a rate would slow convergence.

Concerning the question of how many cycles to run the system, one approach would be to define a fixed number of cycles. Another approach would be to define a more sophisticated stopping condition. A common form of stopping condition is a convergence criterion, for example, stopping when agents are no longer updating their performance deviations during the interactions. This normally occurs when no agent is hearing a performance better than its own performance. Another option is to base convergence on the average performance, that is, the average deviations across the whole of the population. Once this ceases to change by a significant amount per cycle – that amount defined by the user – convergence may be considered to have been achieved.

Three experiments with IMAP will be detailed below, which test the system in terms of capability of expression generation, generation of diversity, and controlling the direction of the diversity.

4.3   Experiments and Evaluation

The melody of the piece Étude No. 3, Op. 10 by Frédéric Chopin (see bottom of Fig. 4.4) was used in the experiments that follow. Although IMAP is able to process whole pieces of (monophonic) music, for the sake of clarity, only the first five bars of Chopin's piece were considered below.

4.3.1 Experiment 1: Can Agents Generate Performances Expressing Their "Preference" Weights?

The purpose of this experiment is to demonstrate that the agents generate performances that express their "preference" weights. In order to show this clearly, two weight sets were used: set (A) $w_{Tem} = 1$, $w_{1Tem} = 1$, and all other weights $= 0$; and set (B) $w_{Lou} = 1$, $w_{3Lou} = 1$, and all other weights $= 0$. The first set of weights will only lead to preference rule 1 being applied and only apply it to tempo. The second set of weights will lead to preference rule 3 being applied and only apply it to loudness. If agents express the music structure through their weights, then a multi-agent system where agents have only the weight set A should generate performances whose tempo deviations clearly express the grouping structure (LBDM) of the music as defined by the preference rule 1. Similarly, if the agents are given the weight set B, then the generated loudness deviations should express the accentuation curve as implemented by the preference rule 3.

Two groups of experiments were run: 5 with weight set A and 5 with weight set B. A system of 15 agents was used, and 20 iterations were used for each run. For each run in the experiment with weight set A, the initial agent performances were randomized. For comparison purposes, exactly the same set of initial performances was used for the parallel run with weight set B; hence, the 10 runs only use 5 sets of 15 random initial performances. In order to enable meaningful results for the scenario with the weight set A, a new curve was defined: the *transferred LBDM* curve. The transferred LBDM curve is our own adaptation of the LBDM curve into a form more easily comparable with the grouping expression. The transferred curve will have maxima at the boundary points on the LBDM curve and minima at the turning points within each note group. The transferred LBDM is concave between boundary points. An example is shown in Fig. 4.3. The preference rule 1 can then be interpreted as saying that tempo curves should move in the opposite direction to the transferred LBDM curve or equivalently that the reciprocal of the tempo curve should move in the same direction as the transferred LBDM curve.

In this experiment the average performance across all agents was used to represent the performances evolved by the system: thus, the deviations of the tempo and loudness generated by the system are represented by the deviations of the tempo and loudness in the average performance. The results of scenarios with weight sets A and B can be seen in Table 4.2, which shows the average correlations $Corr(x, y)$ across the five runs for:
(a) $x =$ the transferred LBDM curve $tLBDM$
(b) $x =$ the accentuation curve Acc
(c) $y =$ the reciprocal of performance tempo $rTem$
(d) $y =$ the performance loudness Lou.

It can be seen that for the weight set A (a weight set that should cause grouping structure to be expressed and use tempo deviations to express it), there is an increase in correlation between the transferred LBDM and the reciprocal performance tempo: $Corr(tLBDM, rTem) = 0.11$. For the weight set B (a weight set that

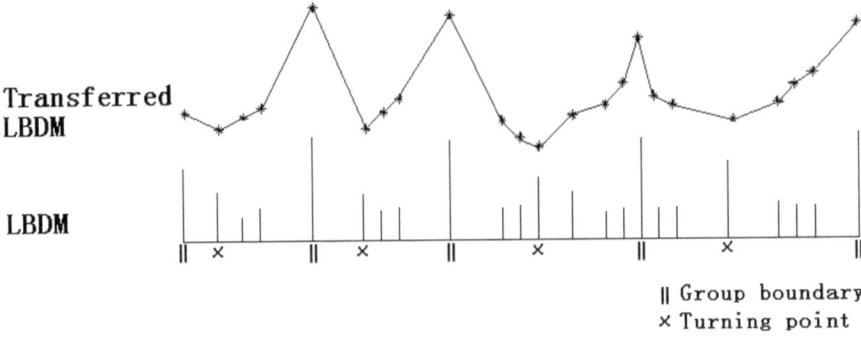

Fig. 4.3 Example of a transferred LBDM curve for a melody from Chopin's Étude No. 3, Op. 10, shown at the *bottom* of figure. The *horizontal axis* is time. As for the *vertical axis*, LBDM values do not have units as such. They indicate relative "boundary strength," rather than absolute values. The fitness function only needs to know the direction of the transferred LBDM curve rather than its absolute value. In the *lower graph* the LBDM values are plotted for each note pair/interval. The group boundaries and turning points are shown on the *horizontal axis*. It can be seen that the transferred LBDM curve in the *upper graph* is concave between boundaries, has maxima at boundaries, and has minima at the turning points

Table 4.2 Results from experiment 1 showing correlations for average performance across a population of agents

	Before iterations	After iterations	Increase
Weight set A (Tem)			
Corr(tLBDM, rTem)	0.49	0.61	0.11
Corr(tLBDM, Lou)	0.52	0.52	0
Corr(Acc, Lou)	0.5	0.52	0.02
Weight set B (Lou)			
Corr(tLBDM, rTem)	0.49	0.49	0
Corr(tLBDM, Lou)	0.52	0.48	−0.04
Corr(Acc, Lou)	0.5	0.7	0.2

An increase in correlation between the transferred LDBM and reciprocal performance tempo shows that the tempo deviations are expressing the grouping structure of the music. An increase in correlation between the accentuation curve and loudness shows that the loudness is expressing elements of the metric, melodic, and harmonic structure of the music, as defined in the accentuation curve

should cause the accentuation curve to be expressed by loudness deviations), the only increase in correlation is between the accentuation curve and the loudness: *Corr(Acc, Lou)* = 0.2. These results show that the average agent performances are expressing the preference weights in the system. Figure 4.4 shows expressive deviations evolved by two agents for the Chopin's melody.

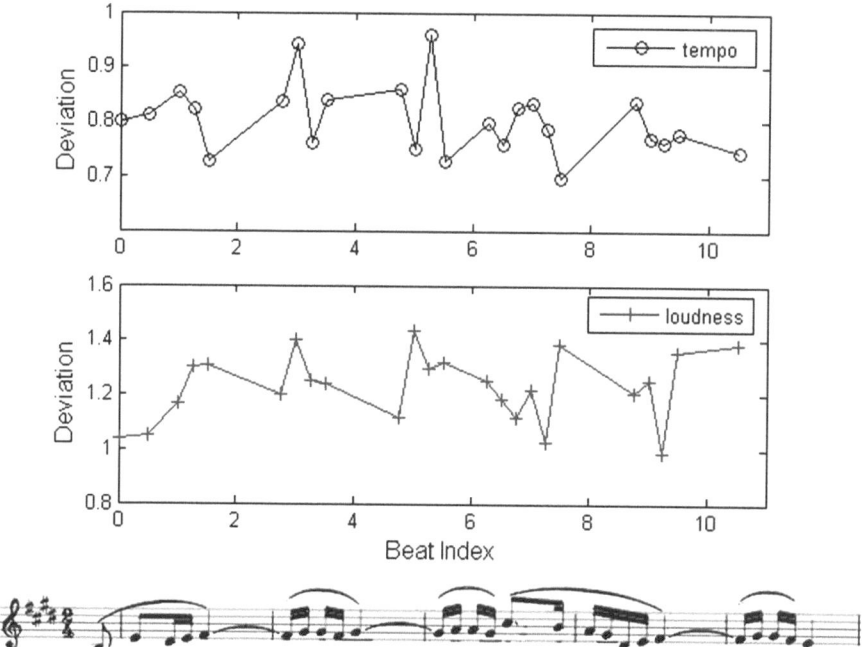

Fig. 4.4 Expressive deviations of two agents from experiment 1 after 20 iterations for the first 5 bars of the melody of Chopin's Étude No. 3, Op. 10. (Each point in the plots corresponds to a note in the score, excepting the last point in each plot.) The *top graph* (*circles*) shows the weight set A of an agent (tempo expression only), hence only tempo expression is plotted. The *bottom graph* (*crosses*) shows the weight set B of another agent (loudness evaluation only), hence only loudness expression is plotted

4.3.2 Experiment 2 Can One Control the Extent of the Performances' Diversity?

The purpose of this experiment was to demonstrate that IMAP can generate a diversity of performances and that the user can control that diversity. In the experiment a group of 15 agents was used, each with randomly initialized performance deviations. A set of default weights W for Table 4.1 was defined. The experiment was set with two conditions. In condition (i), agents were assigned weights that could vary by no more than 10% from the corresponding default weight in set W. In condition (ii) this variation was raised to 60%. So in condition (ii) the preference weights varied much more widely across agents than in condition (i). In each condition 4.30 iterations were done and the coefficient of variation was calculated for deviations across the population, that is, the ratio of standard deviation to mean for both tempo and loudness deviations. This experiment was repeated

10 times, each time with different initial random performance deviations. After 30 iterations in condition (i), the resulting average coefficient of variation for tempo and for loudness deviations were 0.2%. In condition (ii), with the more diverse preference weights, the value was 1.9%. This supports the ability of IMAP to generate a diversity of performances and to control that diversity using the spread of preference weights.

4.3.3 Experiment 3 Controlling the Direction of the Performances' Diversity

The purpose of this experiment was to demonstrate that if agent preferences are biased a certain way in a subset of the population, then the resulting performances will become affected by that preference. This demonstrated that although a diversity of performances can be produced as shown by experiment 2, changing the distribution of weights enables one to change the distribution of outcomes in a coherent way. In order to show this, we used the same two weight sets as in experiment 1: (A) $w_{Tem} = 1$, $w_{1Tem} = 1$, and all other weights $= 0$ and (B) $w_{Lou} = 1$, $w_{3Lou} = 1$, and all other weights $= 0$. Thus, the weight set A only affects timing and the weight set B only affects loudness. The two weight sets do not overlap in their effect. In this experiment the population of 15 agents from experiment 1 had another 5 agents added to it. The 15 agents (labeled group G2) are assigned weight set B and the 5 additional agents (labeled group G1) are assigned weight set A. The objective is to demonstrate that the addition of G1 to G2 leads to G1 influencing the performances of G2, in spite of the fact that G1 and G2 have mutually exclusive weight sets.

Before running the experiment, it is necessary to benchmark the level of random relative increase in evaluation that can be generated in the system. Specifically, given an agent system of 15 agents with preference weights that only affect loudness, how much would we expect their expressive tempo evaluation to increase relative to the increase in their expressive loudness evaluation, solely due to random fluctuations in tempo during iterations? These random fluctuations come from the randomized initial performances influencing each other. This was measured by taking a system of 15 agents with loudness-only weights (i.e., weight set B) and doing 5 runs of 25 cycles. (The authors ran a number of versions of these experiments, and it was clear that as little as 5 runs of 25 cycles were sufficient to generate meaningful random fluctuations in this contex.) The results are shown in Table 4.3. The column and row headings in this table are defined as follows: "Lou" refers to the expressive loudness evaluation by Eq. 4.3, "Tem" refers to the expressive tempo evaluation by Eq. 4.2, "Before" is the average evaluation before iterations, "After" is the average evaluation after 25 iterations, "Change" is the change in evaluation before and after 20 iterations, and "TempoRatio" is the change in tempo evaluation divided by the change in loudness evaluation.

Table 4.3 Result of benchmarking the level of random fluctuations. After 25 iterations, the increase in loudness, evaluation, and tempo evaluation were measured with Eqs. 4.3 and 4.2, respectively. The ratio of tempo evaluation increase to loudness evaluation increase was calculated

Set B	Run1		Run2		Run3		Run4		Run5	
	Lou	Tem	Lou	Tem	Lou	Tem	Lou	Tem	Lou	Tem
Before	0.19	0.19	0.213	0.213	0.223	0.223	0.21	0.213	0.301	0.301
After	0.315	0.19	0.325	0.19	0.306	0.248	0.35	0.208	0.374	0.292
Change	0.125	0	0.112	−0.02	0.083	0.025	0.137	−0.005	0.073	−0.009
TempoRatio	0		−0.205		0.301		−0.037		−0.123	

Essentially, this ratio is a measure of the increase of tempo expressiveness relative to the increase of loudness expressiveness, as shown in Eq. 4.11:

$$Tempo\ Ratio\ (P) = \frac{Increase_{in_{E_{Tem}(P)}}}{Increase_{in_{E_{Lou}}}(P)} \quad (4.11)$$

The average value of *TempoRatio* across the five runs is equal to −0.013. This will be used as a measure of relative tempo evaluation increase due to random fluctuations in performance since during these five runs there was no evaluation function pressure to increase tempo expressiveness. This particular *TempoRatio* = −0.013 is referred to as the *baseline value* of *TempoRatio*.

Next, another set of runs were done with 5 agents added to the system of 15 agents described above. As has been mentioned, the 5 agents (group G1) were assigned tempo-only weight set A, as opposed to the 15 agents (group G2) who had loudness-only weight set B. The results after 25 iterations are shown in Table 4.4. The column heading "AP2" is the average performance deviation of agents in G2. For instance, $G1(AP2) = 0.255$ is G1's average evaluation of G2's performances in run 2 after 25 iterations.

The key measurements in Table 4.4 are G1's evaluations of G2's performances AP2; this will be written as *G1(AP2)*. Note that all values in "Increase G1(AP2)" row are smaller than all the values in the "Increase G2(AP2)" row. These values are shown before and after iterations in rows 1 and 2 of Table 4.4, respectively. *G1 (AP2)* is calculated using Eq. 4.12, but this equation can be simplified into Eq. 4.13 because w_{LouG1} is equal to 0 and w_{TemG1} is equal to 1 (weight set A):

$$G1(AP2) = E_{G1}(AP2) = w_{TemG1} * E_{TemG1}(AP2) + w_{LouG1} * E_{LouG1}(AP2) \quad (4.12)$$

$$G1(AP2) = E_{TemG1}(AP2) \quad (4.13)$$

Thus, because G1's evaluation functions measure only tempo expressivity, *G1 (AP2)* provides a measure of the expressive tempo evaluation of G2's performance. So the difference between $G1(AP2)$ before and after the iterations is a measure of how much G2's expressive tempo evaluation has increased, as evaluated by G1. Similarly the measure of G2's expressive loudness evaluation is found by calculating G2's evaluation of its own performance, $G2(AP2)$, as shown in Eq. 4.14, which

Table 4.4 Results for a 20 agents system made up of 15 agents with weight set B (labeled as G2) and 5 agents with weight set A (labeled as G1). After 25 iterations, the increase in loudness evaluation and tempo evaluation for the average performance of G2 was measured for both groups. The ratio of tempo evaluation increase to loudness evaluation increase (*Cross Group TempoRatio*) was then calculated

		Run1 AP2	Run2 AP2	Run3 AP2	Run4 AP2	Run5 AP2
G1(AP2)	*Before*	0.245	0.273	0.239	0.269	0.255
	After	0.252	0.255	0.274	0.276	0.291
G2(AP2)	*Before*	0.21	0.236	0.284	0.24	0.234
	After	0.335	0.307	0.349	0.322	0.305
Increase G1(AP2)		0.007	−0.018	0.035	0.007	0.036
Increase G2(AP2)		0.125	0.071	0.065	0.082	0.071
Cross group TempoRatio		0.056	−0.253	0.538	0.085	0.507

can be simplified into Eq. 4.15 because w_{TemG2} is equal to 0 and w_{LouG1} is equal to 1 (weight set B):

$$G2(AP2) = E_{G2}(AP2) = w_{TemG2} * E_{TemG2}(AP2) + w_{LouG2} * E_{LouG2}(AP2) \quad (4.14)$$

$$G2(AP2) = E_{TemG2}(AP2) \quad (4.15)$$

The increase in $G2(AP2)$ before and after iterations gives the increase in G2's loudness expressivity as a result of iterations. The ratio of these two values is shown in Eq. 4.16 and is the increase of expressiveness of G2's tempo deviations relative to the increase in expressiveness of G2's loudness deviations. This could be interpreted as a form of "cross group" *TempoRatio* (*CGTR*) of G2's performance AP2. However, Eq. 4.16 is not G1's actual *TempoRatio* as defined in Eq. 4.11; otherwise, the numerator in Eq. 4.16 would have to be *Increase in* $E_{TemG2}(AP2)$. A *TempoRatio* based on this numerator would always be equal to 0 since G2's evaluation function E_{TemG2} is defined by weight set B, which has all weights in E_{TemG2} set equal to 0. Therefore, the only meaningful tempo ratio has G1's E_{TemG1} in the numerator. This is not just meaningful, but also relevant: the purpose of this experiment was to investigate how G1's view of expressive performance has influenced G2. Thus, when looking at the influence of G1's evaluation function on G2, the function to use is G1's evaluation function, hence the use of the cross group *TempoRatio*, or CGTR. This is calculated in the last row of the Table 4.4. The average value of CGTR for G2's performance is equal 0.219:

$$\frac{Increase_{in_{G1(AP2)}}}{Increase_{in_{G2(AP2)}}} = \frac{Increase_{in_{E_{TemG1}(AP2)}}}{Increase_{in_{E_{LouG1}}}(AP2)} = CGTR(AP2) \quad (4.16)$$

It would be tempting to say that the average CGTR = 0.219 supports the hypothesis that G1's tempo weights have influenced G2's tempo expression, just because it is a positive value. However on its own, this positive average CGTR may just represent the result of random fluctuations in G2's tempo deviations caused during the iterations. But recall that we have shown in a previous set of 5 runs that the baseline value *TempoRatio* due to random fluctuations in a dynamics-only agent set was of the order of −0.013. By comparing G2's CGTR of 0.219 to the baseline value *TempoRatio* of −0.013 and considering that G1 and G2 have mutually exclusive weight sets, one can see that the expressiveness of G2's tempo deviations relative to the expressiveness of G2's loudness deviations is significantly larger than could likely be explained by random fluctuations. This supports the hypothesis that G1 has significantly influenced the increase in G2's tempo expressivity relative to its loudness expressivity. This in turn supports the idea that if agent preferences are biased a certain way in a subset of the population, then the whole system's performances will become affected by that preference.

4.3.4   Conclusions and Recommendations for Further Work

This chapter introduced an imitative multi-agent system approach to generate expressive performances of music, based on agents' individual parameterized musical rules. We have developed a system called IMAP (imitative multi-agent performer) to demonstrate the approach. Aside from investigating the usefulness of such an application of the imitative multi-agent paradigm, there was also a desire to investigate the inherent feature of diversity and control of diversity in this methodology: a desirable feature for a creative application, such as synthesized musical performance. In order to aid this control of diversity, parameterized rules were utilized based on previous expressive performance research. These were implemented in the agents using previously developed musical analysis algorithms. When experiments were run, it was found that agents were expressing their preferences through their music performances and that diversity could be generated and controlled.

In addition to the possibility of using IMAP in practical applications, there are also potential applications of IMAP in an area that multi-agent systems are frequently used: modeling for sociological study, specifically in the sociological study of music performance [39]. However the focus of this chapter was on the practical application of imitative multi-agent systems to generate expressive performance, rather than to investigate social modeling.

A priority piece of future work for IMAP would be to conduct formal listening tests to measure human judgments of automatically generated performances. Only then we would be in a better position to evaluate whether or not IMAP would indeed be more practical and more beneficial for music-making than simply allowing the user to control parameters directly. Another area of work would be listening experiments on how adjusting parameters such as the pitch and interonset interval weights in the LBDM would affect performances and how other variables such as the number-of-bars horizon in the key change part of the accentuation curve impacts performances.

The effectiveness of IMAP is to a significant degree decided by the effectiveness of the analysis level. We acknowledge that the algorithms we have used are not absolutely perfect; for example, LBDM is known to only be a partial solution to the detection of local boundaries. Different analysis algorithms should be tested. The same could be said of the rule level: other sets of rules could be experimented with. In both the case of the rule level and the analysis level, such work could include the investigation of explicitly polyphonic analysis functions and rules. Furthermore, despite the initial experience and thoughts regarding convergence criteria for the system, such criteria are by no means obvious in a creative application; so further work should be done at this front.

We believe that advanced learning rate functionality would be a fruitful area for further investigation. For example, agents with learning rates of 0% have the power to influence but not be influenced by the system. Another area of investigation is interaction control. The system currently assumes that all agents can always interact with all agents. In multi-agent systems there are often "popularity" or "connection" measures [46, 47] that define which agents interact with which. The addition of a social network, which could change conditionally over time, would be worth investigating.

IMAP has the potential to be influenced by human performances and this is certainly an area worth investigating further. Suppose, the system is set up with 50% of agents supplied with performance deviations from a single performance M by a human performer A. The other 50% would have random performances. Depending on preference weightings, the resulting performances would be influenced to a degree by performer A's performance. Another approach would be to reverse engineer evaluation function weights from performer A's performance using a parameter search optimization technique [48]. Performer A's preference weights would affect the performances more strongly than just using performer A's initial performances. The preference function would not necessarily contain performer A's real preference, and there would not be a one-to-one relationship between function weights and a single performance. Nevertheless, such an approach would be worth investigating as a tool for generating new expressive performances. In fact one could envision a "recipe book" of different agent preferences generated by deviations from different professional performers. These agents could then be added to IMAP in the proportions desired by the user. For example, "I would like a performance repertoire of Bach's Piano Partita No. 2 based 30% on Daniel Barenboim's performance, 50% on Glen Gould's performance, and 20% based on the preference weights I explicitly specify."

Another suggested future work for IMAP would be to study the effect of agent communication noise on the convergence of the system. For instance, Kirke and Miranda [49] have introduced a multi-agent system in which agents communicate musical ideas and generate new ideas partially through errors in the communication. Similarly, allowing agents in IMAP to make small errors in their performances could be viewed as an imitative equivalent of a GA mutation operator. This would potentially lead to agents generating performances that more closely match their preferences.

Also, one should consider extending IMAP to expressive performance indicators other than tempo and loudness. However, the limitations of MIDI make this difficult with our current framework. Ideally, we should address this extension once we are in a position to deal directly with audio rather than MIDI.

Acknowledgments This work was financially supported by the EPSRC-funded project "Learning the Structure of Music," grant EP/D062934/1. Qijun Zhang was partially supported by the Faculty of Technology, University of Plymouth. An earlier version of this chapter was published in Computer Music Journal Vol. 34, No. 1, pp. 80–96. The authors thank MIT Press for permission to publish this chapter.

Questions

1. What is evolutionary computation?
2. What is the difference between a genetic algorithm and a multi-agent system with imitation?
3. Why is the potential for diversity a desirable trait for a system generating novel expressive music performances?
4. What two communication functions does each agent in IMAP have?
5. What is the difference between the rule level and the analytics level in an IMAP agent's evaluation function?
6. What are performance curves?
7. What four elements does an IMAP agent represent a score with?
8. Give one method of controlling the extent of performances' diversity in IMAP.
9. What does the TempoRatio represent?
10. What type of sociological study does IMAP have the potential to be useful for?

References

1. Park TH (2009) An interview with Max Mathews. Comput Music J 33(3):9–22
2. Boulanger R (ed) (2000) The Csound book: perspectives in software synthesis, sound design, signal processing and programming. The MIT Press, Cambridge
3. Widmer G, Goebl W (2004) Computational models of expressive music performance: the state of the art. J New Music Res 33(3):203–216
4. Kirke A, Miranda ER (2010) A survey of computer systems for expressive music performance. ACM Surv 42(1):1–49
5. Sundberg J, Askenfelt A, Frydén L (1983) Musical performance. A synthesis-by-rule approach. Comput Music J 7:37–43
6. Bresin R, Friberg A (2000) Emotional coloring of computer-controlled music performances. Comput Music J 24(4):44–63
7. Clynes M (1986) Generative principles of musical thought: integration of microstructure with structure. Commun Cogn 3:185–223
8. Livingstone SR, Muhlberger R, Brown AR, Loch A (2007) Controlling musical emotionality: an affective computational architecture for influencing musical emotions. Digit Creat 18(1):43–53
9. Johnson ML (1991) Toward an expert system for expressive musical performance. Computer 24(7):30–34
10. Ishikawa O, Aono Y, Katayose H, Inokuchi S (2000) Extraction of musical performance rule using a modified algorithm of multiple regression analysis. In: Proceedings of the international computer music conference. International Computer Music Association, San Francisco, pp 348–351

11. Canazza S, Drioli C, De Poli G, Rodà A, Vidolin A (2000) Audio morphing different expressive intentions for multimedia systems. IEEE Multimed 7(3):79–83
12. Bresin R, Vecchio C (1995) Neural networks play Schumann. In: Proceedings of the KTH symposium on grammars for music performance, Stockholm. Department of Speech Communication and Music Acoustics, KTH, Stockholm, pp 5–14
13. Camurri A, Dillon R, Saron A (2000) An experiment on analysis and synthesis of musical expressivity. In: Proceedings of 13th colloquium on musical informatics, L'Aquila, Italy
14. Grindlay GC (2005) Modelling expressive musical performance with Hidden Markov Models. Master's thesis, University of California Santa Cruz, USA
15. Raphael C (2001) Synthesizing musical accompaniments with Bayesian belief networks. J New Music Res 30(1):59–67
16. Widmer G, Tobudic A (2003) Playing Mozart by analogy: learning multi-level timing and dynamics strategies. J New Music Res 32(3):259–268
17. Ramirez R, Hazan A (2005) Modeling expressive performance in Jazz. In: Proceedings of 18th international Florida artificial intelligence research society conference. AAAI Press, Palm Beach, pp 86–91
18. Zhang Q, Miranda ER (2006) Evolving musical performance profiles using genetic algorithms with structural fitness. In: Proceedings of the 8th annual conference on Genetic and evolutionary computation. ACM Press, New York, pp 1833–1840
19. Ramirez R, Hazan A, Maestre E, Serra X (2008) A genetic rule-based model of expressive performance for jazz saxophone. Comput Music J 32(1):38–50
20. Friberg A, Sundberg J (1999) Does music performance allude to locomotion? A model of final ritardandi derived from measurements of stopping runners. J Acoust Soc Am 105:1469–1484
21. Seashore CE (1938) Psychology of music. McGraw-Hill, New York
22. Palmer C (1997) Music performance. Annu Rev Psychol 48:115–138
23. Gabrielsson A (2003) Music performance research at the millennium. Psychol Music 31:221–272
24. Clarke EF (1988) Generative principles in music performance. In: Generative processes in music: the psychology of performance, improvisation, and composition. Clarendon Press, Oxford, pp 1–26
25. Juslin P (2003) Five facets of musical expression: a psychologist's perspective on music performance. Psychol Music 31(3):273–302
26. Miranda ER, Biles JA (eds) (2007) Evolutionary computer music. Springer, London
27. Goldberg DE (1989) Genetic algorithms in search, optimization, and machine learning. Addison-Wesley, Colchester
28. Dissanayake E (2001) Birth of the arts. Nat Hist 109(10):84–92
29. Zentall T, Galef BG (1988) Social learning: psychological and biological perspectives. Lawrence Erlbaum Associates, Hillsdale
30. Boyd R, Richerson PJ (2005) Solving the puzzle of human cooperation. In: Levinson S (ed) Evolution and culture. MIT Press, Cambridge, MA, pp 105–132
31. Miranda ER (2002) Emergent sound repertoires in virtual societies. Comput Music J 26(2):77–90
32. Noble J, Franks DW (2004) Social learning in a multi-agent system. Comput Inform 22(6):561–574
33. De Boer B (2000) Emergence of vowel systems through self-organisation. AI Commun 13:27–29
34. Hashida M, Nagata N, Katayose H (2006) Pop-E: a performance rendering system for the ensemble music that considered group expression. In: Proceedings of 9th international conference on music perception and cognition, Spain, pp 526–534
35. Todd NP (1985) A model of expressive timing in tonal music. Music Percept 3:33–58
36. Ben-David A, Mandel J (1995) Classification accuracy: machine learning vs. explicit knowledge acquisition. Mach Learn 18(1):109–114
37. Friberg A, Bresin R, Sundberg J (2006) Overview of the KTH rule system for musical performance. Adv Cogn Psychol 2(2):145–161
38. Todd NP (1992) The dynamics of dynamics: a model of musical expression. J Acoust Soc Am 91(6):3540–3550

39. Clarke EF, Davidson JW (1998) The body in music as mediator between knowledge and action. In: Thomas W (ed) Composition, performance, reception: studies in the creative process in music. Oxford University Press, Oxford, pp 74–92

40. Sundberg J (2000) Grouping and differentiation two main principles of music. In: Nakada T (ed) Integrated human brain science: theory, method application (music). Elsevier, Amsterdam, pp 299–314

41. Cambouropoulos E (2002) The local boundary detection model (LBDM) and its application in the study of expressive timing. In: Proceedings of the 2001 international computer music conference. International Computer Music Association, San Francisco. Available online: http://hdl.handle.net/2027/spo.bbp2372.2001.021. Assessed on 05 Oct 2009

42. Lerdahl F, Jackendoff R (1983) A generative theory of tonal music. The MIT Press, Cambridge

43. Thomassen JM (1982) Melodic accent: experiments and a tentative model. J Acoust Soc Am 71(6):1596–1605

44. Krumhansl C (1991) Cognitive foundations of musical pitch. Oxford University Press, Oxford

45. Bresin R (1998) Artificial neural network based models for automatic performance of musical scores. J New Music Res 27(3):239–270

46. Kirke A (1977) Learning and co-operation in mobile multi-robot systems. PhD thesis, University of Plymouth

47. Wooldridge M (2004) An introduction to multi-agent systems. Wiley, Malden

48. Winston WL, Venkataramanan M (2002) Introduction to mathematical programming: applications and algorithms. Duxbury Press, Pacific Grove

49. Kirke A, Miranda ER (2011) Using a biophysically-constrained multi-agent system to combine expressive performance with algorithmic composition. In: Miranda ER (ed) A-life for music: music and computer models of living systems. A-R Editions, Middleton

Modeling, Analyzing, Identifying, and Synthesizing Expressive Popular Music Performances

5

Rafael Ramirez, Esteban Maestre, and Alfonso Perez

Abstract

Professional musicians manipulate sound properties such as pitch, timing, amplitude, and timbre in order to add expression to their performances. However, there is little quantitative information about how and in which contexts this manipulation occurs. In this chapter, we describe an approach to quantitatively model and analyze expression in popular music monophonic performances, as well as identifying interpreters from their playing styles. The approach consists of (1) applying sound analysis techniques based on spectral models to real audio performances for extracting both inter-note and intra-note expressive features, and (2) based on these features, training computational models characterizing different aspects of expressive performance using machine learning techniques. The obtained models are applied to the analysis and synthesis of expressive performances as well as to automatic performer identification. We present results, which indicate that the features extracted contain sufficient information, and the explored machine learning methods are capable of learning patterns that characterize expressive music performance.

R. Ramirez (✉)
DTIC, Universitat Pompeu Fabra, Tànger, 122-140, 08018 Barcelona, Spain
e-mail: rafael.ramirez@upf.edu

E. Maestre
CCRMA, Stanford University, 660 Lomita Dr, 94350 Stanford, CA, USA
e-mail: esteban@ccrma.stanford.edu

A. Perez
CIRMMT and IDMIL, Schulich School of Music, McGill University,
555 Sherbrooke St. West Montreal, Quebec H3A 1E3, Canada
e-mail: alfonso.perezcarrillo@mail.mcgill.ca

A. Kirke and E.R. Miranda (eds.), *Guide to Computing for Expressive Music Performance*, 123
DOI 10.1007/978-1-4471-4123-5_5, © Springer-Verlag London 2013

5.1   Introduction

Music performance plays an important role in our culture nowadays. Most people are able to distinguish between different types of expression in performances. However, there is little quantitative information about how and in which contexts expressive performance occurs. Expressive music performance research (for an overview, see [1, 2]) investigates the manipulation of sound properties such as pitch, timing, and amplitude in an attempt to understand and recreate expression in performances.

5.1.1   Overview of Previous Work

One of the first attempts to provide a computer system with musical expressiveness is that of Johnson [3]. Johnson developed a rule-based expert system to determine expressive tempo and articulation for Bach's fugues from *The Well-Tempered Clavier*. The rules were obtained from two expert performers. A long-term effort in expressive performance modeling is the work of the KTH group [4–6]. Their *Director Musices* system incorporates rules for tempo, dynamic, and articulation transformations. The rules are obtained from both theoretical musical knowledge, and experimentally by using an analysis-by-synthesis manual approach. The rules are divided into *differentiation rules* which enhance the differences between scale tones, *grouping rules*, which specify what tones belong together, and *ensemble rules* which synchronize the voices in an ensemble.

Canazza et al. [7, 8] implemented a system to analyze the relationship between the musician's expressive intentions and his/her performance. The analysis reveals two expressive dimensions, one related to loudness (dynamics) and another one related to timing (*rubato*). Dannenberg and Derenyi [9] investigated the trumpet articulation transformations using manually generated rules. They developed a trumpet synthesizer, which combines a physical model with an expressive performance model. The performance model generates control information for the physical model using a set of rules manually extracted from the analysis of a collection of performance recordings.

More recently, there have been several approaches to computationally modeling expressive performance by applying machine learning techniques [10]. Lopez de Mantaras and Arcos [11] report on SaxEx, a performance system capable of generating expressive solo saxophone performances in jazz. Their system is based on case-based reasoning, a type of analogical reasoning where problems are solved by reusing the solutions of similar, previously solved problems. In order to generate expressive solo performances, the case-based reasoning system retrieves from a memory containing expressive interpretations those notes that are *similar* to the input inexpressive notes. The case memory contains information about metrical strength, note duration, and so on and uses this information to retrieve the appropriate notes. One limitation of their system is that it is incapable of explaining the predictions it makes.

Ramirez et al. [12, 13] have explored and compared diverse machine learning methods for obtaining expressive music performance models for jazz saxophone that are capable of both generating expressive performances and explaining the expressive transformations they produce. They propose an expressive performance system based on inductive logic programming which learns a set of first-order logic rules that capture expressive transformation both at an inter-note level (e.g., note duration, loudness) and at an intra-note level (e.g., note attack, sustain). Based on the theory generated by the set of rules, they implemented a melody synthesis component, which generates expressive monophonic output (MIDI or audio) from inexpressive melody MIDI descriptions.

With the exception of the work by Lopez de Mantaras et al. and Ramirez et al., most of the research in expressive performance using machine learning techniques has focused on classical piano music and thus on *global* timing and dynamics (i.e., loudness) transformations. This contrasts most other musical instruments, which have additional hard-to-measure ways of varying the performance of each note (e.g., vibrato, glissando, and the ability to vary the dynamics throughout the note).

Widmer [14, 15] reported on the task of discovering general rules of expressive classical piano performance from real performance data via inductive machine learning. The performance data used for the study are MIDI recordings of 13 piano sonatas by W.A. Mozart performed by a skilled pianist. In addition to these data, the music score was also coded. The resulting substantial data consists of information about the nominal note onsets, duration, metrical information, and annotations. When trained on the data, an inductive rule-learning algorithm discovered a small set of quite simple classification rules that predict a large number of the note-level choices of the pianist.

Tobudic and Widmer [16] describe a relational instance-based approach to the problem of learning to apply expressive tempo and dynamic variations to a piece of classical music at different levels of the phrase hierarchy. The different phrases of a piece and the relations among them are represented in first-order logic. The description of the musical scores through predicates (e.g., *contains(ph1,ph2)*) provides the background knowledge. The training examples are encoded by another predicate whose arguments encode information about the way the phrases were played by the musician. Their learning algorithm recognizes similar phrases from the training set and applies their expressive patterns to a new piece.

Other inductive approaches to rule learning in music and musical analysis include [17, 18]. In [17], Dovey analyzes piano performances of Rachmaninoff pieces using inductive logic programming and extracts rules underlying them. In [18], Van Baelen extended Dovey's work and attempted to discover regularities that could be used to generate MIDI information derived from the musical analysis of the piece.

The use of expressive performance models (either automatically induced or manually generated) for identifying musicians has received little attention in the past. Saunders et al. [19] apply string kernels to the problem of recognizing famous pianists from their playing style. The characteristics of performers playing the same piece are obtained from changes in beat-level tempo and beat-level loudness. From such characteristics, general performance alphabets can be derived, and pianists' performances can then be represented as strings. They apply both kernel partial least squares and support vector machines to these data.

Stamatatos and Widmer [20] address the problem of identifying the most likely music performer, given a set of performances of the same piece by a number of skilled candidate pianists. They propose a set of very simple features for representing stylistic characteristics of a music performer that relate to a kind of "average" performance. A database of piano performances of 22 pianists playing two pieces by Frédéric Chopin is used. They propose an ensemble of simple classifiers derived by both subsampling the training set and subsampling the input features. Experiments show that the proposed features are able to quantify the differences between music performers.

Ramirez et al. [21] develop a machine learning approach to jazz saxophone performer identification by analyzing the pitch, timing, amplitude, and timbre of individual notes, as well as the timing and amplitude of individual intra-note events. They identify performers by establishing a performer-dependent mapping from inter-note features (essentially a "score" whether or not the score physically exists) to a repertoire of inflections characterized by intra-note features. Thus, their approach to interpreter identification strongly relies on the performances' timbre content, which makes sense in performances in jazz saxophone. In this chapter, we consider violin performances. The work described here combines and extends previous work on expressive performance modeling reported in [13, 22].

Molina et al. [23] proposed an approach for identifying violinists in monophonic audio recordings. They considered a database of sonatas and partitas for solo violin by J.S. Bach and identified performers by capturing their general expressive footprint based on a characterization of the way melodic patterns are played as a set of frequency distributions. Performances were transcribed focusing on the melodic contour, and melodic segments were tagged according to Narmour's implication/realization model [24].

5.1.2 Chapter Overview

In this chapter, we describe a general approach to computationally model, analyze, synthesize, and identify interpreters in expressive performances. The approach applies machine learning algorithms to automatically discover regularities and patterns from a corpus of real performance data. The aim is to allow the computational algorithms to learn autonomously the relevant musical contexts and their corresponding expressive patterns. The approach attempts to answer a variety of musicological questions, such as:

- How consistent are the performances of individuals?
- How different are the performance styles of different interpreters?
- Is it possible to automatically identify interpreters from their playing styles?
- How close can a computer-generated performance approximate the expression introduced by human professional musicians in their performances?

The study of these questions is important in order to:

1. Increase our understanding of the strategies employed by talented professional musicians to produce expression and emotions in their performances. We believe

that by examining our trained models, it is possible to gain musicological insight into the complex task of performing a musical piece expressively.

2. Enable music information retrieval applications such as performer search and classification. Given the explosion of online music and the rapidly expanding digital music collections, the development of music information retrieval applications such as performer search and classification is an important application of the work reported here.

3. Implement next generation postproduction systems able to mimic human expressive performance. Implementing this kind of postproduction systems would bring great advantages to composers, allowing them to listen to their music as it is likely to be performed and thus guiding them during the composition process. It is also easy to imagine expressive automatic accompaniment systems for soloists or even tutoring systems that could evaluate and critique student performances.

The rest of the chapter is organized as follows: Section 5.2 describes how audio recordings are processed in order to extract information about both the internal structure of notes (i.e., intra-note information) and the musical context in which they appear (i.e., inter-note information). Section 5.3 describes our approach to expressive performance modeling and style-based automatic interpreter identification, and finally, Sect. 5.4 presents some conclusions and indicates some areas of future research.

5.2 Audio Analysis

In this section, we outline how we extract a symbolic description of a performed melody for monophonic recordings (for a comparison of the method reported here and other methods, see [25]). We use this melodic representation to provide description of the performances and apply machine learning techniques to this representation. Our interest is to obtain, for each performed note, a set of symbolic features from the audio recording.

5.2.1 Energy and Fundamental Frequency Computation

First of all, we perform a spectral analysis of a portion of sound, called an analysis frame, whose size is a parameter of the algorithm. This spectral analysis consists of multiplying the audio frame with an appropriate analysis window and performing a discrete Fourier transform (DFT) to obtain its spectrum. In this case, we use a frame width of 46 ms, an overlap factor of 50%, and a Keiser-Bessel 25-dB window. Then, we compute a set of low-level descriptors for each spectrum: energy and an estimation of the fundamental frequency. From these low-level descriptors, we perform a note segmentation procedure. Once the note boundaries are known, the note descriptors are computed from the low-level values. The main low-level descriptors used to characterize note-level expressive performance are instantaneous energy and fundamental frequency.

The energy descriptor is computed on the spectral domain using the values of the amplitude spectrum at each analysis frame. In addition, energy is computed in different frequency bands as defined in [26].

For the estimation of the instantaneous fundamental frequency, we use a harmonic matching model derived from the two-way mismatch procedure (TWM) [27]. For each fundamental frequency candidate, mismatches between the harmonics generated and the measured partials frequencies are averaged over a fixed subset of the available partials. A weighting scheme is used to make the procedure robust to the presence of noise or absence of certain partials in the spectral data. The solution presented in [27] employs two mismatch error calculations. The first one is based on the frequency difference between each partial in the measured sequence and its nearest neighbor in the predicted sequence. The second is based on the mismatch between each harmonic in the predicted sequence and its nearest partial neighbor in the measured sequence. This two-way mismatch helps to avoid octave errors by applying a penalty for partials that are present in the measured data but are not predicted and also for partials whose presence is predicted but which do not actually appear in the measured sequence. The TWM mismatch procedure has also the benefit that the effect of any spurious components or partial missing from the measurement can be counteracted by the presence of uncorrupted partials in the same frame.

First, we perform a spectral analysis of all the windowed frames, as explained above. Secondly, the prominent spectral peaks of the spectrum are detected from the spectrum magnitude. These spectral peaks of the spectrum are defined as the local maxima of the spectrum which magnitude is greater than a threshold. The spectral peaks are compared to a harmonic series and a two-way mismatch (TWM) error is computed for each fundamental frequency candidates. The candidate with the minimum error is chosen to be the fundamental frequency estimate.

Note segmentation is performed using a set of frame descriptors, which are energy computation in different frequency bands and fundamental frequency. Energy onsets are first detected following a band-wise algorithm that uses some psychoacoustical knowledge [26]. In a second step, fundamental frequency transitions are also detected.

5.2.2 Note Descriptors

We compute note descriptors using the note boundaries and the low-level descriptors values. The low-level descriptors associated to a note segment are computed by averaging the frame values within this note segment. Pitch histograms have been used to compute the pitch note and the fundamental frequency that represents each note segment, as found in [28]. This is done to avoid taking into account mistaken frames in the fundamental frequency mean computation. First, frequency values are converted into cents by the following formula:

$$c = 1200 \cdot \log_2 \left(\frac{f}{f_{ref}} \right) \qquad (5.1)$$

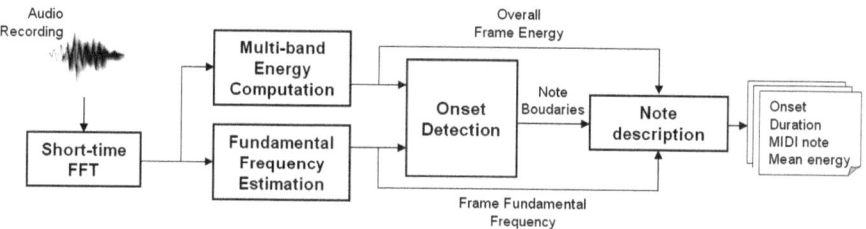

Fig. 5.1 Schematic view of the melodic description process. Note onsets are extracted based on the study of energy and fundamental frequency

where $f_{ref} = 8.176$ (f_{ref} is a the reference frequency of the C_0). Then, we define histograms with bins of 100 cents and hop size of 5 cents and we compute the maximum of the histogram to identify the note pitch. Finally, we compute the frequency mean for all the points that belong to the histogram. The MIDI pitch is computed by quantization of this fundamental frequency mean over the frames within the note limits. Figure 5.1 shows an overview of the melodic description process.

5.2.3 Note Transitions

For characterizing note detachment, we also extract some features of the note-to-note transitions describing how two notes are detached. For two consecutive notes, we consider the transition segment starting at the first note's release and finishing at the attack of the following one. Both the energy envelope and the fundamental frequency contour (schematically represented by E_{XX} and f_0 in Fig. 5.2) during transitions are studied in order to extract descriptors related to articulation. We measure the energy envelope minimum position t_c (see also Fig. 5.2) with respect to the transition duration as in (5.2). This descriptor has proven useful when reconstructing amplitude envelopes during transitions.

We compute a legato descriptor as described next. The relevance of this descriptor was assessed in [29]. From Fig. 5.2, we join start and end points on the energy envelope contour by means of a line L_t representing the smoothest case of detachment. Then, we compute both the area A_2 below the energy envelope and the area A_1 between the energy envelope and the joining line L_t and define our legato descriptor as shown in (5.3):

$$E_{TPOS_{min}} = \frac{t_c}{t_{end} - t_{init}} \tag{5.2}$$

$$LEG = \frac{A_1}{A_1 + A_2} = \frac{\int_{t_{init}}^{t_{end}} (L_t(t) - E(t))dt}{\int_{t_{init}}^{t_{end}} L_t(t)dt}. \tag{5.3}$$

Fig. 5.2 Schematic view of the transition segment characterization

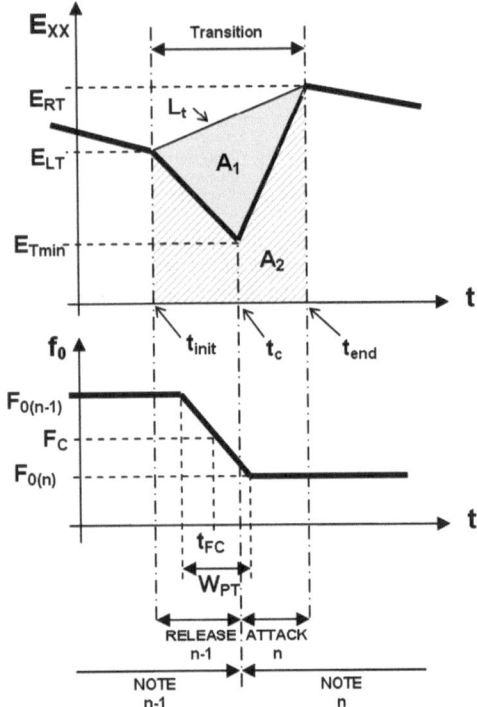

5.2.4 Musical Analysis

After having computed the note descriptors as above, and as a first step towards providing an abstract structure for the recordings under study, we decided to use Narmour's theory of perception and cognition of melodies [24, 30] to analyze the performances.

The implication/realization model proposed by Narmour is a theory of perception and cognition of melodies. The theory states that a melodic musical line continuously causes listeners to generate expectations of how the melody should continue. According to Narmour, any two consecutively perceived notes constitute a melodic interval, and if this interval is not conceived as complete, it is an *implicative interval*, i.e., an interval that implies a subsequent interval with certain characteristics. That is to say, some notes are more likely than others to follow the implicative interval. Two main principles recognized by Narmour concern *registral direction* and *intervallic difference*. The principle of registral direction states that small intervals imply an interval in the same registral direction (a small upward interval implies another upward interval and analogously for downward intervals), and large intervals imply a change in registral direction (a large upward interval implies a downward interval and analogously for downward intervals). The principle of intervallic difference states that a small (five semitones or less)

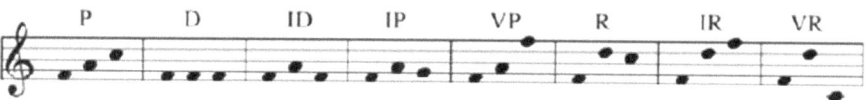

Fig. 5.3 Prototypical Narmour structures

Fig. 5.4 Narmour analysis of a melody fragment

interval implies a similarly sized interval (plus or minus 2 semitones), and a large interval (seven semitones or more) implies a smaller interval. Based on these two principles, melodic patterns or groups can be identified that either satisfy or violate the implication as predicted by the principles. Such patterns are called structures and are labeled to denote characteristics in terms of registral direction and intervallic difference. Figure 5.3 shows prototypical Narmour structures. A note in a melody often belongs to more than one structure. Thus, a description of a melody as a sequence of Narmour structures consists of a list of overlapping structures. We parse each melody in the training data in order to automatically generate an implication/realization analysis of the pieces. Figure 5.4 shows the analysis for a melody fragment.

5.2.5 Gesture Acquisition

We have acquired bowing motion data by means of two 3D motion tracker sensors, one mounted on the violin and the other on the bow. We are able to estimate with great precision and accuracy the position of the strings, the bridge, and the bow. With the collected data we compute, among others, the following bowing performance parameters: bow distance to the bridge, bow transversal position, velocity and acceleration, bow force, and string being played.

In order to detect bow direction, it is not enough to use detected zero crossings of bow speed for extracting bow direction because of the possible performed bowed triplets. Instead, we compute bow speed histograms for each of the note segments after alignment and get the sign of the histogram maximum as the indicator for the bow direction. We also detect ornamentations (mordents). Detection of mordents is carried out after note segmentation and can be summarized as follows. For each segmented note, pitch and aperiodicity function is calculated. Pitch curve segments with high aperiodicity or very short segments are not considered for the detection. The remaining intra-note pitch curve is then quantized to semitones, and notes with changes of one tone or semitone inside the note are considered to be part of an ornament.

5.3   Expressive Performance Modeling and Interpreter Identification

In this section, we describe our approach to music performance modeling and interpreter identification. In particular, we describe how the learnt computational expressive models can be used for understanding and generating expressive performances as well as for identifying interpreters based on their playing style.

5.3.1   Training Data

In this work, we focus on Celtic jigs. Celtic jigs are a form of lively folk dance, as well as the accompanying dance tune, originating in England in the sixteenth century and today most associated with Irish dance music. Celtic jigs are fast tunes but slower than reels that usually consist of eighth notes in a ternary time signature (6/8 time) with strong accents at each beat. The training data used in this research are monophonic recordings of nine Celtic jigs, each performed by three professional violinists (the pieces were recorded in the Audiovisual Institute's recording studio at the Pompeu Fabra University, expressly for the experiment). Apart from the tempo (they played following a metronome), the musicians were not given any particular instructions on how to perform the pieces.

5.3.2   Note Descriptors

We characterize each performed note by a set of inter-note features representing both properties of the note itself and aspects of the musical context in which the note appears (see Fig. 5.5). Information about the note includes note pitch (*Pitch*), note duration (*dur*), and note metrical strength (*MetrStr*) while information about its melodic context includes the relative pitch and duration of the neighboring notes (*PrevPitch, PrevDur, NextPitch, NextDur*), i.e., previous and following notes, as well as the Narmour structures in which the note appears in first, second, and third position (*Nar1, Nar2, Nar3*). The note's Narmour structures are computed by performing the musical analysis described in the previous section. The metrical strength of a note is computed based on the note's position within the bar in which it appears. In a 4/4 piece, it is defined as *very strong, strong, medium, weak,* and *very weak* if the note appears in beat 1, 3, 2, or 4, offbeat or anywhere else, respectively. Thus, each performed note N is contextually characterized by the tuple:

   N = (*Pitch, Dur, MetrStr, PrevPitch, PrevDur, NextPitch, NextDur, Nar1, Nar2, Nar3*)

We also extract other note features, as described in Sect. 5.3. These features are the amount of legato with the previous note, the amount of legato with the following note, and mean energy.

Fig. 5.5 Inter-note descriptors

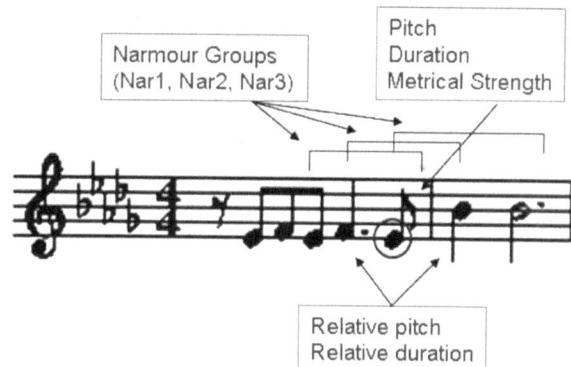

5.3.3   Evaluation

The results reported in the following sections have been obtained by performing the standard tenfold cross validation in which 10% of the data is held out in turn as test data while the remaining 90% is used as training data. When performing the tenfold cross validation, we leave out the same number of data per class. In order to avoid optimistic estimates of the classifier performance, we explicitly remove from the training set all repetitions of the hold-out data. This is motivated by the fact that musicians are likely to perform a melody fragment and its repetition in a similar way. Thus, the applied tenfold cross validation procedure, in addition to holding out a test example from the training set, also removes repetitions of the example.

5.3.4   Expressive Performance Modeling

5.3.4.1 Learning Task

We are concerned with expressive transformations on note duration and note energy, as well as bow direction and melody alteration. In the case of note duration and note energy, we have approached the problem both as a classification task and a regression task. By approaching the problem as a classification task, our aim is to obtain interpretable rules that can serve as a mean to understand expressive performance while the regression task allows to obtain model capable of generating expressive performances of new pieces by considering the score as the sole input. In the case of bow direction and melody alteration, we have approached the problem as a classification task only. The reason is that here we are interested in predicting a class, either up or down for bow direction, and ornamented or not ornamented for melody alteration. The prediction of these two resulting classifiers is used for synthesizing an expressive performance of a particular piece. The exact ornamentation to be performed is determined by applying a nearest neighbor algorithm on an ornamentation database extracted from the performances.

The performance classes that interest us are *lengthen, shorten,* and *same* for duration transformation; *soft, loud,* and *same* for energy variation; *up* and *down* for bow direction; and *ornamentation* and *none* for melody alteration. A note is considered to belong to class *lengthen* if its performed duration is 20% longer (or more) than its nominal duration, e.g., its duration according to the score. Class *shorten* is defined analogously. A note is considered to be in class *loud* if it is played louder than its predecessor and louder than the average level of the piece. Class *soft* is defined analogously. We decided to set these boundaries after experimenting with different ratios. The main idea was to guarantee that a note classified, for instance, as lengthen was purposely lengthened by the performer and not the result of a performance inexactitude. A note is considered to belong to class *ornamentation* if a note or group of notes not specified in the score has been introduced in the performance to embellish the note in the melody and to class *none* otherwise.

As a regression task we are interested in predicting duration, onset, and energy deviations expressed as a ratio of the values specified in the score (for energy which is not specified in the score we take the score value as the average of the energy of all the notes in the piece). For instance, for duration a predicted value of 1.14 represents a prediction of 14% lengthening of the note with respect to the score. In the case of onset prediction, this same value represents a 14% of a quarter note onset delay, and in the case of energy, it indicates that the note should be played a 14% louder than the average energy in the piece. For generating expressive performances, we do not treat melody alterations (e.g., ornamentations) as a regression problem; instead, we simply classify whether a note should be ornamented, in which case we adapt an ornamented note in the training data to the new context of the note being generated.

5.3.4.2 Learning Algorithm

We have applied Tilde's top-down decision tree induction algorithm [31]. Tilde can be considered as a first-order logic extension of the C4.5 decision tree algorithm [32]: instead of testing attribute values at the nodes of the tree, Tilde tests logical predicates. This provides the advantages of both propositional decision trees (i.e., efficiency and pruning techniques) and the use of first-order logic (i.e., increased expressiveness). The increased expressiveness of first-order logic may provide a more elegant specification of the musical context of a note, and in some cases it provides a more accurate predictive model [11]. Tilde can also be used to build multivariate regression trees, i.e., trees able to predict vectors. In our case, the predicted vectors are the duration and energy transformations.

We have applied the learning algorithm with the following target predicates: duration/2, energy/2, bowdir/2, and alteration/2 (where/n at the end of the predicate name denotes the number of arguments the predicate takes). Each target predicate corresponds to a particular type of transformation: duration/2 refers to duration transformation, energy/2 to energy transformation, bowdir/2 to bow direction, and alteration/2 refers to melody alteration (see Fig. 5.6). For learning a definition of each target predicate, we use the complete training data specialized for the particular type of transformation, e.g., for duration/3, we used the complete data set information on duration transformation (i.e., the performed duration

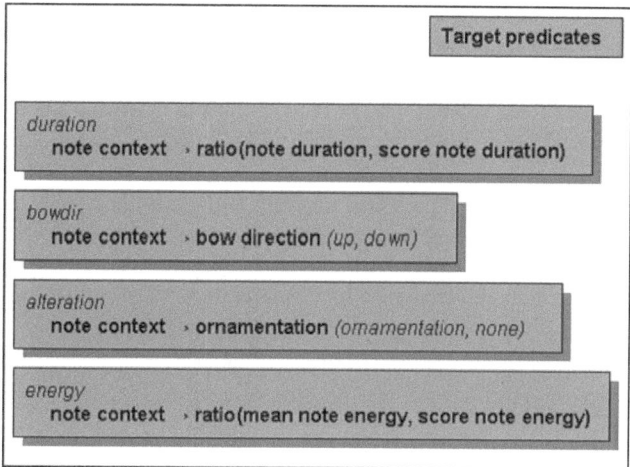

Fig.5.6 Target predicates

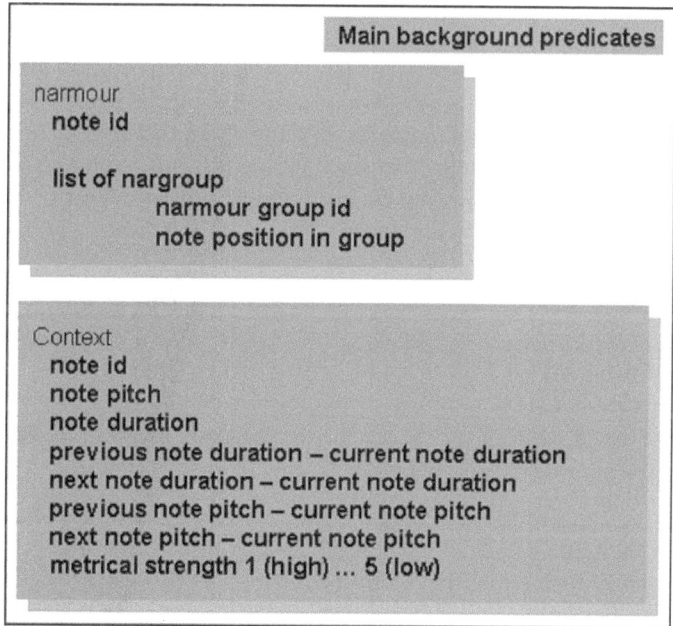

Fig.5.7 Main background predicates: context/8 and narmour/2

transformation for each note in the data set). The arguments are the musical piece, the note in the piece, and performed transformation.

We use (background) predicates to specify both note musical context and background information. The predicates we consider include context/7, narmour/ 2, succ/2, prevdur/2, nextdur/2, prevint/2, nextint/2, metricstr/2, and member/3. Figure 5.7 illustrates the main background predicates. Predicate context/8 specifies the local context of a note. Its arguments are note identifier, note's nominal duration, duration of previous and following notes, extension of the pitch intervals between the note and the previous and following notes, and tempo at which the note is played. Predicate narmour/2 specifies the Narmour groups to which the note belongs. Its arguments are the note identifier and a list of Narmour groups. Predicate succ (X,Y) means Y is the successor of X, prevdur(X,Y), nextdur(X,Y), prevint(X,Y), nextint(X,Y), mean Y is the previous duration ratio, the next duration ratio, the previous interval, and the next interval of X, respectively. Predicate metricstr(X,Y) means that Y is the metrical strength of note X, and predicate member(X,L) means X is a member of list L. Note that succ(X,Y) also means X is the predecessor of Y. The succ(X,Y) predicate allows the specification of arbitrary size note context by chaining a number of successive notes together: succ(X_1,X_2), succ(X_2,X_3), . . ., succ (X_{n-1},X_n), where X_i ($1 < i < n$) is the note of interest.

5.4   Results

We trained a separate model for each of the three violinists. The induced classification rules are of different types. Some focus on features of the note itself while others focus on the Narmour analysis. Rules referring to the local context of a note, i.e., rules classifying a note solely in terms of the timing, pitch, and metrical strength of the note and its neighbors, as well as compound rules that refer to both the local context and the Narmour structure were discovered. Some of the induced rules seem to capture performance principles while others seem to be of less musical interest. The following are examples of induced rules:

[Rule 1]
duration(A, lengthen):-
        succ(A, B),
        context(A,0.5,_,_,_,_,_),
        nextdur(A,1),
        metricstr(A,1).
"Lengthen a note if it is on a very strong metrical position and both the note and the following note duration are eighth notes"

[Rule 2]
duration(A, shorten):-
        succ(B, A),
        context(A,0.5,_,_,_,_,_),
        prevdur(A,1),
        metricstr(A,4).
"Shorten a note if it is on a weak metrical position and both the note and the previous note duration are eighth notes"

Rules 1 and 2 are complementary and are consistent with previous research, which noted that traditional Irish fiddle music contains *swing* timing deviations at the eighth-note level [33]. See later for further evidence provided by the regression model.

[Rule 3]
duration(A, shorten):-
      metricstr(A,4),
      narmour(A,[nargroup(reverse id,1),
      nargroup(reverse id,2),nargroup(ir,3)]).
"Shorten a note if it is on a weak metrical position and it appears in reverse ID, reverse ID, and IR Narmour groups in 1st, 2nd, and 3rd position, respectively."

For the classification tasks and first interpreter, we obtained a correctly classified instances percentage of 90%, 87%, 86%, and 92% for duration, dynamics, ornamentation, and bow direction prediction, respectively. For the second and third interpreters, we obtained accuracies of 86%, 85%, 88%, and 90% and 76%, 81%, 79%, and 90%, respectively. As mentioned before, these numbers were obtained by performing tenfold cross validation on the training data. For the regression task and first interpreter, we obtained correlation coefficients of 0.88 and 0.83 for the duration and energy transformations, respectively. For the second and third interpreters, we obtained 0.91 and 0.85 and 0.82 and 0.74, respectively. We have compared the model's transformation predictions and the actual transformations performed by the musician on pieces not considered in the training stage. Figure 5.8 contrasts the note duration deviations predicted by the model and the deviations performed by the first violinist for a particular piece. Similar results were obtained for the other two violinists. As illustrated in Fig. 5.8, the induced models seem to capture accurately the expressive transformations the musician introduces in the performances.

Expressive deviations at the note level occur in many different musical styles and depend on the metrical position in the musical structure. For instance, some jazz pieces are characterized by a particular pattern of timing deviations: the *swing* where consecutive eighth notes are performed as long-short patterns [34]. It has been noted that traditional Irish fiddle music also shows comparable timing deviations at the eighth-note level [33]. It turned out that the learned duration model captures this kind of timing deviation. Figure 5.9 compares, at the eighth-note level, the average predicted duration deviation ratio of notes in strong metrical position and their successor notes in weak metrical positions.

Synthesis. We fed a violin synthesizer with the prediction results of the models. We make use of a sample-based spectral concatenative synthesizer that uses an annotated database of samples from real recordings and segmented using the techniques described before. The database consists of several musical phrases combining different dynamics, durations, pitch, and articulations. Note annotations include bowing information (note bow direction and whether a note is slurred or tied). Sample selection is based on a weighted Euclidean distance measure with strict matching for bow direction in a similar way as presented in [35]. After the sample selection stage, pitch shift and time stretch transformations are applied in order to match note characteristics in the model's output. In order to obtain a particular ornamentation instance in addition to a prediction of class ornamented, we apply a nearest neighbor algorithm (with Euclidean distance on the note properties) in the ornamentation database, i.e., the set of ornamented note

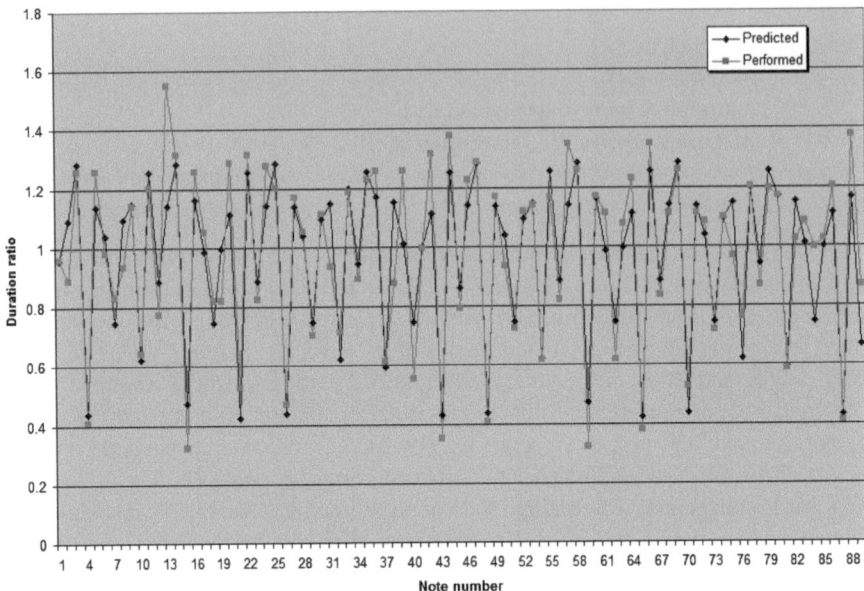

Fig. 5.8 Note deviation ratio for a tune with 89 notes. Comparison between performed and predicted duration ratios

Fig. 5.9 Average predicted note deviation ratio for notes in strong metrical position and following notes in weak metrical positions

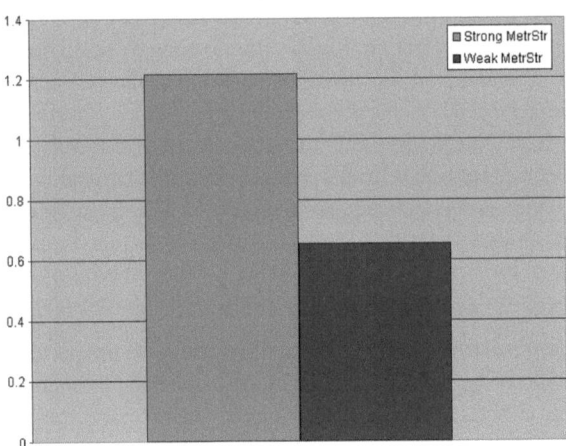

examples. Once a score note has been classified as ornamented, we compute its distance to every note which was performed ornamented and select the one with minimum distance. We then retrieve the corresponding ornamentation. We compute the distance as follows:

$$\sqrt{Pitchdif^2 + DurationDif^2 + MetrStrengthDif^2}$$

where *PitchDif* is the normalized difference between the pitch of the score note and the pitch of a note in the predicted class. Similarly, *DurationDif* is the normalized difference between the duration of the score note and the duration of a note in the predicted class, and *MetrStrengthDif* is the normalized difference between the two notes' metrical strength. The selected ornamentation is then transposed to fit the new note melodic context.

5.4.1 Identifying Performers by Their Playing Style

5.4.1.1 Learning Task

We are interested in obtaining a classifier F of the following form:

$$F(MelodyFragment(N_1, \ldots, N_k)) \rightarrow Performers$$

where $MelodyFragment(N_1, \ldots, N_k)$ is the set of melody fragments (composed of notes $N_1, \ldots, N_k$) and *Performers* is the set of possible performers to be identified. For each performer Pi to be identified, we learn an expressive performance model M_i predicting the performer timing, energy, and note transitions expressive characteristics (characterized by the note duration, energy mean, and legato descriptors described in Sect. 5.3):

$$M_i(Note) \rightarrow (PerfDur, PerfEner, PerfLeftTrans, PerfRightTrans)$$

where *Note* is a note in the score represented by its context features, i.e., *Note* is represented by the tuple (Pitch, Dur, PrevPitch, PrevDur, NextPitch, NextDur, Nar1, Nar2, Nar3) as described before, and the vector (*PerfDur,PerfEner, PerfLeftTrans,PerfRightTrans*) contains the model's prediction for how Performer P_i would play the note in terms of note duration (*PerfDur*), energy (*PerfEner*), and transitions (*PerfLeftTrans,PerfRightTrans*).

5.4.1.2 Learning Algorithm

For training each Model Mi, we have explored several machine learning techniques, including support vector machines [36] with 2nd order polynomial kernel, artificial neural networks [37] fully connected with one input neuron for each attribute, and one hidden layer with six neurons, k-nearest neighbor ($k=2$), model trees, and ensemble methods (bagging, boosting, voting, and stacking).

All the recorded pieces are segmented into fragments representing musical phrases. Given a fragment denoted by a list of notes $[N_1, \ldots, N_m]$ and a set of possible performers denoted by a list of performers $[P_1, \ldots, P_n]$, classifier F identifies the performer as follows:

$F([N_1, \ldots, N_m], [P_1, \ldots, P_n])$
    for each performer P_i
        $Scorei = 0$
    for each note N_k

$FN_k = $ features(N_k)
$Mi(FN_k) = (PD_k, PE_k, PLT_k, PRT_k)$
for each performer P_i
    $ScoreNK_i = dist([D(NK), E(N_k), LT(N_k), RT(N_k)], [PD_k, PE_k, PLT_k, PRT_k])$
    $Score_i = Score_i + ScoreNK_i$
return P_i *(i in {1,...,m})* with minimum score,

where

$$dist([X_1, X_2, X_3, X_4], [Y_1, Y_2, Y_3, Y_4,]) = \sqrt{(X_1 - Y_1)^2 + (X_2 - Y_2)^2 + (X_3 - Y_3)^2/2 + (X_4 - Y_4)^2/2}$$

For each note in the melody fragment, the classifier F computes the set of the note contextual features. Once this is done, for each note N_k and for each performer P_i, performance model M_i predicts the expected duration, energy, and transitions for N_k. This prediction is based on the note's contextual features. The score $Score_i$ for each performer i is updated by taking into account the Euclidean distance between the note's actual duration, energy, and transitions and the predicted values. Finally, the performer with the lower score (i.e., the smaller accumulated distance) is returned. Clearly, the expressive models M_i play a central role in the output of classifier F. Note that in computing this distance, we have balanced the weight of the duration, energy, and transition differences by dividing by 2 the left and right transition differences. The reason for this is that we consider the left and right transitions as one prediction.

5.5   Results

There were a total of 806 notes available for each performer. For evaluating the classification function F, we segmented each of the performed pieces in phases and obtain a total of 92 phrases for each performer. The classification accuracy of the baseline classifier (one which chooses randomly one of the three performers) is 33% (measured in correctly classified instances percentage). The average accuracy and the accuracy obtained for the most successful trained classifier was 76.1% and 81.2%, respectively. The correctly classified instances percentage for each learning method is presented in Table 5.1. The results seem to indicate that it is indeed feasible to train successful classifiers to identify performers from their playing style using the considered features.

5.6   Discussion

Regarding the modeling of expressive deviations, the obtained results indicate that the features extracted contain sufficient information to detect performance patterns of particular interpreters and that the machine learning techniques considered are suitable for learning these patterns. One interesting question is how different the

Table 5.1 Classification accuracy for the 1-note and short phrases (in correctly classified instances percentage)

Algorithm	1-note	Phrase
Decision trees	29.1	69.3
Support vector machines	35.7	80.7
Artificial neural networks	32.9	76.5
k-Nearest neighbor	30.6	72.9
Bagging (decision trees)	31.2	78.1
Boosting (decision trees)	30.5	74.1
Voting (decision trees, SVM, ANN, 1-NN)	32.9	76.5
Stacking (decision trees, SVM, ANN, 1-NN)	31.7	81.2

performance styles of different interpreters are. We have indirectly investigated this question by training classifiers for automatically identifying the different interpreters based on their playing styles. On this line, we found that the difference between the classification results obtained and the accuracy of a baseline classifier indicates that the features extracted contain sufficient information to identify the studied set of performers and that the methods explored are capable of learning performance patterns that distinguish these performers. It is worth noting that every learning algorithm investigated (decision trees, SVM, ANN, k-NN, and the reported ensemble methods) produced considerably better than random classification accuracies. This supports our statement about the feasibility of training successful classifiers for the case study reported.

We selected two types of musical segment lengths: 1-note segments and short-phrase segments. Evaluation using 1-note segments results in poor classification accuracies, while short-phrase segments evaluation results in accuracies well above the accuracy of a baseline classifier. The poor results of the 1-note evaluation may indicate that although the extracted features are relevant, it is not sufficient to consider them in a one-note basis. Just as a human expert would have problems identifying interpreters from listening to one-note audio files, the trained classifiers are not able to identify the performers reliably given this limited information. As soon as there are more notes involved together with the context in which they appear, the trained classifier (just as a music expert) is able to identify the interpreter.

One issue, which is not clear from the reported results, is what features are mostly responsible for the identification results. In order to investigate this, we have performed an additional experiment in which we have applied each model separately. For the duration model, the obtained best accuracy and average accuracy are 51.1 and 46.7, respectively. For the energy model, the obtained best accuracy and average accuracy are 47.6 and 43.0, respectively. Finally for the transition model, the obtained best accuracy and average accuracy are 43.9 and 41.6, respectively. These results seem to indicate that there is some performer-specific information in the isolated duration, energy, and transition models, but the models are certainly more accurate at identifying interpreters when considered together.

5.7 Conclusions

In this chapter, we outlined past research on modeling expressive performance using machine learning techniques and presented a particular approach to quantitatively model and identify interpreters in expressive audio performances. The approach is based on the application of sound analysis techniques to monophonic audio recordings in order to extract pitch, timing, amplitude and transition features, characterizing both the notes and the musical context in which they appear. Different machine learning techniques were explored to train computational models characterizing different aspects of expressive performance, and the resulting models were used to analyze and generate expressive performances as well as to automatically identify performers. The results indicate that the features extracted contain sufficient information and the explored machine learning methods are capable of learning patterns that characterize expressive music performance.

Questions

1. What are the four musicological questions that this study attempts to answer?
2. Name three areas that could be helped by answers to these questions.
3. How is note segmentation done on the audio stream?
4. What are the two main principles recognized by Narmour in his theory?
5. How many prototypical Narmour structures are there?
6. How is bow direction detected in the gesture acquisition?
7. What levels of metrical strength are defined in the note descriptors?
8. What are some of the traditional deviations found in Irish jig music?
9. Why might the results be poor for the 1-note experiments?
10. What were the most successful and least successful classifiers in the results?

References

1. Gabrielsson A (1999) The performance of music. In: Deutsch D (ed) The psychology of music, 2nd edn. Academic, New York, 579 pages
2. Gabrielsson A (2003) Music performance research at the millennium. Psychol Music 31(3):221–272
3. Johnson ML (1992) An expert system for the articulation of Bach fugue melodies. In: Baggi DL (ed) Readings in computer-generated music. IEEE Computer Society, Los Alamitos, pp 41–51
4. Bresin R (2001) Articulation rules for automatic music performance. In Proceedings of the international computer music conference. International Computer Music Association, San Francisco, pp 294–297
5. Friberg A, Bresin R, Fryden L (2000) Music from motion: sound level envelopes of tones expressing human locomotion. J New Music Res 29(3):199–210
6. Friberg A, Bresin R, Sundberg J (2006) Overview of the KTH rule system for musical performance. Adv Cogn Psychol Spec Issue Music Perform 2(2–3):145–161

7. Canazza S, De Poli G, Roda A, Vidolin A (1997) Analysis and synthesis of expressive intention in a clarinet performance. In Proceedings of the 1997 international computer music conference. International Computer Music Association, San Francisco, pp 113–120
8. Canazza S, De Poli G, Drioli C, Roda A, Vidolin A (2004) Modeling and control of expressiveness in music performance. Proc IEEE 92(4):286–701
9. Dannenberg RB, Derenyi I (1998) Combining instrument and performance models for high-quality music synthesis. J New Music Res 27(3):211–238
10. Mitchell TM (1997) Machine learning. McGraw-Hill, New York, 542 pages
11. de Mantaras RL, Arcos JL (2002) AI and music, from composition to expressive performance. AI Mag 23(3):43–57
12. Ramirez R, Hazan A (2006) A tool for generating and explaining expressive music performances of monophonic jazz melodies. Int J Artif Intell Tools 15(4):673–691
13. Ramirez R, Hazan A, Maestre E, Serra X (2008) A genetic rule-based expressive performance model for jazz saxophone. Comput Music J 32(1):38–50
14. Widmer G (2001) Discovering strong principles of expressive music performance with the PLCG rule learning strategy. In Proceedings of the 12th European conference on machine learning (ECML'01), Germany. Springer, Berlin, pp 552–563
15. Widmer G (2002) Machine discoveries: a few simple, robust local expression principles. J New Music Res 31(1):37–50
16. Tobudic A, Widmer G (2003) Relational IBL in music with a new structural similarity measure. In Proceedings of the international conference on inductive logic programming. Springer, pp 365–382
17. Dovey MJ (1995) Analysis of Rachmaninoff's piano performances using inductive logic programming. In European conference on machine learning. Springer, pp 35–38
18. Van Baelen E, De Raedt L (1996) Analysis and prediction of piano performances using inductive logic programming. In International conference in inductive logic programming, pp 55–71
19. Saunders C, Hardoon D, Shawe-Taylor J, Widmer G (2004) Using string kernels to identify famous performers from their playing style. In Proceedings of the 15th European conference on machine learning (ECML'2004), Pisa, Italy, pp 384–395
20. Stamatatos E, Widmer G (2005) Automatic identification of music performers with learning ensembles. Artif Intell 165(1):37–56
21. Ramirez R, Maestre E, Serra X (2010) Automatic performer identification in commercial monophonic jazz performances. Pattern Recognit Lett 31:1514–1523
22. Ramirez R, Perez A, Kersten S, Maestre E (2008) Performer identification in celtic violin recordings. In International Society of Music Information Retrieval (ISMIR) conference, Philadelphia, USA, pp 483–488
23. Molina-Solana M, Arcos JL, Gomez E (2010) Identifying violin performers by their expressive trends. Intell Data Anal 14(5):555–571
24. Narmour E (1990) The analysis and cognition of basic melodic structures: the implication realization model. University of Chicago Press, Chicago, 358 pages
25. Gómez E, Klapuri A, Meudic B (2003) Melody description and extraction in the context of music content processing. J New Music Res 32:33–54
26. Klapuri A (1999) Sound onset detection by applying psychoacoustic knowledge. In Proceedings of the IEEE international conference on acoustics, speech and signal processing, ICASSP, pp 3089–3092
27. Maher RC, Beauchamp JW (1994) Fundamental frequency estimation of musical signals using a two-way mismatch procedure. J Acoust Soc Am 95:2254–2263
28. McNab RJ, Smith LA, Witten IH (1996) Signal processing for melody transcription, working paper 95/22, Hamilton, New Zealand, University of Weikato, Department of Computer Science
29. Maestre E, Gomez E (2005) Automatic characterization of dynamics and articulation of monophonic expressive recordings. In Proceedings of the 118th AES convention, Barcelona, Spain, pp 36–40
30. Narmour E (1991) The analysis and cognition of melodic complexity: the implication realization model. University of Chicago Press, Chicago, 321 pages

31. Blockeel H, De Raedt L, Ramon J (1998) Top-down induction of clustering trees. In Shavlik J(ed) Proceedings of the 15th international conference on machine learning, Madison, Wisconsin, USA. Morgan Kaufmann, pp 53–63
32. Quinlan JR (1993) C4.5: programs for machine learning. Morgan Kaufmann, San Francisco, 305 pages. ISBN 1–55860–238–0
33. Rosinach V, Traube C (2006) Measuring swing in Irish traditional fiddle music. In Proceedings of international conference on music perception and cognition, pp 1168–1171
34. Friberg A, Sundstrom J (2002) Swing ratios and ensemble timing in jazz performances: evidence for a common rhythmic pattern. Music Percept 19(3):333–349
35. Maestre E, Hazan A, Ramirez R, Perez A (2006) Using concatenative synthesis for expressive performance in jazz saxophone. In Proceedings of international computer music conference, New Orleans, pp 82–85
36. Cristianini N, Shawe-Taylor J (2000) An introduction to support vector machines. Cambridge University Press, Cambridge, 190 pages. ISBN 0–521–78019–5
37. Chauvin Y, Rumelhart ED (eds) (1995) Backpropagation: theory, architectures and applications. Lawrence Erlbaum Assoc, Hillsdale, 549 pages. ISBN 0–8058–1259–8

Statistical Approach to Automatic Expressive Rendition of Polyphonic Piano Music

6

Tae Hun Kim, Satoru Fukayama, Takuya Nishimoto, and Shigeki Sagayama

Abstract

In this chapter, we discuss how to render expressive polyphonic piano music through a statistical approach. Generating polyphonic expression is an important element in achieving automatic expressive piano performance since the piano is a polyphonic instrument. We will start by discussing the features of polyphonic piano expression and present a method for modeling it based on an approximation involving melodies and harmonies. An experimental evaluation indicates that performances generated with the proposed method achieved polyphonic expression and created an impression of expressiveness. In addition, performances generated with models trained on different performances were perceptually distinguishable by human listeners. Finally, we introduce an automatic expressive piano system called Polyhymnia that won the first place in the autonomous section of Performance Rendering Contest for Computer Systems (RenCon) 2010.

T.H. Kim (✉)
Audio Communication Group, Technische Universitat Berlin, Einsteinufer 17c, 10587 Berlin, Germany
e-mail: t.kim@campus.tu-berlin.de

S. Fukayama
Graduate School of Information Science and Technology, The University of Tokyo, Japan
e-mail: fukayama@hil.t.u-tokyo.ac.jp

T. Nishimoto
Olarbee Japan, Hiroshima, Japan
e-mail: nishimotz@olarbee.com

S. Sagayama
Graduate School of Information Science and Technology, The University of Tokyo, Japan
e-mail: sagayama@hil.t.u-tokyo.ac.jp

A. Kirke and E.R. Miranda (eds.), *Guide to Computing for Expressive Music Performance*, 145
DOI 10.1007/978-1-4471-4123-5_6, © Springer-Verlag London 2013

6.1   Introduction

Human music performance includes expression that is not explicitly scored. This is one of the reasons that people prefer music performed by accomplished musicians rather than performances directly rendered from the score by a computer, without any expressiveness. More specifically, humans would perform a musical piece with tempo, loudness, and tone-color variations, which are not explicitly written in the score, and those variations result in the preferred emotional expressivity.

Automatic performance rendering is the problem of generating an expressive performance from a given musical score by machine. It is a challenging problem since performing a musical piece is one of the most complex human behaviors – the mechanisms of expressive performance are still not clear. However, such technology has many applications, for example, studying human expressive performances through developing computational models, providing copyright-free performances for general users, and supporting computer-aided music creation and performance. This research field can be considered as a branch of artificial intelligence and robotic musical performance.

Music can be performed with many different types of instruments. Since each instrument has a different mechanical design for enabling expressiveness, developing a universal method for automatic renditions for all musical instruments would be extremely difficult. We are focusing here on piano renditions because there are a large number of solo compositions available for the instrument, and therefore, it is clearly a useful application for computer-aided musical performance. Thanks to its relatively simple mechanical design, much musical expression in piano music can be represented with only three parameters: instantaneous tempo, loudness (velocity), and performed duration. Such a basic parametric representation allows us to develop a simple model of musical expression and can be easily encoded in MIDI format.

Although piano has such a relatively simple mechanical design, the instrument has a wide range of expression. One of the key factors in the expressiveness of the piano is its capability for solo polyphonic performances. This means that multiple notes can be played simultaneously, and each note can be expressed differently. Various combinations of note expressiveness create various sounds, and this makes the piano highly expressive. Therefore, generating polyphonic expression is one of the most important issues in developing automated piano performance.

Several computational methods for automatic expressive performance rendering have been proposed. The synthesis-by-rule approach [21] attempts to implement explicit performance rules on a computer – these are extracted by musical experts based on the analysis-by-synthesis method [6]. Extracting such rules is a hard and time-consuming task, and it is difficult to extract all of performance rules without generating contradictory rules. The query-by-example approach [22] attempts to generate an expressive performance through concatenating musically expressive segments selected from a performance database with a searching algorithm. It allows the generation of an expressive performance without explicitly extracting performance rules. However, the approach requires a huge amount of performance data to allow it to generalize to arbitrary musical pieces. Both of those approaches are mainly focusing on using the hierarchical structures of given pieces for rendering expressive performances. They utilize conventional music theories, such as generative theory of tonal music (GTTM) [13] and modern mathematical music theory [14].

Our approach is, however, based on the statistical modeling approach [8] that focuses on the statistical relationship between the compositional structure and musical expression, on a note-by-note basis. This approach has a number of benefits. Firstly, it avoids the need for developing explicit rules. Statistical relations between note-level compositional structures and musical expressivity can be learned automatically from human expressive performance data. Secondly, this approach can be more robust for generalization to unknown piano pieces. Once statistical relations have been learned from a broad enough data set, many types of piano pieces can be rendered using those learned relations. A third advantage is that relatively small collection of performance data is all that is necessary for an automatic expressive performance rendering. For example, an automatic piano performance system called Usapi learned to generate musical expression from only five human expressive performances and reported good experimental results [23]. Finally, this approach facilitates the generation of expressive performances with more diverse styles. Statistical models of a wide range of styles can be generated by training with different performance date sets, and these can be used for inferring expressive performances with a wide range of styles. The statistical modeling approach has recently become popular because of the above advantages.

It is informative to consider the analogy between speech synthesis and musical performance rendering: the first two approaches discussed above that focus on musical hierarchy are analogous to speech prosody generation. The approach in this chapter, focusing on note-wise expression, is analogous to phoneme generation. Just as a combination of both prosody and phoneme generation is necessary for a successful speech synthesis system, so a combination of phrase-wise and note-wise expressiveness is the basis of successful expressive piano rendering. An automated rendition of a high-quality music performance remains a hard problem. As a first step in solving this, we aim to eliminate the *machine-likeness* in a computer-rendered piano performance through the statistical modeling of expressive polyphonic piano.

In this chapter, we will start by discussing polyphonic expression in piano music based on what is known about human expressive piano performances. Then, we discuss an approximation to the polyphonic dependency of note expression with melodic and harmonic dependencies and present a model of them using conditional random fields. Finally, we introduce an automated expressive piano performance system called Polyhymnia that is able to learn and predict a diverse collection of polyphonic expressiveness and to interpret musical notation automatically. The system participated in Performance Rendering Contest for Computer Systems (RenCon) 2010 and won the first place in the autonomous section of that contest.

6.2   Polyphonic Expression in Piano Music

There are many score elements influencing musical expression in piano music, for example, performance-related musical notation, the hierarchical structures of the score, and the note-level compositional structures. We now discuss how such elements affect piano music expression. An expressive piano performance has both monophonic and polyphonic features, though polyphonic features are more complex than monophonic features. We will discuss how both elements contribute to musical expression in piano performance.

6.2.1 Influential Elements

There are various performance-related musical notation symbols in a piano score that provide performers with a basic guideline for an expressive performance. There are many talks by noted pianists citing that the proper execution of such symbols is vital for a good piano performance [7, 12]. Tempo marks, such as andante and allegro, indicate basic tempo. Dynamic markings, such as *pp* and *ff,* indicate basic loudness. In terms of MIDI, these can be mapped into concrete values of BPM (beat per minute) and MIDI velocity, for computer MIDI performances. Wedges, such as *cresc.*, *dim.*, *rit.*, and *acc.*, indicate gradual changes of instantaneous tempo and loudness, and their executions may vary from instance to instance. This means that a parametric mathematical representation of symbol execution may be advantageous in automated performance. Articulation marks, such as *tenuto* and *staccato*, indicate actual note duration in performance, and their execution varies according to context. Hence, a statistical method may help in determining concrete note durations for each occurrence of these symbols. Some musical symbols – such as trills, mordents, and turns – indicate that the annotated notes should have additional notes added to them during performance. Grace notes are notes that "decorate" their parent note. These additional notes can be automatically executed with the help of noise-based models simulating human motor error. Some symbols such as *con brio*, *cantabile*, and *vivace* indicate the emotive interpretation for a given piece. The relationship between emotion and expression is still not clear, and therefore – compared to other notation markings – it is relatively hard to automatically execute such emotion-specific symbols.

It is well known that most Western piano composition has a hierarchical structure, such as phrase and passage structures. This structural hierarchy is of significant importance in the performance of the piano piece [16]. Phrase boundaries are important cues for an expressive performance. For example, the beginning of a phrase is often performed with a gradual acceleration in tempo, with the end of a phrase performed with a gradual deceleration in tempo. However, there is rarely a single unique interpretation of a piece's structure – it is difficult to analyze hierarchical structures of a given musical piece automatically.

Although musical notation symbols and the hierarchical structure provide rough guidance for an expressive performance, musical expression in piano music has many more contributing factors. Figure 6.1 shows an example of musical expression in a human expressive performance. In measures 17 and 18, there are no musical symbols providing performance instructions. However, based on an example measured expert performance, it can be seen that all of the expressive parameters are varying in spite of this. A number of previous researchers propose

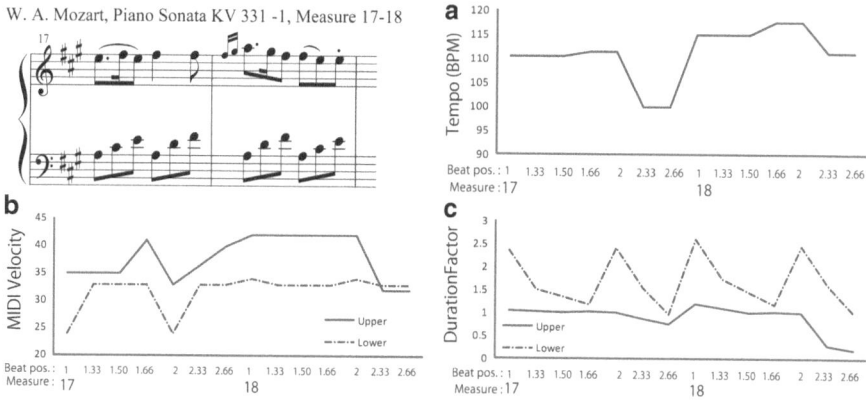

Fig. 6.1 Musical expression of voices in a human expressive performance (Ingrid Haebler, from CrestMuse PEDB [9]). Fluctuations of instantaneous tempo (**a**), MIDI velocity (**b**), and ratio of performed duration to nominal duration (**c**)

that these fluctuations are based on the note-level compositional structure. This is one of the most important characteristics of an expressive piano performance. These note-level structures also have a significant influence on polyphonic expression relative to notation symbols and the hierarchical structure. We propose that note-level structures are the most important element influencing polyphonic expression in piano music.

There are a number of other elements involved in piano musical expression. For example, pedal playing is regarded as a key performance technique, and there are many pedaling methods [12]. It is possible to encode some pedaling in a digital format such as MIDI; however, synthesis of piano with pedaling effects is still an unsolved problem. Sometimes performers incorporate expressive additional notes – not written in the score. For example, many musicians perform the pieces of J. S. Bach with additional notes as part of their musical expression. These additions can be viewed as a form of musical improvisation, and their generation is a different class of problem. For the above reasons, we have not incorporated pedaling and improvisation into the system described in this chapter.

6.2.2   Polyphonic Features of Musical Expression in Piano Music

Figure 6.1 is an example of the musical expression of voices. Looking at musical expression of the uppermost voice in the figure, which can be regarded as a monophonic melody, we can see that instantaneous tempo, loudness, and performed duration are fluctuating over time, and tempo in each measure changes in an arch form (because a phrase boundary exists between the measures).

Incorporated into these observations, the following elements of musical expression in monophonic performances can be observed:

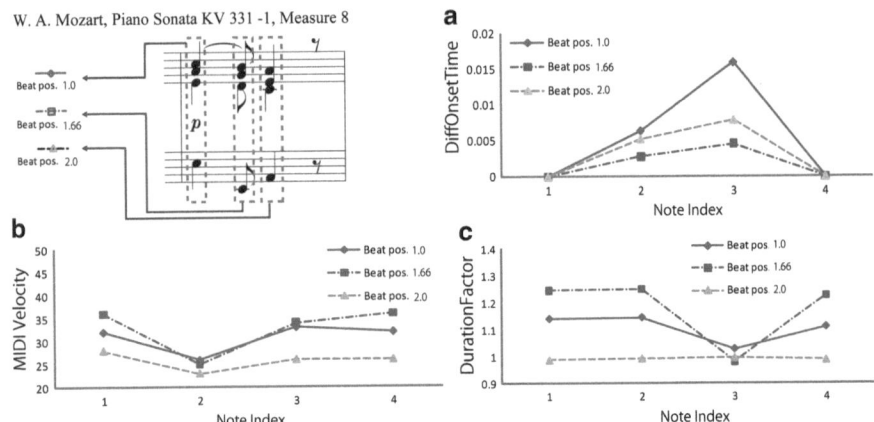

Fig. 6.2 Musical expression of harmonies in a human expressive performance (Ingrid Haebler, from CrestMuse PEDB). Note index is the index of harmonic notes sorted in a descending order. Note onset-time differences of various harmonic notes calculated based on the uppermost voice, where 1.0 is the length of a quarter note (**a**), MIDI velocities of various harmonic notes (**b**), and ratio of performed duration to nominal duration of various harmonic notes (**c**)

- Instantaneous tempo, loudness, and performed duration are fluctuating over time.
- These fluctuations are not random as they are generated by artistic intention.

   Musical expression in polyphonic performances is significantly more complex than in monophonic performance. Looking at all voices in Fig. 6.1, we can see that instantaneous tempo, loudness, and performed duration are fluctuating in each voice, and these fluctuations are musically meaningful. For example, the lowest note A in the lowermost voice is performed as *legato*. The expressive actions in both the uppermost and lowermost voices are not identical. Figure 6.2 illustrates some of these issues in relation to harmonies (i.e., focusing on the related expressiveness of notes in a single chord, rather than the expressive relationships in a melodic sequence). From the figure, we can see that each harmonic note is expressed differently, including note onset-time differences. Such an asynchrony of harmonic note expression causes different sonic effects from a given harmony.

   These observations highlight some features of musical expression in polyphonic performances:

- Musical expression in each voice can have all of the features found in a monophonic performance.
- Musical expression for a voice is not always the same as the expression found in other voices.
- Musical expression for a note in harmony is not always the same as the expression of the other notes.
- Onset-time differences in harmonic notes play an important role in harmonic musical expression.

W. A. Mozart, Piano Sonata, KV. 331-1, Measure 5-8

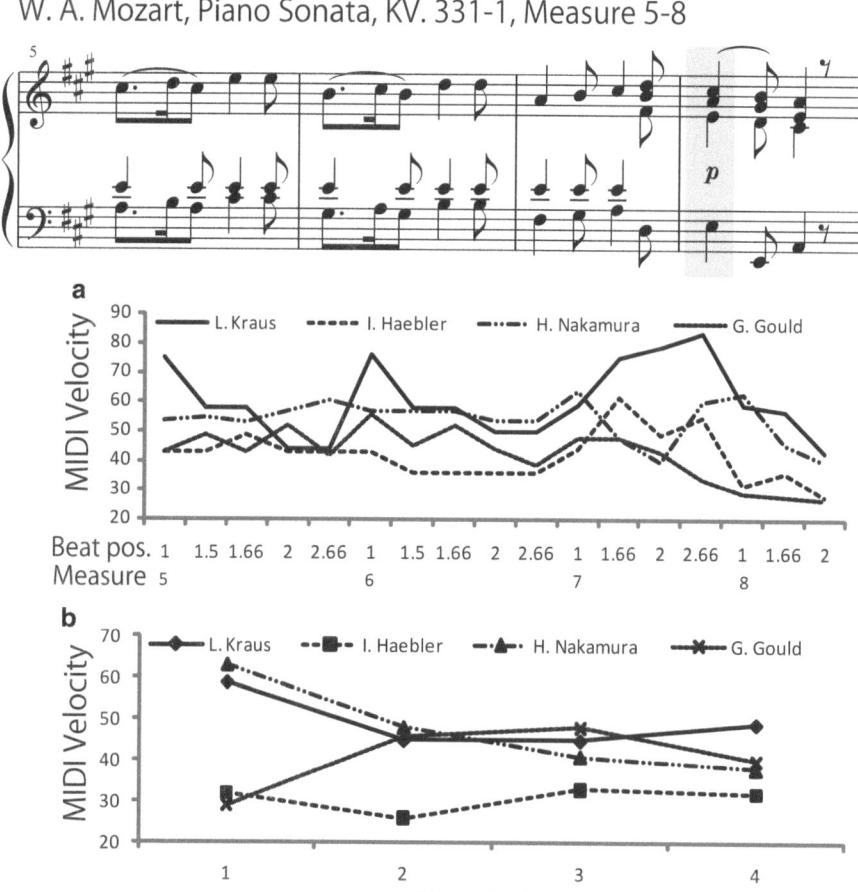

Fig. 6.3 Performances by four different human performers. Various velocity fluctuations of the uppermost voice (**a**). Various combinations of harmonic note expressions by playing the first harmony at the measure 8 (**b**). All performances are from CrestMuse PEDB

6.2.3 Diversity of Polyphonic Expression

A piano score can be performed with a diverse range of styles. Musicological research on human piano performance indicates that there is both *commonality* and *diversity* in piano performance [19]. The level of a performer's skill and their personal preferences in interpreting the piece generate their individual performance style – leading to the *diversity* of piano performance. However, there are certain tendencies that almost all of performers have; these are the *commonalities* of piano performance.

Figure 6.3 shows performances of W. A. Mozart, Piano Sonata, KV. 331, first movement by four different performers. Here, we can see that each performer performed the same piece with different expressive elements. For example, the velocity for the four performances differs significantly. In addition, the performers performed a harmony with different combinations of harmonic note expression. Generating such diverse performances for a piano piece while keeping its common musical expression is a challenge for an automatic piano performance system.

6.3   Statistical Modeling of Polyphonic Piano Renditions

We now present a method for expressive polyphonic piano renditions through statistical modeling. In case of polyphonic expression, the dependency of a note's expressive actions is based on so many elements that it is hard to make models tractable and a huge amount of training data is necessary. To reduce the impact of these complexities, we present an approximation to polyphonic dependency with a combination of melodic and harmonic dependencies. This approximation allows the modeling of melodic and harmonic dependencies through any statistical models with hidden state transition functionality, for example, dynamic Bayesian networks, hidden Markov models, and conditional random fields. We present a model based on conditional random fields and discuss the learning of model parameters from human piano performances, and the generalization of the trained system to infer musical expression for a previously unseen piano piece.

6.3.1   Probabilistic Formulation

One of the most important characteristics of expressive piano performance is that expressive parameters vary based on note-level compositional structure. To estimate those fluctuations, we focus on statistical relationships between compositional structure and note expression. A compositional structure of note expression can be represented with a score feature vector $S = \{s_1, s_2, s_3, \ldots, s_m, \ldots, s_M\}$, where S_m is the mth score feature and M is the number of score features. Then, a piano score $\mathbf{S}$ can be represented as a sequence of S such as $\mathbf{S} = \{S_1, S_2, S_3, \ldots, S_n, \ldots, S_N\}$ where S_n is a score feature vector of the nth note and N is the number of notes in a given score $\mathbf{S}$. The musical expression applied to a note will be represented with three parameters:

- Instantaneous tempo
- Loudness
- Performed duration

which for simplicity we will assume are independent of each other.

Let d be one of those three expression parameters. Then, a sequence of note expressions D in a given piano piece can be represented as a sequence $D = \{d_1, d_2, d_3, \ldots, d_n, \ldots, d_N\}$, where d_n is the musical expression of the nth note and N is the number of notes. If we assume that a sequence of note expressions is probabilistically conditioned on a sequence of score feature vectors, then we can assume a conditional probability distribution $P(D|\mathbf{S}; \Theta)$, where Θ is a set of model parameters. Such a distribution is hard to determine manually because in many cases relations between **S** and D are not explicit. However, it can be estimated from a set of human expressive performances with machine learning techniques.

The estimation of the probability distribution $P(D|\mathbf{S}; \Theta)$ can be accomplished by learning model parameters Θ from a training data set. Training data should consist of set of pairs of a score $\tilde{\mathbf{S}}_k$ and its corresponding musical expression $\tilde{D}_k$, where k is the index of piano pieces in a training data set. Let S be a set of scores and **D** be a set of corresponding musical expressions in the training data such that $S = \{\tilde{\mathbf{S}}_1, \tilde{\mathbf{S}}_2, \tilde{\mathbf{S}}_3, \ldots, \tilde{\mathbf{S}}_k\}$ and $\mathbf{D} = \{\tilde{D}_1, \tilde{D}_2, \tilde{D}_3, \ldots, \tilde{D}_k\}$, where K is the number of the training pieces. Then, model parameters Θ can be learned by

$$\hat{\Theta} = \arg \max {}_{\Theta} \mathcal{L}(\Theta; S, \mathbf{D}) \qquad (6.1)$$

where $\mathcal{L}(\Theta; S, \mathbf{D})$ is a likelihood function of Θ, given S and **D**.

Once the model parameter $\hat{\Theta}$ is estimated, then we can infer an expressive performance with a given piano score by computing $\hat{D}$ such that

$$\hat{D} = \arg \max {}_D P\left(D| \mathbf{S}; \hat{\Theta}\right) \qquad (6.2)$$

By modeling piano renditions of a monophonic melody, a compositional structure S_n can be represented with a simple set of score features, such as pitch, duration, note interval, and duration ratio between the current and previous notes. Previous work argues that each note expression d_n is dependent on the other note expressions [4, 24], and therefore, we cannot simply assume that the d_n are independent of each other. If we assume that d_n is only dependent on d_{n-1}, a sequence of note expressions D can be modeled as a linear Markov chain, in the case of monophonic renditions. Such modeling enables a computationally tractable model with a reasonably sized training data set, thanks to its Markov assumption.

However, modeling polyphonic piano renditions is a significantly more complex problem. Figure 6.4 shows an example of note expression dependency in a polyphonic performance. A score feature vector representing a compositional structure will be significantly complex because there are many more score patterns than in the monophonic case. For example, note intervals and duration ratios between several notes should be considered because there could be a set of multiple notes preceding the current note. Dependencies between note expressions will be complex for the same reason, and therefore, it is difficult to assume the Markov property in modeling those dependencies. Such a complex model is usually not computable, and a huge amount of training data is necessary for learning the model parameters Θ.

Modeling polyphonic piano renditions with computational tractability requires an approximation. There are a number of possible approximations. For example, consider only the melody voice that is most noticeable to a listener – the attentive melody. It could then be assumed that the other voices have the same expression the attentive melody has. Obviously, a simple model is possible based on this approximation, but this is an oversimplification for modeling the polyphonic

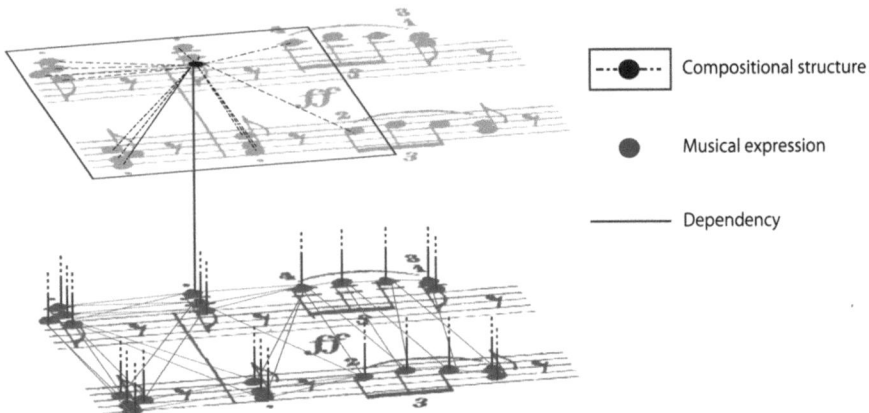

Fig. 6.4 Example of note expression dependency in a polyphonic performance. A note's expression is dependent on its compositional structure and the other note expressions. Such dependencies are highly complex

features of an expressive piano performance. Another possible approximation: a polyphonic piano piece can be considered a combination of multiple voices. Each voice is a monophonic melody, and therefore, a combination of simple models is possible. However, such an approximation is usually impossible because many piano pieces are not simply segmentable into multiple voices. A third approach is to treat a polyphonic piano piece as a monophonic melody by sorting the notes in time and pitch orders. A simple model is possible with this approximation, but then the musical structure of the piece will be lost.

6.3.2 Approximation with Melodic and Harmonic Dependencies

Polyphonic piano renditions can be approximated through renditions of the uppermost voice, the lowermost voice, and the harmonies. As discussed in Sect. 6.2, each voice in a polyphonic piece has its own individual expression, and listeners are able to perceive them simultaneously. Additionally, it is well known that listeners perceive the performance expression of the uppermost and lowermost voices more clearly than the expression of the inner voices [10, 17]. If more than three voices are sounding simultaneously, the performance expression of the inner voices is blurred, and therefore, it is difficult for a listener to perceive them. Combinations of expressive note performance in a harmony contribute to the sonic effect of the harmony, and clearly a listener is able to perceive such sound differences. These psychoacoustic characteristics indicate that the proposed approximation, which is based on a combination of outer voices and harmonies, should promise a perceptually acceptable rendition.

Figure 6.5 shows a dependency network based on the proposed approximation. A voice can be regarded as a monophonic melody, and therefore the structural

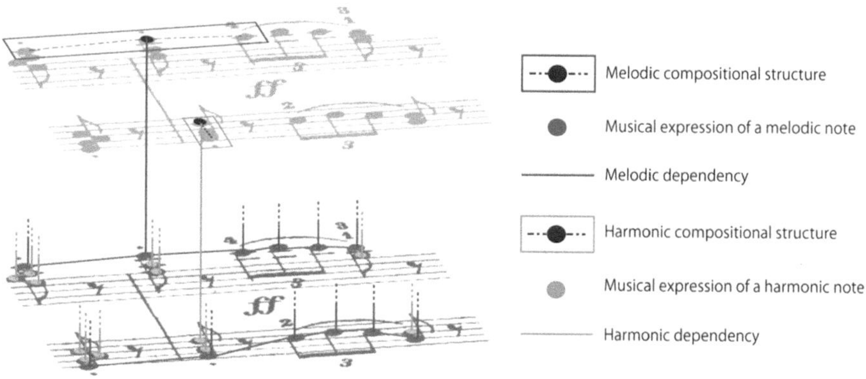

Fig. 6.5 Note expression dependency based on an approximation using melodies and harmonies. The dependency network is simplified by introducing these melodic and harmonic dependencies

elements of a melodic note can be represented with a simple set of score features. In addition, we can assume the Markov property for modeling dependencies between the expressive performance of melodic notes. Hence, it will be assumed that the performance expression of a melodic note is conditioned on its structural elements and the expressive performance of the previous note. This approximation will be labeled *melodic dependency*.

Harmonic expression can be also regarded as a one-dimensional sequence by sorting the notes in the chord into pitch order. Therefore, the structural elements of a harmonic note can also be represented with a simple score feature set, and we can assume the Markov property for modeling dependencies between harmonic note expressive performances. Hence, it will be assumed that performance expression of a harmonic note is conditioned on its harmonic structure and the expressive performance of the previous higher (or lower) note. This approximation will be labeled *harmonic dependency*.

Assuming that the performance expressions of the uppermost voice, lowermost voice, and the chords in the upper staff are independent of the harmonies in the lower staff, $P(D|\mathbf{S}; \Theta)$ can be approximated such that

$$
\begin{aligned}
P(D|\mathbf{S}; \Theta) = &P(D^{m^u}|\mathbf{S}^{m^u}; \Theta^{m^u}) \cdot P(D^{m^l}|\mathbf{S}^{m^l}; \Theta^{m^l}) \cdot \\
&\prod_{h^u=1}^{H^u} P(D^{h^u}|\mathbf{S}^{h^u}; \Theta^{h^u}) \cdot \prod_{h^l=1}^{H^l} P(D^{h^l}|\mathbf{S}^{h^l}; \Theta^{h^l}),
\end{aligned}
\tag{6.3}
$$

where D^{m^u} and D^{m^l} are expressive performances of the uppermost and lowermost voices, respectively. $\mathbf{S}^{m^u}$ and $\mathbf{S}^{m^l}$ are the score feature vectors of the uppermost and lowermost voices, respectively. D^{h^u} and $\mathbf{S}^{h^u}$ are the expressive performances and score feature vectors of a harmony in upper staff h^u, respectively. H^u is the number of harmonies in upper staff for a given piano piece. D^{h^l} and $\mathbf{S}^{h^l}$ are the expressive performances and score feature vectors of a harmony in lower staff h^l, respectively. H^l is the number of harmonies in the lower staff for the given piano piece.

We will assume that melodic and harmonic compositional structures can be represented with simple sets of score features, and melodic and harmonic note expression dependencies obey the Markov assumption. As a result, it is possible to learn the model parameters $\Theta^{m^u}, \Theta^{m^l}, \Theta^{h^u}$, and Θ^{h^l} with a reasonable size of training data.

Based on those discussions, we now present the following strategy for learning and estimating polyphonic expressive piano performances.

6.3.2.1 Learning Model Parameters with Training Performances

1. Split piano scores in the training data set into upper and lower staff.
2. Extract the sequence of highest notes in the upper staff and the sequence of the lowest notes in the lower staff. Those two sequences are regarded as the outer voices. Extract harmonies for each staff.
3. Learn $\hat{\Theta}^{m^u}$ and $\hat{\Theta}^{m^l}$ with the corresponding expressive performance for the extracted outer voices.
4. Learn $\hat{\Theta}^{h^u}$ and $\hat{\Theta}^{h^l}$ with the corresponding expressive performance for the extracted harmonies.

6.3.2.2 Predicting Expressive Performance for a Given Piano Score

1. Split the input score into upper and lower staff.
2. Extract the sequence of the highest notes, and estimate their expressive performance based on $P\left(D^{m^u}|\mathbf{S}^{m^u};\hat{\Theta}^{m^u}\right)$. Extract the sequence of the lowest notes, and estimate their musical expression based on $P\left(D^{m^l}|\mathbf{S}^{m^l};\hat{\Theta}^{m^l}\right)$.
3. Estimate the expressive performance of the harmonies in the upper staff based on $P\left(D^{h^u}|\mathbf{S}^{h^u};\hat{\Theta}^{h^u}\right)$, and estimate expressive performance of harmonies in lower staff based on $P\left(D^{h^l}|\mathbf{S}^{h^l};\hat{\Theta}^{h^l}\right)$.
4. Combine the four estimated expressive performances.

6.3.3 Modeling with Conditional Random Fields

Since the proposed approximation enables the Markov assumption for both the melodic and harmonic expressive performance, these can be modeled with statistical models with hidden state transitions, such as dynamic Bayesian networks, hidden Markov models (HMMs), and conditional random fields (CRFs). Considering that our goal is to estimate a note expression sequence, given a piano score represented as a sequence of score feature vectors, we believe selected CRF as the framework for modeling those dependencies.

CRFs [11] are discriminative and undirected graphical models and can be considered as a generalization of HMMs since they give constant transition probabilities to arbitrary functions varying across the position in the hidden state sequence, depending on the input sequence. HMMs factorize a joint probability such as $P(D, \mathbf{S})$, where $\mathbf{S}$ is a given (or observed) and D is hidden. To factorize $P(D, \mathbf{S})$, it is necessary to model $P(\mathbf{S})$ since $P(D, \mathbf{S}) = P(D|\mathbf{S}) \cdot P(\mathbf{S})$. This means that all of the possible S should be enumerated and an emission probability should be given for each possible S. This is difficult since we want to be able to handle new and unknown piano scores, and thus, the number of possible S will be significantly large.

Unlike HMMs, CRFs factorize a conditional probability $P(D|\mathbf{S})$ directly. This means that it is not necessary to model $P(\mathbf{S})$ as it is never used during the learning and inferring procedures. Since we do not need to consider a model of the given sequence $\mathbf{S}$, enumerating all of the possible S is not necessary any more. Therefore, CRFs for expressive piano renditions should be more robust to dealing with unknown piano pieces. We now present the detailed modeling of melodic and harmonic dependencies with CRFs.

6.3.3.1 Melodic Dependency
Expression Parameters
Expressive performance of a melody note will be represented with three expressive parameters: instantaneous tempo, loudness, and performed duration.

Human perception of tempo changes logarithmically not linearly. Therefore, instantaneous tempo should be defined on a logarithmic scale based on the average tempo of a given piece. Since a piano performance contains expressive performance based on musical symbols and hierarchical structures, defining instantaneous tempo based on the average tempo of the entire piece is not sufficient. Instantaneous tempo of the nth note can be represented with TempoFactor_n and defined based on the average tempo of the notes in a limited scope, such that

$$\text{TempoFactor}_n = \log\left(\frac{\text{Tempo}_n}{\text{Tempo}_{\text{avg}}^{\text{scope}}}\right), \tag{6.4}$$

where $\text{Tempo}_{\text{avg}}^{\text{scope}}$ is the average tempo across a number of notes in the scope, whose size can be decided experimentally. It was found that a scope size of five tempo values Tempo_{n-3}, Tempo_{n-2}, Tempo_{n-1}, Tempo_n, and Tempo_{n+1} gave the best performance.

Similarly, loudness of the nth note can be represented by Loudness_n defined as

$$\text{Loudness}_n^m = \log\left(\frac{\text{Velocity}_n}{\text{Velocity}_{\text{avg}}^{\text{scope}}}\right), \tag{6.5}$$

where $\text{Velocity}_{\text{avg}}^{\text{scope}}$ is the average velocity of Velocity_{n-3}, Velocity_{n-2}, Velocity_{n-1}, Velocity_n, and Velocity_{n+1}. The influence of dynamic markings and wedges can be eliminated by calculating Loudness_n^m based on $\text{Velocity}_{\text{avg}}^{\text{scope}}$.

Human perception of performed duration is also not linear but logarithmic. Hence, performed duration of the nth note is represented with DurationFactor_n defined as

Table 6.1 Score features for a melodic compositional structure

Instantaneous tempo	Loudness	Performed duration
–	Pitch	–
–	Duration^{score}	Duration^{score}
NoteInterval I, II, III, IV	NoteInterval I, II, III, IV	NoteInterval I, II, III, IV
DurationRatio I, II, III, IV	DurationRatio I, II, III, IV	DurationRatio I, II, III, IV
Metric I, II	Metric I, II	Metric I, II
ArticulationMarks	ArticulationMarks	ArticulationMarks

$$\text{DurationFactor}_n^m = \log\left(\frac{\text{Duration}_n^{\text{perf}}}{\text{Duration}_n^{\text{score}}}\right), \tag{6.6}$$

where Duration$_n^{\text{score}}$ and Duration$_n^{\text{perf}}$ are the nominal duration in the score and the performed duration, respectively.

Let d_n^m be one of the nth melodic expression parameters such as TempoFactor$_n$, Loudness$_n^m$, and DurationFactor$_n^m$, and let D^m be a sequence of d_n^m. Since a standard CRF is not able to deal with continuous hidden variables, d_n^m will be quantized into discrete values. This is done here using the k-means algorithm. The number of classes k determines the number of labels, which is equivalent to the resolution of quantization. By providing initial values of class centers based on the prior probability of d_n^m estimated from a given training data set, a nonlinear quantization is possible. For example, more probable values of d_n^m can be quantized into small size bins.

Compositional Structure

Let $\mathbf{S}^m$ be a sequence of melodic structures. Previous studies on human expressive piano performances address that a melodic structure S_n^m can be represented with a score feature vector, whose elements vary based on each expression parameter [5, 21]. We used score features, as shown in Table 6.1. Pitch is an absolute pitch given as a MIDI note number, and Duration^{score} is the nominal duration in the score. NoteInterval I, II, III, IV are note intervals of the pairs (n_{t-3}, n_{t-2}), (n_{t-2}, n_{t-1}), (n_{t-1}, n_t), and (n_t, n_{t+1}), respectively, where n_t is the current note. DurationRatio I, II, III, IV are duration ratios of the pairs above. Metric is a variable that has a value from $\{very\_strong, strong, weak\}$, and Metric I, II are the metric of the previous and current notes, respectively. ArticulationMarks is an articulation mark such as *staccato*, *accent*, and *fermata*.

CRFs for Melodic Dependency

Let f_j^m be a function of a sequence containing melodic structures, the nth note expression, the $(n-1)$th note expression, and the position n. Such a function will be called a *local feature function*, and it can have arbitrary forms and return values. Note that f_j^m will be defined for every triple in the training data of a score feature, discrete value of $(n-1)$th note expression, and discrete value of nth note expression. Hence, there could be a large set of local feature functions. An example of those functions is

$$f_{10}^{\mathrm{m}}\left(d_{n-1}^{\mathrm{m}}, d_n^{\mathrm{m}}, \mathbf{S}^{\mathrm{m}}, n\right) = \begin{cases} 1, & \text{if } d_{n-1}^{\mathrm{m}} = l_5, \, d_n^{\mathrm{m}} = l_3 \text{ and } s_{n,3}^{\mathrm{m}} = -2 \\ 0, & \text{otherwise} \end{cases}, \qquad (6.7)$$

where l_3 and l_5 are the third and fifth discrete values of note expression, respectively, and $s_{n,3}^{\mathrm{m}} = -2$ means that the third score feature of the nth compositional structure is -2. If $s_{n,3}^{\mathrm{m}}$ is defined as NoteInterval I, -2 means that the pitch of the $(n-1)$th note is 2 units chromatically higher than the pitch of the nth note.

Let us define another function, $F_j^{\mathrm{m}}(D^{\mathrm{m}}, \mathbf{S}^{\mathrm{m}})$, that indicates how many times the jth triple occurred in the whole melodic expression. This function is called the global feature function, or for brevity's sake, the *feature function*. Mathematically, it is defined as

$$F_j^{\mathrm{m}}(D^{\mathrm{m}}, \mathbf{S}^{\mathrm{m}}) = \sum_{n=1}^{N} f_j(d_{n-1}^{\mathrm{m}}, d_n^{\mathrm{m}}, \mathbf{S}^{\mathrm{m}}, n). \qquad (6.8)$$

We are interested here in which global feature functions have important roles for certain expressive performance elements. Hence, a weighting variable is introduced for the jth feature function θ_j^{m}. Then, the model parameters Θ^{m} are a set of weights for all the feature functions. We will assume that the best probability distribution $P(D^{\mathrm{m}}|\mathbf{S}^{\mathrm{m}}; \Theta^{\mathrm{m}})$ is the one with the largest entropy – subject to known constraints $\theta_j^{\mathrm{m}} F_j^{\mathrm{m}}(D^{\mathrm{m}}, \mathbf{S}^{\mathrm{m}})$ for all $j = 1 \dots J$, i.e., we assume that an unknown score feature has probabilistically no influence on determining the current note expression. As a result, according to the principle of maximum entropy, $P(D^{\mathrm{m}}|\mathbf{S}^{\mathrm{m}}; \Theta^{\mathrm{m}})$ can be defined as

$$P(D^{\mathrm{m}}|\mathbf{S}^{\mathrm{m}}; \Theta^{\mathrm{m}}) = \frac{1}{Z^{\mathrm{m}}(\mathbf{S}^{\mathrm{m}}, \Theta^{\mathrm{m}})} \exp \sum_j \theta_j^{\mathrm{m}} F_j^{\mathrm{m}}(D^{\mathrm{m}}, \mathbf{S}^{\mathrm{m}}), \qquad (6.9)$$

where $Z^{\mathrm{m}}(\mathbf{S}^{\mathrm{m}}, \Theta^{\mathrm{m}})$ is a normalization factor such that

$$Z^{\mathrm{m}}(\mathbf{S}^{\mathrm{m}}, \Theta^{\mathrm{m}}) = \sum_{D'^{\mathrm{m}}} \exp \sum_j \theta_j^{\mathrm{m}} F^{\mathrm{m}}(D'^{\mathrm{m}}, \mathbf{S}^{\mathrm{m}}) \qquad (6.10)$$

where D'^{m} is across all of the possible note expression sequences.

6.3.3.2 Harmonic Dependency
Expression Parameters

Since the onset-time differences between harmonic notes have an important role in the expressive performance of a harmony, expressive performance of a harmonic note will be represented here by loudness, performed duration, and onset-time difference.

Human perception of the loudness of a harmonic note is not linear but logarithmic, based on the loudness of other notes performed in parallel. Once the

Table 6.2 Score features for a harmonic compositional structure

Instantaneous tempo	Loudness	Performed duration	Onset-time difference
Pitch	Pitch	Pitch	Pitch
Duration^{score}	Duration^{score}	Duration^{score}	Duration^{score}
NoteDistance	NoteDistance	NoteDistance	NoteDistance
OuterNote	OuterNote	OuterNote	OuterNote

simultaneous harmonic notes are sorted into pitch order, then loudness of the ith harmonic note can be represented with Loudness$_i^h$ defined as

$$\text{Loudness}_i^h = \log\left(\frac{\text{Velocity}_i}{\text{Velocity}_0}\right), \tag{6.11}$$

where Velocity$_i$ is the velocity of the current note to be performed and Velocity$_0$ is the velocity of the note in a given harmony that belongs to the uppermost or lowermost voice.

Similarly, the performed duration of the ith harmonic note is represented as DurationFactor$_i^h$ which is defined as

$$\text{DurationFactor}_i^h = \log\left(\frac{\text{Duration}_i^{\text{perf}}}{\text{Duration}_0^{\text{perf}}}\right), \tag{6.12}$$

where Duration$_0^{\text{perf}}$ and Duration$_i^{\text{perf}}$ are the performed duration of the note in a given harmony which belongs to the uppermost or lowermost voice and the performed duration of the current note, respectively.

The onset-time difference of the ith harmonic note is represented as DiffOnsetTime$_i$ defined as

$$\text{DiffOnsetTime}_i = \text{OnsetTime}_0 - \text{OnsetTime}_i, \tag{6.13}$$

where OnsetTime$_0$ is the onset time of the note in a given harmony which belongs to the uppermost or lowermost voice. OnsetTime$_i$ is the onset time of the current note being performed. DiffOnsetTime$_i$ is a difference in onset times, where the length of a quarter note is defined as 1.0 (for further details, see [9]).

Let d_i^h be one of the ith harmonic expression parameters such as Loudness$_i^h$, DurationFactor$_i^h$, and DiffOnsetTime$_i$, and let D^h be a sequence of d_i^h. Since a standard CRF is not able to deal with continuous hidden variables, d_i^h should be quantized into discrete values, and this can be done using the same approach used for quantizing melodic note expression described earlier.

Compositional Structure

Let S^h be a sequence of harmonic compositional structures. We assume that a harmonic compositional structure S_i^h can be represented using the score features shown in Table 6.2. Pitch is the absolute pitch represented as a MIDI note number, and Duration^{score} is the nominal duration in the score. NoteDistance is measured by the interval between the pitch of the uppermost or lowermost voice and the current note being performed. OuterNote is a variable that is *true*, if the current note is an outer note of the harmony, and *false*, otherwise.

CRFs for Harmonic Dependency

CRFs for harmonic dependency can be defined in a similar way to that done in the modeling of melodic dependency.

Let f_j^h be a function of a sequence of harmonic compositional structures, the ith note expression, the $(i - 1)$th note expression, and the score position i. Then, an example of harmonic local feature functions would be

$$f_5^h(d_{i-1}^h, d_i^h, \mathbf{S}^h, i) = \begin{cases} 1, & \text{if } d_{i-1}^h = l_2, d_i^h = l_1 \text{ and } s_{i,3}^h = 3 \\ 0, & \text{otherwise} \end{cases}, \tag{6.14}$$

where l_2 and l_1 are the second and first discrete values of note expression, respectively. $s_{i,3}^h = -2$ means that the third score feature of the ith harmonic compositional structure is 3. If $s_{i,3}^m$ represents NoteDistance, 3 means that the chromatic pitch distance between the ith note and the note belonging to uppermost or lowermost voice is 3.

Global feature functions of harmonic dependency $F_j^h(D^h, \mathbf{S}^h)$ can be written as

$$F_j^h(D^h, \mathbf{S}^h) = \sum_{i=1}^{I} f_j(d_{i-1}^h, d_i^h, \mathbf{S}^h, i). \tag{6.15}$$

Let θ_j^h be a weight of $F_j^h(D^h, \mathbf{S}^h)$ and Θ^h be a set of such weights. According to the principle of maximum entropy, then, $P(D^h|\mathbf{S}^h; \Theta^h)$ can be written as

$$P(D^h|\mathbf{S}^h; \Theta^h) = \frac{1}{Z^h(\mathbf{S}^h, \Theta^h)} \exp \sum_j \theta_j^h F_j^h(D^h, \mathbf{S}^h), \tag{6.16}$$

in which $Z^h(\mathbf{S}^h, \Theta^h)$ is a normalization factor such that

$$Z^h(\mathbf{S}^h, \Theta^h) = \sum_{D'^h} \exp \sum_j \theta_j^h F_j^h(D'^h, \mathbf{S}^h), \tag{6.17}$$

where D'^h is all of the possible note expression sequences.

6.3.3.3 Learning and Estimation

For convenience in the following derivations, we will denote $\mathbf{S}^{m''}$, $\mathbf{S}^{m'}$, $\mathbf{S}^{l''}$, and $\mathbf{S}^{h'}$ as $\mathbf{S}$, and $D^{m''}$, $D^{m'}$, $D^{h''}$, and $D^{h'}$ as D. Similarly we will denote $\Theta^{m''}$, $\Theta^{m'}$, $\Theta^{h''}$, and $\Theta^{h'}$ as Θ. Learning the musical expression of a performance is equivalent to estimating Θ from k score and performance pairs $\{S,D\}_k$. Equations 6.9 and 6.16 can be rewritten such that

$$P(D|S;\Theta) = \frac{1}{Z(S,\Theta)} \exp \sum_j \theta_j F_j(D, S), \tag{6.18}$$

where

$$Z(S,\Theta) = \sum_{D'} \exp \sum_j \theta_j F(D', S). \tag{6.19}$$

Assuming that the k pairs of $\{S,D\}_k$ are distributed identically and independently, a log-likelihood function of Θ can be written as

$$\mathcal{L}(\Theta; \mathcal{S}, \mathbf{D}) = \sum_k \mathcal{L}\left(\Theta; \tilde{S}_k, \tilde{D}_k\right)$$

$$= \sum_k \left[\log \frac{1}{Z\left(\tilde{S}_k, \Theta\right)} + \sum_j \theta_j F_j\left(\tilde{D}_k, \tilde{S}_k\right) \right]. \tag{6.20}$$

Hence, the parameter values $\hat{\Theta}$ can be computed by Eq. 6.1.

Since the function $\mathcal{L}(\Theta; \mathcal{S}, \mathbf{D})$ is concave, it guarantees convergence to the global maximum. To find the global maximum, we differentiate the likelihood function $\mathcal{L}(\cdot)$ with respect to parameter θ_j and set the derivate to 0. Unfortunately, such an approach does not always yield a closed form solution, and therefore, analytical determination of parameter values $\hat{\Theta}$ that maximize the log-likelihood is not always possible. Instead, maximum-likelihood parameters can be estimated with iterative algorithms, such as iterative scaling [1, 3, 18] and other gradient-based methods [2, 20, 25].

Once Θ is learned using a set of training performances, we can estimate the musical expression D of a given score S by computing Eq. 6.2. Since $Z(\cdot)$ is a constant value and exponential functions are monotonically increasing, Eq. 6.2 can be rewritten such as

$$\hat{D} = \arg \max_D \sum_j \hat{\theta}_j F_j(D, S), \tag{6.21}$$

and this can be solved efficiently with the dynamic programming technique. $Z(\cdot)$ has the form of the partition function, and it can be efficiently computed with the forward-backward algorithm [11].

6.3.4 Experimental Evaluation

We have proposed an approach to the statistical modeling of polyphonic piano performances which focuses on the relationship between note-level compositional

Table 6.3 Training performances for rendering a *known* piece. Four performances of a Mozart's piano sonata were used in total. All performances are from CrestMuse PEDB

Piece	Performer
Piano Sonata KV331, 1st movement	Hiroko Nakamura
Piano Sonata KV331, 1st movement	Norio Shimizu
Piano Sonata KV331, 1st movement	Ingrid Haebler
Piano Sonata KV331, 1st movement	Lily Kraus

Table 6.4 Training performances for rendering an *unknown* piece. Fourteen performances of 14 of Chopin's piano pieces were used in total. All performances are from CrestMuse PEDB

Pieces	Performer
Prelude Op. 28, No. 1, 4, 7, 15, and 20 (five pieces)	Vladimir Ashkenazy
Etude Op.10-3, 10–4, and 25–11 (three pieces)	Vladimir Ashkenazy
Waltz Op. 18, 34–2, 64–2, 69–1, and 69–2 (five pieces)	Vladimir Ashkenazy
Nocturne No. 2, Op. 9–2 (one piece)	Vladimir Ashkenazy

structures and note expressions. To avoid an overly complex model which leads to computational intractability and requires a huge amount of training data, we have proposed a method based on an approximation using melodic and harmonic representations. To examine if the proposed methods are able to generate polyphonic musical expression, we have conducted generative experiments for both *known* and *unknown* piano pieces, i.e., those that the system has been trained for as well as those it has not. In addition, we have conducted listening experiments on the generated performances to see how humans perceive them and whether modeling polyphonic expression is actually effective for automatic expressive piano renditions.

6.3.4.1 Generative Experiments

Two experiments for rendering known and unknown pieces were conducted. First, the proposed method was evaluated on a piece known to the system. The proposed models for melodic and harmonic expression were trained with four human performances of W. A. Mozart's Piano Sonata, KV. 331 (the 1st movement as shown in Table 6.3). The same piece was used as the test piece. The selected piece contains several harmonies, which makes it ideal for examining if the proposed method is able to generate polyphonic expression for a known piano piece.

In the second evaluation, the proposed method was tested on a score previously unknown to the system. The proposed models for melodic and harmonic expression were trained with 14 pieces of F. Chopin, which were performed by Vladimir Ashkenazy, as shown in Table 6.4. As the test piece, we used F. Chopin, Nocturne No. 10, Op. 32 (the 2nd movement), a score that was not included in the training data set. This piece was selected because it contains mixed melodies and harmonies and, therefore, is a good piece for testing how well the proposed method is able to generate polyphonic expression for an unknown piano piece.

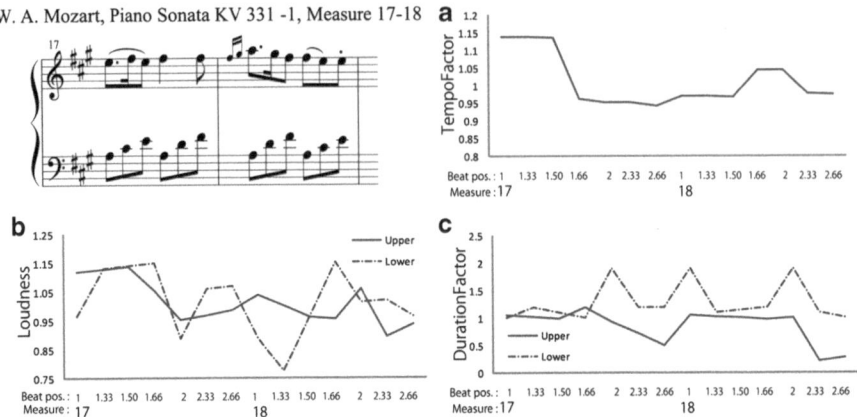

Fig. 6.6 Expressive performance of voices in a generated performance of the piano piece from training set. Trajectory of instantaneous tempo calculated by Eq. 6.4 (**a**), trajectory of loudness calculated by Eq. 6.5 (**b**), and trajectory of performed duration calculated by Eq. 6.6 (**c**)

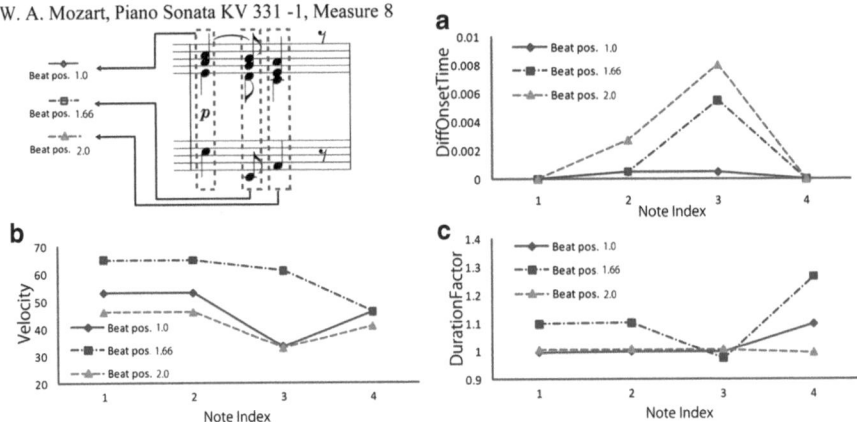

Fig. 6.7 Expressive performance of harmonies in a generated performance of the piano piece from training set. Onset-time differences calculated by Eq. 6.13 (**a**), velocities (**b**), and performed durations calculated by Eq. 6.12 (**c**) of harmonic notes in several harmonies

Figure 6.6 shows an excerpt of melodic expression in the generated performance of the Mozart (known) test piece. It has been mentioned that the musical expression of individual voices in an expressive piano performance is not always the same. This is probably because each voice has a different musical role, for example, the uppermost voice having the role of a melody and the lowermost voice having the role of an accompaniment, as is the case in Fig. 6.6. The experimental results show that the generated performance actually exhibited different expressive performance actions for the different voices.

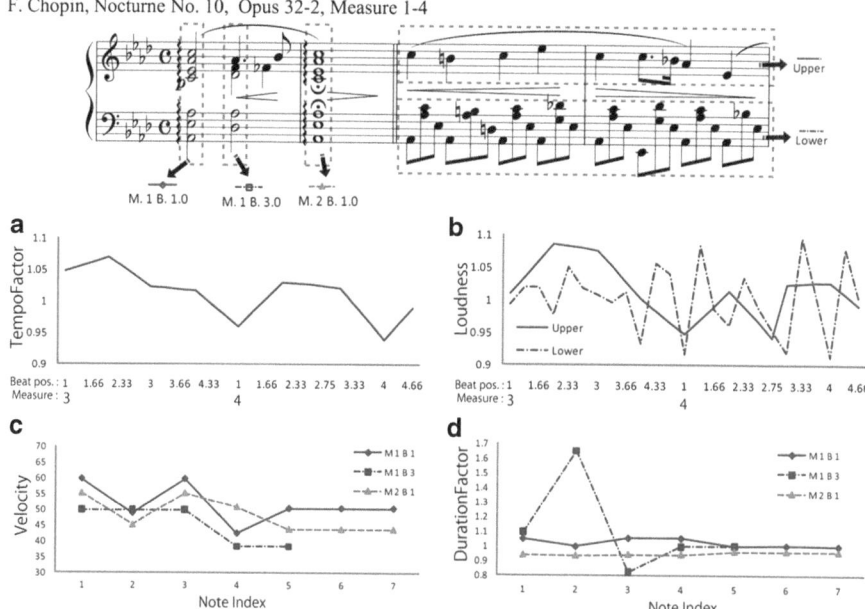

Fig. 6.8 Melodic and harmonic expression in the generated performance of a piano piece not in training set. Fluctuation of instantaneous tempo calculated by Eq. 6.4 (**a**). Loudness fluctuation in melodic expression calculated by Eq. 6.5 (**b**). Velocities of harmonic notes in several harmonies (**c**). Performed note durations of harmonic notes calculated by Eq. 6.12 (**d**). Fluctuation of performed note durations in melodic expression and onset-time differences of harmonic notes are omitted due to space limitations

The trajectories of all expression parameters were found to not be random but to have musical meaning. For example, changes in expressively performed duration in the lowermost voice exhibited a certain pattern such that the lowest note A was performed as *legato*.

Figure 6.7 shows an excerpt of harmonic expression in the generated performance of the known test piece. It has been mentioned that musical expressions of notes in a given harmony are not always the same as each other. This is probably caused by the artistic intentions of performers and their characteristic fingerings. The experimental result shows that the performance generated with the proposed method exhibits different musical expressive actions for each harmonic note. This experimental result indicates that the performance of a *known* piano piece generated with the proposed method exhibits this element of polyphonic expression that can be found in a human's expressive piano performance.

Figure 6.8 shows an excerpt of the melodic and harmonic expression in the system-generated performance of F. Chopin, Nocturne No. 10, Op. 32 (2nd movement), a piece not included in the system's training set. The experimental result indicates that the uppermost and lowermost voices exhibited different musical expression, and the harmonic notes in given harmonies exhibited different musical expression to each other. As in the known piece, these expressive performance actions were not random but had musical meaning. For example, instantaneous tempo exhibited an arch-like form over each measure. The experimental result indicates that the performance of an unknown piano piece generated with the proposed method exhibits elements of the polyphonic expression that can be found in a human expressive piano performance.

The results of both generative experiments indicate that the performances of known and unknown pieces generated with the proposed method exhibited multiple polyphonic expressive actions that can be found in human expressive performances.

6.3.4.2 Listening Experiments

The results of the generative experiments show that the proposed methods were able to generate expressive performances of polyphonic piano pieces. In addition to those generative experiments, we conducted listening experiments to see how a human perceives the generated performances and how efficient modeling polyphonic expression is for automatic piano renditions.

We prepared three performances generated with the proposed method. Three piano pieces were used: W. A. Mozart, Piano Sonata, KV. 331, the 1st movement (SNT331-1); F. Chopin, Nocturne No. 10, Op. 32, the 2nd movement (NCT010); and W. A. Mozart, Piano Sonata, KV. 545, the 3rd movement (SNT545-3). For SNT331-1 and NCT010, we used the performances from the generative experiments above. For SNT545-3, we used a new performance generated from a model trained with six of Mozart's piano sonatas: KV. 279–1, 279–2, 279–3, 331–1, 545–1, and 545–2 (performed by M. J. Pires). Note that the test piece, KV545-3, was not included in the training data.

In addition, three more performances were utilized for each piece (giving 12 samples in total): a performance generated without any expression, a performance by a human performer, and a generated performance without polyphonic expression. Generated performances without polyphonic expression had expression generated only in uppermost voice, and this was copied to the other voices. Hence, the uppermost voice, the lowermost voices, and the harmonies had the same expression. The purpose of preparing generated performance without polyphonic expression was to see if the proposed method that models polyphonic piano renditions is effective for automatic piano renditions.

"Human likeness" and musicality of each sound sample were evaluated by 25 participants[1] using two 6-level scales. For "human likeness," 1 was defined as *not at all like a human playing* and 6 as *very much like a human playing*. For musicality, 1 was defined as *not at all musical* and 6 as *very musical*. The properties of the sample music were unknown to the participants. At the beginning of the experiment, there was a "training phase," participants listened to the four prepared sound samples for

---

[1] Six nonmusicians, 17 hobbyist musicians, and 2 professional musicians participated in the experiment.

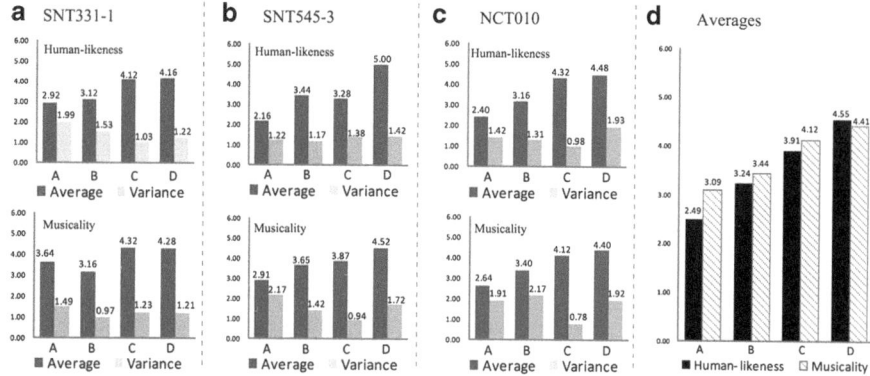

Fig. 6.9 Results of listening experiments for SNT331-1 (**a**), SNT545-3 (**b**), and NCT010 (**c**); average "human likeness" and musicality of the 3 pieces (**d**). Performance A is without expression ("deadpan"), B is the performance generated without polyphonic expression, C is the performance generated with polyphonic expression, and D is the performance by a human performer. Note that human performance includes expressive interpretation of musical symbols

each piece without evaluation, and after that they listened to the four sound samples once again while evaluating each of them (the "evaluation phase").

Figure 6.9 shows the results of the listening experiments. In this figure, we can see that the performances generated with the proposed method – incorporating the polyphonic expression – were evaluated by listeners as sounding more humanlike and more musical, when compared with the nonexpressive performances, for all three pieces. In the case of SNT331-1 and NCT010, participants evaluated them with the scores close to the performances by a human performer. An ANOVA test[2] with $p < 0.05$ in fact indicates that these differences were not significant. Thus, for SNT331-1 and NCT010, the performances generated with the proposed polyphonic method sounded much closer to human expressive performances.

In the case of SNT545-3, the performance generated with polyphonic expression was scored relatively low by listeners compared to the human performance. One possible reason for this is that the expressive interpretation of musical symbols and structures plays a more important role when performing this Mozart piano sonata with fast tempo. Since the performance by a human performer included this expressive interpretation of musical symbols and structures, this may explain the comparatively lower score.

However, the mean "human likeness" and musicality of the three pieces shows that the performances generated with the proposed polyphonic expression method lead to a better score than performances generated without polyphonic expression. The overall "human likeness" and musicality of the performances generated with the proposed method of polyphonic expression were the closest to the performances

---

[2] Differences in the average scores were tested using analysis of variance and its post-hoc test using TukeyHSD algorithm implemented in GNU R.

by a human performer, when compared with the other generated samples in the experiment ($p < 0.05$). This is probably because the performances generated with polyphonic expression had a more profound expressive content than the performances generated without polyphonic expression.

These results show that the proposed method is effective in generating expressive performances of polyphonic piano pieces, with the generated results being significantly "humanlike" and with a significant degree of musicality.

6.4   Polyhymnia: An Automated Piano Performance System

We introduce an automated expressive piano performance system called Polyhymnia.[3] To our knowledge, it is the first system that is able to generate polyphonic expression through statistical models and to provide a diversity of performances for a given piano piece. Polyhymnia was entered into the Performance Rendering Contest for Computer Systems ("RenCon") in 2010 and won first place in the autonomous section of the contest.

6.4.1   System Overview

To obtain an expressive piano performance with Polyhymnia, users are only required to input a piano score in MusicXML [15] format; no other input is required. Unlike the MIDI format, MusicXML is able to encode almost every form of musical symbol in a machine-readable format. Extracted expressive musical symbols (*p, mf, f, crescendo, ritardando*, etc.) are interpreted using our proposed model based on the analysis of human expressive performances. A learned polyphonic expression model predicts using conditional random fields the melodic and harmonic expressive actions. The intensity of expression ("expressive depth") of a generated performance is controlled using a scaling ratio. Users can obtain expressive performances in both MP3 and MIDI formats (Fig. 6.10).

Expressive musical symbols are key in performing a piano piece because they provide basic instructions for the expressive performance. Hence, automatic interpretation of musical symbols is essential for automatic piano rendition. Polyhymnia interprets musical symbols with a proposed exponential model and a Gaussian noise model based on an analysis of human piano performances.

---

[3] Polyhymnia is one of the nine muses in Greek mythology, and it also means *choral poetry* or *multiple hymns*.

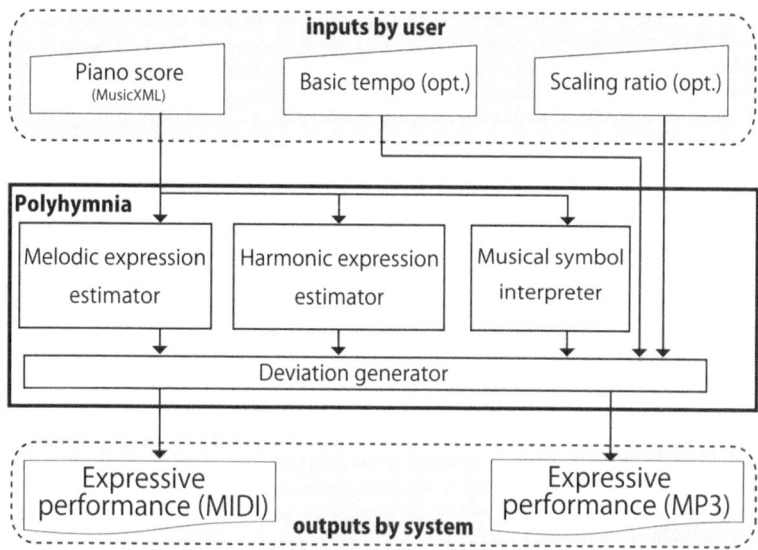

Fig. 6.10 Polyhymnia architecture

Table 6.5 Statistics of human performer interpretation of dynamic markings. Averages and standard deviations were estimated from 15 performances of F. Chopin's piano pieces interpreted by V. Ashkenazy in CrestMuse PEDB. Note that *ppp* and *mp* did not occur in the analyzed performances

	ppp	*pp*	*p*	*mp*	*mf*	*f*	*ff*	*fff*
Upper staff								
Occurrence (frequency)	–	157	2,087	–	67	1,490	418	19
Average (MIDI velocity)	–	50	52	–	58	67	76	98
Std. deviation (MIDI velocity)	–	14	15	–	8	15	16	2
Lower staff								
Occurrence (frequency)	–	150	3,169	–	53	1,538	353	12
Average (MIDI velocity)	–	37	37	–	47	57	73	101
Std. deviation (MIDI velocity)	–	13	11	–	9	20	19	11

6.4.2   Automatic Interpretation of Expressive Musical Symbols

6.4.2.1 Expression Markings

Dynamic markings such as *p*, *mf*, and so forth can be mapped to concrete MIDI velocity values. To develop a set of mappings, 15 performances of V. Ashkenazy in CrestMuse PEDB were statistically analyzed. Table 6.5 shows the result and indicates that the interpretations of each marking were widely distributed and that the interpretations in upper and lower staff were different for all dynamic marks.

More specifically, the lower staff markings were performed more softly than those in the upper staff. When interpreting dynamic markings automatically, a given marking could be mapped to multiple possible concrete values. However for the sake of simplicity, Polyhymnia maps given markings to the estimated mean values for upper and lower staff for that marking, respectively. (This could easily be extended to a more advanced mapping system for different marking occurrences.)

Wedges such as *crescendo*, *diminuendo*, and *ritardando* should be mapped into gradual changes of loudness or tempo. Human perception is that loudness and instantaneous tempo change gradually when sound intensity and tempo in BPM are changing exponentially. Furthermore, human performers implement such changes in various exponential strategies. In the case of *ritardando*, the human interpretation of the mark can be modeled using Eq. 6.22. d_0 is the start velocity or tempo, β is the parameter for an expression depth, and α is the parameter for the change trajectory "shape." If α is set to 1.0, then energy and tempo in BPM change exponentially, and this will be perceived by a listener as natural gradual change.

$$d_t = d_0(\beta \cdot t^\alpha + 1), \tag{6.22}$$

where d_t is loudness and t is time.

With different settings of α and β, each occurrence of a wedge can be mapped onto various exponential forms. For the sake of simplicity, Polyhymnia interprets all occurrences of a particular wedge with the same parameter values. However, as with dynamic markings, this can be easily improved by the automated determination of separate parameter values for separate occurrences of a wedge.

6.4.2.2 Ornaments

Mordents, turns, trills, and grace notes are performed with additional notes. Since such additional notes decorate their parent note, we will assume that their loudness is determined using their parent note. However, a human performer is not able to implement a note sequence with a constant velocity. If we assume that these motor errors follow a Gaussian distribution, loudness in MIDI velocity of the ith successive note d_i can be modeled as

$$d_i = d_0 + \mathcal{N}(0, \sigma^2) \tag{6.23}$$

where d_0 is the loudness of the parent note. σ^2 controls the fluctuation range of the loudness.

Arpeggios indicate that the onset time of each note in a chord should be delayed successively. Since a human performer is not able to implement a constant delay between notes, we will assume that such a delay contains Gaussian noise. Then, the onset time of ith chord note d_i can be modeled as

$$d_i = d_0 + i \cdot \Delta + \mathcal{N}(0, \sigma^2) \tag{6.24}$$

where Δ is a delay time and d_0 is the onset time of the lowest chord note.

Table 6.6 Test pieces for the experimental evaluation. Note that not all of the test pieces were included in the training performances for both models

ID	Composer	Piece	Tempo
CF	F. Chopin	Mazurka No. 5, Op. 7-1	Fast
CS	F. Chopin	Sonata No. 2–3, Op. 35, Trauer Marsch	Slow
MF	W. A. Mozart	Sonatina No. 5–3, KV. 439	Fast
MS	W. A. Mozart	Marche Funebre, KV. 453a	Slow
RT	S. Joplin	The Entertainer (ragtime)	Middle
GR	E. Grieg	7 Lyric Pieces, 7 Remembrance, Op. 71	Slow

6.4.3 Experimental Evaluation

An automatic music performance system should be able to render pieces *not included in its training set* in various compositional styles. In order to evaluate Polyhymnia in this respect, piano pieces in various compositional styles were rendered with the system, and 19 human listeners[4] evaluated them. We rendered six out-of-training-set pieces with Polyhymnia, as shown in Table 6.6. Note that the test pieces included not only F. Chopin and W. A. Mozart's pieces but also E. Grieg and S. Joplin's pieces, whose compositional styles are quite different to those of the training pieces.

In order to test rendering expressive performances with different performance styles, we trained two different models: the *Ashkenazy model* trained with 15 performances[5] of V. Ashkenazy and the *Gould model* trained with seven performances of G. Gould.[6] We prepared five performances for each piece: without expression (D), by musical symbol interpretation only (E), generated with *Ashkenazy model* (S1), generated with *Gould model* (S2), and by a human performer (H). Details of these generated pieces were unknown to the listeners, and once again their "human likeness" and musicality were evaluated using 6-level scales.

Figures 6.11 and 6.12 show the generated performances of CS and RT, respectively, performed with the *Ashkenazy model* and *Gould model*. From those figures, we can see that the two generated performances are expressively differentiated. For example, instantaneous tempo and loudness exhibit different fluctuations in the two models, and those fluctuations have different ranges. Specifically, the fluctuation range of the *Ashkenazy model* is wider than that found in the *Gould model*. In addition, many more notes were found to be performed *staccato* in the performance generated with the *Gould model*.

---

[4] Two professional musicians, 13 hobbyist musicians, and 2 nonmusicians participated in the listening experiments.

[5] F. Chopin, Prelude No. ~ 1, 4, 7, 15, 20, Etude Op. ~ 10-3, 10–4, 25–11, Waltz Op. ~ 18, 34–2, 64–2, 69–1, 69–2, Nocturne No. ~ 2 and 10.

[6] W. A. Mozart, Piano Sonata KV279-1, 279–2, 279–3, 331–1, 545–1, 545–2 and 545-3.

F. Chopin, Piano Sonata No. 2-3, Opus 35, Trauer Marsch, Measure 13-16

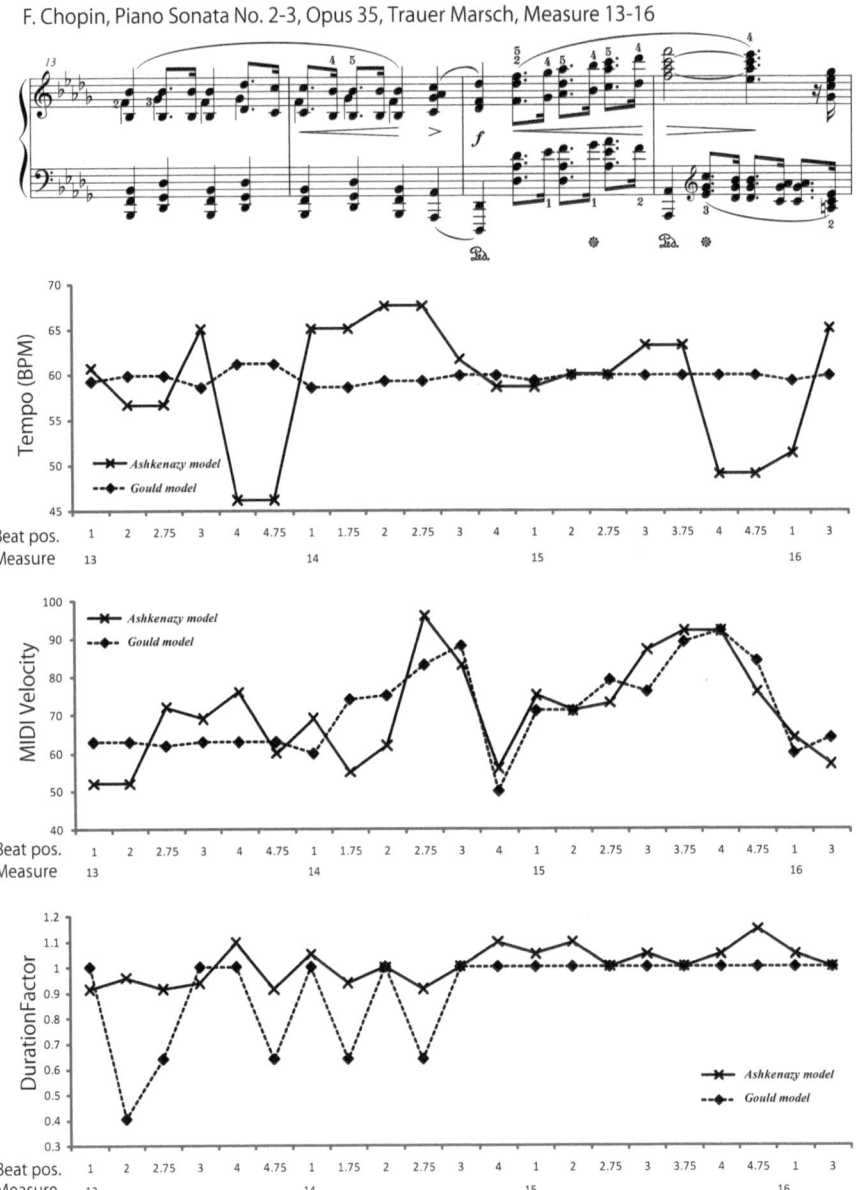

Fig. 6.11 Generated performances of F. Chopin, Piano Sonata No. 2, the 3rd movement, Trauer Marsch, Op. 35 with *Ashkenazy model* and *Gould model*. Note that DurationFactor was calculated with Eq. 6.6, and only the expression of the uppermost voice is shown due to the space limitation

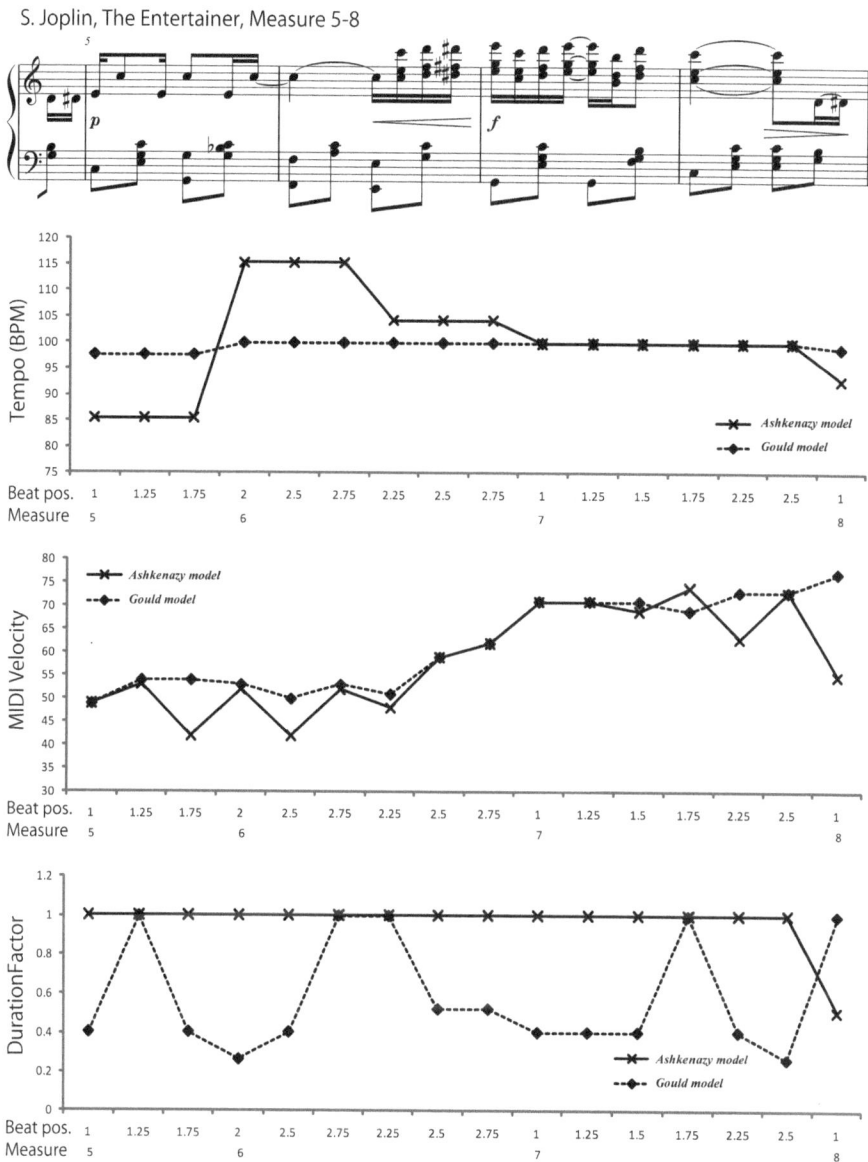

Fig. 6.12 Generated performances of S. Joplin, The Entertainer, with *Ashkenazy model* and *Gould model* (excerpts). Note that DurationFactor was calculated with Eq. 6.6, and only the expression of the uppermost voice is shown due to the space limitation

Figure 6.13 shows the results of the listening experiments for generation quality (human likeness and musicality). Looking at the average scores of the six test pieces, analysis of variance on those average differences with $p < 0.05$ indicates that E, S1, and S2 achieved better scores than D. This indicates that

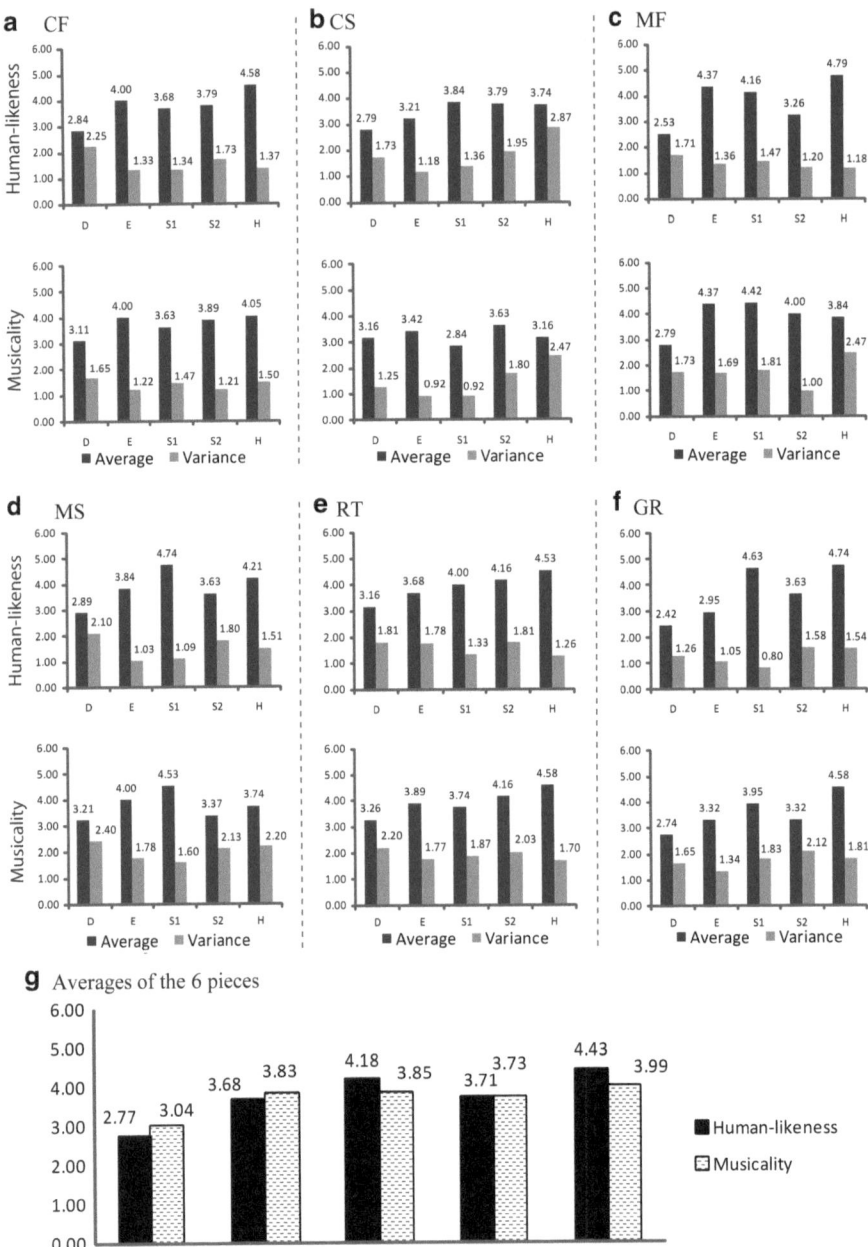

Fig. 6.13 Results of the listening experiments for generation quality. Average scores and variances of each piece (**a–f**). Average human likeness and musicality of the six pieces (**g**)

performances generated by Polyhymnia sounded better than nonexpressive performances. Score differences between S1 and H were not significant. This means that performances generated with the *Ashkenazy model* gave the impression of human expressive performance. In some piece, score differences between S2 and H were not significant. This means that only some performances generated by the *Gould model* gave the impression of human expressive performance. These experimental results show that the system is able to obtain two different expressive performances with two different models.

This means that it should be possible to obtain various performances utilizing models trained with different data sets.

In order to render an automatic performance in a specific style, the trained model should reflect the style found in training data set. To examine whether models were successfully reflecting certain performance styles, we conducted listening experiments for style identification. In these experiments, we used the performance samples S1 and S2 for the six pieces. Each listening experiment was divided into the two parts: a training phase and an evaluation phase. In the training phase, participants listened to three performances of three pieces[7] generated with the *Ashkenazy model* and another three performances of the same three pieces generated with the *Gould model*. The purpose of the training phase was to give familiarity with the styles that the *Ashkenazy model* and *Gould model* were reflecting and to train participants to distinguish these styles. Note that the pieces used in the training phase were completely different from the pieces used in the evaluation phase. In the evaluation phase, participants listened to S1 and S2 for the six pieces, as shown in Table 6.6, in a random order, and they evaluated each sample by answering which style they attributed to the given performance sample. Participants were limited to selecting one of the two possible answers, S1 or S2.

Figure 6.14 shows the results of these listening experiments for style identification. In the case of the performances generated with *Ashkenazy model*, five out of the six performances were identified as S1 by over 50% of the participants, and the average identification rate was 73.6%. This supports the idea that the *Ashkenazy model* reflected the style exhibited by its training performances. However, 63% of the participants identified Chopin's mazurka (CF) as S2, not as S1. A mazurka piece has a waltz-like accompaniment, which is usually performed in a *staccato*-like way. Such a *staccato*-like performance style is one of the distinguishable characteristics of S2, a possible reason for CF-S1 being ambiguously identified.

In case of the performances generated with *Gould model*, five out of the six performances were identified as S2 by over 50% of the participants, and the average identification rate was 73.6%. This means that *Gould model* was also reflecting the style found in the training performances. However, 58% of the participants identified Grieg's piece (GR) as S1, not as S2. The notes of the uppermost voice in GR-S2 were

---

[7] W. A. Mozart, Klavierstück, KV. 33, W. A. Mozart, Sonatina No. 41, KV. 439, F. Chopin, Mazurka No. 19, Op. 30.

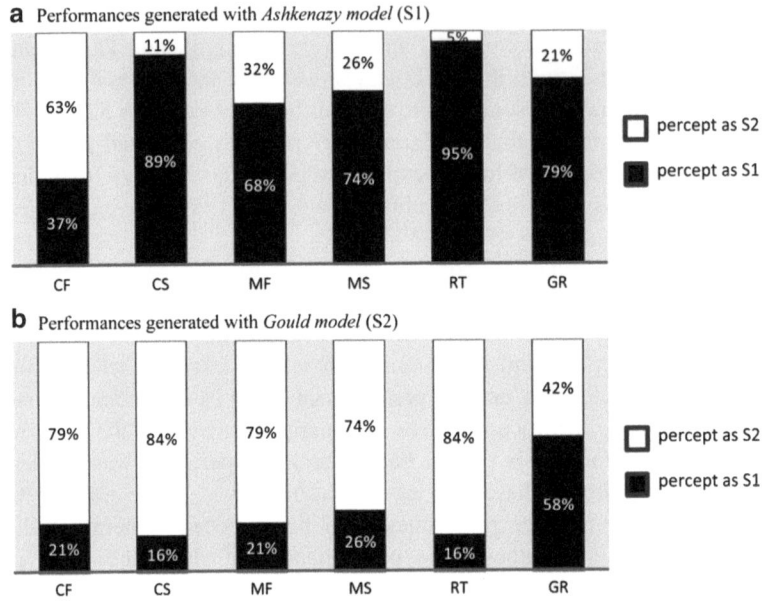

Fig. 6.14 Results of the listening experiments for style identification. Identification results of 6S1 that were predicted with *Ashkenazy model* (**a**) and 6S2 that were predicted with *Gould model* (**b**)

not performed in a *staccato*-like way, due to its melodic compositional structure, and this may be a possible reason why GR-S2 was ambiguously identified.

Those results indicate that both the *Ashkenazy model* and the *Gould model* reflected the performance styles of the training data sets and that the performances generated with each model had a consistent performance style. This means that it should be possible to obtain a variety of models reflecting different performance styles utilizing our proposed methodology.

6.5   Conclusion

In this chapter, we have presented a statistical model for expressive polyphonic piano rendition. We have discussed polyphonic expression in piano music, including key influencing elements in a piano score, monophonic and polyphonic features in musical expression, and the diversity of polyphonic expression. We have also discussed the modeling of statistical relationships between compositional structures and note expression based on an approximation of melodic and harmonic relations and presented a modeling of these relations using conditional random fields. Experimental results indicated that generated performances with the model exhibited polyphonic expression and created the impression of humanlike expressiveness. We have introduced an automatic expressive piano performance system called Polyhymnia which incorporates mathematical models for automatic interpretation of musical symbols. Experimental results for Polyhymnia indicated that the system generated expressive piano performances, that the performances reflected learned performance styles from training performances, and that they were perceptually distinguishable by human listeners.

Performing a piano piece is a complex human behavior, so a number of challenging problems still remain in improving machine-rendered piano performance. One is the improving of the interpretation of musical symbols. Although musical symbols have explicit meanings, their actual interpretation varies according to context. To generate these variations, we proposed mathematical parametric models for musical symbol interpretation. However, Polyhymnia automatically interprets musical symbols with fixed parameter values, and we believe that a statistical approach to determine parameter values for each occurrence of a musical symbol would improve the machine-rendered expressiveness of a piano performance. Another challenging problem is to model the coupling between tempo and loudness. Our approach incorporates a strong assumption that all expression parameters in the piano performance are independent of each other. However, some studies of human expressive piano performance show that tempo and loudness are sometimes coupled. For example, a tempo decrease sometimes leads to a loudness decrease [26]. We believe that modeling tempo-loudness coupling could improve a machine-rendered performance. The final challenge we highlight here is the need for a method for the accurate extraction of score information, a key part for constructing a robust automatic performance system. The effective range of some musical symbols is ambiguous. For example, it is easy to find a *rit.* mark without an *a tempo* mark. A human performer still can understand where the tempo should return to its original value. However, this is a difficult task for computers since there are no explicit rules for determining such a termination. A false extraction of score information could lead to an unpleasant performance, and therefore, a method for accurate extraction will greatly help the construction of a robust automatic performance system.

Acknowledgments This work was partially funded by CrestMuse Project of Japan Science and Technology Agency and supported by Samsung Scholarship Foundation.

Questions

1. What is one of the key factors in the expressive ability of the piano?
2. Name three benefits of the statistical modeling approach for modeling expressive performance.
3. Highlight four features of musical expression in polyphonic performances.
4. What is the difference in the model between harmonic dependency and melodic dependency?
5. What dynamic programming technique can be efficiently used to calculate the musical expression?

6. In what forum has Polyhymnia been independently evaluated, and what was the result?
7. What statistical method with hidden state transition functionality is at the heart of Polyhymnia's learning and modeling algorithm?
8. Why is MusicXML able to encode much better than MIDI?
9. In a crescendo or diminuendo, if sound intensity is changing exponentially, what is the human perception of the loudness?
10. In Polyhymnia, how is loudness determined for mordents, turns, trills, and grace notes?

References

1. Berger AL (1997) The improved iterative scaling algorithm: a gentle introduction, Carnegie Mellon University
2. Bottou L (1991) Stochastic gradient learning in neural networks. In Proceedings of Neuro-Nimes 91
3. Darroch J, Ratcliff D (1972) Generalized iterative scaling for log-linear models. Ann Math Stat 43:1470–1480
4. Flossmann S, Grachten M, Widmer G (2009) Expressive performance rendering: introducing performance context. In Proceedings of the SMC, pp 155–160
5. Friberg A, Bresin R, Sundberg J (2006) Overview of the KTH rule system for musical performance. Adv Cogn Psychol 2(2):145–161
6. Gabrielsson A (1985) Interplay between analysis and synthesis in studies of music performance and music experience. Music Percept 3:59–86
7. Gieseking A, Leimer K (1972) Piano technique. Dover, New York
8. Grindlay G, Helmhold D (2006) Modeling, analyzing, and synthesizing expressive piano performance with graphical models. Mach Learn 65:361–387
9. Hashida M, Matsui T, Katayose H (2008) A new database describing deviation information of performance expressions. In Proceedings of the ISMIR, pp 489–494
10. Huron D, Fantini D (1989) The avoidance of inner-voice entries: perceptual evidence and musical practice. Music Percept 7(1):43–48
11. Lafferty J, McCallum A, Pereira F (2011) Conditional random fields: probabilistic models for segmenting and labeling sequence data. In Proceedings of the ML, pp 282–289
12. Lehvinne J (1972) Basic principle in pianoforte playing. Dover, New York
13. Lerdahl F, Jackendoff R (1983) A generative theory of tonal music. MIT Press, Cambridge, MA
14. Mazzola G (2002) The topos of music – geometric logic of concept, theory, and performance. Birkenhäuser, Basel/Boston
15. MusicXML, Recordare llc., http://www.recordare.com/musicxml
16. Palmer C (1997) Music performance. Ann Rev Psychol 48:115–138
17. Pancutt R (2003) Accents and expression in piano performance. In: Niemöller KW (ed) Perspektiven und Methoden einer Systemischen Musikwissenschaft, Systemische Musikwissenschaft. Peter Lang, Frankfurt am Main, pp 163–185
18. Pietra SD, Pietra VD, Lafferty J (1995) Inducing features of random fields. Technical Report, CMU-CS-95-144, Carnegie Mellon University
19. Repp BH (1992) Diversity and commonality in music performance: an analysis of timing microstructure in Schumann's "Trämerei". J Acoust Soc Am 92(5):2546–2568
20. Sha F, Pereira F (2003) Shallow parsing with conditional random fields. In Proceedings of Human Language Technology, NAACL
21. Sundberg J, Askenfelt A, Frydén L (1983) Musical performance: a synthesis-by-rule approach. Comp Music J 7(1):37–43

22. Suzuki T, Tokunaga T, Tanaka H (1999) Case-based approach to the generation of musical expression. In Proceedings of the IJCAI, pp 642–648
23. Teramura K, Okuma H (2008) Gaussian process regression for rendering music performance. In Proceedings of the ICMPC
24. Teramura K, Maeda S (2010) Statistical learning of tempo variation for imitating piano performance (in Japanese). IPSJ Tech Rep., vol. 85, no. 12
25. Wallach HM (2002) Efficient training of conditional random fields. Master's thesis, University of Edinburgh
26. Widmer G, Dixon S, Goebl W, Pampalk E, Tobudic A (2003) In search of the Horowitz factor. AI Mag 24(3):111–130

Evaluation of Computer Systems for Expressive Music Performance

7

Roberto Bresin and Anders Friberg

Abstract

In this chapter, we review and summarize different methods for the evaluation of CSEMPs. The main categories of evaluation methods are (1) comparisons with measurements from real performances, (2) listening experiments, and (3) production experiments. Listening experiments can be of different types. For example, in some experiments, subjects may be asked to rate a particular expressive characteristic (such as the emotion conveyed or the overall expression) or to rate the effect of a particular acoustic cue. In production experiments, subjects actively manipulate system parameters to achieve a target performance. Measures for estimating the difference between performances are discussed in relation to the objectives of the model and the objectives of the evaluation. There will be also a section with a presentation and discussion of the Rencon (Performance Rendering Contest). Rencon is a contest for comparing the expressive musical performances of the same score generated by different CSEMPs. Practical examples from previous works are presented, commented on, and analysed.

7.1 Introduction

Once a computer system for expressive music performance has been designed and implemented, the next step is to evaluate it. Evaluation has been briefly discussed in the first chapter of this book, but will now be looked at in more detail. Evaluation can focus on different aspects of a computer-generated performance. For example,

R. Bresin (✉) • A. Friberg
Department of Speech, Music & Hearing, KTH Royal Institute of Technology,
Lindstedtsvägen 24, 100 44 Stockholm, Sweden
e-mail: roberto@kth.se; afriberg@kth.se

A. Kirke and E.R. Miranda (eds.), *Guide to Computing for Expressive Music Performance*, 181
DOI 10.1007/978-1-4471-4123-5_7, © Springer-Verlag London 2013

it is common practice among researchers to verify if the effect produced by a new performance rule corresponds to what a musician would have done in the same musical situation. However, the performance produced by a musician is much complex than the effect produced by a single rule; it is therefore important to verify if the particular CSEMP produces realistic performances, i.e. if they sound as if they were created by a human player. The quality of automatic performances can vary on a scale that goes from as *performed by a beginner* at the bottom to as *performed by an expert musician* at the top.

While drawing conclusions from, for example, measured data is difficult, a model in the sense we discuss here attempts to generalize the conclusions even further by predicting outcome for new data. Thus, the evaluation of a model becomes even more important. It is not so simple that one could devise one evaluation method that would fit all models. On the contrary, testing and evaluation is a multifaceted process that is strongly coupled to both the method used and the specific research questions addressed and as suggested by Widmer and Goebl [1] – possibly even a separate research question in itself.

So what is it that we want to evaluate? Music performance is a complex human activity involving a number of human and cultural aspects. The decisions of the performer are influenced by a number of factors of which only a few of them are related to the score. These can include past experience, analysis of the score, expressive intention, cultural context and conventions, the audience, the room, etc. Thus, as is also evident in recordings, a given piece can be interpreted in a number of ways even by the same performer, implying that a model using only the score as input data can never fit perfectly to recorded performances. Many of the early computational models focused almost entirely on the relationship between the score and the performance. In the last decade or so, there has been an expansion of the horizon to include also the expressive intention of the performer in terms of different semantic descriptions such as the emotional expression (e.g. [2, 3]).

Two main evaluation methods can be identified. One could either do a fit to measurements by comparing the outcome of the model with measured performances or perform a perceptual evaluation using listening experiments in which subjects rate different aspects of the performances produced by the model.

There are a number of different aspects relating to the evaluation and to the aim of the study:

- Generality – how well does the model describe (or differentiate between) different performers, pieces, musical genres, and so forth?
- Flexibility – does the model try to approximate and generalize only existing performances, or can it adapt to different expressive intentions?
- Properties of the model – many aspects can be identified, such as simplicity, number of parameters, explicit/implicit description, and closeness to human models/perception.

In its simplest form, a CSEMP can be seen as a *black box* that receives a musical score in input and produces an expressive performance at the output (see Fig. 7.1). In the following sections, we will learn some of the methods that make it possible to evaluate this black box.

Fig. 7.1 A CSEMP can be seen as a black box that receives a musical score in input and produces an expressive performance at the output

7.2 Evaluation Methods

7.2.1 Comparison with Ground Truth Data

It is often relatively straightforward to compare the outcome of a model with measurements of performances by real musicians. Two different methods can be identified: comparison with manual expert annotation and comparison with real performance data.

7.2.1.1 Data from Expert Musicians

This usually involves data that are not direct performance measurements. For example, it could be an analysis of the score. One such example of this is the punctuation rule described below. A key issue dealing with evaluation is the quality of the ground truth data. It is not feasible to obtain one set of data that is consistent in all cases. Although models of performance use the score to infer the resulting performance, in most cases it is not only the surface structure in terms of the symbols in the score that is needed as input. Often some kind of analysis of the score is required for utilization in further processing. For example, if a phrasing rule is modelled, the system needs to know where the phrases start and end. This implies that two models are needed in a chain: the analysis model and the performance realization model. The analysis model could be the time-span reduction analysis as used by Todd [4], a manual annotation by an expert, or even inferred automatically from performances. Initially, one might hope that the analysis ground truth is rather consistent. That is, different experts provide the same analysis for the same piece. Unfortunately, this is not the case. Most methods of musical analysis include an interpretative element. However, on some elementary level, most listeners and experts will agree. Cases like this include the start and end positions of major phrases, clear chord changes, or clear rhythmic groupings. On a deeper level, it is not trivial to provide a general analysis. This becomes dependent on the whole area of music perception and cognition – the complicated process of how we form perceptual higher-level structures from an auditory stream. This is not helped by composers, since a common compositional tool is to work with the boundaries of this perception by contrasting the expected (easily perceived structure) with unexpected or contrasting elements. While this creates tension and interest in the listener, it makes the modelling more difficult.

If we go back to the expert annotation, the conclusion is that generating the ground truth data based on analysis can be rather problematic. A further complication is that the variances in two computational models due to these types of differences are usually non-linear. For example, if a certain analysis approach was used for a phrasing model, while a performer uses a different analysis model (which in most cases will not be explicit anyway), then the resulting fit for the measurement comparison will not be good. In order to deal with this problem, the ground truth data needs to be carefully collected and analysed. In order to ensure some generality, data from several experts should be collected and the results analysed in terms of general trends. The problem of non-linearity implies that it is usually not possible to take an average value over all the experts, possibly leading to the constraint that only individual results can be used. Previous work in this direction has been sparse, and there is a need for further studies in this area.

As an example, we will look at the *punctuation rule* in the KTH rule system (a system discussed in other chapters in this book). When we developed the punctuation rule [5], we ultimately used the annotation of one expert only, namely Lars Frydén, our long-term collaborator and inspirer for the rule system. In this rule, we aimed to automatically identify small melodic units consisting of approximately 1–7 notes. The aim was not primarily to find the melodic grouping as investigated in previous work (e.g. [6, 7]), which was based on a more theoretical and perceptual ground, but rather to find boundaries that were suitable to mark in the performance with a small micro-pause. One concrete difference is that the punctuation also allows for groups consisting of a single note.

The rule was first developed using analysis-by-synthesis on a step-by-step basis, adding different sub-rules that each used a small context of five notes (inspired by Gestalt principles). About 50 different melodies were manually annotated, giving the position of the melodic boundaries, i.e. the punctuation positions. The final weights of the different sub-rules were optimized using an automatic procedure on half of the annotated melodies. Due to the non-linearity of the system (e.g. a small change in a weight can result in a switch of note position), a simple grid-based search was done on the weight parameters to find the optimal solution given the annotated melodies.

Unfortunately, we do not have any data on the accuracy of the punctuation rule in its initial formulation, but there was certainly a notable increase in the accuracy after optimization. Our interpretation was that this procedure successfully found the optimal solution within the limitation given by the context of the low-level sub-rules. Thus, the differences could mainly be attributed to aspects not covered in the model such as the influence of metre, text, and higher-level grouping.

Using one expert in this way leads to results that are limited in scope. As discussed earlier, it is clear that a general model that suits everybody and that defines the 'average' point-of-view cannot be formulated, in this case due to the non-linear behaviour of the problem itself. However, if the underlying principles (in this case, the sub-rules) are expressing important aspects that the experts have in common, it is then possible to model an interpretation of various experts through different combinations of weights operating on the underlying principles.

A parallel model for punctuation was also developed, using a neural network design based on previous models used for modelling music performance [8]. We were then able to compare two completely different design methods: the rather ad hoc-developed analysis-by-synthesis method, with a more general data prediction algorithm (although the latter also includes an element of ad hoc design methodology). The neural network model was, for technical reasons, optimized on a rather small subset of the annotated melodies. Given that the rule used to train the network was developed and annotated by the same expert, it was not surprising that the automatic system using neural networks performed slightly worse than the purely rule-based model. (The network did, however, exhibit some of the same behaviour in relation to the basic Gestalt principles.)

7.2.1.2 Data from Measurements

A straightforward method for involving data from measurements is optimizing a model based on a set of measurements of performances. The evaluation is then, to a certain extent, given, considering the development method. That is, a measure of closeness-of-fit for the model development procedure will also provide a measurement for evaluation. An obvious characteristic of a method developed in this way is its strong coupling to the measurements, which can be both a drawback and an advantage. One positive effect is that the scope of the rule is clearly defined by the database that has been used. If, however, a model is trying to capture a more general principle of performance, then it has to be evaluated using a large number of different examples.

Obtaining good data can be a tedious and/or challenging process. For an overview of measurement techniques, see [9, 10]. An ecological element seems to be key in these cases. That is, the best measurements may be obtained from commercial recordings in which playing errors are minimal and the resulting performance is close to the intention of the performer. However, working with commercial recordings implies that the performance data often needs to be extracted manually for each note in a tedious procedure using a waveform or spectrogram display (e.g. [11, 12]). Such extraction is also limited to timing data, mostly onsets. Other parameters such as dynamics are difficult to extract, although in this case a reasonable approximation can be obtained from the instantaneous sound level (e.g. [13]). Recently, automatic and semi-automatic methods have been used with some success. If the automatic recognition of, for example, tone onsets is combined with a computer tool for manual correction, then the whole annotation procedure can be made more efficient [9, 10].

As discussed by De Poli [14], the evaluation metrics for estimating the closeness-of-fit to data are more or less an open issue. This makes it problematic to compare the outcome of different studies. First of all, one has to choose the proper representation of the data. For example, when investigating timing, a number of different possibilities are available. When looking at temporal variations on the note level, the absolute IOI (inter-onset interval) of a fixed note value can be used, or the relative IOI from a baseline performance (e.g. a nominal or a neutral performance [2]), or the instant tempo (the inverse of the IOI).

One possible standard method for the comparison of different performances would be to use the Euclidian distance (root mean squared difference). This is the standard statistical measure in, for example, regression analysis. Other possibilities are the mean of the absolute difference ([15]; see below) or the maximum difference. A key issue here is to relate the evaluation metrics to a more general perceptual model of the parameter variation. Unfortunately, such a model is still largely unformulated. One approach is to relate it to the just noticeable deviation (JND) of the musical parameters. This then defines the floor at which a certain performance variation remains unnoticed. For this purpose, previous timing studies have been summarized according to different classes of timing variations, such as the displacement of a single onset or a change in tempo [16]. This showed that the JND behaves in two different ways depending on if the IOI is higher or lower than about 250 ms. However, this data based on isolated cases (isochronous sequences) can be hard to apply in a complex musical situation. Also, the JND is highly dependent on the context, such that an expected lengthening is much harder to detect [17]. Nevertheless, the use of the JND baseline can be useful, in particular, for estimating the relative importance of performance variables such as dynamics and timing, as applied by Zanon and De Poli [18, 19].

To give an example, we will discuss the development of the *phrase arch rule* in the KTH system (also discussed in Chap. 1) and its comparison with performance measurements [15] (see also [1]). The phrase arch rule was developed as an extension and alteration of the phrasing model presented by Todd [4, 20]. While the model by Todd was based on a time-span reduction analysis, providing a rather fixed result based on the analysis, this formulation was parameterized into a tool that would allow modelling of a larger number of different performances as observed in measurements. Thus, the problem was largely to find a model with the smallest number of parameters that could still reasonably fit the data. One basic restriction was that all phrases belonging to the same hierarchical level were performed in the same manner, i.e. with the same amount of deviation from score. It resulted in a set of eight parameters that could modify the phrase shape for a specified phrasing level. Later, the rule was modified so that curves mimicking human hand gestures could be also used [21].

The model was tested on 28 performances of Schumann's *Träumerei* as measured by Repp [11]. In this case, we used a multi-phrase arch operating on different levels, resulting in a total of 18 parameters that were optimized using a simple greedy algorithm. The final fit could, on average, explain almost 50% of all performance variations, however with rather large individual variations. Apparently, some of the performers used a similar phrasing approach, while others used differing performance principles. Using only one rule, phrase arch, meant we did not a priori expect to predict all variations. An example of good fit is shown in Fig. 7.2.

Subsequent testing has been done using a Mozart piano performance [22], which revealed a positive and significant correlation between the performance and the phrase arch rule in most parts of the piece.

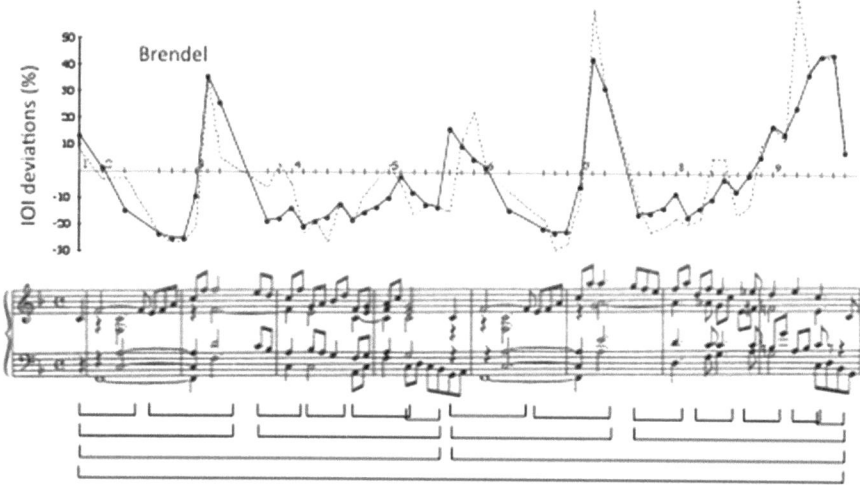

Fig. 7.2 An example of the resulting parameter optimization of the phrase arch rule. The solid line is the rule-generated performance, and the dotted line a performance by Brendel

Zanon and De Poli [18] made an extensive and independent study trying to match the KTH rule system to performance measurements. They defined a distance measure in a so-called pre-Hilbert space that would allow a better optimization of the rule parameters. By using weights in the distance measure related to the just noticeable differences (JND), they optimized all the rule parameters simultaneously using a composite distance measure, including IOI, duration, and sound level. They used one composition performed multiple times with different expressive intentions on a Yamaha Disklavier by one pianist. For different versions of a 'natural' performance, the phrase arch was found to be used in moderate positive quantities. Other rules (e.g. punctuation rule, negative duration contrast) were more pronounced than this, while some other rules obtained rather weak couplings. It was also found that there were consistent variations of the rules for the different expressive intentions, mostly in accordance with previous literature. Trying to overcome the limitation of a fixed rule amount, they also tried to fit a model in which the rule quantities were allowed to vary for different sections of the piece. However, the results were rather mixed results [19].

The fitting of the phrase arch rule (and other rules) to performance data has, in general, yielded mixed results. However, the rule has been in use for a long time, and it is immediately apparent for a listener that the rule is effective for marking the phrases. This has also been confirmed in studies using rule-generated performances (e.g. the GERM model [21]). Thus, there is a discrepancy between evaluation of generated performances with listening experiments and the fitting of data to measurements. This is natural if it is assumed that the generated performances are just a subspace of all possible performances within a certain musical tradition (see also [23]).

So in summary, the phrase arch rule has been tested in three different studies. However, only one musical example was used for each study, and two of them included only one performer. This is obviously not sufficient for drawing any general conclusions about a performance model. It did reveal that the limitation of keeping the rule amount constant during a whole piece is not in accordance with data from real performances. Unfortunately, letting the rule parameters vary for each phrase is not an alternative due to the resulting excessive number of parameters. This indicates that there is need for a refined formulation of the phrase arch rule.

7.2.1.3 Machine Learning Methods

Another modelling approach is to define the modelling as a general data prediction task, similar to methods used in, for example, music information retrieval. Then, given a sufficiently large and diverse database, any general method used in machine learning can be tested, for example, neural networks, support vector regression, or Bayesian modelling (e.g. [24]). While these approaches rarely utilize underlying principles – for example, in music perception – they have the advantage of a strong mathematical foundation with many powerful tools and methods. These can help to validate the modelling and thus also the evaluation, for example, feature selection methods and cross-validation. These methodologies and approaches can, to a certain extent, also be applied in more traditional studies using, for example, multiple linear regression. Cross-validation involves testing the predictive power of the model on data that has not been used for the optimization, switching which data is used for modelling and which for testing. While this is an obvious method of evaluation for any model, it is still seldom used outside the field of machine learning.

Generally, models using machine learning methods are developed using some kind of learning phase in which the model is trained on data from measurements. Thus, as was mentioned earlier, the default evaluation method is implicit in the methodology and provided by the measure of closeness-of-fit to the data.

Modelling of performance data with machine learning methods can be done in a 'black box' fashion. So various machine learning methods can be applied to a problem on a trial and error basis – and then the best performing algorithm, chosen. This is mathematically very elegant and powerful. However, it is often the case that they provide little insight into the underlying process; they can also be difficult to analyse in terms of how the final system works. So with this approach, we have a well-defined evaluation in terms of the fit to data, but there are significant evaluative aspects missing.

Other elements which can be further examined are the errors themselves. Are the errors small in some sense? Are they close to the target values, or are they more random in character? Often, results are reported stating that the errors are such that a neighbouring performance action class is selected instead of the correct one, but these errors are seldom quantified. Another evaluation approach is to do a listening test with the produced examples. This can provide a more direct perceptual evaluation (in contrast to the model fit, which is only indirectly coupled to perception through the deviation of the different parameters). The complicating factor here is that the perceptual impact of a performance deviation is strongly coupled to the musical structure in the sense that we are more sensitive to variations in important events and less sensitive to expected variations [17]. One example is the study by Friberg and Sundberg [25] (see also [26]) where a model of the *final ritard* was developed using measurements; this was then further evaluated in a listening experiment.

Another example of a model trained on measured data is that of an artificial neural network-based system (ANN) for automatic performance of musical scores developed by Bresin [8]. In this model, ANNs were trained using data from a performance by a professional pianist. The ANNs were able to learn the main expressive strategies used by the pianist, and these could be matched to some of the rules of the KTH rule system.

The research group led by Gerhard Widmer in Vienna and Linz has a long tradition of applying machine learning methods to music performance, some of which is discussed in Chap. 3. They have modelled different aspects such as local-level performance principles, phrasing, and characterizing different performers and have also looked at visualizing expressive parameters. Many of these studies used the complete set of Mozart sonatas as performed by one pianist on a computer-controlled piano and from which most of the performance details were extracted. In a study of local-level performance variations, Widmer [27] developed an inductive rule-learning algorithm that automatically produced a set of 17 classification rules that could explain a surprisingly large proportion of the total variation. The advantage with this approach is that the results are, in many cases, rules that are easy to interpret and understand, and in fact, some of the produced rules were similar to the rules in the KTH rule system.

The evaluation was, in this case, strongly coupled to the method and the outcome of the model. Here, the result was not primarily a performance prediction but a set of general principles. Thus, these generated rules can be evaluated by comparing them to other rule systems, but they can also be investigated in terms of the generality across different performances and other aspects.

7.2.2 Listening Experiments

Listening experiments are among the most popular methods for evaluating CSEMPs. Listening experiments can be of various kinds. For example, subjects may be asked to rate a particular higher-level expressive feature in a performance, such as the emotion conveyed or the overall expression. Or they may be asked to rate the effect of a certain performance feature such as melody lead. In this next section, we present some of the most common methods employed in listening tests.

7.2.2.1 Analysis-by-Synthesis Method

The analysis-by-synthesis method has been used in the design of many CSEMPs. The method involves a designer attempting to formalize a performance principle, applying it to the performance of a score, evaluating the effects with an online listening test, and then adjusting the formalization of the performance principle until the desired expressive effect is achieved.

Most of the performance rules included in the KTH rule system for musical performance (Director Musices) have been designed applying the analysis-by-synthesis method [28]. In this case, either the knowledge of a musical expert, Lars Frydén, or information extracted from real performances was translated into performance rules by a programmer. The effect produced by each performance rule was evaluated by the expert musician and/or by the programmer through listening tests. The rule was then either modified towards producing the desired effect or directly inserted into the performance system.

An example of performance rules designed using the analysis-by-synthesis method is the articulation rules implemented in Director Musices [29], the design and evaluation of which are described in the next section.

Articulation Rules

Music scores often include *legato* and *staccato* marks indicating how to perform certain notes. In this section, we briefly describe how it is possible to design and evaluate rules for the automatic rendering of such notations so that they sound as musically convincing as a human musician performing them.

The starting point of the design was the analysis of the performances recorded on a computer-monitored grand piano, involving two databases. The first database consisted of performances by five skilled pianists of the *Andante* movement of W. A. Mozart's Piano Sonata in G major, KV 545. They were asked to play the piece with nine different expressive intentions: glittering, dark, heavy, light, hard, soft, passionate, flat, and natural. The second database consisted of recordings of 13 Mozart piano sonatas played by a concert pianist. From the databases, we collected the performances of all the notes that were marked staccato and legato in the scores. By comparing the deviations of note durations from their nominal values and by correlating them to the pianists' expressive intentions and the composer's expressive indications in the score (i.e. *adagio, allegro, presto*), we were able to extract trends and to design performance rules that simulated the pianists' deviations in different expressive contexts. Briefly, the *score staccato articulation* rule introduces a micro-pause after a *staccato* tone and shortens its duration. This rule can be used to control the quantity of *staccato* articulation. It is applied to notes marked *staccato* in the score. The *score legato articulation* rule produces an overlap of tones, or *legato*. The rule affects and controls the amount of the overlap time between adjacent tones. The rule can be applied to notes that are marked *legato* in the score (see [29] for a detailed description of the rules).

These two rules have been evaluated by checking that the deviations that they produce roughly reproduce the effects measured in the two databases used for extracting the two rules. Since then, the articulation rules have been successfully used, and indirectly evaluated, in the generation of emotionally expressive performances that have been correctly classified in agreement with the hypotheses made in the GERM model [21].

7.2.2.2 Rating the Effect of a Specific Performance Feature

In many cases, CSEMPs implement a number of rules and principles that produce different effects in the performance. It is therefore desirable to validate in isolation the effect produced by each rule on a certain performance feature. In this section, we present the procedures for rating the effect on two important performance features in piano performance: melody lead and legato articulation.

Melody Lead

In professional performances of piano music, the melody voice tends to anticipate the accompaniment by 20–30 ms. This may be an intuitive attempt at dynamic differentiation. The melody voice is usually played louder than the accompaniment, which may also cause the melody to lead (since the tone production in a grand piano is based on hammers being accelerated towards strings). A hard key strike results in a high hammer velocity, whereas a soft key strike results in a low hammer velocity. Consequently, the hammers will arrive at the strings asynchronously if the keys are depressed with varying force [30]. Presuming that the player strives at playing synchronously, this can easily be modelled and provide more natural performances of piano music played by CSEMPs.

A model of note synchronization [31] has been implemented in pDM, a program for real-time expressive performance [32] which has already been discussed in Chap. 2. The model, based on measurements of the mechanics of a real piano, has been evaluated in a listening test with experienced pianists [33]. The model provides as an emergent effect the so-called melody lead effect, as well as more naturalness in automatic performance of piano music (as shown in Fig. 7.3).

Seven expert pianists (one female, six male, average age 42) took part in an experiment for testing the melody lead effect. The test was divided in two parts. In the first part of the test, the seven participants listened to five pieces of music: 'Träumerei' and 'Der Dichter Spricht' by Schumann, 'Etude op. 10/3' by Chopin, 'KV1e' by Mozart, and 'Emigrantvisa', a Swedish folksong arranged by Jan Johansson. For each example, participants were instructed to adjust the two parameters tempo and synchronization to make it sound 'as realistic as possible'. These five musical examples were presented in random order. To control the two parameters, participants used two physical sliders on an input device. Visual feedback was provided on the screen when the slides were moved. The value of tempo slider ranged between 50% and 200% of the original tempo for each stimulus. The absolute value of the synchronization slider corresponded to the amount of melody lead (or inverted melody lead) being added (implemented as percent of travel time) to each note. Participants could therefore exaggerate the effect of both melody lead and inverted melody lead (similar to a lag effect) by up to 200%. The key expectation was that if participants selected a performance feature as the preferred one, they would not choose the inverted effect, since it would sound unnatural. To force participants to really use their ears, the synchronization slider was randomly mirrored for each stimulus, so that its upper value could correspond either to inverted melody lead or to normal melody lead.

In the second part of the test, the same five pieces were presented. Participants once again adjusted the tempo with a slider but chose the synchronization value by selecting one of three fixed alternatives on the computer screen, in a forced choice fashion. The three alternatives, presented to the participants with non-identifiable

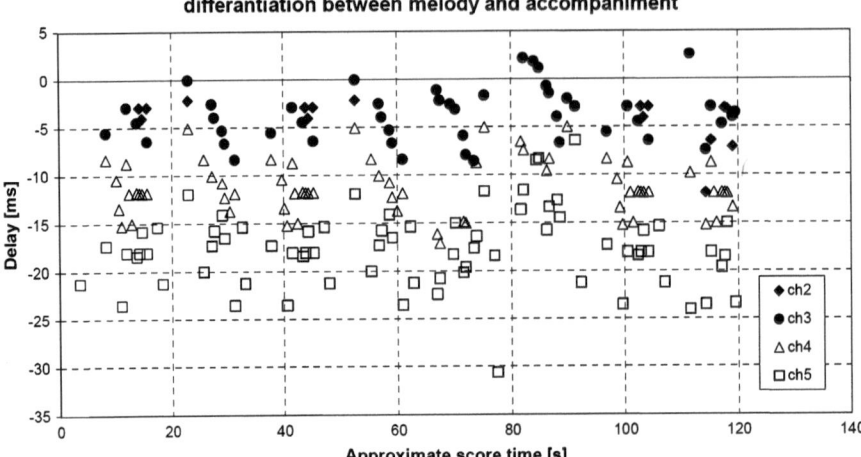

Fig. 7.3 Delay times in Schumann's 'Träumerei' played with a nominal performance, the model of note synchronization applied, and no dynamic differentiation between melody and accompaniment. ch2, ch3, ch4, and ch5 indicate the different voices associated to a specific MIDI channel

labels, corresponded to (1) perfect synchronization, (2) full melody lead effect, and (3) full inverted melody lead effect. The musical examples were presented in random order, and the three versions were randomly distributed among the alternatives. Once again, the participants were instructed to select the preferred tempo with the tempo slider and choose the alternative for synchronization that they perceived as most realistic.

The key results for the first part of the test showed that on average participants-selected positive synchronization values (normal melody lead). 'Etude op. 10/3' by Chopin was the piece performed with the highest level of melody lead. 'Der Dichter Spricht' by Schumann received the lowest average value of melody lead (close to zero).

Results (see Fig. 7.4) indicate that participants preferred positive synchronization (i.e. melody lead) inversely correlated with tempo (−0.76 on a 0.01-level Pearson correlation), and this result matches actual human performance approaches [30]. Negative synchronization values (inverted melody lead effect) were independent from the particular tempo. Negative synchronization is a concept not found in piano music but used for the purpose of this test, and the arbitrary relation to tempo seems thus logical.

Of all the stimuli in the second part of the test, the participants selected full inverted melody lead effect only 6 times; perfect synchronization was selected 20 times, and full melody lead effect 9 times. Results therefore indicate that the melody lead model evaluated in the test simulates subjective perception of typical asynchronous onsets found in piano music.

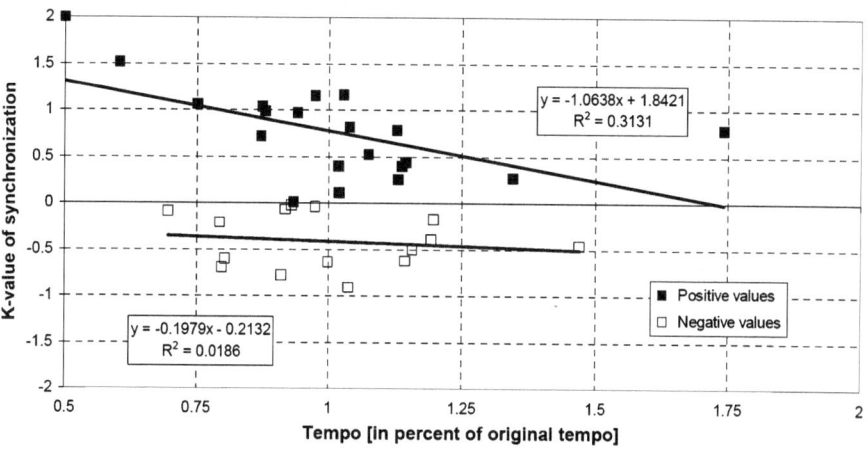

Fig. 7.4 Positive and negative synchronization values plotted separately

Legato Articulation

As has been mentioned, articulation is one of the most important features for the control of expression in music performance. Players make use of *legato* and *staccato* articulations both when following the composer's notation and in the communication of emotional intensions (for an overview, see [34] and [35]; for research experiments on legato articulation, see [36, 37]).

In a study for the identification of the best legato articulation in piano performance, Bruno Repp [36] conducted two experiments, one listening experiment and a production experiment.

In the listening experiment, 15 participants (five of them pianists), with a musical experience ranging from casual music making to more than 10 years of instrument training, were asked to adjust the amount of key overlap times (KOTs) interactively, so as to achieve a specified degree of legato (best legato, minimal legato, maximal legato) in continuously ascending and descending 5-tone sequences. With the term 'best legato', the author meant a legato in which the tones seemed 'optimally connected'. Participants could control the amount of KOT in real time through a software interface running on a computer connected to a computer-controlled grand piano – a Yamaha Disklavier. Each sequence was played in three different registers (second, fourth, and sixth octaves), three different tempi (inter-onset intervals of 520, 779, and 1,039 ms), and with three step sizes between tones (1 semitone, 2 semitones, 3 semitones). This gave a total of 27 conditions.

Among the main results of the listening experiment, it was observed that a key determinant in each of the three degrees of legato was register. In particular, the average KOT for optimal 'best' legato increased from 73 ms in the second octave to 145 ms in the fourth octave and up to 169 ms in the sixth octave. This effect was due to the faster decay of high tones, which reduces acoustic overlap.

In the production experiment, Repp asked nine musically trained pianists (six female, three male) to each perform 36 scores on a Yamaha Disklavier. The pianists were instructed to play the same sequences as used in the perception experiment, at a fixed metronome tempo but in a natural way – and not necessarily with mechanical precision. The intended IOIs were approximately 250, 500, and 1,000 ms. A main result – as in the production experiment – was the observation of a significant register effect: KOTs increased with register.

While a clear difference was found in the perception experiment between the 1-semitone and 2-semitone conditions, this difference was small (and non-significant) in the production experiment. This was probably due to the fact that participants relied on the acoustic feedback only in the perception experiment – they did not have a haptic feedback from the keyboard that was available in the production experiment. Kinematic and haptic feedback is probably also the cause of the increased KOTs from medium to slow tempo in the production experiment (opposite to the effect observed in the listening experiment).

7.2.3   Rating of High-Level Properties: Emotions

There are cases in which investigators are interested in evaluating high-level properties of a performance generated by a CSEMP, such as the overall expression, the degree of naturalness, or the emotional intention. Only a few studies have evaluated the emotional expression of performances generated by CSEMPs. In this section, we briefly present one.

In the evaluation of a computational model of expression in music performance, the GERM model, Juslin and colleagues [21] evaluated the effect of four sources of variability in music performance. The four sources were G *(generative rules)*, which communicate the generative structure in a musical manner; E *(emotional expression)*, which is controlled by the performer's expressive intention; R *(random variations)*, which simulate internal timekeeper variance and motor delay variance; and M *(movement principles)*, which account for the biological motion found in certain features of the performance. The four sources were simulated by the deviations produced by different performance rules included in the Director Musices CSEMP [28]. For example, the G-source was generated by those performance rules that produce effects that help to convey the musical structure to listeners.

A listening test based on a factorial design was conducted for evaluating the effects produced by the four factors, G, E, R, and M. The stimuli were produced using a sampled piano sound and consisted of 16 performances of a simple polyphonic piece of music (Carl Michael Bellman's Epistel No. 48): 2 generative rule conditions (present/absent) × 2 emotional expression conditions (present/absent) × 2 random variation conditions (present/absent) × 2 motion principle conditions (present/absent). Twelve musically trained listeners (six male, six female), aged 21–41 years (mean = 30.5), participated to the listening experiment. All of them had played a musical instrument for at least 2 years, and eight were also members of a choir.

The emotional expression condition was defined by a set of three performance rules producing respectively slower tempo (nominal IOI lengthened by 30%), softer sound level (nominal sound level decreased by 6 dB), and legato articulation. The same rules were found to be effective in communicating sadness in a previous study [3].

Participants were asked to rate the 16 performances on six adjective scales supposed to reflect the four different components: Clear, Gestural, Human, Musical, Sad, and Expressive. As expected by the experimenters, these adjectives were found to be positively correlated with the four GERM components in the following way: Clear (G), Gestural (M), Human (R, M), Musical (G, E, M), Sad (E), and Expressive (G, E, R, M). In particular, the stimuli with the emotional expression condition present were rated as more Sad than other stimuli. This result confirmed that the performance rules used for generating the emotional component were successfully perceived as communicating sadness.

7.2.4 Interactive Listening

A particular form of evaluation that has been made possible by technological developments in more recent years is based on the interactive participation of subjects who manipulate performance parameters in real time, trying to achieve a target performance.

This kind of test can be called an *interactive listening test* and puts the participant in the centre of a production-perception loop. The participant continuously makes changes to the performance of a piece of music until the acoustic result matches the requested quality of the target performance. The requested quality could be a specific emotional intention ('the performance should sound happy') or match the behaviour of a single performance feature ('the performance must be played with the most satisfying level of legato'). The latter case has already been presented in the 'Legato Articulation' section [36].

In this section, we will briefly describe the design of an interactive listening test in which the authors asked 20 participants (2 female, 18 male) to manipulate seven musical variables: tempo, sound level, articulation, phrasing, register, instrument, and attack speed. They were asked to communicate five different emotional expressions (neutral, happy, scary, peaceful, sad) for each of four different scores [38]. The average age of the participants was 33, and they played a musical instrument on average for 22.5 years. The musical structure of the four scores was specifically composed[1] for communicating four different emotions: happiness, sadness, fear, and peacefulness. In particular, the scores differed in pitch height and default tempo.

The equipment used for the experiment consisted of a sound synthesizer (the Vienna Symphonic Library controlled by the Kontakt 2 sampler) and a gesture controller designed and built for the experiment – a box with eight sliders, only seven of which were used for the experiment, with a look similar to that of an

---

[1] The scores were polyphonic and were selected from a battery of stimuli specially composed at Montreal University (www.brams.umontreal.ca/plab/downloads/Emotional_Clips.zip). This battery consisted of 14 scores per emotion. All 14 × 4 scores were rated along four adjective scales (happy, sad, scary, and peaceful) in a previous study [39]. The highest rated and least ambiguous score for each emotion was selected as stimulus in our experiment.

audio mixer. There was also a program for running psychophysical experiments (Skatta[2]) and an adapted version of the pDM tool for interactive expressive control of music performance [32].

For each of the stimuli, Skatta automatically selected the next stimulus (music score to be played) and communicated it to pDM. pDM automatically started playing the new score using the sound sampler Kontakt 2. pDM received data from the slider controller held by the participant which communicated with pDM via the UDP protocol. Skatta logged the changing values of the musical variables based on the participant's manipulation of the seven sliders on the gesture controller; this being done while the participant was rendering the score in an attempt to match the emotion requested by Skatta (through a text message on the computer screen.) Each slider was associated to one of the seven musical variables. Participants were asked to use the gesture controller for adjusting the values of the seven musical variables for communicating five different emotional expressions – neutral, happy, scary, peaceful, and sad – for each of four different scores described in the stimuli section above. Skatta presented the requested emotional expression and the music scores in random order for each participant, for a total of 5 × 4 stimuli per subject. Participants were told to regulate the positions of the sliders to achieve the target performance by changing the performance in real time. Participants were free to pause/stop/repeat each score as many times they wished. When they were satisfied with their rendering of the stimulus, they could move on to the next one by clicking a 'next' button on the Skatta user interface. The last value logged for each slider was used in the analysis of the performances. The next stimulus would then automatically start playing with the same slider values of the previous one. As a consequence, participants were never presented with the original version of the scores, and if it happened, it was by chance. The duration of the experiment was 35 min on average, with a standard deviation of 13 min.

The set-up of this experiment allowed a methodical analysis of the interaction between the emotion of each score and the emotional expression intended by performers. There were two main results: (1) the musical variables were manipulated by participants in the same direction as that reported in previous research on emotional expressive music performance; (2) the mean values of the five musical variables – tempo, sound level, articulation, register, and instrument – were identified for each of the five emotions and found to be independent from the particular score and its emotion. This means that the pDM CSEMP allows for generalization, and the performances that it can generate are independent in expression from the starting score. In conclusion, the performance rules used for the expressive performance rendering are of general applicability.

---

[2] http://skatta.sourceforge.net

7.3 Evaluation in Performance Rendering Contests

Rencon (Performance Rendering Contest) is an international contest initiated in 2002 for comparing expressive performances of the same score generated by different CSEMPs [40–44]. There has been some discussion of Rencon in Chap. 1, but it will now be addressed in detail. Rencon's goal is to foster research into computational models of and methods for the generation of expressive musical performances. The ultimate goal of the Rencon initiative is the development of a performance-rendering machine that will win 'Chopin Concours' by 2050. This can be compared to RoboCup, whose goal is described as: 'By mid-21st century, a team of fully autonomous humanoid robot soccer players shall win the soccer game, complying with the official rules of FIFA, against the winner of the most recent World Cup'. The process of achieving Rencon's goals is expected to span many interrelated research fields and yield several interesting and innovative findings and solutions.

In the past, Rencon has been organized as a workshop with an associated musical contest that provides a forum for presenting and discussing the latest research in automatic performance rendering and, more generally, computer-based music performance research. The methods used for evaluating the performances have changed over the history of Rencon. In the following sections, we present two of the methods used in the past: the one used for the ICMC 2005 Rencon[3] and that used for SMC 2011 Rencon.[4] For more information about the different instantiations of Rencon, please refer to the website http://renconmusic.org.

7.3.1 Evaluation with Formal Listening Tests (Rencon 2005)

For the ICMC 2005 Rencon event, a formal listening test was run to evaluate the performances produced by four different CSEMPs: COPER [45], Director Musices [23], pDM [32], and Pop-E [46]. Ten participants (two female, eight male), average age 30 (min 22, max 40), who played an instrument in average for 16 years (min 4, max 30), were asked to rate the performances along six 'low-high' 11-point scales (0 = very low, 10 = very high):
1. *Level of technical skill* – if a performance sounds like it is technically skilled
2. *Rhythmic accuracy* – level of rhythmic accuracy in the performance
3. *Human* – if a performance sounds like a human created it
4. *Musical* – how musical the performance is
5. *Expressive* – how expressive the performance is
6. *Overall quality* – the overall performance quality

---

[3] http://renconmusic.org/icmc2005/
[4] http://smc2011.renconmusic.org/

Table 7.1 Results of ICMC 2005 Rencon evaluation listening test

System name	Technical	Rhythmic accuracy	Human	Musical	Expressive	Overall quality	Average
Pop-E	5.80	4.98	7.18	5.78	5.79	7.50	5.91
DM (default)	6.94	6.80	5.30	5.54	5.30	5.80	5.98
pDM (fixed)	3.99	50	4.49	3.23	2.88	3.62	3.92
pDM (moving)	68	4.64	5.43	5.62	6.56	5.62	5.67
COPER	2.85	1.77	4.12	2.10	3.74	33	2.92

The detailed instructions given to the participants are shown below:

You will now listen to different versions of a brief piece of music. Your task is to judge each version of the piece by indicating a value (using the computer mouse) on each of the six 'adjective' scales that you can see in front of you. The more you think that a particular 'adjective' applies to a given version, the higher value you should indicate on the corresponding 'adjective' scale. Ten represents maximum of this attribute, and zero represents minimum. The meaning of each 'adjective' will be explained on a separate sheet. Read it carefully, so that you are fully aware of what each scale refers to. Note that you do not have hurry. There is no time limit for the experiment. The important thing is that you are satisfied with your ratings of each version before you move on to the next.

When you have completed the ratings of a certain version, you simply click on the Next-button: this will start the next version. Sometimes, it may feel difficult to make a judgment. Still, try to do your best, and remember that your judgments should be made in relation to the other versions that you hear.

If you like to, you can go back to the previous version by clicking on the Previous-button, and to the first or last versions by clicking on the First-button or on the Last-button respectively.

Please feel free to ask any questions you like before we start the experiment.

The results of the evaluation test are reported in Table 7.1. The pDM program was evaluated based on two performances. One performance (*moving*) was produced by manipulating rule parameters in real time; the other one (*fixed*) was obtained with fixed values for the rule parameters. The performance by Director Musices (DM) was obtained applying its *default* rule palette.

7.3.2 Two-Stage Evaluation Method (Rencon 2011)

For the SMC-Rencon 2011 event, a two-stage evaluation method was adopted. In the first stage (stage I), an expert panel consisting of six experts rated both the scientific novelty of the competing CSEMPs and their usefulness, on a scale from 1 to 5.[5] For each of the CSEMPs, the experts based their judgment both on a written scientific description of the performance system and on the performance of

---

[5] Strong accept = 5, weak accept = 4, borderline = 3, weak reject = 2, strong reject = 1.

Table 7.2 Results of Rencon 2011, stage I

System name	Place number of musicality						Place number of technical quality								
	R1	R2	R3	R4	R5	Rank (a)	R1	R2	R3	R4	R5	R6	Rank (b)	(a) + (b)	Final rank
No. 1 DM	2	4	4	3.5	2	**3**	4	2	1	7	–	3	**2**	5	2
No. 2 usapi	6	4	5	6.5	1	**5**	7	3	6	2	5	6	**7**	12	6
No. 3 Kagurame II	5	6.5	6	5	7	**6**	1	7	2	4	4	7	**4**	10	5
No. 4 VP	4	1	3	1	4	**2**	6	4	4	5	2	5	**5**	7	3
No. 5 Kagurame III	7	6.5	7	6.5	6	**7**	3	6	5	3	6	4	**5**	12	6
No. 6 Shunji System	3	4	2	3.5	5	**4**	5	5	3	6	3	2	**3**	7	3
No. 7 YQX	1	2	1	2	3	**1**	2	1	-	1	1	1	**1**	2	1

R1–R6 means Reviewer 1, Reviewer 2, etc. Each number in the table is the rank calculated from the obtained points by each reviewer. The ranks were calculated on a scale from 1 to 7; 1 corresponds to the highest ranking, and 7 to the lowest
DM Director Musices, *VP* VirtualPhilharmony

a compulsory piece of music, 'A Little Consolation', composed by Tadahiro Murao (2011). A music committee made up of five experts rated the CSEMP performances, also on a scale from 1 to 5. The CSEMPs were then ranked according to their ratings, and these were successively averaged to determine the final ranking. Results of stage I are reported in Table 7.2.

At stage II, the listeners from the SMC audience (77 participants) and Internet voters (about 15) evaluated the performances produced onsite by the CSEMPs on a computer-controlled Yamaha Disklavier grand piano. The competing performances can be found at the Rencon website.[6] At stage II, research groups competing with their CSEMP had to produce onsite an expressive performance of the same piece of music within a 1-h time limit. The piece chosen was an excerpt (the first 61 bars, until the fermata) of the third movement (Rondo – Allegro) of Beethoven Piano Sonata No. 8 Op 13.,[7, 8] Results of Rencon 2011 stage II are reported in Table 7.3.

---

[6] http://smc2011.renconmusic.org/2011/07/15/evaluation-results-stage-ii/

[7] http://imslp.info/files/imglnks/usimg/f/fb/IMSLP30364-PMLP01410-Beethoven_Sonaten_Piano_Band1_Peters_Op13.pdf

[8] http://smc2011.renconmusic.org/2011/07/15/selected-setpiece/

Table 7.3 Results of Rencon 2011, stage II

System name	Performance A			Performance B			(A) + (B)
	Internet	Onsite	Total (A)	Internet	Onsite	Total (B)	
No. 1 CaRo 2.0	56	464	**520**	61	484	**545**	**1065**
No. 2 YQX	64	484	**548**	65	432	**497**	**1045**
No. 3 VirtualPhilharmony	46	452	**498**	32	428	**460**	**958**
No. 4 Director Musices	33	339	**372**	13	371	**384**	**756**
No. 5 Shunji System	24	277	**301**	20	277	**297**	**598**

Internet means the total ratings collected from Internet voters. *Onsite* means the total ratings collected by voters listening at the live performances on site (Note that the CaRo 2.0 system did not participate to stage I of Rencon 2011)

The SMC-Rencon 2011 Award was given to YQX [47], the system reaching the highest total points in both stages. This system is detailed in Chap. 3.

7.4 Conclusion

In this chapter, we have presented the main methods that have been applied in recent years for the evaluation of CSEMPs. It can be seen from this overview that the evaluation methods are heterogeneous and a standard evaluation method has not yet been established. Rencon is one possible way of establishing an evaluation approach that can be applied to different CSEMPs. Therefore, in order to advance the field of computer systems for expressive music performance, we can identify at least two crucial aspects.

Firstly, the evaluation in general has to be taken more seriously. As it is a complicated process, it is natural that a CSEMP is developed with rather limited evaluation. An important aspect is the independent evaluation by other researchers, as this often is leading to lower evaluation scoring. Reasons for this could be that the model is less well understood by other researchers and thus not optimally applied on the examples, or that it is applied on examples that were not the target of the model's original research. Or it may be that an independent testing is simply more objective.

The second major issue concerns the lack of performance data or the limited test material that has been used in many previous system evaluations. The whole field of computer systems for expressive music performance would improve in scientific quality through the creation of new databases of variety of performances, which could then serve as a baseline for comparing different models. It would be particularly useful to initiate a common effort in the research community in similar way to other fields such as in music information retrieval or speech research.

Questions

1. What are the two main evaluation methods that can be identified overall in CSEMPs?
2. What is the difference between generality and flexibility in a model?
3. For the comparison with ground truth data approach, name the three ways of modelling and evaluating a system.
4. In which of the above three approaches is the default evaluation method implicit in the methodology?
5. Describe the analysis-by-synthesis modelling approach.
6. What are the elements which may cause the melody lead effect in human piano playing?
7. Describe an *interaction listening test*.
8. What is one possible way of establishing an evaluation method which could be applied to different CSEMPs?
9. What is an important aspect which could contribute towards evaluation being done more seriously?
10. How might the major issue of lack of performance data and limited test material be addressed by the research community?

References

1. Widmer G, Goebl W (2004) Computational models of expressive music performance: the state of the art. J New Music Res 33(3):203–216
2. Canazza S, De Poli G, Drioli C, Roda A, Vidolin A (2004) Modeling and control of expressiveness in music performance. Proc IEEE 92(4):686–701
3. Bresin R, Friberg A (2000) Emotional coloring of computer controlled music performance. Comput Music J 24(4):44–63
4. Todd NPMcA (1985) A model of expressive timing in tonal music. Music Percept 3:33–58
5. Friberg A, Bresin R, Frydén L, Sundberg J (1998) Musical punctuation on the microlevel: automatic identification and performance of small melodic units. J New Music Res 27(3):271–292
6. Cambouropoulos E (1988) Towards a general computational theory of musical structure. PhD thesis, Faculty of Music and Department of Artificial Intelligence, University of Edinburgh
7. Ahlbäck S (2004) Melody beyond notes. A study in melody cognition. PhD thesis, Department of Musicology, Göteborg University
8. Bresin R (1998) Artificial neural networks based models for automatic performance of musical scores. J New Music Res 27(3):239–270
9. Goebl W, Dixon S, De Poli G, Friberg A, Bresin R, Widmer G (2008) Sense in expressive music performance: data acquisition, computational studies, models. In: Polotti P, Rocchesso D (eds) Sound to sense - sense to sound: a state of the art in sound and music computing. Logos Verlag, Berlin, pp 195–242
10. Goebl W, Widmer G (2009) On the use of computational methods for expressive music performance. In: Crawford T, Gibson L (eds) Modern methods for musicology: prospects, proposals and realities. Ashgate, Aldershot, pp 93–113
11. Repp BH (1992) Diversity and commonality in music performance: an analysis of timing microstructure in Schumann's "Träumerei". J Acoust Soc Am 92(5):2546–2568
12. Friberg A, Sundström A (2002) Swing ratios and ensemble timing in jazz performance: evidence for a common rhythmic pattern. Music Percept 19(3):333–349

13. Repp BH (1999) A microcosm of musical expression: II. Quantitative analysis of pianists' dynamics in the initial measures of Chopin's Etude in E major. J Acoust Soc Am 105:1972–1988
14. De Poli G (2004) Methodologies for expressiveness modeling of and for music performance. J New Music Res 33(3):189–202
15. Friberg A (1995) Matching the rule parameters of Phrase arch to performances of *"Träumerei"*: a preliminary study. In: Friberg A, Sundberg J (eds) Proceedings of the KTH symposium on Grammars for music performance, 27 May 1995, pp 37–44
16. Friberg A, Sundberg J (1995) Time discrimination in a monotonic, isochronous sequence. J Acous Soc Am 98(5): 2524–2531.
17. Repp BH (1995) Detectability of duration and intensity increments in melody tones: a partial connection between music perception and performance. Percept Psychophys 57(8):1217–1232
18. Zanon P, De Poli G (2003) Estimation of parameters in rule systems for expressive rendering in musical performance. Comput Music J 27:29–46
19. Zanon P, De Poli G (2003) Estimation of time-varying parameters in rule systems for music performance. J New Music Res 32(3):295–316
20. Todd NPMcA (1989) A computational model of rubato. Contemporary Music Review 3:69–88
21. Juslin PN, Friberg A, Bresin R (2002) Toward a computational model of expression in performance: the GERM model. Musicae Scientiae, Special issue 2001–2002, 63–122
22. Sundberg J, Friberg A, Bresin A (2003) Attempts to reproduce a pianist's expressive timing with Director Musices performance rules. J New Music Res 32(3):317–326
23. Friberg A, Battel GU (2002) Structural communication. In: Parncutt R, McPherson GE (eds) The science and psychology of music performance: creative strategies for teaching and learning. Oxford University Press, New York, pp 199–218
24. Marsland S (2009) Machine learning: an algorithmic perspective. Chapman & Hall/CRC, Boca Raton
25. Friberg A, Sundberg J (1999) Does music performance allude to locomotion? A model of final ritardandi derived from measurements of stopping runners. J Acoust Soc Am 105(3):1469–1484
26. Widmer G (2003) Discovering simple rules in complex data: a meta-learning algorithm and some surprising musical discoveries. Artif Intell 146(2):129–148
27. Widmer G (2002) Machine discoveries: a few simple, robust local expression principles. J New Music Res 31:37–50
28. Friberg A, Bresin R, Sundberg J (2006) Overview of the KTH rule system for musical performance. Adv Cogn Psychol Spec Issue Music Perform 2(2–3):145–161
29. Bresin R (2001) Articulation rules for automatic music performance. In: Schloss A, Dannenberg R, Driessen P (eds) Proceedings of the international computer music conference – ICMC 2001. ICMA, San Francisco, pp 294–297
30. Goebl W (2001) Melody lead in piano performance: expressive device or artifact? J Acoust Soc Am 110(1):563–572
31. Bjurling J (2007) Timing in piano music - a model of melody lead. Master of Science thesis, KTH Royal Institute of Technology, School of Computer Science and Communication, Stockholm, Sweden. ISSN-1653–5715. http://www.nada.kth.se/utbildning/grukth/exjobb/rapportlistor/2007/rapporter07/bjurling_johan_07115.pdf
32. Friberg A (2006) pDM: an expressive sequencer with real-time control of the KTH music performance rules. Comput Music J 30(1):37–48
33. Bjurling J, Bresin R (2008) Timing in piano music – testing a model of melody lead. In Proceedings of ICMPC 10, Sapporo
34. Gabrielsson A, Lindström E (2010) The role of structure in the musical expression of emotions. In: Juslin PN, Sloboda JA (eds) Handbook of music and emotion: theory, research, applications. Oxford University Press, Oxford, pp 367–400
35. Juslin PN, Timmers R (2010) Expression and communication of emotion in music performance. In: Juslin PN, Sloboda JA (eds) Handbook of music and emotion: theory, research, applications. Oxford University Press, Oxford, pp 453–489: 2001–2002
36. Repp BH (1997) Acoustics, perception, production of legato articulation on a computer-controlled grand piano. J Acoust Soc Am 102(3):1878–1890

37. Bresin R, Battel GU (2000) Articulation strategies in expressive piano performance. Analysis of legato, staccato, repeated notes in performances of the Andante movement of Mozart's sonata in G major (K 545). J New Music Res 29(3):211–224
38. Bresin R, Friberg A (2011) Emotion rendering in music: range and characteristic values of seven musical variables. Cortex 47(9):1068–1081
39. Vieillard S, Peretz I, Gosselin N, Khalfa S, Gagnon L, Bouchard B (2007) Happy, sad, scary and peaceful musical excerpts for research on emotions. Cogn Emot 22(4):720–752
40. Hashida M, Nakra M, Katayose H, Murao T, Hirata K, Suzuki K, Kitahara T (2008) Rencon: performance rendering contest for automated music systems. In: Proceedings of international conference on music perception and cognition (ICMPC 2008)
41. Hiraga R, Hashida M, Hirata K, Katayose H, Noike K (2002) RENCON: toward a new evaluation method for performance rendering system. In: Proceedings of internatioal computer music conference, pp 357–361
42. Hiraga R, Bresin R, Hirata K, Katayose, H (2003) Rencon in 2002. In Proceedings of IJCAI-03 rencon workshop, Acapulco, Mexico, pp 59–64
43. Hiraga R, Bresin R, Hirata K, Katayose H (2004) Rencon 2004: turing test for musical expression. In NIME '04: proceedings of the 4th international conference on New interfaces for musical expression, Hamamatsu, Shizuoka, Japan, pp 120–123
44. Hiraga R, Bresin R, Katayose H (2006) Rencon 2005. In Proceeding of the 20th annual conference of the Japanese Society for Artificial Intelligence (1D2–1)
45. Noike K, Toyoda K, Katayose H (2005) An initial implementation of corpus based performance rendering system "COPER". Info Process Soc Jpn (IPSJ) 2005(14):67–70
46. Hashida M, Nagata N, Katayose H (2005) A study of description capability of performance characteristics on PopE. In: The 19th annual conference of JSAI
47. Widmer G, Flossmann S, Grachten M (2009) YQX plays chopin. AI Mag 30(3):35–48

Computational Music Theory and Its Applications to Expressive Performance and Composition

8

Masatoshi Hamanaka, Keiji Hirata, and Satoshi Tojo

Abstract

This chapter describes a musical analysis system based on a generative theory of tonal music (GTTM). Music theory provides methodologies for analyzing and transcribing such knowledge, experiences, and skills from a musician's perspective. Our concern is whether the concepts necessary for musical analysis are sufficiently externalized in musical theory. Given its ability to formalize musical knowledge, GTTM is considered here to be the most promising theory among the many that have been proposed because it captures the aspects of musical phenomena based on the gestalt in the music and follows relatively rigid rules. This chapter also describes music expectation and melody morphing methods that can use the analysis results from the music analysis system. The music expectation method predicts the next notes needed to assist musical novices in playing improvisations. The melody morphing method generates an intermediate melody between two melodies in a systematic order in accordance with a specific numerical measure.

M. Hamanaka (✉)
Intelligent Interaction Technologies, University of Tsukuba, 1-1-1 Tenodai, Tsukuba 305-8577, Japan
e-mail: hamanaka@iit.tsukuba.ac.jp

K. Hirata
Faculty of Systems Information Science, Future University Hakodate, 116-2 Kamedanakano-cho, Hakodate, Hokkaido 041-8655, Japan
e-mail: hirata@fun.ac.jp

S. Tojo
School of Information Science, Japan Advanced Institute of Science and Technology, 1-1 Asahidai, Nomi, Ishikawa, Japan
e-mail: tojo@jaist.ac.jp

A. Kirke and E.R. Miranda (eds.), *Guide to Computing for Expressive Music Performance*, 205
DOI 10.1007/978-1-4471-4123-5_8, © Springer-Verlag London 2013

8.1   Introduction

Our goal is to create a system that will enable a musical novice to manipulate a piece of music (an ambiguous and subjective medium) according to his/her intentions. It is important to make it possible to create a musical system useable by novices which can:

1. Easily manipulate a piece of music
2. Capture the user's intentions

Note that the higher the abstraction level of the objects for manipulating the music, the more difficult it becomes to reflect the user's intentions. For example, it is difficult for musical novices to manipulate music with commercial music sequencer software that only operates on the surface structure of music, that is, the pitch and note, on timing of each note. On the other hand, GarageBand [1] can create a piece of music through simple manipulations, that is, by just concatenating prestored phrases. However, when it is desired to specifically arrange a portion of a melody in a phrase, it is necessary to manipulate the surface structure of the music. A musical novice would find it difficult to manipulate such software to mirror his/her intentions in that case.

Music theory, in particular, focuses on traditionally score-notated pieces, giving us a methodology for analyzing and understanding a piece as well as explaining in a comprehensive way deeper structure, musical knowledge, experiences, and skills. Implementing music theory on a computer would bring great benefits because it could provide a theoretical basis for developing a support system for musical activities. For instance, advantages include expressive performance rendering [2–4] and music summarization for practical use when displaying the results of a music information retrieval system [5].

Systems for music analysis have been developed called ATTA [6, 7] and FATTA [8] based on a music theory called generative theory of tonal music (GTTM) [9]. ATTA and FATTA can generate a time-span tree as the result of a GTTM analysis. The GTTM consistently represents multiple aspects of music in a single framework. This feature is important when developing a musical system to assist a novice in manipulating musical structures. For example, if one considers a simple operation that splits a melody, the split operations may vary depending on the relevant musical structure. Therefore, it is preferred that the splitting position of the melody and that of the ornamented melody be identical. Unless a system of consistent operations for melody, rhythm, and harmony is developed, the resulting splitting position may not be identical.

In terms of to how the software should reflect the user's intentions, consider the example of composing a melody where it is supposed that a user wants to arrange melody A by adding some musical nuances to it that he/she knows from melody B. If a user could use a system with such a morphing function, they could, for example, utilize the function "add the nuance of melody B to melody A," which can accurately incorporate the user's intentions. The system can generate multiple versions of melody A each incorporating more and more nuances of melody B. The advantage

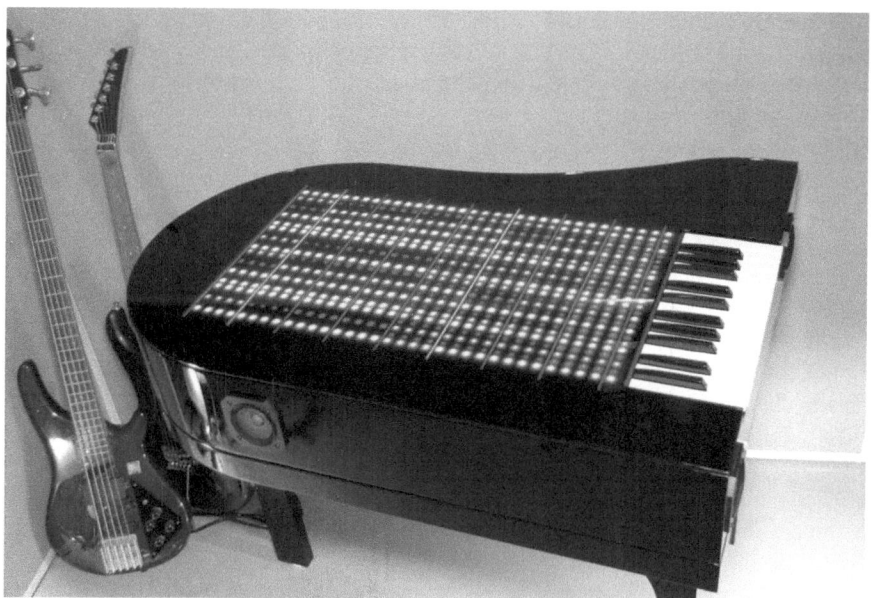

Fig. 8.1 Expectation piano

of such morphing is not only its simple and accurate transferability and manipulability but also its ease of understanding the relationship between inputs and outputs.

Many previous music systems [10–12] have their own approach to musical analysis, from which it is difficult to acquire deeper musical structures, and thus these systems are difficult to manipulate in a way that reflects the user's intention. On the other hand, Hirata [13] defines a representation method and primitive operation for polyphony, which indicates the potential for constructing a melody-arranging algorithm.

A melody morphing method has been developed in which monophonies A and B are input, and then intermediate melodies between melodies A and B are generated with a systematic order according to a certain numerical measure, by configuring the parameters that determine the level of influence of the features of melodies A and B [14, 15]. Our system exploits melody morphing to make it possible for novices to create melodies reflecting their intentions.

Melody prediction is one of the most difficult problems in musical information retrieval because composers and players may or may not create melodies that conform to expectations. The development of a melody expectation methodology is thus a key part of building a system that supports musical novices – melody expectation is one of the most basic skills for a musician.

Our melody prediction method helps a novice construct a melody or play an improvisation by displaying next note candidates. This method is designed for use with the "expectation piano" (Fig. 8.1), which was developed to assist musical novices play improvisations. On the lid of this piano, there is a 32 × 25 full-color LED matrix that displays a piano-roll view that scrolls down in time with the music.

Two key requirements have been identified to make a melody expectation method useable by musical novices playing an improvisation on the expectation piano:

1. Candidate notes are predicted and output even if the input melody is novel.
2. The output is musically appropriate.

Two approaches were considered during the development of this method: statistical learning and musical theory. With the statistical learning approach, the predictions depend on the characteristics of the data used for learning, for example, composer, genre, period, country, etc. [16, 17]. Another aspect of this approach comes from predicting candidate notes for a novel melody. This can be problematic because the system may not be able to find a similar melody in the learning data and thus may be unable to evaluate whether particular notes are appropriate candidates or not. However, with the music theory approach, the predictions do not depend on the characteristics of the data used for learning. It can thus be applied more successfully to novel melodies.

Unlike most statistical learning methods for note prediction, the methodology utilized here evaluates the appropriateness of a candidate note from the view point of music theory. Although many music theories have been proposed [18–21], GTTM is the most suitable for predicting notes in a melody because it can be used to represent multiple musical elements in a single framework. In particular, our prediction method uses a concept based on GTTM's melody stability, and the tonal pitch space (TPS) [22] to evaluate the appropriateness of a melody. (Tonal pitch space [22] is a music theory for chord progression composed by Lerdahl, who is one of the authors of the GTTM.) The method can thus predict candidate next notes not only using the surface structure of the melody but also from the deeper melodic structure, as acquired by GTTM and tonal pitch space analysis.

The organization of this chapter is as follows. In Sect. 8.2, we briefly describe the GTTM music theory, discuss the problems with implementing GTTM and how to solve them, and then propose exGTTM as extension of GTTM. In Sect. 8.3, we describe an interactive analyzer for GTTM which enables the seamless adjustment of the automatic analysis process with the ATTA (automatic time-tree analyzer), and a manual edit process with a GTTM manual editor. In Sect. 8.4, the melody expectation method for predicting following notes is described, designed for assisting musical novices in improvisation. In Sect. 8.5, we explain our melody morphing methodology which generates intermediate melodies between two other melodies, with a systematic similarity of musical features according to a defined numerical measure. In Sect. 8.6, we evaluate the performance of the implemented system. Finally in Sect. 8.7, we conclude with a summary and overview of future work.

8.2   Implementing GTTM on a Computer

GTTM is a music theory consisting of four subtheories: grouping-structure analysis, metrical-structure analysis, time-span reduction, and prolongational reduction. It attempts to simulate the listening insights of an "experienced listener."

Grouping-structure analysis hierarchically divides a series of notes in a homophony into phrases or motives, similar to the way a singer looks for breathing points

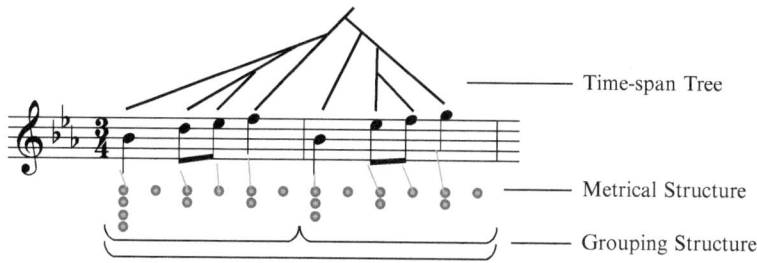

Fig. 8.2 Grouping structure, metrical structure, and time-span tree. Groups are graphically presented as several levels of arcs below the music staff. Stronger beats are illustrated by more dots at multiple levels below the music staff

Fig. 8.3 The *left side* shows a melody and its corresponding time-span tree, where a single note, called a head (note C4 shown in *right side*), represents the time-span denoted by <—> containing the two notes

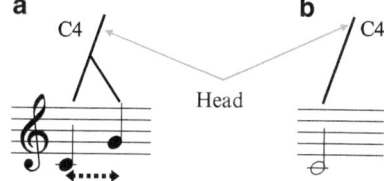

when singing a long melody (Fig. 8.2). The metrical-structure analysis identifies strong and weak beats at multiple metrical levels: quarter note, half note, whole note, two measures, and four measures. Essentially, it is looking for the beats at which a listener beats time with his/her hands to the music, or through which a conductor swings his/her baton. Time-span reduction distinguishes important parts of a melody from less important ones, yielding a binary tree called a time-span tree, such that each structurally important note belongs to a stem (Fig. 8.3) at each level. The prolongational reduction method generates a tree structure representing subordinate relationships between chords – doing so by explicitly indicating harmonic retention and change.

Each subtheory of GTTM is described by two types of rules: a well-formedness rule prescribes the conditions and constraints that must always be satisfied, and a preference rule prescribes which structure is most preferred among the structures satisfying the well-formedness rules. Thus, depending on the situation, some preference rules hold and others do not.

Methodologies for implementing three of the four subtheories are presented in this section: grouping-structure analysis, metrical-structure analysis, and time-span reduction [6–8, 23, 24]. The prolongational reduction is still evolving and is currently more controversial; hence we have not implemented it at present.

8.2.1 GTTM Implementation Issues

When we wish to make GTTM rules operate on a computer, we have to give a "fuzzy" concept a firm definition and supplement any elements lacking. Roughly speaking,

Fig. 8.4 GPR3a ("register") is applied between notes *3* and *4*, and GPR6 ("parallelism") is applied between notes *4* and *5*. A boundary cannot be deduced at both *3-4* and *4-5* because GPR1 ("alternative form") strongly implies that note *4*, by itself, cannot form a group

these tasks correspond to parameterization and externalization, respectively. Here, we discuss the problems occurring in the process of parameterization and externalization.

Ambiguous Concepts Defining Preference Rules. GTTM uses some imprecisely defined terms that can create ambiguities in the analysis. For example, GTTM has rules for selecting structures in discovering similar melodies (called parallelism) but does not have a clear definition of similarity itself. To solve this problem, we attempted to formalize the criteria for deciding for a rule being applicable.

Conflict Between Preference Rules. Conflict between rules often occurs and results – there is no strict order for applying the preference rules, causing ambiguities in the analysis. Figure 8.4 shows a simple example of a conflict between grouping preference rules (GPR). To solve this problem, we introduced adjustable parameters that enable us to control the relative strength with which each rule is applied.

Lack of Algorithmic Form. Knowledge represented in the GTTM rules is, in general, declarative. A system is required to perform automatic reasoning using the declaratively described knowledge. GTTM provides few descriptions of the reasoning and algorithms needed to compute analysis results.

8.2.2 Solution: Proposal of exGTTM

We have extended the GTTM theory through externalization and parameterization, devising a machine-executable extension of GTTM: exGTTM. The externalization includes introducing an algorithm for generating the hierarchical structure of a time-span tree in a mixed top-down/bottom-up manner. Such an algorithm has not previously been available for GTTM. The parameterization includes a parameter for controlling the priorities of rules to avoid conflicts among them, as well as parameters for controlling the shape of the hierarchical time-span tree. Although it has been suggested that such parameters are required in GTTM, they have not explicitly presented previously.

We distinguish two types of ambiguity in music analysis: one involving musical understanding by humans and the other involving the representation of music theory. The former kind of ambiguity derives from the ambiguity in music itself. The latter type of ambiguity – a part of GTTM – is due to the lack of a mechanization concept or of it only being presented in an implicit way. The former (musical) kind of ambiguity leads us to assume there is more than one correct result. We attempt to avoid the latter (analysis) type of ambiguity through full externalization and parameterization.

8.2.2.1 Full Externalization and Parameterization

The significance of a fully externalized and parameterized approach is twofold: more precise controllability and reproducing the manual results. Whenever we find a correct result that exGTTM cannot generate, we introduce new parameters and give them appropriate values so that exGTTM can then generate this result. In this way, we repeatedly externalize and introduce new parameters until we have obtained all of the results that are generally considered correct. In total, we have introduced 15 parameters for grouping-structure analysis (Table 8.1), 18 for metrical-structure analysis (Table 8.2), and 13 for time-span reduction (Table 8.3).

We supplied lacking parameters where appropriate and made any implicit parameters explicit.[1] The parameters introduced by exGTTM are categorized as Identified, Implied, and Unaware.

A parameter in the first category has already been identified in GTTM but is not assigned concrete values. Hence, we provide values for such parameters. For example, the resulting value of the GPR2a application, D_{GPR2a}, is binary. If the rule applies, then D_{GPR2a} is 1, and if it does not apply, 0. On the other hand, since GPR6 always applies to some degree, the resulting value of GPR6 – D_{GPR6} – varies continuously between 0 and 1.

A parameter of the second category (Implied) is only implied by GTTM. We make it explicit. For example, to resolve preference rule conflicts, we introduce parameters that express the priority of each preference rule (S^{GPRR}, S^{MPRR}, and S^{TSRPRR} in Tables 8.1, 8.2, and 8.3). Since each preference rule has its own priority, all of the possible priority patterns are realized – an example of full parameterization.

For the third category (Unaware), we develop parameters that are not utilized in the original theory, because they lack clear musicological meaning. For example, GPR6 in exGTTM requires extra parameters for controlling the properties of parallel segments, including the weighting of pitch-oriented matching versus timing-oriented matching.

There are also intermediate variables utilized in calculation, denoted as D and B. The domain of all the intermediate variables is constrained to the range 0–1, and to ensure this, such variables are normalized at every computation stage. Thanks to this property, exGTTM can flexibly combine any of the intermediate variables (and possibly other parameters) and cascade as many weighted-mean calculations as required. This facilitates more precise controllability.

---

[1] In this chapter, the word "parameter" is used not only for parameters used to control a system externally but also for internal variables (intermediated variables) that connect submodules.

Table 8.1 The 15 adjustable parameters for the grouping-structure analyzer

Parameters	Description
$S_{GPRR}(0 \leqq S_{GPRR} \leqq 1)$	Strength of each grouping preference rule. The larger the value, the stronger the rule action. $R \in \{2a, 2b, 3a, 3b, 3c, 3d, 4, 5, \text{and } 6\}$
$\sigma(0 \leqq \sigma \leqq 0.1)$	Standard deviation of a Gaussian distribution, the average of which is the GPR5 boundary. The larger the value is, the wider its "skirt" becomes
$W_m(0 \leqq W_m \leqq 1)$	Balance between temporal similarity of attack points in GPR6 and that of pitch difference. The larger the value is, the more the system focuses on pitch difference
$W_l(0 \leqq W_l \leqq 1)$	Weight for the length of parallel phrases. The larger the value is, the more that length of parallel phrases is prioritized in GPR6
$W_s(0 \leqq W_s \leqq 1)$	Balance determining for GPR6 whether note i becomes the ending note of a group or the beginning note of the following group. The larger the value is, the more the note tends to become an ending note
$T_{GPR4}(0 \leqq T_{GPR4} \leqq 1)$	Threshold at which the effects of GPR2 and GPR3 are considered to be salient in GPR4. The smaller the value is, the more probable it is that GPR4 is applied
$T^{low}(0 \leqq T^{low} \leqq 1)$	Threshold for the lower-level boundary. The smaller the value is, the more salient that boundary becomes

Table 8.2 The 18 adjustable parameters for the metrical-structure analyzer

Parameters	Description
$S_{MPRR}(0 \leqq S_{MPRR} \leqq 1)$	Strength of each metrical preference rule. The larger the value is, the more strongly the rule acts. $R \in \{1, 2, 3, 4, 5a, 5b, 5c, 5d, 5e, \text{and } 10\}$.
$W_m(0 \leqq W_m \leqq 1)$	Balance in MPR1 between the temporal similarity of attack points and that of pitch difference. The larger the value, the more the system focuses on the pitch difference
$W_l(0 \leqq W_l \leqq 1)$	Weighting for the length of parallel phrases in MPR1. The larger the value, the more the length of parallel phrases is prioritized
$W_s(0 \leqq W_s \leqq 1)$	Balance determining for MPR1 whether the note i becomes the ending note of a group or the beginning note of the following group. The larger the value, the more the note tends to be an ending note
$T_{MPRR}(0 \leqq T_{MPRR} \leqq 1)$	Value for the threshold deciding whether each rule is applicable. $R \in \{4, 5a, 5b, 5c\}$

Table 8.3 The 13 adjustable parameters for the time-span tree analyzer

Parameters	Description
$S_{TSRPRR}(0 \leqq S_{TSRPRR} \leqq 1)$	Strength of each rule. The larger the value, the stronger the rule action. $R \in \{1, 2, 3, 4, 5a, 5b, 5c, 5d, 5e, \text{and } 10\}$
$W_m(0 \leqq W_m \leqq 1)$	The balance in TSRPR4 between the temporal similarity of attack points and that of the pitch difference. The larger the value, the more the system focuses on pitch difference
$W_l(0 \leqq W_l \leqq 1)$	The weighting for the length of parallel phrases in TSRPR4. The larger the value, the more the length of parallel phrases is estimated
$W_s(0 \leqq W_s \leqq 1)$	The balance determines in TSRPR4 for whether a note i becomes the ending note of a group or the beginning note of the following group. The larger the value, the more the note tends to become the ending note

8.2.2.2 Algorithm for Analyzing a Hierarchy

The problem of analyzing hierarchical structures in the grouping-structure/ metrical-structure analyses and the time-span tree reduction can be regarded as a constraint satisfaction problem (CSP). This is because the GTTM rule form only represents the properties to be satisfied within the hierarchical. Neither constraints on nor order of the generation hierarchical structures is determined in advance in GTTM.

The constraints stipulated by the GTTM rules are divided into two categories: local and global. The former includes GPR2 (proximity) and TSRPR1 (strong metrical position). The latter includes GPR5 (symmetry) and MPR1 (parallelism). It is important to handle global constraints carefully when generating hierarchical structures. For example, GPR5 in Fig. 8.5: given a group at layer 1, an inner boundary probably occurs around the center of the group, that is, either between notes 1 and 2 or between notes 2 and 3. We can consider two cases. In case 1, the boundary between notes 1 and 2 is selected (taking into account the effects of some other rules). Then in each subgroup in layer 2, the inner boundary of the subgroup may occur to the left-hand side of a center note. In case 2, on the other hand, the boundary between notes 2 and 3 is selected. Thus, the inner boundary may occur to the right-hand side of a center note.

In light of the above considerations, we develop algorithms for generating hierarchical structures for exGTTM so that nodes are generated either from the bottommost nodes or from the topmost node incrementally and so that each time the nodes in a layer are calculated, global information is recalculated before moving onto an adjacent layer.

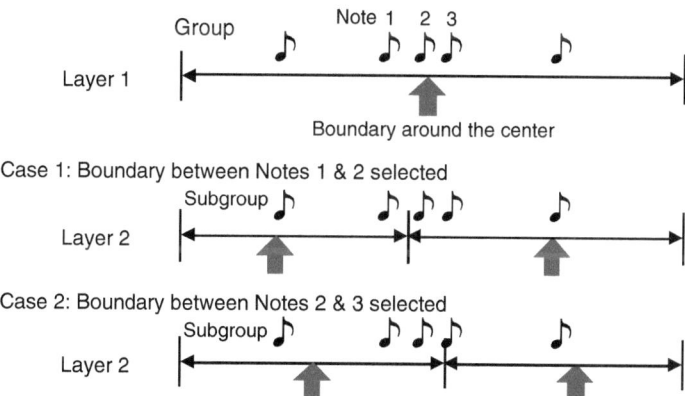

Fig. 8.5 In computing GPR5, the determined boundary position influences the identification of remote boundaries in lower layers. We take into account up-to-date global information every time. That is, a global constraint is inevitably dynamic

8.2.3 FATTA: Fully Automatic Time-Span Tree Analyzer

We have implemented a time-span tree analyzer, called the automatic time-span analyzer (ATTA), utilizing exGTTM. Although ATTA can automatically acquire a time-span tree, the parameters are manually controlled – and it takes too much time to find a set of optimal parameters. Therefore, we have also developed a method for automatically estimating the optimal parameters [8].

There are two preference rules in GTTM [9] not implemented in ATTA – GPR7 and TSRPR5. These rules require that information from later processes, such as time-span/prolongational reductions, be utilized in earlier processes:

> GPR7 (time-span and prolongational stability): Prefer a grouping structure that results in a more stable time-span and/or prolongational reduction.
>
>   TSRPR5 (metrical stability): When choosing the head of time-span T, prefer a choice that results in a more stable choice of metrical structure.

These are calculated as part of FATTA, a process flow shown in Fig. 8.6, which consists of the ATTA and a loop for the GPR7 and TSRPR5. To estimate the optimal parameters automatically, the structural stability of the analysis results derived by ATTA is evaluated. GPR7 and TSRPR5 are used to calculate the level of stability.

8.2.3.1 Implementation of GPR7 with Tonal Pitch Space

GPR7 is applied during the loop between the time-span/prolongational reduction and the grouping-structure analysis. This rule leads to a preference for grouping structures that lead to more stable time-span and/or prolongational reductions. The holding level of GPR7, which varies continuously between 0 and 1, is defined as

$$D_{\text{GPR7}} = \frac{\sum_{i} \text{distance}\,(p(i),s(i)) \times \text{size}(i)^2}{\sum_{i} \text{size}(i)^2}. \tag{8.1}$$

where i indicates the head of the time-span with primary and secondary branches denoted by $p(i)$ and $s(i)$, respectively. Distance(x, y) indicates the distance between notes x and y in the tonality of the piece – as defined using Lerdahl's tonal pitch space [2]. This distance is normalized here between 0 and 1. The size(i) indicates the length of the time-span with head i. When calculating D_{GPR7}, the square of size (i) is used for the weighting (for empirical reasons).

In the tonal pitch space, the distance between chord x $= C_1/\mathbf{R_1}$ and chord y $= C_2/\mathbf{R_2}$ is defined as follows:

$$\delta(x \rightarrow y) = i + j + k, \tag{8.2}$$

where i is region distance, j is chord distance, and k is basic space difference. The region distance is the smallest number of steps along the regional circle of fifths

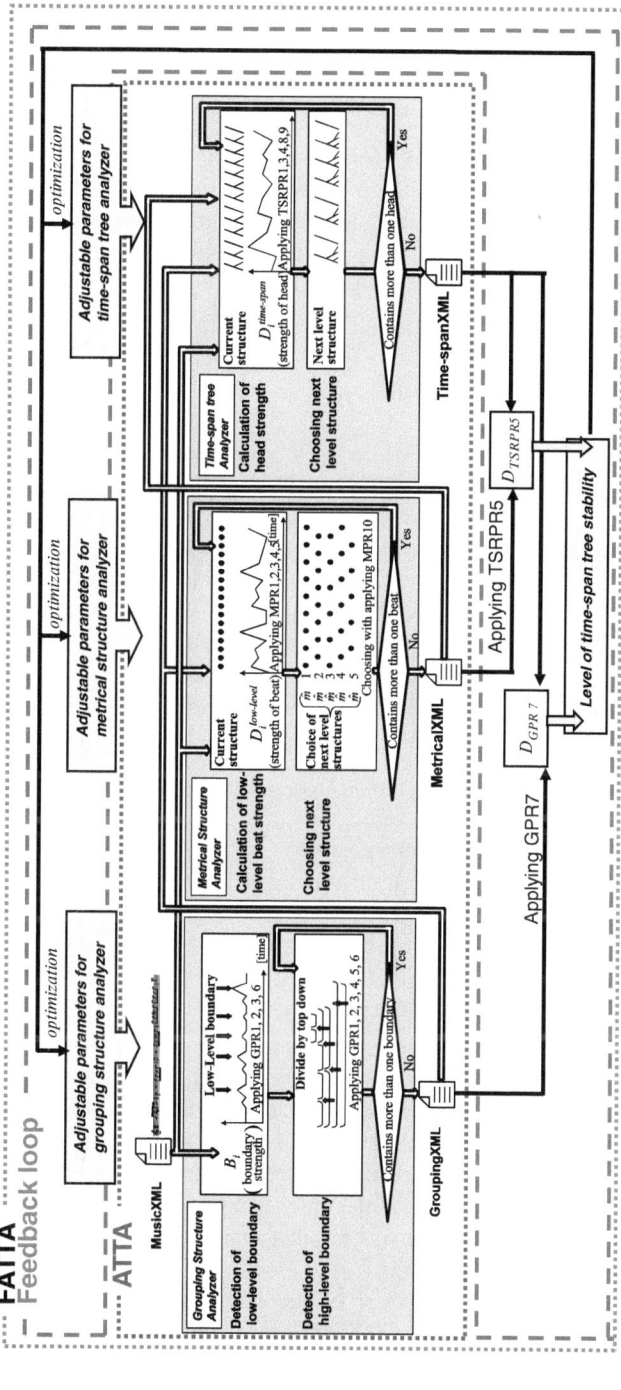

Fig. 8.6 Processing flow for the fully automatic time-span tree analyzer (FATTA)

between $\mathbf{R_1}$ and $\mathbf{R_2}$. The chord distance is the smallest number of steps along the chordal circle of fifths between the roots of C_1 and C_2 within each region. The basic space distance is a specially weighted to define each chord and region. Note that pitch class only has a meaning in terms of the elements of the sets that define chords and regions, and chords are always understood as functioning within some region.

8.2.3.2 Implementation of TSRPR5

TSRPR5 is applied during the loop between the time-span reduction and metrical-structure analyzer and results in a more stable metrical structure when choosing the head of a time-span. The holding level of TSRPR5, which varies continuously between 0 and 1, is defined as

$$D_{\text{TSRPRS}} = \frac{1}{\sum\limits_i \text{size}(i)^2} \times \sum\limits_i \begin{cases} \text{size}(i)^2 & \text{dot}(p(i)) \geq \text{dot}(s(i)), \\ 0 & \text{dot}(p(i)) < \text{dot}(s(i)). \end{cases} \quad (8.3)$$

where $dot(x)$ indicates the number of metrical dots for note x.

8.2.3.3 Optimization of Adjustable Parameters

The optimal set of ATTA parameters is obtained by maximizing the average of D_{GPR7} ($0 \leq D_{\text{GPR7}} \leq 1$) and D_{TSRPR5} ($0 \leq D_{\text{TSRPR5}} \leq 1$). The parameters and default values are $S_{\text{rules}} = 0.5, T_{\text{rules}} = 0.5, Ws = 0.5, Wr = 0.5, Wl = 0.5$, and $\sigma = 0.05$. Because there are 46 parameters, a significant amount of time is needed to calculate all parameter combinations. To minimize the calculation time, an algorithm was constructed as follows:

1. Maximize average of D_{GPR7} and D_{TSRPR5} through changing a parameter from its minimum to its maximum value.
2. Repeat (8.1) for all parameters.
3. Iterate (8.1) and (8.2) as long as the average of D_{GPR7} and D_{TSRPR5} is higher than that of the previous iteration.

8.3   Interactive GTTM Analyzer

Figure 8.7 is a screenshot of the viewer for the interactive GTTM analyzer. A sequence of notes is displayed in piano-roll format. Below the notes is the grouping structure graphically presented as several levels of arcs. Below the grouping structure is the metrical structure. Strong beats are illustrated as several levels of bars. Above the notes is the time-span tree, and below the time-span tree is the prolongational tree (a binary tree that expresses the structure of tension and relaxation in a piece of music).

Figure 8.8 gives an overview of the interactive GTTM analyzer structure. It consists of an ATTA [6, 7], a GTTM manual editor, and a GTTM process editor. The ATTA is made up of analyzers for grouping structure, metrical structure, and time-span tree. A prolongation tree analyzer is also being developed.

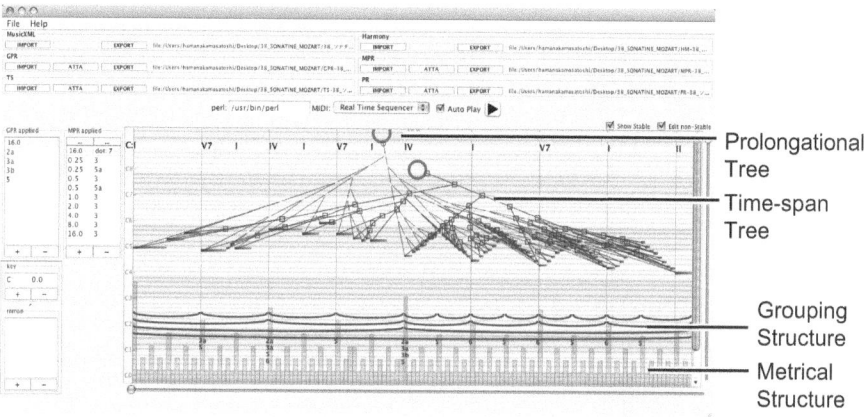

Fig. 8.7 Screenshot of interactive GTTM analyzer

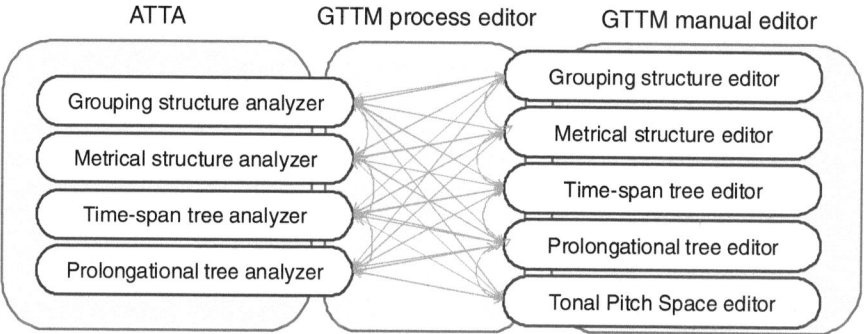

Fig. 8.8 Overview of interactive GTTM analyzer

The GTTM manual editor is made up of editors for grouping, metrical, time-span, prolongational, and tonal pitch space. Although the GTTM includes rules that require the analysis results of chord progression, the ATTA utilizes rules based on the results of the tonal pitch space approach.

The analysis process for the ATTA and GTTM manual editor can be complex, and sometimes a user becomes confused as to what they should do next in the analysis; there are three analyzing processes in the ATTA and five editing processes in the GTTM manual editor. Furthermore, a user may iterate through the ATTA and manual edit processes multiple times. To address this issue, a further GTTM *process* editor is proposed – one which presents to the user candidates for the next stage of the analysis process. The user can then simply select the next analysis from these candidates.

An XML format is used for all the input and output data structures in the interactive GTTM analyzer. Each analyzer and editor of the system work independently, but they are integrated through the XML-based data structure.

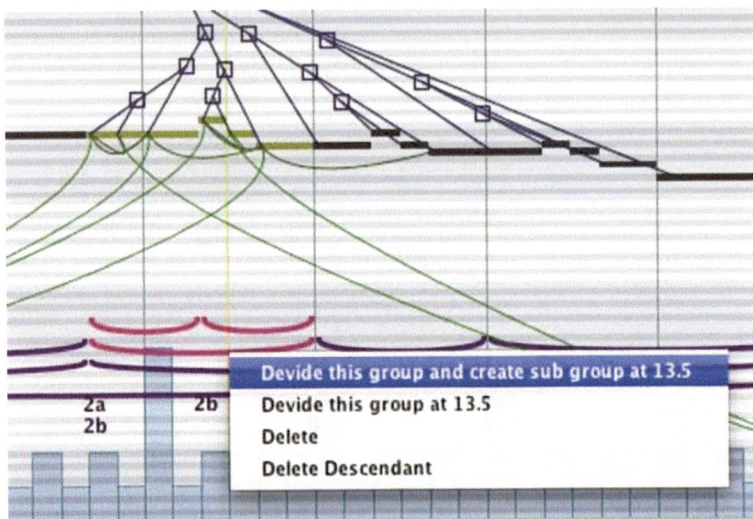

Fig. 8.9 Screenshot of grouping-structure editor

8.3.1 GTTM Manual Editor

The ATTA may not always produce a result which reflects the user's interpretation. When a user desires to adjust the analysis result according to preference, they can use the GTTM manual editor. Methods for editing and constructing a GTTM musical structure using the GTTM manual editor are now described.

8.3.1.1 Grouping-Structure Editor

Figure 8.9 is a screenshot of the interactive GTTM analyzer during the process of a grouping-structure edit. The color of the target group and all its subgroups turns red after selection with the mouse. Then a pop-up menu can be opened by right clicking, with four operations: (1) divide this group and create subgroup, (2) divide this group, (3) delete, and (4) delete descendant.

To change a position of a grouping boundary, the user first deletes the groups which adjoin the boundary, and then divides the upper level (global level) group and creates new subgroups at the point they desire to create a boundary. By left clicking a grouping boundary, the user will see the rules that are applied to the boundary, and they can add or delete these rules.

8.3.1.2 Metrical-Structure Editor

Although the metrical-structure analyzer in the ATTA performs fairly well [24], a user may still desire to perform minor edits on the resulting metrical analyses. To do this, the user can change the strength level of a beat in the editor by dragging a bar up or down. Furthermore, the user can see the rules that are applied to that bar and can add to, or delete from, these rules.

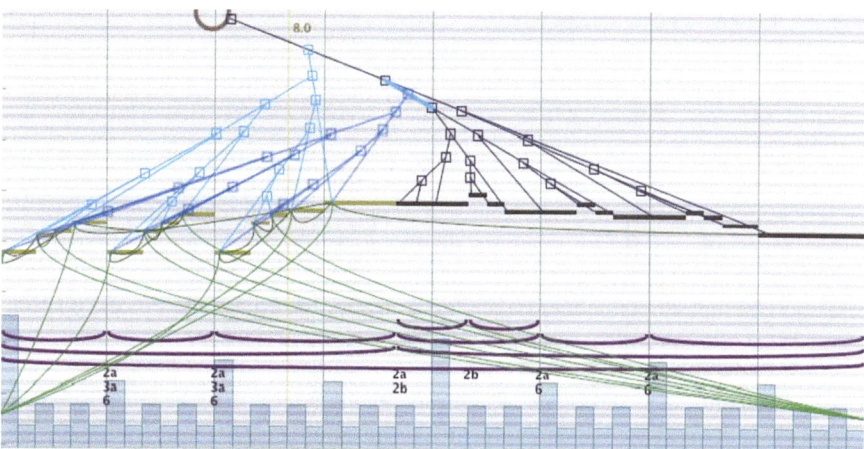

Fig. 8.10 Screenshot of when dragging head

While editing beat strength, a user may also distort hierarchical metrical structures. In other words, the results of the metrical-structure editor may sometimes contradict the metrical preference rules. This problem can be addressed using the GTTM process editor discussed in Sect. 8.3.2.

8.3.1.3 Time-Span Tree Editor

In the time-span tree editor, each branch of the time-span tree has a head represented by a square, and the user moves the head by dragging another branch. Figure 8.10 shows a screenshot of a head being moved. The light blue branch is the former position, and the dark blue branch is the new position. A user selects a type for each head through a pop-up menu from the options: (1) ordinary, (2) fusion, (3) transformation, and (4) cadential retention.

8.3.1.4 Prolongational Tree Editor

The prolongational tree editor has a similar user interface to that used for the time-span tree editor. The prolongational tree is constructed by connecting heads based on the time-span tree. There are head connection constraints for the prolongational tree. When a head connection of a prolongational tree is ill-formed, the GTTM process editor automatically opens the pop-up menu and displays candidate solutions to make it well-formed.

8.3.1.5 Tonal Pitch Space Editor

A tonal pitch space editor is included in the interactive GTTM analyzer because it provides quantitative grounds for the prolongational tree to be hierarchical. As a result, analyzing the tonal pitch space in line with the prolongational tree improves analysis performance.

8.3.2 GTTM Process Editor

In GTTM, the analysis sequence proceeds in the following order: grouping structure, metrical structure, time-span tree, and finally, prolongational tree. However, the GTTM contains feedback links from higher- to lower-level structures. For example, grouping preference rule 7 (GPR7) (time-span and prolongational stability) prefers a grouping structure that results in a more stable time-span and/or prolongation reduction. Therefore, analysis involving feedback-linked rules requires a number of analysis processes by trial and error. The GTTM process editor aids this repetition through three functions: data input, history recording, and process control.

8.3.2.1 Data Input

Data input helps with the input of analysis results which have been prepared by another user or analysis. For example, there is no automated analyzer for tonal pitch space [22] in the interactive GTTM analyzer; however, attempts have been made to implement the tonal pitch space system, so those results can be used as an input [25].

New rules can be added to the ATTA using the data input functionality. For example, grouping preference rule 6 (GPR6) is a rule for parallelism in a grouping structure; however, the GTTM does not define the decision criteria for deciding whether two or more segments are parallel. Therefore, multiple implementations of GPR6 are possible, although our system utilizes only one. By adding a new rule to the ATTA, a new adjustable parameter for a new rule implementation of GPR6, say GPR6+, can be manipulated.

8.3.2.2 History Recording

This function records all analysis operations so a user can return to the previous phase of analysis at any point. History recording enables the copying and pasting of several analysis operations while editing parallel phrases.

GTTM contains few descriptions of the algorithms needed to compute actual analysis results, in particular with the time-span and prolongational trees. Through the use of history recordings, we hope to develop an analysis knowledge base, which can be used to improve automated analyses.

8.3.2.3 Process Control

Process control enables the seamless adjustment of the analysis process by using the GTTM manual editor acting on the ATTA. The representation method differs depending on the number of candidates suggested for the next process.

When there is only one candidate, the process-control function automatically executes the process. For example, when the user edits the strongest beat in Fig. 8.11a in the second level, the hierarchical metrical structure is "broken" because in level 3 of Fig. 8.11b, there are three weak continuous beats, and the metrical well-formedness rule 2 (MWFR2) no longer holds. MWFR2 requires that strong beats are spaced either two or three beats apart at each metrical level. The process editor automatically produces alternate strong and weak beats in level 3 (Fig. 8.11c). If there is a higher metrical structure than level 3, the ATTA metrical

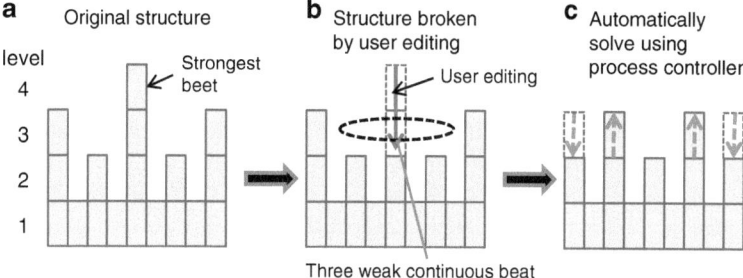

Fig. 8.11 Automatically correcting "broken" metrical structure

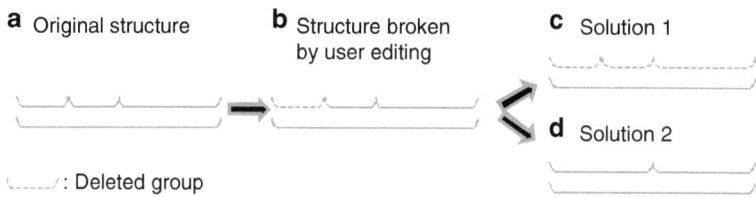

Fig. 8.12 Two types of solutions for "broken" grouping structure

analyzer automatically analyzes past level 3 and constructs a hierarchical metrical structure, hopefully reflecting the user's intention.

When there are multiple candidates, the process-control function automatically opens the pop-up menu which displays these candidates as options. For example, consider the grouping structure shown Fig. 8.12a, and suppose the user deletes a group as in Fig. 8.12b. Then the grouping structure of Fig. 8.12b is "broken" because grouping well-formedness rule 3 (GWFR3) no longer holds. To solve this problem, there are only two process options:

1. Delete all the groups at the same level of the deleted group (Fig. 8.12c).
2. Extend the grouping boundary of the left end of the right group of the deleted group, to the left end of that deleted group (Fig. 8.12d).

The next process would be executed by selecting one of the two process options displayed in the pop-up menu.

When there are a larger number of candidates, the process-control function selects and shows the top-ten candidates based on the history recording. The candidates are ordered depending on their similarity to the edit history. For example, after editing a time-span tree with the time-span tree editor, executing a grouping analyzer or metrical analyzer in the ATTA would be ranked high in the candidate list because there are rules for feedback links, such as GPR7 or metrical preference rule 9 (MPR9). GPR7 (time-span and prolongational stability) is a link from the time-span and prolongational trees to the grouping structure, and MPR9 (time-span interaction) is a link from the time-span tree to the metrical structure.

In this section, we omit the details of the implementation of GPR7 and MPR9 due to space limitations.

8.4   Melody Expectation

The melody expectation method presented here predicts candidate notes using their level of stability in a time-span tree defined in FATTA. A single expected, following tone cannot always be specified; thus, our "expectation piano" simply suggests multiple candidates from among pitch events with higher stability. The FATTA system only deals with monophonic western tonal music. Thus, the expectation method can predict only monophonic musical structures for western tonal music as well.

8.4.1   Melody Expectation Method

A key element of the melody expectation method here is that it is not based solely on the local melody (i.e., a few notes previous to a relevant note). The stability of the entire melody up to the note to be predicted is calculated. Previous melody expectation methods based on music theory (e.g., Steve Larson's theory of musical forces [21]) derive an expected note from the local melody. Music tends to be more interesting when it does not match the listener's expectations, such as a delayed note, and this may result in tension and relaxation. A composer will deliberately construct such music, making it difficult to accurately predict the next note in the melody. For example, they may use ornamentation notes. However, FATTA can evaluate the stability of the entire structure of the time-span tree, including branches connected to main notes and leaves connected to ornament notes. Hence, the method here can predict candidate notes even in this situation.

8.4.1.1 Real-Time Extension for FATTA

To be able to predict notes using GTTM, FATTA must run in real time. However, several minutes are needed to finish an analysis. Hence, the algorithm needed adjustment for real-time operation. To speed up the iteration described in Sect. 8.2.2, the set of optimal parameter values for the previous melody is reused as an initial parameter set. This is an approximation because the previous melody is one note shorter than the present melody. To further increase speeds, an analysis window is utilized by ATTA. The size of the window is the longest group length within 16 measures of the present position. This length is acquired through preprocessing using the grouping-structure analyzer in ATTA. If there is no grouping boundary within 16 measures from the present position, 16 measures is used as the window size.

8.4.1.2 Calculating Level of Stability for Melodies

FATTA is used to evaluate the appropriateness of a candidate melody by calculating its stability. The average of D_{GPR7} and D_{TSRPR5} is used as the level of stability.

Figure 8.13 shows the calculated stability level for a series of notes. The level of stability can only begin to be calculated after the third note because GTTM analysis requires at least four notes.

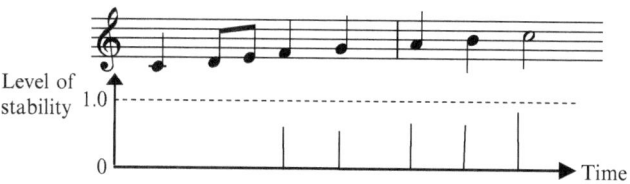

Fig. 8.13 Level of stability over time

In this score, the first note is a tonic of the region, and the final note is also a tonic of the region. This leads to a large stability value at the tail of the melody and a smaller value in the middle. Thus, the higher the stability level of a note, the relatively closer it is to the tonic of the region. The region of the melody and chord progression are estimated in GPR7 here by applying tonal pitch space methods.

8.4.2 Expectation Piano

The expectation piano assists novices learning musical improvisation by displaying predicted notes on the piano lid. When the novice is stuck, they can continue the improvisation – without impairing tonality – by playing a note displayed on the lid.

8.4.2.1 Overview
The process flow of the expectation piano is as follows. Firstly, the MIDI signal for the music played on the piano is sent to the computer. The signal is quantized, and a MusicXML version of the melody is created An adaptive quantization method [26] is used to eliminate deviations in onset times – these are aligned to the normalized positions. The MusicXML is fed into FATTA. Then the predicted notes are displayed on the piano lid.

8.4.2.2 Scrolling LED Piano Roll
Below the piano lid, which is made of semitransparent acrylic resin, there is a 32×25 full-color LED matrix. The predicted candidate notes are displayed in a piano-roll format. The roll scrolls down at a constant speed. The 32 lights represent two measures when the resolution is a sixteenth note; 25 is the number of keys on the keyboard. When the level of stability is high, the LED shows yellow; when it is low, it shows black; and when it is neither, it shows red. There is also a 32×20 blue LED matrix that displays the bar lines for the piano roll.

8.4.2.3 Construction
The piano is 953 mm long and 710 mm wide and resembles a grand piano. It consists of a MIDI keyboard, the LED display, a computer, a power supply, and four speakers. The LED display is 630 mm long and 390 mm wide. The colors of the LEDs are controlled by MAX6972, which is a 16-output, 12-bit pulse-width-modulation

(PWM) LED driver. There is a 5-mm gap between the LEDs and piano lid to protect the acrylic resin lid from the heat of the LEDs. A half-mirror sheet is bonded to the back side of the acrylic resin so that the lights of the LEDs show on the surface of the piano lid rather than 5 mm below it. The LED drivers are controlled using the computer via a network cable, which sends the data for the LED colors through the user datagram protocol.

8.5 Melody Morphing

The melody morphing system takes as input an initial melody A and a target "nuance" melody B and gives a resulting morphed melody C. The system utilizes the following constraints (constraints 1 and 2 are for melody C; 3 and 4 are methodological constraints):

1. The similarity between A and C must be closer than that of A and B, and the similarity between B and C must be closer than that of A and B.
2. If B is the same as A, C will be the same as A.
3. The features of melody C depend on parameters that decide the level of influence of melodies A and B.
4. If A and B are monophonic, then C is monophonic.

8.5.1 Using GTTM for Melody Morphing

The melody morphing method uses time-span trees acquired by analyzing the results of a GTTM analysis of melodies A and B. Figure 8.14 shows how an example melody abstraction process can be obtained using a time-span tree. In the figure, the time-span tree for melody D embodies the results of the GTTM analyses. More important notes are connected to a branch nearer the root of the tree. The least important notes are connected to the leaves of the tree. An abstracted melody E can be obtained by slicing the tree horizontally using line E and omitting notes that are connected to branches under line E. In the same manner, slicing the tree higher up at line F, a more abstracted melody F is obtained. This abstraction of melody can be regarded as a kind of melody morphing because melody E is a form of "intermediate" melody between melody E and melody F.

In order to fully implement the melody morphing, a set of primitive operations are used: the subsumption relation (written as $\sqsubseteq$), meet (written as $\sqcap$), and join (written as $\sqcup$), as proposed in Hirata [13]. The subsumption relation represents the relation an instantiated object is subsumed by a more abstract object (see Fig. 8.15a). This is written as "instantiated object" $\sqsubseteq$ "more abstract object." For example, the relationship among TD, TE, and TF, which are the time-span trees (or reduced time-span trees) of melodies D, E, and F in Fig. 8.2, can be represented as follows:

$$TF \sqsubseteq TE \sqsubseteq TD \tag{8.4}$$

Fig. 8.14 Abstraction of melody

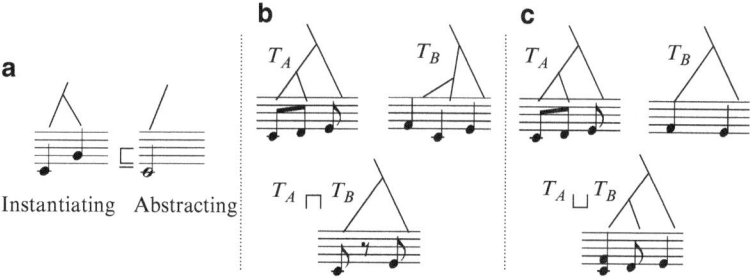

Fig. 8.15 Examples of subsumption ⊑, meet ⊓, and join ⊔

The meet operator for two melodies extracts the largest common part or the most common information from the time-span trees of the two melodies, in a "top-down" manner (see Fig. 8.15b). The join operator joins two time-span trees in a top-down manner as long as the structures of two time-span trees are consistent (see Fig. 8.15c).

8.5.2 Overview of Melody Morphing Method

The word morph usually means transforming one image into another through a visually seamless transition. For example, a morphing method for a face picture creates intermediate pictures through the following operations:

1. Link characteristic points such as on the eyes, nose, etc., in the two pictures (Fig. 8.16a).
2. Rate the intensities of shape (position), color, etc., in each picture.
3. Combine the pictures.

Fig. 8.16 Examples of linking two pictures/melodies

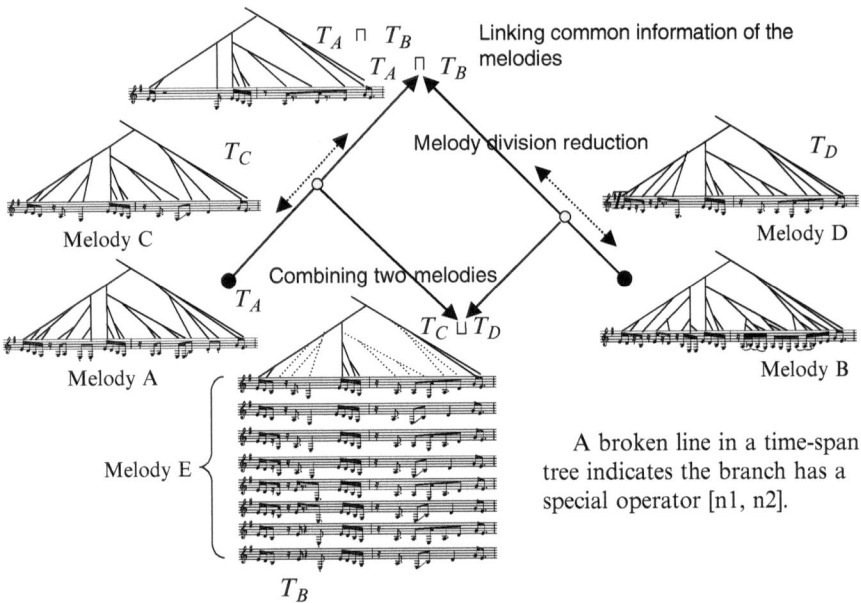

Fig. 8.17 Overview of melody morphing procedure

Similarly, the melody morphing method creates intermediate melodies with the following operations:

1. Link the most common information of the time-span trees of two melodies (Fig. 8.16b).
2. Abstract the notes of a melody in the difference branch of the time-span tree using the melody divisional reduction method.
3. Combine both melodies.

The melody morphing method is illustrated in Fig. 8.17.

8.5.3 Linking Information Common to Melodies

Note that from this point on in this chapter, all melodies discussed will be assumed to be monophonic. FATTA [8] can generate a time-span tree from the score automatically but can only deal with monophonic input.

By using the time-span trees T_A and T_B from melodies A and B, the most common information $T_A \sqcap T_B$ – which is not only the essential parts of melody A but also those of melody B – can be calculated. The meet operation $T_A \sqcap T_B$ result is abstracted from T_A and T_B, and those notes discarded in the abstraction process are defined as the *difference in information* between T_A and T_B.

When calculating $T_A \sqcap T_B$ – by extracting the largest common part of T_A and T_B in a top-down manner – the result may change depending on whether the same note in different octaves (e.g., C4 and C3) are distinguished. If octave notes are discriminated, C4 $\sqcap$ C3 will be empty $\perp$. If they are not distinguished, the result is just C, that is, abstracted of the octave information. For the system here a note and the octave note are regarded as different notes because processing is found to be more difficult if the octave information is not defined.

8.5.4 Melody Division Reduction

A method is introduced now for smoothly increasing or decreasing the presence of the features found in the difference information of T_A and T_B. The melody divisional reduction method abstracts the notes of the melody in the difference branch of the time-span tree by applying the abstraction described in Sect. 8.5.1.

In the melody divisional reduction method, melodies Cm ($m = 1, 2, ..., n$) are acquired from T_A and $T_A \sqcap T_B$ using the following algorithm. The index m of Cm indicates the number of notes in the difference information of the time-span trees that are included in T_{Cm} and not included in $T_A \sqcap T_B$:

Step 1: Define the Level of Abstraction
A user sets the parameter value L that determines the level of abstraction of the melody. L ranges from 1 to the number of notes in the difference information of the time-span trees that are included in T_A but not included in $T_A \sqcap T_B$.

Step 2: Abstraction of Notes in the Difference Information
This step selects and abstracts a note which has the fewest number of dots in the difference information. The number of dots can be acquired from the GTTM analysis results [3]. If two or more notes have the fewest dots, the first one in the list is selected.

Step 3: Iteration
Iterate step 2 L times.
Subsumption relations will hold as follows for the time-span trees T_{Cm} constructed with the above algorithm:

$$T_A \sqcap T_B \not\sqsubseteq T_{Cn} \not\sqsubseteq T_{Cn-1} \not\sqsubseteq \ldots \not\sqsubseteq T_{C2} \not\sqsubseteq T_{C1} \not\sqsubseteq T_A \qquad (8.5)$$

In Fig. 8.17, there are nine notes included in T_A but not included in $T_A \sqcap T_B$. Therefore, the value of n is 8, and eight kinds of melodies Cm ($m = 1, 2, \ldots, n$) can be acquired between T_A and $T_A \sqcap T_B$ (Fig. 8.18).

In the same way, a melody D can be acquired from T_B and $T_A \sqcap T_B$ as follows:

$$T_A \sqcap T_B \not\sqsubseteq T_D \not\sqsubseteq T_B \tag{8.6}$$

8.5.5 Combining Two Melodies

Given melodies C and D, which are results of the divisional reduction using time-span tree of melodies A and B, the join operator is used to combine C and D. The simple join operator is not sufficient for combining T_C and T_D, because $T_C \sqcup T_D$ is not necessarily monophonic, even if T_C and T_D are monophonies. In other words, the result of the operation has chords when the time-span structures are overrides and the pitches of the notes are different. Thus, the result would violate condition 4 in Sect. 8.3.

To avoid this problem, a special operator [n1, n2] is introduced, which outputs note n1 or note n2, as a result of n1 $\sqcup$ n2. Then, the result of $T_C \sqcup T_D$ is all combinations of monophonic melodies produced by the operator.

8.6 Experimental Results

It is difficult to compare the performance of this system with that of previous systems because the approaches taken are so different. The method used here, based on music theory, evaluates the appropriateness of the notes from a musical point of view. Hence, the evaluation approach will be to quantitatively evaluate each step in the method and then detail an example result.

8.6.1 Evaluation of ATTA and FATTA

The performance of the music analyzer was analyzed using an F-measure given by the weighted harmonic mean of precision and recall (as utilized in pattern recognition system evaluation):

$$F_{\text{measure}} = 2 \times \frac{P \times R}{P + R} \tag{8.7}$$

This evaluation required the availability of a "correct" analysis grouping structure, metrical structure, and time-span tree. A hundred sections of 8-bar-length, monophonic, classical music pieces were collected. Musicology experts manually analyzed them utilizing GTTM and using the manual-edit mode of the interactive

Fig. 8.18 Melody divisional
reduction

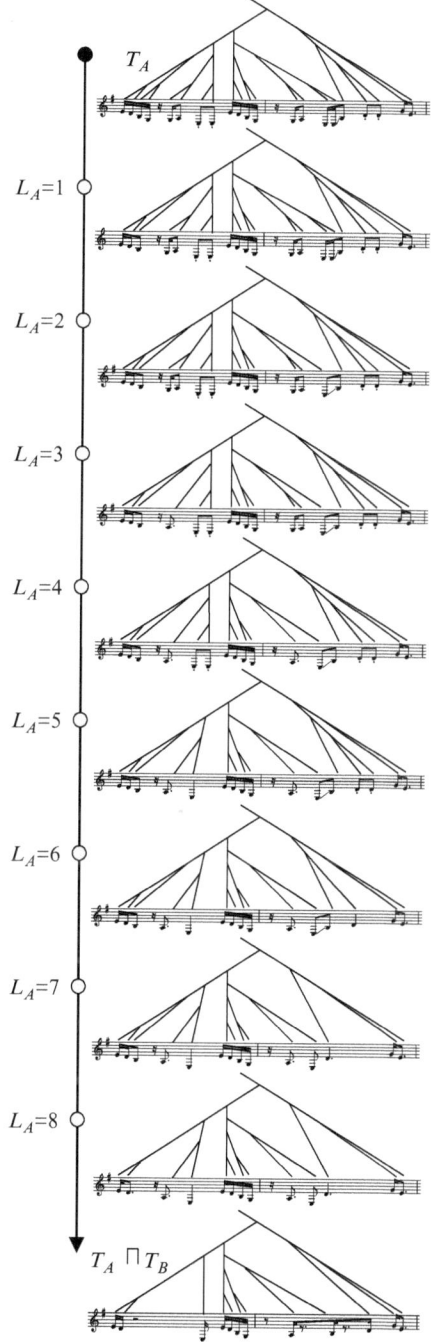

Table 8.4 F-measure of analyzer outperformed the baseline

Melodies	Grouping-structure analyzer		Metrical-structure analyzer		Time-span tree analyzer	
	Baseline performance	System with configured parameters	Baseline performance	System with configured parameters	Baseline performance	System with configured parameters
1. Moments Musicaux	0.18	0.56	0.95	1.00	0.71	0.84
2. Wiegenlied	0.76	1.00	0.83	0.85	0.54	0.69
3. Traumerei	0.60	0.87	0.76	1.00	0.50	0.63
4. An die Freude	0.12	0.73	0.95	1.00	0.22	0.48
5. Barcarolle	0.04	0.54	0.72	0.79	0.24	0.60
⋮	⋮	⋮	⋮	⋮	⋮	⋮
⋮	⋮	⋮	⋮	⋮	⋮	⋮
Total (100 melodies)	0.46	0.77	0.84	0.90	0.44	0.60

GTTM analyzer to assist in developing the grouping structure, metrical structure, and time-span tree. Three other further experts crosschecked these manually produced results.

To evaluate the baseline performance of the system, the following default parameters were used in the analysis: $S^{rules} = 0.5$, $T^{rules} = 0.5$, $Ws{,}=0.5$ $Wr =0.5$, $Wl = 0.5$, and $\sigma = 0.05$.

In this test, the parameters were configured manually because the optimal values of the parameters depend on the piece of music. When a user changes the parameters, the hierarchical structures change as a result of the new analysis.

It took an average of approximately 10 min per piece to find each plausible tuning for the set parameters set (Tables 8.1, 8.2, 8.3). After configuration, the F-measures of our analyzer outperformed the fully manual baseline (Table 8.4).

Next, the set of parameters was optimized using FATTA. The average F-measures became 0.48, 0.89, and 0.49 for grouping, metrical, and time-span tree structures, respectively – thus still outperforming the baseline performance.

8.6.2 Evaluation of Interactive GTTM Analyzer

The time taken to perform an analysis with the interactive GTTM analyzer was compared to the GTTM manual editor without an ATTA. For the analysis, 100 pieces from the 300 scores (with human-validated grouping-structure analysis, metrical structure, and time-span tree) were utilized. The prolongational tree was not included in this, because its analyzer is still under development. It was found

Table 8.5 Operation time of interactive GTTM analyzer and GTTM manual editor

Melodies	Interactive GTTM analyzer (in seconds)	GTTM manual editor (in seconds)
1 Grande Valse Brillante	326	624
2. Moments Musicaux	541	791
3. Turkish March	724	1,026
4. Anitras Tanz	621	915
5. Valse du Petit Chien	876	1,246
	:	:
Total (100 melodies)	575	891

that the interactive GTTM analyzer outperformed the GTTM manual editor without an ATTA (Table 8.5).

8.6.3 Evaluation of Melody Morphing Method

One method of evaluating the melody morphing M is to test that any extrapolative melody M is an interpolative melody of melodies A and B. This is formalized by the expressions in (8.8):

$$\{R(A,M)<R(A,B) and\ R(B,M)<R(A,B)\} \tag{8.8}$$

where $R(X,Y)$ denotes the similarity between melodies X and Y.

To measure the similarity between melodies X and Y, the $R_N(X, Y)$ measure in (8.9), defined by Hirata [13], is used. It indicates how much information is lacking from the two melodies as a result of the meet operation:

$$R_N(X,Y) = \frac{|meet\ (X,Y)|}{max\left(|X|_N, |Y|_N\right)} \tag{8.9}$$

where $|X|_N$ denotes the number of notes in melody X.

Ten pairs of sample melodies were selected for A and B. It was found that all the extrapolative melodies M from melodies A and B satisfied expression (8.8).

8.6.4 ShakeGuitar

As well as the evaluation approaches described above, the ShakeGuitar has been developed as a demonstration system for the melody morphing method. It works with the iPhone/iTouch and enables users to enjoy the simulated experience of guitar playing even if they are musical novices (Fig. 8.19). Shaking the iPhone/iTouch with varying degrees of strength influences the level of guitar-melody difficulty. This smoothly changes in real time from soft backing to heavy soloing using the melody morphing method. Users can identify the difficulty level visually through the color of the guitar body changes, corresponding to the level.

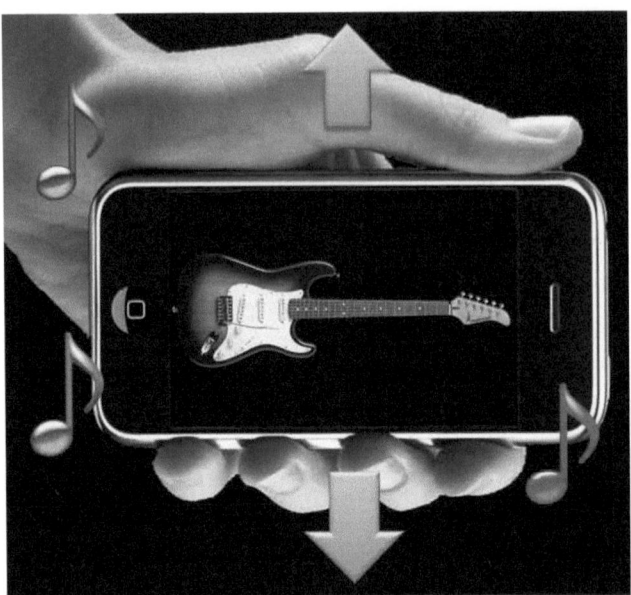

Fig. 8.19 ShakeGuitar

8.7   Conclusion

We have developed music analyzing systems called ATTA and FATTA, which can be used to derive the GTTM time-span tree. A music analyzer has been introduced – the interactive GTTM analyzer – which can derive the grouping structure, metrical structure, time-span tree, and prolongational tree based on GTTM. The analyzer also derives analysis results for chord progressions based on the tonal pitch space theory. A melody expectation method and a melody morphing method have also been proposed, based on the time-span tree of GTTM. The main results of this study can be summarized in the following five points.

Extended GTTM. An extended GTTM (exGTTM) was proposed for use in computer implementation. The difficulty with computer implementation of GTTM has been discussed many times, but previously no radical solution has been proposed. The rules can be reformalized using numerical expressions with adjustable parameters. As a result, it is possible to separate the definition and ambiguity from the material analyzed.

Implemented Music Analyzer. An actual working system has been implemented which can acquire the hierarchical grouping structure, metrical structure, and time-span tree. This interactive GTTM analyzer consists of an automated GTTM analyzer, the ATTA, a GTTM manual editor, and a GTTM process editor. By using the process editor, a user can seamlessly change the analysis process of the ATTA and that of the manual editor. The experimental results show that this interactive GTTM analyzer outperforms the GTTM manual editor without an ATTA.

Experiments with Human-Verified Analyses. The experiment results showed that, with preconfigured parameters, the music analyzer outperformed the baseline F-measure. One hundred expert-verified analyses were performed, which is the largest database of analyzed results of GTTM thus far. As a contribution to the research of music analysis, the interactive GTTM analyzer and a dataset of 300 pairs of scores and analysis results by musicologists are available on the website http://music.iit.tsukuba.ac.jp/hamanaka/gttm.htm.

Melody Expectation Method. A melody expectation was presented, which predicts candidate notes on the basis of GTTM and the tonal pitch space theory (TPS). It is designed to be used with an expectation piano, which displays the predicted notes on its lid, thereby supporting musical novices in performing improvisation.

Melody Morphing Method. A melody morphing method was constructed for generating interpolative melodies between two input melodies A and B using melody divisional reduction. The melody divisional reduction smoothly decreases the difference information in the melodies. So to generate interpolative melodies, all that is required is to select two input melodies and configure the parameters for controlling the reduction or augmentation level of each melody. The actual final development of an interactive melody generator and the evaluation of the melody morphing method are planned in future work.

It is planned to develop further systems, using time-span trees and the results of the music analyzer, for musical tasks such as harmonizing, voicing, ad-lib, etc. These will help to further explore the effectiveness of implementing GTTM for providing such musical knowledge.

Questions

1. Why are the systems in this chapter potentially so important to automated systems for expressive music performance?
2. What musicological system are ATTA and FATTA designed to automate?
3. What is prolongation reduction?
4. What is a time-span tree?
5. What do parameterization and externalization partially deal with, thus allowing an analysis to be automated on a computer?
6. When is TSRPR5 applied and what does it result in?
7. What are the meet and join operations?
8. How are meet and join used to morph melodies?
9. Give one method for evaluating melody morphing.
10. How could the melody morphing method be used to smoothly change the ShakeGuitar backing in real time from soft backing to heavy soloing?

References

1. Apple – GarageBand (2012). http://www.apple.com/ilife/garageband/
2. Todd N (1985) A model of expressive timing in tonal music. Music Percept 3(1):33–58
3. Widmer G (1983) Understanding and learning musical expression. In: Proceeding of the 1983 international computer music conference (ICMC1983), New York, pp 268–275
4. Hirata K, Hiraga R (2003) Ha-Hi-Hun plays Chopin's Etude. In: Working notes of IJCAI-03 workshop on methods for automatic music performance and their applications in a public rendering contest, Acapulco, pp 72–73
5. Hirata K, Matsuda S (2003) Interactive music summarization based on generative theory of tonal music. J New Music Res (JNMR) 32(2):165–177
6. Hamanaka M, Hirata K, Tojo T (2007) Implementing "a generating theory of tonal music". J New Music Res (JNMR) 35(4):249–277
7. Hamanaka M, Hirata K, Tojo S (2005) ATTA: automatic time-span tree analyzer based on extended GTTM. In: Proceedings of the 6th international conference on music information retrieval conference (ISMIR2005), London, pp 358–365
8. Hamanaka M, Hirata K, Tojo S (2007) FATTA: full automatic time-span tree analyzer. In: Proceedings of the 2007 international computer music conference (ICMC2007), Copenhagen, vol 1, pp 153–156
9. Lerdahl F, Jackendoff R (1983) A generative theory of tonal music. MIT Press, Cambridge, MA
10. Balaban M (1996) The music structures approach to knowledge representation for music processing. Comput Music J 30(2):96–111
11. Cope D (1996) Experiments in musical intelligence. A-R Editions, Inc., Madison
12. Dannenberg R (1997) Machine tongues XIX: Nyquist, a language for composition and sound synthesis. Comput Music J 21(3):50–60
13. Hirata K, Aoyagi T (2003) Computational music representation based on the generative theory of tonal music and the deductive object-oriented database. Comput Music J 27(3):73–89
14. Hamanaka M, Hirata K, Tojo S (2009) Melody extrapolation in GTTM approach. In:Proceedings of the 2009 international computer music conference (ICMC2009), Montreal, pp 89–92
15. Hamanaka M, Hirata K, Tojo S (2008) Melody morphing method based on GTTM. In:Proceedings of the 2008 international computer music conference (ICMC2008), Belfast, pp 155–158
16. Mozer M (1994) Neural network music composition by prediction: exploring the benefits of psychoacoustic constraints and multi-scale processing. Connect Sci 6(2–3):247–280
17. ManYat Lo, Simon M. Lucas S (2006) Evolving musical sequences with N-Gram based trainable fitness functions. In: Proceedings of the 2006 IEEE Congress on evolutionary computation, Vancouver, pp 604–614
18. Cooper G, Meyer LB (1960) The rhythmic structure of music. The University of Chicago Press, London
19. Narmour E (1990) The analysis and cognition of basic melodic structure. The University of Chicago Press, Chicago
20. Temperley D (2001) The cognition of basic musical structures. MIT Press, Cambridge
21. Larson S (2004) Musical forces and melodic expectations: comparing computer models with experimental results. Music Percept 21/4:457–498
22. Lerdahl F (2001) Tonal pitch space. Oxford University Press, New York
23. Hamanaka M, Hirata K, Tojo S (2004) Automatic generation of grouping structure based on the GTTM. In: Proceeding of 2004 international computer music conference (ICMC2004), Miami, pp 141–144
24. Hamanaka M, Hirata K, Tojo S (2005) Automatic generation of metrical structure based on the GTTM. In: Proceeding of 2005 international computer music conference (ICMC2005), Barcelona, pp 53–56
25. Sakamoto S, Tojo S (2009) Harmony analysis of music in tonal pitch space. Information Processing Society of Japan SIG technical report, vol 2009 (in Japanese)
26. Hamanaka M, Goto M, Asoh H, Otsu N (2003) A learning-based quantization: unsupervised estimation of the model parameters. In: Proceedings of 2003 international computer music conference (ICMC2003), Singapore, pp 369–372

Anthropomorphic Musical Robots Designed to Produce Physically Embodied Expressive Performances of Music

9

Jorge Solis and Atsuo Takanishi

Abstract

The recent technological advances in robot technology, musical information retrieval, artificial intelligence, and so forth, may enable anthropomorphic robots to roughly emulate the physical dynamics and motor dexterity of humans while playing musical instruments. In particular, research on musical robots provides opportunity to study several aspects outside of robotics, including understanding human motor control from an engineering point of view, understanding how humans generate expressive music performances, and finding new methods for interactive musical expression. Research into computer systems for expressive music performance has been more frequent during the recent decades; such systems are usually being designed to convert a musical score into an expressive musical performance typically including time, sound, and timbre deviations from a deadpan realization of the score and then reproducing this for a MIDI-enabled instrument. However, the lack of a physical response (embodiment) limits the unique experience of the live performance found in human performances. New research paradigms can be conceived from research on musical robots which focuses on the production of a live performance by mechanical means. However, there are still several technical issues to be solved – enabling musical robots to analyze and synthesize musical sounds as musicians do, to understand and reason about music, and to adapt behaviors accordingly.

J. Solis (✉)
Department of Physics & Electrical Engineering, Karlstad University,
Universitetsgatan 2, 651 88 Karlstad, Sweden

Research Institute for Advanced Science and Engineering, Waseda University,
2-2 Wakamatsu-cho, Shinjuku-ku 162-8480 Tokyo, Japan
e-mail: solis@ieee.org

A. Takanishi
Department of Modern Mechanical Engineering & Humanoid Robotics Institute,
Waseda University, 2-2 Wakamatsu-cho, Shinjuku-ku 162–8480 Tokyo, Japan
e-mail: contact@takanishi.mech.waseda.ac.jp

A. Kirke and E.R. Miranda (eds.), *Guide to Computing for Expressive Music Performance*, 235
DOI 10.1007/978-1-4471-4123-5_9, © Springer-Verlag London 2013

In this chapter, an overview on the current research trends on wind-instrument-playing musical robots will be given by detailing some examples. In particular, the development of an anthropomorphic flutist robot will be presented by describing its mechanical design, the implementation of intelligent control strategies, and the analysis of a number of musical parameters which enable the robot to play an instrument with expressiveness.

9.1   Introduction

The development of musical robots has interested researchers from the golden era of automata up to the present day. There are some classic examples of automata displaying humanlike motor dexterity in playing instruments, such as "The Flute Player" developed by Jacques de Vaucanson. This automaton was designed and constructed as a means to better understand the human breathing mechanism [1]. Vaucanson presented "The Flute Player" to the Academy of Science in 1738. For the occasion, he wrote a lengthy report carefully describing how his flutist could play exactly like a human. The design principle was that every single mechanism corresponded to every muscle. Thus, Vaucanson had arrived at those sounds by mimicking the very means by which a man would make them. Nine bellows were attached to three separate pipes; these led into the chest of the figure. Each set of three bellows was attached to a different weight leading to varying degrees of air pressure, which led to all pipes and joined into a single one, equivalent to a trachea, continuing up through the throat, and widening to form the cavity of the mouth. The lips, which bore upon the hole of the flute, could open and close, and move backward or forward. Inside the mouth was a moveable metal tongue, which governed the airflow and created pauses.

Other early robotic developments include the integration of automated actuation systems on musical instruments such as the piano, percussion instruments, and woodwinds ([2–8], or [9, 10] for a historical overview). More recently, researchers have been developing not only sound-making devices that automatically play musical instruments but also musical robots whose perceptual abilities allow musical collaboration with human musicians [11–15]. In fact, thanks to the advances in electronics, computer science, and so forth, a number of musical-instrument-playing robots have been developed, which produce live performances using enhanced dexterity and perceptual capabilities. Research on musical robots now provides a means for studying a number of aspects of human behavior, such as understanding human motor control and how humans communicate ideas and finding new modes of musical expression.

As a result, research on musical robots has attracted the interest of researchers from multiple fields, including robotics, computer science, arts, and entertainment. In 1984, Waseda University pioneered this work by developing an anthropomorphic musical robot. Most notably, WABOT-2 was able to play a concert organ [11]. Then, in 1985, WASUBOT, also built at Waseda University, was able to read a musical score and play a repertoire of 16 tunes on a keyboard instrument. WABOT-2's key developer, Professor Kato, argued that an artistic activity such as playing a keyboard instrument would require humanlike intelligence and dexterity. After the development of WABOT-2, several researchers have gone on to develop different types of robots capable of playing conventional musical instruments. The Musician Robot (MUBOT), developed at the University of Electro-Communications in 1989, was designed to automatically play a violin or cello [2]. The MUBOT was developed with the premise that music should be played by a robot without the need to remodel the musical instruments at all. This kind of violin performance robot was developed to act both as an entertainment robot and performance robot and as an approach for studying robot and musical engineering. At Hosei University, Takashima [6] has being developing different music performance robots for playing wind instruments such as saxophone, trumpet, trombone, and shakuhachi (traditional Japanese bamboo flute). The saxophone-playing robot has been developed using the philosophy of instruments not be changed or remodeled. This robot consists of an artificial mouth, fingering mechanisms, and an air-supplying system. Due to the complexity of replicating the motion of human fingers, the fingering mechanism is composed instead of 23 fingers, one for each key of the saxophone. Weinberg and Driscoll [17] at Georgia Institute of Technology have produced a percussionist robot capable of interacting with musical partners. The robot, called Haile, has two controllable arms for striking a drum. Both arms can be made to strike in different locations on the drum to change pitch. In addition, the velocity of the arms is controllable, allowing changes in loudness. The right arm is controlled by a solenoid actuator to enable faster hits, and the left arm is controlled by a linear motor to enable more powerful strikes. However, Haile's instrumental abilities were percussive and not melodic, and its motion range was limited to a small space around the robot's body. The same authors addressed these limitations with Shimon, a robot that plays a (melodic) instrumental marimba [13]. Shimon consists of four arms, each controlled by a voice-coil linear actuator at its base. The arms run along a shared rail in parallel to the marimba's long side. The robot's trajectory can cover the marimba's full 4 octaves.

Shimojo [5] has also been developing at the University of Electro-Communications a violin-playing robot, built consisting of a commercial 7-DOF manipulator that holds the bow and a fingering mechanism with 2 DOFs. A bowing holder was designed and is attached to the end effector of the multilink manipulator. Some companies such as Toyota [18] have been introducing musical performance robots, for example, a trumpet-playing robot, as a way of introducing novel methods of entertainment and assistance for elderly care. Toyota has developed artificial lips that move in a way similar to human lips and humanlike hands that enable the robot to play trumpets in a more humanlike way. These robots are also able to walk while performing.

The development of musical performance robots opens the opportunity of studying humans from different points of view [10], for example, human–robot interaction (tools for understanding their interaction with humans), human motor control (benchmarks for better understanding how humans are able of synchronizing multiple degrees of freedom), arts/entertainment (new modes of musical expression that may have been hidden behind the rubric of musical intuition and were thus not revealed by conventional musical techniques), and education (advanced musical educational tools). It is worth mentioning that the research with wind instrument robots has been focused on understanding human motor control.

In the following subsection, an overview of the current research on wind-instrument-playing robots is presented.

9.1.1 Wind-Instrument-Playing Musical Robots

Since 1990, the development of the anthropomorphic Waseda Flutist Robot has been focused on mechanically emulating the anatomy and physiology of the organs involved in flute playing. For this reason, the organs involved during the flute playing have been mechanically reproduced. This has resulted in the development of the Waseda Flutist Robot No. 4 Refined IV (WF-4RIV). The WF-4RIV is composed of 41 DOFs designed to reproduce the functions of the lungs, vocal cord, oral cavity, tongue, lips, neck, arms, and fingers (the next section will detail the WF-4RIV).

The "Flute Playing Machine" developed by Martin Riches [19] is designed to play a specially made flute, somewhat in the manner of a pianola, though all of the working parts are clearly visible. The Flute Playing Machine consists of an alto flute, blower (lungs), electromagnets (fingers), and various electronics. The design principle is transparent in a dual sense. The visual scores can be easily followed so that the visual and acoustic information is synchronized. The pieces it plays are drawn with a felt-tip pen on a long transparent music roll which is then optically scanned by the photocells of a reading device. The machine has a row of 15 photocells which read felt-tip pen markings on the transparent roll. Their amplified signals operate the 12 keys of the flute and the valve which controls the flow of air into the embouchure. The two remaining tracks are used for regulating the dynamics or sending timing signals to a live performer when performing a duet.

One of the first attempts to develop a saxophone-playing robot has been that of Takashima at Hosei University [6]. Named APR-SX2, the robot utilizes three main components: a mouth mechanism (a pressure-controlled oscillating valve), the air supply mechanism (a source of energy), and fingers (to make the column of air in the instrument shorter or longer). The artificial mouth consists of flexible artificial lips and a reed pressing mechanism. The artificial lips are made of a rubber balloon filled with silicon oil with appropriate viscosity. The air-supplying system ("lungs") consists of an air pump and a diffuser tank with a pressure control system – the supplied air pressure is regulated from 0.0 to 0.02 MPa. The APR-SX2 was designed based on the principle that the instrument itself should not need to be adjusted for robot playing. A total of 23 fingers, actuated by solenoids, were configured to play the saxophone's keys, and a modified mouth mechanism was designed to attach it to the mouthpiece. No tonguing mechanism was implemented, although it was included in the communication format. The control system implemented for the APR-SX2 is a single computer dedicated to the control of the key fingering, air pressure and flow, pitch of the tones, tonguing, and pitch bending. In order to synchronize all these for performance, the musical data is sent to the control computer using real-time MIDI. The SMF format was selected to specify the status of the tongue mechanism (on or off), the vibrato mechanism (pitch or volume), and pitch bend (applied force on the reed).

Additionally, the authors have developed the Waseda Saxophonist Robot No. 2 (WAS-2) [20]. The WAS-2 is built using 22 DOFs that reproduce the physiology and anatomy of the organs involved during saxophone playing as follows: 3 DOFs to control the shape of the artificial lips, 16 DOFs for the humanlike hand, 1 DOF for the tonguing mechanism, and 2 DOFs for the lung system. The control system implemented on the WAS-2 is integrated with a PC control and a PC sequencer. The PC control handles the information for each of the degrees of freedom of the saxophonist robot, as well as controls the airflow/pressure to produce the desired sound. The PC control receives MIDI data as input, as well as a music pattern generator for calibration. The music pattern generator produces the calibration parameters required to produce a particular saxophone sound. Inspired by the principle of sound production for single-reed instruments, the WAS-2 requires the control of the following parameters: lower lip position, valve closing rate, airflow, and pressure. Of particular importance is the accurate control of the air pressure and the lower lip's position, which is required during saxophone performance.

A detailed description on the development of the Waseda Flutist Robot will now be given.

9.2 Development of the Waseda Flutist Robot

Our focus has been on developing an anthropomorphic flutist robot which imitates human playing by mechanically reproducing the organs involved in human flute performance. Mechanical design of a flutist robot could follow two approaches: one involving a humanlike shape or an approach not requiring a humanlike shape. Anthropomorphic robots can be particularly useful when there is a desire to avoid remodeling the musical instrument. This has the potential to offer the audience a live experience very similar to that of a human musician. Additionally, it highlights a research opportunity for introducing new educational tools in the teaching of the principles of the music. This is because the flutist robot can be used as a human model to explain the physical movements required to play the flute. In contrast, a robot built without humanlike design principles can reduce the multiple technical difficulties that are also encountered by human musicians, and could potentially have additional degrees of freedom in real-time performance, reaching a much higher level of performance flexibility and quality in terms of specific and idiomatic demands. For example, one can imagine a violin being played by a robot musician with hands that have 12 fingers.

The flute is an air-reed woodwind which, because of the absence of a reed, creates sound using an air beam characterized by its length, thickness, angle, and velocity. The lips are used to control the air beam, having a large effect on flute's sound. Humans produce the sound on the flute by applying the air beam to the edge of the embouchure hole and controlling it with the shape of their lips. Ando [21] determined that the following parameters can be used to modify the air beam (Fig. 9.1): thickness T, width W, length L, and angle θ. The pitch, volume, and tone of the flute sound can change depending on the precise state of the beam.

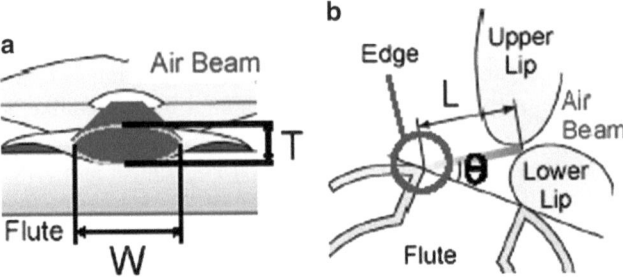

Fig. 9.1 Humans produce a flute sound by applying an air beam to the edge of the embouchure hole and by controlling it with their lip shape. The air beam parameters defined by Ando are shown: (**a**) *front view* and (**b**) *side view*

In our case, the development of the Waseda Flutist Robot is principally based on desire to emulate human levels of flute-playing skill and the application of humanoid robots (which are more useful as tutor systems, entertainment systems, etc). This approach is taken, as opposed to proposing new ways of playing musical instruments. The robot has been designed with a humanlike shape, which can help in the understanding of how humans control the motion of several organs and how humans can communicate and interact with the audience while expressively performing using gestures, body posture, etc. This flutist robot is capable of displaying the basic technical skills required by beginners to flute playing in order for them to produce a sound – fingering, breathe control, air beam control, etc. In addition, extended technical skills have been also implemented (i.e., tonguing, articulation, vibrato, etc.) to enhance the musical expressiveness of the performance. For this purpose, the mechanical design and control strategies are designed to produce more natural-sounding results and smoother transitions between notes, as well as to enhance vibrato production. In the following subsections, the design and control implementation of the Waseda Flutist Robot No. 4 Refined IV (WF-4RIV) are described in detail.

9.2.1 Mechanism Design

The WF-4RIV has a total of 41 DOFs (degrees of freedom) which mechanically simulate the human organs involved during flute playing (Fig. 9.2). It is 1.7 m in height and weighs 150 kg. This new version has improved the design of the lips (3 DOFs) and the tonguing mechanism (2 DOFs). The lips mechanism is designed to produce a more natural sound and the tonguing mechanism, to improve the attack time of the sound (as well as enhancing the double tonguing technique – an extended technical skill). These 5 DOFs, the 1 DOF of the vibrato, and the 2 DOFs of the lungs are key to the expressiveness of the flute performance.

The lung system is meant to be as airtight as possible during the breathing process. The system is composed of two acrylic cases, sealed airtight (Fig. 9.3a). Each contains a bellow controlled by a crank mechanism for breathing air in and out

Fig. 9.2 (**a**) The Waseda
Flutist Robot No. 4 Refined IV

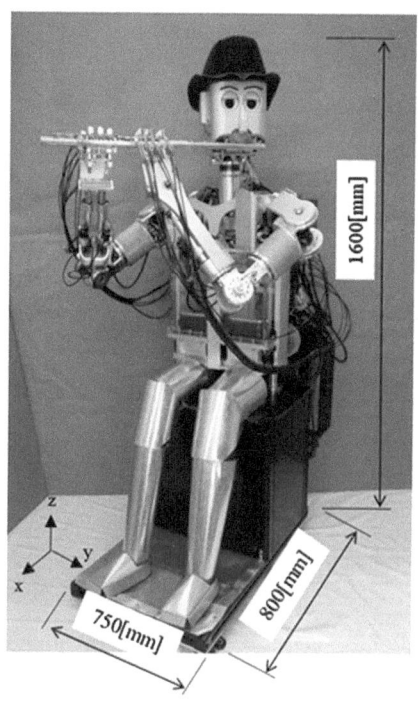

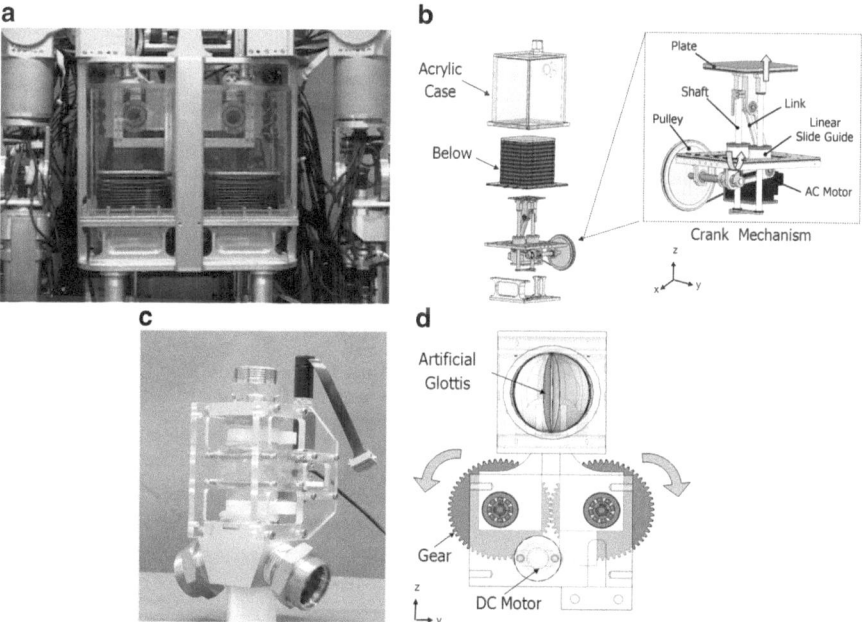

Fig. 9.3 Vocal cord and lung mechanisms of the WF-4RIV: (**a**) The lung mechanism produces the air beam. (**b**) Lung mechanism detail. (**c**) The vocal cord mechanism adds vibrations to the air beam to reproduce the vibrato technique. (**d**) Vocal cord mechanism detail

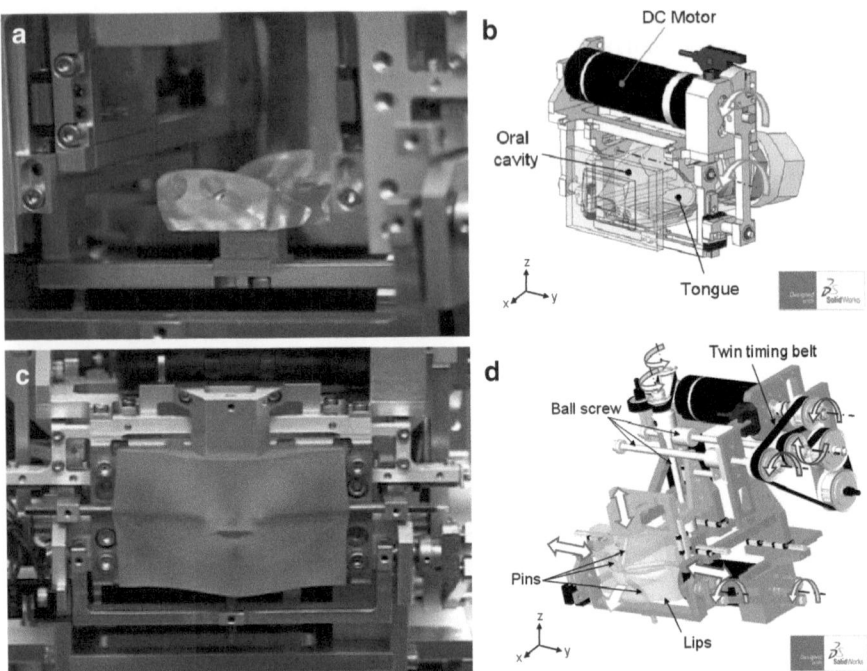

Fig. 9.4 Mouth and tongue mechanisms of the WF-4RIV: (**a**) The tongue mechanism allows for double tonguing and is located inside the artificial oral cavity. (**b**) Tongue mechanism detail. (**c**) The lip mechanism controls the motion of the superior lip, inferior lip, and sideways lips. (**d**) Lip mechanism detail

(Fig. 9.3b). Due to the airtight property of the lung system, the bellows have no contact with the acrylic surface during the breathing cycle. As a result, the quantity of air coming out from the lips has increased in this version, achieving an air conversion efficiency of 81%.

The vocal cord parts are made with a thermoplastic rubber called Septon, fabricated by Kuralay Co. Ltd. This material was selected because of its high stiffness and flexibility (Fig. 9.3a, b). A DC motor linked to a pair of gears adds vibrations to the incoming airstream (1 DOF). The gears are connected to both sides of the vocal folds. This design allows for control of the amplitude and frequency of the glottis aperture. Following the addition of vibrations to the airstream, this stream is then directed through a tube to the robot's oral cavity.

The oral cavity follows the design of a human cavity with a capacity of 30 cc and again uses Septon. This cavity consists of a clamped plate located at the front and a coupler located at the rear. The artificial lips of the robot are attached to the clamped plate, and the tube with the airflow coming from the vibrato mechanism connects to the coupler. A tonguing mechanism is installed inside the oral cavity (Fig. 9.4a). This mechanism, in the WF-4RIV, has 1 DOF and is controlled using a DC motor (Fig. 9.4b). The motor axis is directly connected to a link connected to the tongue.

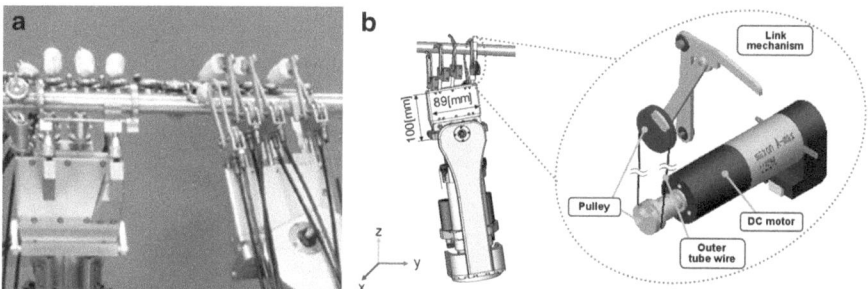

Fig. 9.5 Fingering mechanisms of the WF-4RIV: (**a**) The fingering mechanism enables the robot to push the keys of the flute. (**b**) Fingering mechanism detail

This new cavity design and tonguing mechanism allow the WF-4RIV to implement double tonguing. The double tonguing obstructs airflow using the frontal and back tips of the simulated tongue.

The lip mechanism is composed by 3 DOFs which control the shape of the Septon artificial lip. Septon can easily model a variety of shapes, allowing for more humanlike lips (Fig. 9.4c). An array of pins are set at the top, bottom, and sides of the lips, allowing the lip shape to be changed. The 3 DOFs control the superior, inferior, and side lips (Fig. 9.4d), with the superior lip controlling the thickness of the airstream. The actuation unit for the superior is composed of a DC motor, ball screw, and linear guide. The linear guide converts the rotational motion of the motor into the vertical motion of a link connected to the pin located at the top of the lips. The inferior lip is also used to control the airstream thickness through a similar mechanism connected to the bottom pin. The side lips affect the width and angle of the air beam. Two ball screws are rotated in opposite direction by a toothed timing belt; thus, both side pins on the lips are moved left and right simultaneously.

The fingering system in the WF-4RIV consists of 12 DOFs: The left hand has 5 DOFs, and the right hand has seven DOFs (the index finger has one DOF, and the middle, ring, and small fingers have two DOFs each). The motion of each of the finger phalanges is simulated by a wire drive system actuated by a DC motor (Fig. 9.5a, b). The wire drive has a Teflon coating to reduce friction between the outer tube and the inner cable. The fingertip is silicone RTV rubber (Shin-Etsu Chemical Co., Ltd. Corporation KE12).

The generation of high-quality sound requires more than just correct control of the air beam directed to the embouchure hole. The correct attitude control of the lips by the head and arms also plays a key role. The position of a flutist's head is strongly related to their neck position. If the head is properly balanced on the neck, the flutist is able to bring the arms effortlessly up to the flute without strain. There are a number of common neck movements found during performance: rotation to the left to bring the flute within reach of the left hand and to reduce the horizontal extension at the right shoulder, lateral bending (sideways) to the right to allow the right arm to be lowered, and bending down while playing. Players hold the flute by balancing three forces: the chin, the third phalanx of the left index finger, and the right thumb. This has been the basis for the neck, arm, and flute mounting

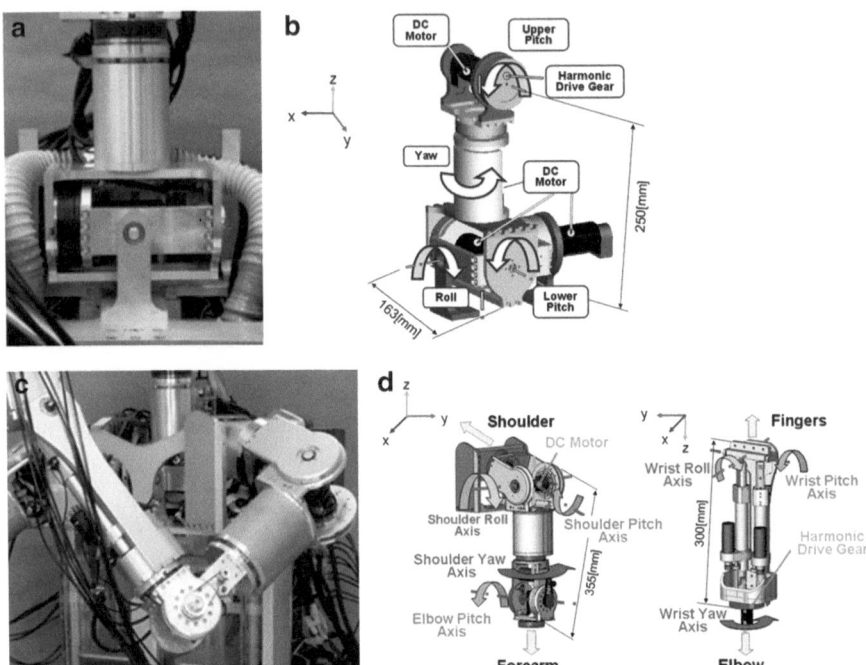

Fig. 9.6 Neck and arm mechanisms of the WF-4RIV: (**a**) The neck mechanism enables the robot to adjust the flute positioning with respect to the lower lips. (**b**) Neck mechanism detail. (**c**) The arm mechanism enables the robot to hold the flute on its own. (**d**) Arm mechanism detail

mechanisms implemented on the WF-4RIV. The neck mechanism has 4 DOFs: upper pitch, lower pitch, yaw, and roll. The neck system expands the range of positioning and attitude control of the lip (Fig. 9.6a). A harmonic drive with a high torque output and high deceleration ratio (Fig. 9.6b) allows for a high positional accuracy. The arm system has 7 DOFs: the upper arm having 4 DOFs and the forearm 3 DOFs (Fig. 9.6c). The upper arm increases the motion range of flute positioning, achieving a high accuracy through a harmonic drive gear and DC motors (Fig. 9.6d). In the case of the forearm, a 2-DOF parallel mechanism is adopted (pitch and roll of the wrist) for high positional accuracy and high mechanical stiffness. The wrist pitch motion involves moving two links in the same direction. The wrist roll motion involves moving two links in opposite directions. Furthermore optical sensors have been attached to each DOF to allow the arm mechanism to be reset from any position to a home position. This ensures the accuracy and consistency of the flute positioning.

The eye system consists of 3 DOFs corresponding to the yaw (horizontal displacement) separately for each eye and pitch (vertical displacement) common to both eyes (Fig. 9.7a). A tendon-driven gimbal mechanism was selected to reduce the mechanical size (Fig. 9.7b). The motion range of the eye is similar to the human range ($-30^{\circ} \sim 30^{\circ}$ for both pitch and roll). Two CCD cameras provide an additional communication channel between the robot and humans.

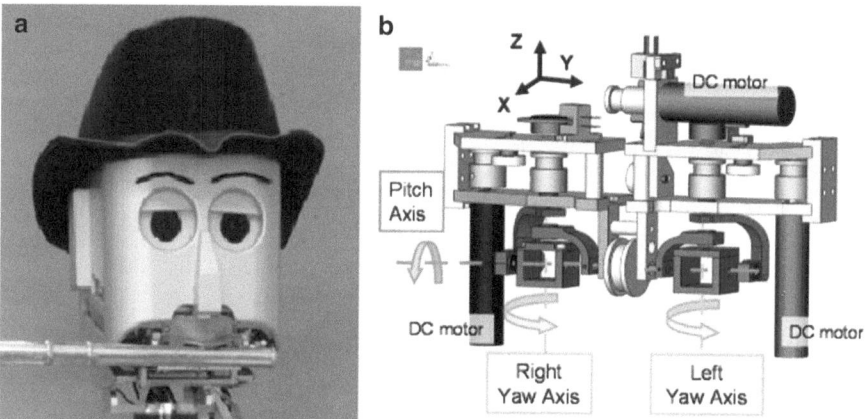

Fig. 9.7 Eye mechanisms of the WF-4RIV: (**a**) The neck mechanism enables the robot to adjust the flute positioning with respect to the lower lips. (**b**) Eye mechanism detail

9.2.2 Musical Performance System

The WF-4RIV's performance control system involves a PC sequencer, PC controller, and PC vision (Fig. 9.8). The PC sequencer generates accompaniment data for the MIDI sound source. It also sends a timing clock to the PC controller to indicate the starting/stopping for robot performance. The PC sequencer is additionally responsible for capturing, recording, and processing any audio data. The PC controller converts musical data into robot control data. Each of the degrees of freedom is controlled to create a performance of the desired score. The PC vision acquires and processes visual information during the interaction. A signal is sent (*via* TCP/IP) to the PC controller to identify when a student is present and to find a human face.

To enable the robot to play a particular musical score, multiple mechanical parameters (lung speed, lip shape, etc.) are calibrated before the performance to assure the quality of the sound produced. Furthermore, an auditory feedback control system is proposed to enhance the expressiveness of the robot performance, as well as to enable the robot to adjust its internal parameters during performance. The proposed system is composed of three main modules (Fig. 9.8): an expressive music generator, a performance control system, and a pitch evaluation system.

9.2.3 Expressive Musical Generator

The principal characteristic of an automatic musical performance system is that it converts a musical score into an expressive musical performance. Typically, this includes time, sound, and timbre deviations from a deadpan realization of the score. Techniques for doing this are discussed in other chapters (with an overview in Chap. 1), but we will revisit this issue to provide immediate context. Two key strategies that have been used for the design of musical performance systems are

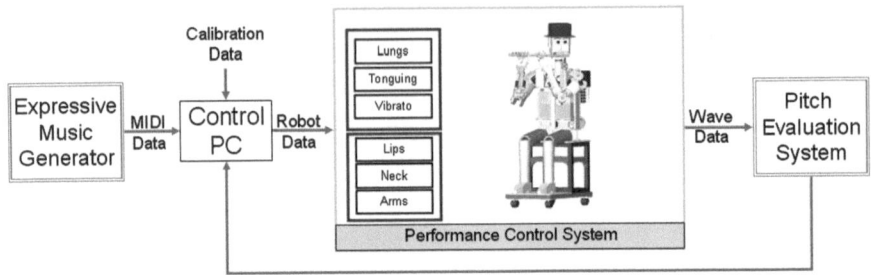

Fig. 9.8 Block diagram of the performance control system

analysis by synthesis and analysis by measurement. In the first method, intuitive nonverbal knowledge and experiences of an expert musician are translated into performance rules. Such rules explicitly contain musically relevant factors. A limitation of this method can be that the rules mainly reflect the musical ideas of specific expert musicians. Professional musicians possess a certain generality in their practice. Rules based on an analysis-by-measurement method are derived from measurements of actual performances – usually recorded. Data is often processed statistically so that rules reflect typical rather than individual deviations from a deadpan performance (even though individual deviations may be musically highly relevant in some cases). The best known analysis-by-synthesis system is the KTH rule system discussed in Chaps. 2 and 7 [22–23].

Machine learning is also another active research stream. Katayose and Inokuchi [29] used inductive artificial intelligence algorithms to infer performance rules from recorded performances. Similar approaches have been proposed by Arcos and Mantaras [24] and Suzuki et al. [25]. There are also several methodologies developed using neural network techniques [26], a fuzzy logic approach [27], and multiple regression analysis [28].

AI approaches have been demonstrated to be capable of generating high-quality humanlike monophonic performances, learning from human performers. However, all of these systems have been tested on computer systems or MIDI-enabled instruments. Such implementations limit the unique experience usually found in live performance. We have implemented an AI approach in the performance control system of the WF-4RIV to enable fuller advantage to be taken from the live performance context. A feed-forward neural network has been implemented to model the musical expressiveness based on the performance of a professional flute player. Using this model, a set of musical performance rules is created to be used by the flutist robot in generating an expressive performance.

A musical score is defined by the note information and its duration. By defining these two parameters, it is possible to notate most common western instruments. However, exactly reproduced, such sound becomes monotonous. Human players add expressiveness to the performance through vibrato, staccato (tonguing), dynamic marks, slurs, and so forth.

There has been no widely accepted scientific approach describing how human players add deviations to express emotions and feelings. We have implemented a

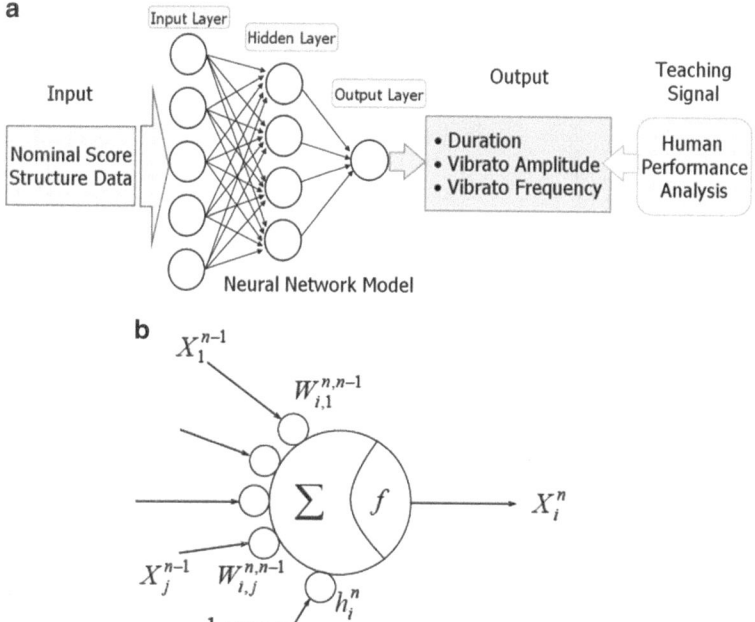

Fig. 9.9 (a) Graphical representation of a feed-forward neural network trained with error back-propagation algorithm. (b) Representation of one unit in a neural network

method called ExMG – designed to output the musical information required to produce an expressive performance. The ExMG takes as input the musical parameters (pitch, volume, tempo, etc.) from the performance of a professional flutist. These parameters are analyzed and extracted using a fast Fourier transform (FFT) tool [30]. A set of musical performance rules are the resulting offline output. These define the deviations introduced by the performer. As has been mentioned, the modeling of expressiveness in the human performance is done using neural networks. Parameters modeled for musical performance rules are note duration, vibrato frequency and vibrato duration, attack time, and tonguing. The resulting musical information is sent directly to the robot's control system using MIDI messages from a sequencer device (PC), enabling a robot musical performance which exhibits expressiveness.

The neural network used was feed-forward and was trained with an error back-propagation algorithm implemented in Borland C++Builder. Feed-forward neural networks are the most widely used models in many practical applications [28]. The network used was a three-layered neural network consisting of n input units, m hidden units, and k outputs units. Each input unit j ($j = 1, 2,..., n$) accepts an input signal x_j and outputs to the hidden units. The output s_i of the hidden unit i is obtained by a weighted summation of the inputs, which are then passed through a nonlinear function known as an activation or transfer function (Fig. 9.9a). The output s_i is calculated using (9.1), where v_{ij} is the connection weight between input unit j and hidden unit i. The transfer function F is a sigmoid function defined as (9.2). As a result, the output of the network y_k is given by (9.3):

$$S_i = F\left(\sum_{j=0}^{n} v_{ij}x_j\right). \tag{9.1}$$

$$F(s) = \frac{1}{1+e^s}. \tag{9.2}$$

$$y_k = F\left(\sum_{i=0}^{m} w_i s_i\right). \tag{9.3}$$

The actual artificial neural network (ANN) implemented is as follows. Three different networks are used to model the expressiveness of the performance: duration rate, vibrato frequency, and vibrato amplitude. For each of the networks, the number of inputs was defined as (Refs. [22, 29], etc.):

1. Duration rate network (14 inputs): slur, crescendo, decrescendo, normalized pitch, pitch difference, note, note time, before breath, after breath, second beat, note from down to up, note accessibility, note up, note down
2. Vibrato duration network (19 inputs): slur, slur on, tie, crescendo, decrescendo, normalized pitch, note, note time, before breath, after breath, first beat, second beat, third beat, note length change, pitch change from down to up, note accessibility, note up start, note down start
3. Vibrato frequency network (18 inputs): crescendo, decrescendo, normalized pitch, note, note time, before breath, after breath, first beat, second beat, third beat, note length change, pitch change from down to up, note accessibility, note up, note down, pitch leap

$$w_i(t+1) = w_i(t) - \eta\left(\frac{\delta E(t)}{\delta w_i}\right). \tag{9.4}$$

$$E(t) = \frac{1}{2}\sum_{K=1}^{N} (y_k(t) - d_k(t))^2. \tag{9.5}$$

The number of hidden layer units for each of the networks was experimentally determined. Seven units were used for the duration rate, five for the vibrato frequency, and seventeen for the vibrato amplitude. Back-propagation algorithm was used to train the ANN, incorporating an external teaching signal (in this case, the performance of a professional flutist). Thus, each output unit is told what the required response to an input signal is (Fig. 9.9b). The weight vectors (w_i) are updated during learning using (9.4), where $E(t)$ is the error between the actual output value (9.5) and desired value, and η is the learning rate. $E(t)$ is the difference between actual output y_k and teaching signal d_k. Coefficient η affects network training speed. There are a number of techniques for selecting this parameter; we experimentally determined $\eta = 0.75$. The ANN was trained to learn the extracted performance rules from the analysis of the professional flutist. It was found that the duration rate converged after 148 steps, the vibrato frequency after 72, and the vibrato amplitude after 49. Note that the small number of hidden layer units and leaning steps was a deliberate strategy to reduce overfitting and increase generalization.

9.2.4 Pitch Evaluation System

At this stage of the research, the analysis of the robot flute sound is only considered in the context of the robot playing alone (i.e., without human accompaniment). The method used to analyze the robot performance is based on the experimental results of Ando [21]. In this, the acoustic properties of the flute sound were analyzed using a mechanical blowing apparatus. The sound quality is measured by analyzing the structure of the harmonics, obtained through the FFT tool developed.

This enabled analysis of pitch (by tracking the maximum amplitude of each FFT frame) and of the sound intensity level of the harmonic structure (through localizing the harmonic, semi-harmonic, and the even and odd-harmonic levels). These were integrated into a sound quality evaluation function (9.6):

$$EvalF = \frac{(M - H) + (L_e - L_o)}{SIL},$$ (9.6)

where M is the harmonic level, L_e is the even-harmonic level, H is the semi-harmonic level, L_o is the odd-harmonic level, and SIL is the sound intensity level.

In (9.6), the sound intensity level is computed as follows. Sound is defined as any pressure variation (in air, water, or other medium) that the human ear can detect. There are two basic properties of the sound which help to understand how the ear can detect and measure the sound: sound power and sound intensity. The *sound power* is the rate at which energy is radiated (energy per unit time) from a sound source. The power of a continuous signal X is the sum of squares of modulus of its Fourier coefficients, as it is shown in (9.7) (N is the frame width, and $/FFT/i$ is the ith sample of frame F). For each frame F of the sampled sound, the root mean square (RMS) value is calculated. RMS is used, rather than the average power of peak level, because it is a more perceptually relevant measurement and has been shown to correspond more closely to the way humans perceive loudness:

$$P_{RMS} = \sqrt{\frac{\sum_{i=1}^{N} \left[|FFT|_i\right]^2}{N}}.$$ (9.7)

$$I = \frac{P_{RMS}}{4\pi r^2}. \tag{9.8}$$

$$SIL = 10 \log 10 \left(\frac{I}{I_0}\right). \tag{9.9}$$

The *sound intensity* is the rate of energy flow through a unit area (Watts/m^2). Sound intensity includes a measure of direction – there will be energy flow in some directions and not in others. Usually the intensity is measured in a direction normal (at 90°) to a specified unit area through which the energy is flowing. Therefore, the sound intensity is measured as it is shown in (9.8). A concept of sound intensity level (*SIL*) is utilized to mimic the ear's response. The *SIL*, in (9.9), is calculated based on the sound intensity using the decibel scale. The reference value I_0 corresponds to the *threshold of hearing intensity* at 1,000 Hz and is 10^{-12} W/m^2.

Using (9.6), the WF-4RIV can detect when it plays a note incorrectly. During a performance, as soon as the pitch evaluation system detects a note played with low sound quality, the note is marked. To improve the sound quality, should the same note be played again, the parameters of the robot are updated based on the "general position" technique. Thus, the WF-4RIV is able to autonomously improve its own performance.

9.3   Auditory Feedback Experiments

A set of experiments have been designed to test the effectiveness of the WF-4RIV system. A short melody was programmed on the WF-4RIV in order to analyze the transitions between notes while implementing the proposed air pressure control system. Furthermore – in order to test if the system is capable of correcting the quality of the flute sound during the performance – the flutist robot was programmed to perform three different scores with different levels of difficulty: Le Cygne (beginner level), Flute Quartet KV. 298 (intermediate level), and Polonaise (advanced level).

The results of programming the WF-4RIV to perform a short melody in order to analyze the transitions between notes are shown in Fig. 9.10. This figure shows the target air pressure and the output response. There are plots for both the open-loop and feed-forward controls. The points marked with circles highlight that the overflow of air pressure is effectively controlled using the feed-forward control system. The correlation coefficients comparing both output responses with the target values have been calculated. The feed-forward control system has a correlation coefficient of 0.535 when compared with the reference value. In contrast, the open-loop control system has a correlation coefficient of 0.458. These results support the effectiveness of the proposed control system in improving the dynamic performance of the WF-4RIV.

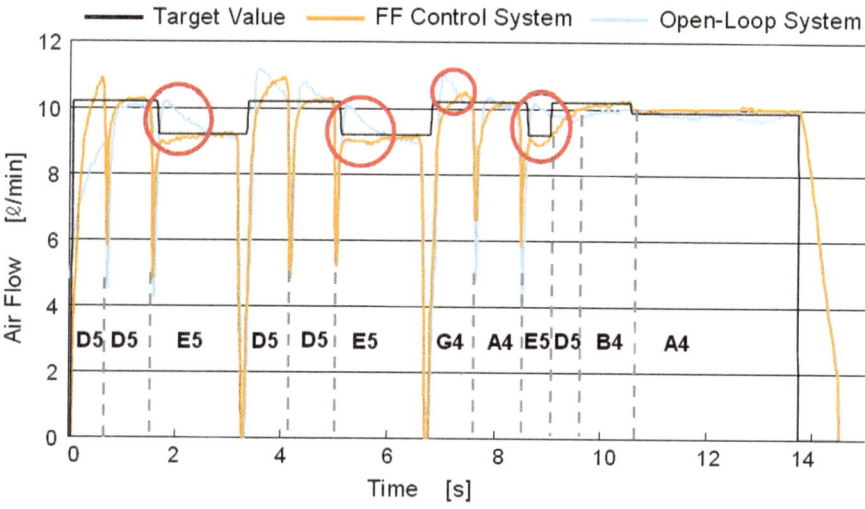

Fig. 9.10 Experimental results comparing the airflow tracking in the open-loop control system with the proposed auditory feedback system

A further set of experiments with the WF-4RIV have been done to examine the effectiveness of the proposed auditory feedback system. The flutist robot has been programmed to perform three different scores, each with a different level of difficulty: Le Cygne (beginner level), Flute Quartet KV. 298 (intermediate level), and Polonaise (advanced level). First, a test was run on the effectiveness of the AFCS to enhance the quality of the produced flute sound and adjust the parameters when an incorrect note was detected by the PES. For each of the scores, the WF-4RIV was tested in two control modes: open-loop and auditory feedback. Each of the recordings was then subjected to the sound evaluation measure in (9.6). Figure 9.11 compares the experimental results with the average of the evaluation score of the control modes for each of the proposed melodies. In all the cases, it can be seen that the quality of the sound was always higher when the proposed AFCS is being used. The collected data was also subjected to a two-way ANOVA statistical analysis to compare the differences between the control methods (open-loop and auditory feedback system) and the differences between the melodies (Le Cygne, Flute Quartet KV. 298, and Polonaise). This should that the effect of the control system on the performance is significant ($p = 0.0340$). However, the effect of different difficulty levels of melodies on the performance was not quite significant ($P = 0.0663$).

A final experiment was done to test if humans could detect improvements due to the feedback-based correction system. For this purpose, 14 subjects (without any musical background) listened to recordings of the robot performance with and without the auditory-feedback-based system. Each of the subjects was asked to evaluate from 1 to 10 the performance of the WF-4RIV, using as a baseline the performance of a professional flutist. They were asked to evaluate both sound

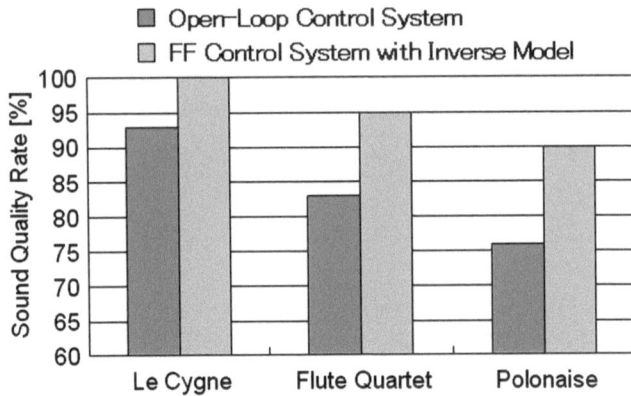

Fig. 9.11 Experimental results of the sound quality rate while comparing the open-loop control system with the proposed auditory feedback system while programming the WF-4RIV to perform different scores

quality and expressiveness. Each of the subjects listened to a recording from the professional flutist several times. Then, both recordings of the robot were played in random order and scored by each subject. Subjects evaluated the performance with the open-loop system with an average of 3.9. The feedback-based system had an average evaluation of 6.1. This experimental result also provides additional support for validity of the evaluation function in (9.6).

9.4   Conclusions and Future Work

This chapter has introduced research on musical performance robots, specifically those which are capable of playing musical instruments. The focus has been on research on wind instruments, which have interested researchers wishing to better understand human motor control from a point of view of robotic human science. Technical details in the development of the Waseda Flutist Robot No. 4 Refined IV (WF-4RIV) have been provided – in particular, the mechanical design of the simulated organs enabling the robot to play flute. This leads to the WF-4RIV being composed of 41 DOFs. Improvements of the WF-4RIV musical performance control system over previous research were detailed, in particular, the proposed control system capable of autonomously improving the quality of the sound. The modules of the control system were presented, and experiments were detailed evaluating the effectiveness of the proposed air pressure feedback control system as well as of the AFCS. The results support the effectiveness of the proposed system in increasing the sound quality.

In regard to future work, the algorithm for estimating the pitch during the flute performance is effective for monophonic sounds. However, this approach is inadequate when the WF-4RIV is playing together with a human partner (e.g., orchestra, band) In relation to this, a long-term goal is to enable the flutist robot to interact more naturally with musical partners, specifically in the context of a jazz band [16]. For this purpose, a musical-based interaction system (MbIS) will be developed to enable the robot to process both visual and aural cues coming through interaction with musicians. For this purpose, more advanced techniques for vision and sound processing (e.g., particle filter for vision and harmonic/rhythmic analysis for sound) will be implemented. Moreover, the proposed MbIS will have two levels of interaction: beginner and extended. The purpose of the two-level design is to make the system more useful to performers with different skill levels.

Acknowledgments A part of this research was done at the Humanoid Robotics Institute (HRI), Waseda University. This research was supported in part by a Gifu-in-Aid for the WABOT-HOUSE Project, by Gifu Prefecture. This work is also supported in part by Global COE Program "Global Robot Academia" from the Ministry of Education, Culture, Sports, Science and Technology of Japan.

Questions

1. What aspects of human behavior does research on musical robots provide a means for studying?
2. Name the three main components utilized by the saxophone-playing robot APR-SX2.
3. What are the four elements that characterize the air beam in a flute?
4. How many degrees of freedom in total does the Waseda flute-playing robot have?
5. Why was the thermoplastic rubber called Septon selected for the vocal cord parts in the flute-playing robot?
6. What are attached to the arm motors to ensure the accuracy and consistency of the flute positioning?
7. What do the three artificial neural networks model?
8. What is the pitch evaluation system used for?
9. How much better percentage-wise was the closed-loop system listener evaluation compared to the open-loop system results?
10. Why might an algorithm that can detect and analyze polyphonic tones be useful in this system?

References

1. de Vaucanson J. Le Mécanisme du Fluteur Automate; An account of the mechanism of an automation: or, image playing on the German-Flute. In: Frans Vester (ed) The flute library, First series (1979) No. 5. Intro. David Lasocki. Buren (GLD). Uitgeverij Frits Knuf, The Netherlands
2. Kajitani M (1989) Development of musician robots. J Robot Mech 1:254–255
3. Singer E, Feddersen J, Redmon C, Bowen B (2004) LEMUR's musical robots. In: International conference on new interfaces for musical expression (NIME), Hamamatsu, Japan. pp 181–184

4. Dannenberg RB, Brown B, Zeglin G, Lupish R (2005) McBlare: a robotic bagpipe player. In: International conference on new interface for musical expression (NIME), Vancouver, Canada. pp 80–84

5. Kuwabara H, Seki H, Sasada Y, Aiguo M, Shimojo M (2006) The development of a violin musician robot. In: IEEE/RSJ international conference on intelligent robots and systems – workshop: musical performance robots and its applications, Beijing, China. pp 18–23

6. Takashima S, Miyawaki T (2006) Control of an automatic performance robot of saxophone: performance control using standard MIDI files. In: IEEE/RSJ international conference on intelligent robots and systems – workshop: musical performance robots and its applications, Beijing, China. pp 30–35

7. Shibuya K (2006) Analysis of human KANSEI and development of a violin playing robot. In: IEEE/RSJ international conference on intelligent robots and systems – workshop: musical performance robots and its applications, Beijing, China. pp 13–17

8. Hayashi E (2006) Development of an automatic piano that produce appropriate: touch for the accurate expression of a soft tone. In: IEEE/RSJ international conference on intelligent robots and systems – workshop: musical performance robots and its applications, Beijing, China. pp 7–12

9. Kapur A (2005) A history of robotic musical instruments. In: International computer music conference, Barcelona, Spain. pp 21–28

10. Solis J, Takanishi A (2007) An overview of the research approaches on musical performance robots. In: International conference on computer music, Copenhagen, Denmark. pp 356–359

11. Kato I, Ohteru S, Shirai K, Matsushima T, Narita S, Sugano S, Kobayashi T, Fujisawa E (1987) The robot musician "WABOT-2" (waseda robot-2). Robotics 3(2):143–155

12. Baginsky NA. The three sirens: a self-learning robotic rock band, accessed 22 May 2012. www.the-three-sirens.info

13. Hoffman G, Weinberg G (2010) Gesture-based human-robot jazz improvisation. In: IEEE international conference on robotics and automation (ICRA), Anchorage, Alaska. pp 582–587

14. Kim Y, Batula A, Grunberg D, Lofaro DM, Oh J, Oh PY (2010) Developing humanoids for musical interaction. In: IEEE/RSJ international conference on intelligent robots and systems – workshop on robots and musical expressions, Taipei, Taiwan. pp 36–43

15. Lim A, Mizumoto T, Cahier LK, Otsuka T, Takahashi T, Komatani K, Ogata T, Okuno HG (2010) Robot musical accompaniment: integrating audio and visual cues for real-time synchronization with a human flutist. In: IEEE/RSJ international conference on intelligent robots and systems (IROS2010), Taipei, Taiwan. pp 1964–1969

16. Petersen K, Solis J, Takanishi A (2010) Musical-based interaction system for the Waseda Flutist Robot: implementation of the visual tracking interaction module. Auton Robot J 28(4):439–455

17. Weinberg G, Driscoll S (2007) The design of a perceptual and improvisational robotic marimba player. In: 16th IEEE international conference on robot and human interactive communication, Jeju, Korea. pp 769–774

18. Toyota Robot Partner, . (2010), accessed 31 July 2010. Available at:.http://www2.toyota.co.jp/en/tech/robot/p_robot/index.html

19. Klaedefabrik KB (2005) Martin Riches – Maskinerne/the machines. Kehrer Verlag, Heidelberg, Germany. pp 10–13

20. Solis J, Petersen K, Yamamoto T, Takeuchi M, Ishikawa S, Takanishi A, Hashimoto K (2010) Design of new mouth and hand mechanisms of the anthropomorphic saxophonist robot and implementation of an air pressure feed-forward control with dead-time compensation. In: International conference on robotics and automation, Anchorage, Alaska. pp 42–47

21. Ando Y (1970) Drive conditions of the flute and their influence upon harmonic structure of generated tone. J Acoust Soc Jpn 26(7):297–305

22. Friberg A, Colombo V, Fryden L, Sundberg J (1991) Performance rules for computer-controlled contemporary keyboard music. Comput Music J 15:49–55

23. Friberg A (1995) A quantitative rule system for musical performance, PhD thesis, Department of Speech, Music and Hearing, Royal Institute of Technology, Stockholm

24. Arcos JL, Mantaras RL (2001) An interactive case-based reasoning approach for generating expressive music. Appl Intell 14:115–129

25. Suzuki T, Tolunaga T, Tanaka H (1999) A case based approach to the generation of musical expression. In: 16th international joint conference on artificial intelligence, Stockholm, Stockholm, Sweden. pp 642–648
26. Bresin R, Poli GD, Ghetta R (1995) A fuzzy approach to performance rules. In: XI colloquium on musical informatics, Bologna, Italy. pp 163–168
27. Ishikawa O, Aono Y, Katayose H, Inokuchi S (2000) Extraction of musical performance rule using a modified algorithm of multiple regression analysis. In: KTH symposium on grammars for music performance, Stockholm, pp 348–351
28. Bishop CM (2004) Neural networks for pattern recognition. University Press, Oxford
29. Katayose H, Inokuchi S (1993) Learning performance rules in a music interpretation system. Comp Hum 27:31–40
30. Solis J, Taniguchi K, Ninomiya T, Takanishi A (2007) Towards an expressive performance of the Waseda Flutist Robot: production of vibrato. In: 16th IEEE international conference on robot and human interactive communication, Jeju, Korea. pp 780–785

Index